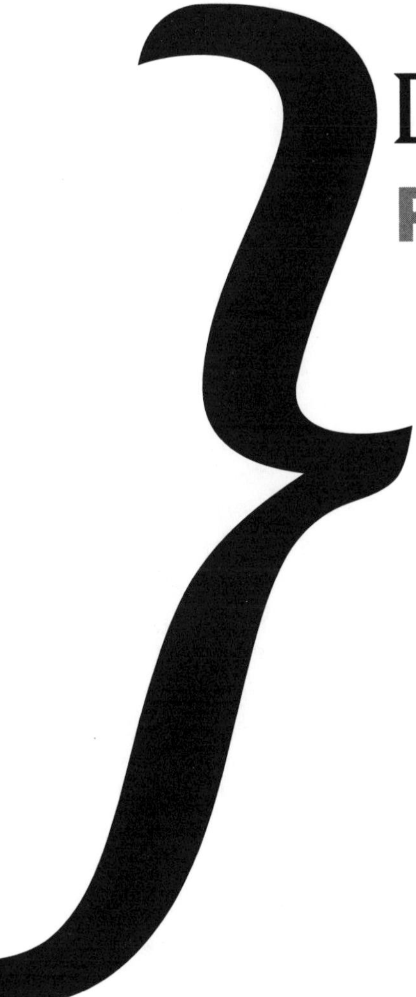

DIGITAL GUITAR POWER!

The Comprehensive Guide

Marc Schonbrun

THOMSON
COURSE TECHNOLOGY
Professional ■ Technical ■ Reference

ISBN: 1-59200-932-8

Library of Congress Catalog Card Number: 2005929768

Printed in the United States of America

06 07 08 09 10 PH 10 9 8 7 6 5 4 3 2 1

Professional ■ Technical ■ Reference

Thomson Course Technology PTR, a division of Thomson Learning Inc.
25 Thomson Place
Boston, MA 02210
http://www.courseptr.com

Publisher and General Manager, Thomson Course Technology PTR:
Stacy L. Hiquet

Associate Director of Marketing:
Sarah O'Donnell

Manager of Editorial Services:
Heather Talbot

Marketing Manager:
Mark Hughes

Acquisitions Editor:
Mark Garvey

Development and Technical Editor:
Orren Merton

Marketing Coordinator:
Jordan Casey

Project and Copy Editor:
Marta Justak

PTR Editorial Services Coordinator:
Elizabeth Furbish

Interior Layout Tech:
Digital Publishing Solutions

Cover Designers:
Mike Tanamachi and Nancy Goulet

Indexer:
Larry Sweazy

Proofreader:
Sean Medlock

This book is dedicated to my wife, Karla, for simply being amazing and enriching my life beyond belief.

Foreword

Guitarists have always struggled to learn the latest guitar technology products and software. The instruction manuals, many of them translated from Japanese and other languages, have created frustration and confusion among guitarists—enter *Digital Guitar Power!* by author Marc Schonbrun.

The goal was to create one authoritative reference for guitarists, providing them with the information they need to understand the latest technology products and make it easier to create their music in digital form.

Mission accomplished. In this well-written text, author Marc Schonbrun gives the reader an understanding of the history of the ever-evolving digital process of making music. He demystifies the concept of modeling amps and guitars. He covers a wide range of software products that guitarists can use for home recording, creating notation, and Tab fingerings and options for live performance or laptop guitar.

Every day more and more musicians seek to use the personal computer with a variety of music software to make music. They want to spend *more* time on the creative part of their music and *less* time on the technical details.

Again, mission accomplished. Marc Schonbrun turns the "complicated" into "easy-to-understand" with concepts for beginners and tips for the more advanced guitarist/user of technology products.

A special note to the 60 million plus guitarists around the globe:

If your music is conceived on a guitar, and you want to explore the world of digital recording and effects, this book is a "must read"!

This extremely well-written book will take you on a journey to understand quickly the important features of these products and begin using a variety of guitar technology products and software to make your own music.

Enjoy!

Patrick G. Cummings

December 20, 2005

President, Brian Moore Guitars/iGuitar Inc.

Acknowledgments

There are far too many people to thank here. Well over 30 companies were involved in this book and each one of them had countless people helping me. Without them, this book wouldn't be possible, so thank you to everyone!

Special thanks to my entire family for their unending support.

Special thanks to Pat Cummings, Jeff Horton, Tobias Thon, Harvey Starr, Brian McConnan, and Jeff Cross—thank you guys for being so involved. Thanks to Barry Diament for changing how I hear audio. Thanks to Mark Robinson and Colin Fairbairn for their expert tips.

Also a big nod to Orren Merton for starting out as my development editor and ending up my friend.

About the Author

Marc Schonbrun graduated magna cum laude from the Crane School of Music. He is an active educator, writer, and performer on the East Coast. Marc's musical resume ranges from classical guitar concertos to jazz trios and rock concerts. He is an active lecturer on guitar and music technology, and he frequently tours the country educating guitarists and musicians. He is also the author of numerous books on music theory, guitar playing, and music technology.

Marc is the author of *The Everything Rock and Blues Guitar Book*, *The Everything Home Recording Book*, *The Everything Reading Music Book*, *The Everything Guitar Chords Book*, *The Efficient Guitarist Book One*, *The Everything Music Theory Book*, and *Mel Bay's "Classical Guitar for Rockers."* Marc is endorsed by Brian Moore Guitars, La Bella Strings, and Flite Sound Speakers. Marc can be found sitting in front of his computer, most of the time.

TABLE OF Contents

Introduction

MIDI guitar has finally taken off, so computer tools for guitarists are multiplying rapidly. *Digital Guitar Power!: The Comprehensive Guide* provides a complete overview into the fusion of computers and guitars and shows you how computer technology and the tools available make your life as a guitarist better and easier. This book has a broad enough focus to appeal to any style and level of guitar player, while still providing the essential information so that you, the player, can embrace digital technology and get the most out of the exciting, cutting-edge tools on the market today.

Whether or not you're taking it slowly and simply, or speeding through looking for information to test out an amp simulator plug-in, you'll find everything you want to know here. If you're ready to make the full leap into MIDI guitar and open up the enormous potential that is only now available to guitarists, I'll show you everything you need to make it work the first time. This book is about making your music and taking it to the next level. I'm here to show you what's there and how to do it without feeling like you need a Ph.D.—which you don't. Creating digital music is easy and fun, and you're going to have a blast getting there.

What You'll Find in This Book

This book is about everything you can do with a guitar and a computer. Computer music production has changed how musicians work. Up until recently, guitar players had not been able to participate in computer recording on a deeper level. Now, with MIDI guitar coming into full-bloom and the world of virtual guitar simulators literally exploding, the guitar can take its rightful place next to the keyboard as the controller and interface of choice for computer musicians.

This book will include discussions of the following topics:

- Guitar amp modeling hardware
- Guitar modeling
- Guitar amp software emulators
- Special digital tools for guitarists
- Recording techniques
- MIDI guitar
- Notation tools for MIDI guitarists
- Virtual instruments
- Live performance with a laptop

Whom This Book Is For

This book is for guitarists who want to take their music to the next level by learning about the revolutionary tools available to them. It's a big field, and I'm here to show you how to make sense out of all the different aspects. It's also for guitarists who have ever tried MIDI guitar and couldn't make it work for them. Things have changed, and MIDI guitar is here to stay. It's staying for a good reason: it may be the coolest innovation in guitar playing since the electric guitar.

This book is also about the computer—our everyday companion that typically has nothing to do with the guitar (other than stealing Internet Tabs). Now computers and guitars are not only commonplace, but they are also becoming an indispensable part of the modern music studio. I think you'll find that this book is the comprehensive guide for making your guitar and computer work in perfect harmony.

How This Book Is Organized

This book is divided into three main sections: hardware, software, and MIDI guitar. The hardware section covers everything from computers to audio interfaces and modeling amplifiers to modeling guitars. The software section goes over all the amazing guitar emulation products on the market today. The MIDI guitar section encompasses what you need to be a MIDI guitarist, how to make it work for you, and what you can do with it, highlighting sequencing, notation, and virtual instruments.

1 Introduction to Digital Guitar

What exactly is "digital guitar?" Let's break open this topic so that you can understand what you, the guitar player of the future, are capable of. Oh, and by the way, the future is now.

Why Digital Guitar?

Let's face it—the computer has transformed the process and art of making music. This revolution has had a long gestation process. The first people in the music industry to reap this particular reward of digital music were keyboard players. The piano keyboard has been the staple of digital music for the longest time, and the earliest synthesizers contained keyboard controllers.

However, as guitar players, our exposure to this technology was largely from the sidelines, mostly as spectators. The closest guitar players ever got to digital technology was a large rack of processors for their sound in the early '80s. Figure 1.1 shows an early synth guitar setup.

Those guitarists who had keyboard skills were able to jump on the bandwagon early and take part in the fun. Early adopters of MIDI guitar technology found that it was quirky and hard to use, so consequently, many guitarists gave up MIDI for good, saying, "It just didn't work."

For the rest of us, the marriage of digital technology and our guitars wasn't even possible… until now. Recently, the computer music world has exploded with plug-ins that emulate our favorite amps and effects. Imagine having a whole virtual room of every great amp ever made, using any speaker you like, selecting different microphones, and applying a whole gamut of effects—all within your computer! This is only one thing that this exciting technology allows us to do. Virtual instruments also enable composers to use virtual versions of instruments that sound so real that it's often hard to tell the difference between the real and the virtual. Finally, now the guitarist can utilize these amazing tools as well. All of this is possible through the digital music explosion that has occurred over the past few years. Figure 1.2 shows what a modern MIDI setup looks like today.

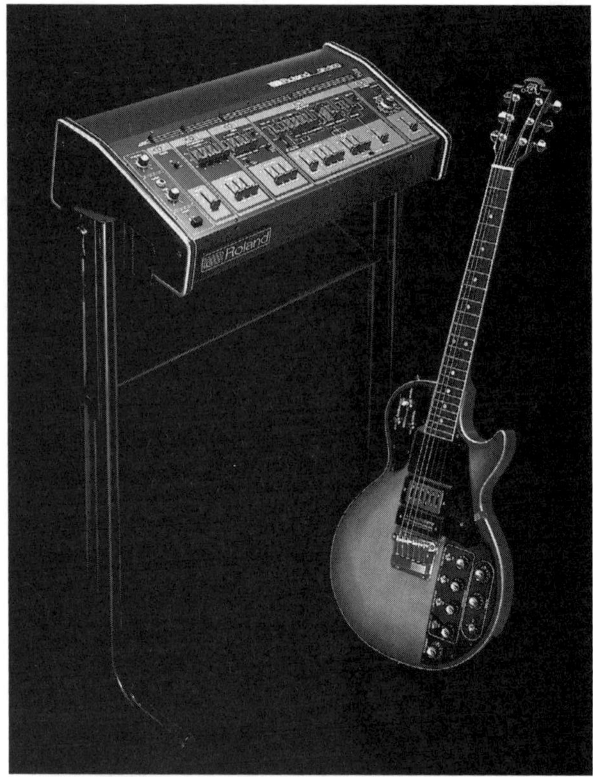

Figure 1.1
An early synth guitar system—the Roland GR-500 and Roland guitar.

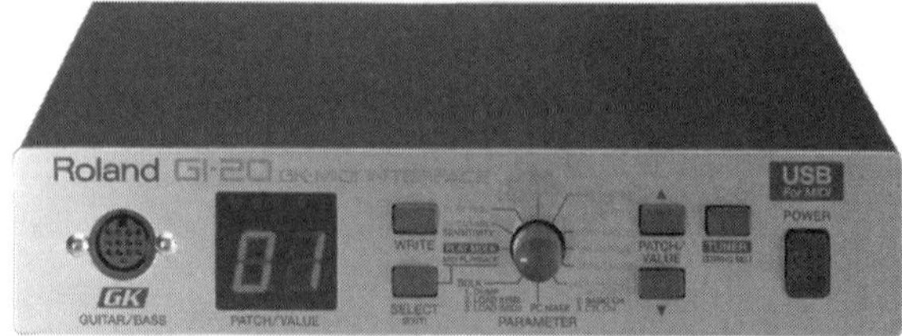

Figure 1.2
A modern MIDI guitar system: the Roland GI-20 guitar to USB MIDI controller.

What Is Digital?

The term "digital" is thrown around often in the music world. More and more it seems as if everything is digital. But I can think of one great example of non-digital technology—the guitar. When many players picture the electric guitar, they picture Jimi Hendrix and his wall of Marshall stacks—this is clearly not digital technology in action. We would refer to this as "analog" technology. Digital technology in some way involves a computer. It may not be a full-blown desktop computer that you surf the Web with; rather, any simple microprocessor capable of processing 0's and 1's will do. This is the heart of digital technology: binary code—0's and 1's.

Sound, as we know it, is composed of sound waves. For the longest time, those sound waves were captured by microphones and converted to electricity. The electricity was stored (usually on tape) and played back as audio. This is the basic premise of an analog audio system. A digital system, on the other hand, converts the sound waves into binary code, which is composed of 0's and 1's. The computer reads the binary code and reinterprets it as music. There's certainly much more to it than that, but those are the basics of digital audio. Because the audio is stored as simply binary numbers, it's very easy to manipulate the audio in various ways—ways that are virtually impossible in the analog world. Basically, digital technology will allow you to meet the keyboard player head-on. Embracing digital guitar will allow you to utilize the following new and revolutionary technology in your music:

- Emulate the sounds of vintage amplifiers.
- Apply the sound of effects pedals without owning any of them.
- Change the sound of your guitar from a Stratocaster to a Les Paul with the turn of a knob.
- Record your guitar with a Fender amp sound and change to a Marshall amp sound later without needing to rerecord.
- Sequence directly with a computer using popular tools such as Pro Tools, Reason, Cubase, Logic, Digital Performer, and others.
- Access synthesizer sounds directly from your guitar using MIDI technology.
- Create notation and tablature directly onscreen, simply by playing your guitar into computer programs such as Sibelius and Finale.
- Create professional guitar tracks at home.

As you can see, this topic is very far-reaching, and we have a lot to cover. That's the fun of digital guitar. It's not just any one thing; rather, it's an expansive and malleable technology. Since digital guitar can be useful to so many different types of players, I'm sure that you will find a home here.

What You'll Learn

The heart of modern music making is the personal computer. Most professional studios are embracing the computer for the majority of their recording and engineering work. The home studio market has literally been revolutionized by digital recording. Only 10 short years ago, the thought of recording an album at home was a dream for most people. Instead, recording took place at expensive pay-by-the-hour facilities that had invested a great deal of money in equipment. Now, with the advances in the home studio market, you can create professional-quality recordings at home. The thought that a personal computer would ship with free, high-quality software capable of creating music (Apple's GarageBand, for example) once seemed more like a dream than a reality; now it's here. Figure 1.3 shows a screenshot of GarageBand in action.

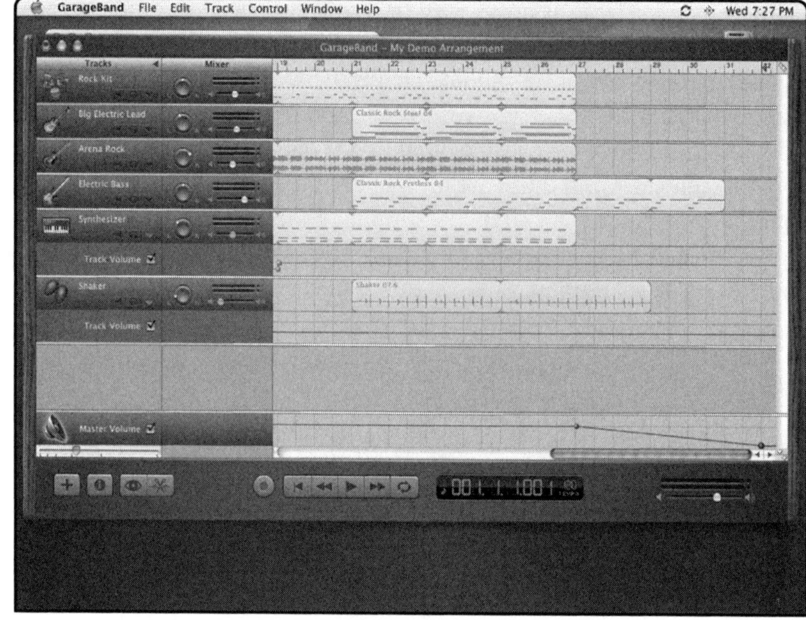

Figure 1.3
GarageBand—The new face of the home studio.

Image from GarageBand Ignite! *©2004 Thomson Course Technology*

While it's amazing that all this power is within your grasp, you will need some pointers on how to use it effectively. This book is broken up into a few major sections that will cover the breadth and depth of digital guitar. Here are the main sections that this book will explore:

- Digital modeling hardware (guitars, amplifiers, and effects)
- Computers and guitars
- Software tools (guitar and amplifier modeling plug-ins)
- Recording and mixing your guitar
- MIDI guitar
- Guitar-driven sequencing
- Educational tools
- Music notation
- Live performance

As you can see, this is a fairly expansive list, which shows just how large a topic this is.

How We'll Get There

Whether you've already been down the digital guitar road or are just starting, let's talk about how this book is going to help you get there. For each chapter and topic, I am going to show you, step by step, all the important points you'll need to understand, no matter how basic. When software titles are discussed, generous screenshots of the software will show you how to use the software. For the more esoteric concepts, like, "How much reverb do I need?," I will give you some garden-variety settings that can get you through almost any musical situation.

More importantly, and this relates to every part of this book, you will understand what each term means. While there may be several guitar amp simulation plug-ins on the market, and they will all look and work differently, you'll see common repeating terms. If you understand this basic vocabulary, no matter what you encounter, including tools not mentioned in this book, you will be able to understand them. I will also include some unique features, including tips from professional musicians and interviews with the brilliant minds who helped to create some of the software covered in this book. This is the heart of this book: lead by clear example.

Who This Book Is For

This book is designed for anyone who plays the guitar and is interested in making music with it. If you play the guitar and own some home recording technology, this book is designed to help you get the most out of your current setup. It will also show you some of the cutting-edge technologies available today and how you can utilize them.

If you play guitar and have always wanted to start recording at home, this book will show you what's out there, what you can afford, and most importantly, what you need to do it right. For the novice, there are so many programs and so many terms to understand. Finding the right software and the best hardware, and understanding how to use it, can appear to be a daunting task. Have no fear—I will get you there with ease.

This book is also designed to bring you up-to-date with what's going on in the industry. The music technology industry is moving at a breakneck pace; it's hard to keep up with all the latest advancements. MIDI guitar is a technology that has been around for a long time and has gone through a rebirth. You may have tried MIDI guitar at some point in the last 15 years and met with limited success. You may have become disillusioned with the technology and resigned yourself to the idea that "it just doesn't work right." If you fall into this camp, this book is for you. MIDI guitar is an integral part of the digital guitar puzzle. The last few years have shown significant advancements in MIDI guitar, and it is now a viable and reliable technology. I am going to show you what's out there. If you've never considered MIDI guitar, prepare for an awakening.

No matter who you are, you and I are brought here by a common goal: We love guitar, and we love music. The goal of this book is to fuse our love of music with digital/computer technology. This is going to be a blast, so grab your ax, boot up your computer, and let's learn about digital guitar!

2 The History of Processing for Guitar

This book is focused on what you can do with a guitar and a computer today. It's easy to understand how, in our technologically advanced world, the guitar and the computer is a good marriage. First, let's look at how the technology has matured. Digital processing for guitar has been around in some form since the early 1980s. The technology has come such a long way in a relatively short time. The '80s: fond memories they are not! "Digital" was a relatively dirty word, and MIDI—well, forget about MIDI. There was no more evil word to a guitarist than MIDI! Let's look at how we got to where we are now.

Analog and Digital Sound

Digital signal processing, or DSP for short, is a fairly revolutionary process. DSP is at the heart of this book, and understanding it will serve you well. The first step is to talk about sound in general.

Sound

Sound is an amazing thing. It's the movement of air, or more specifically, the compression of air molecules. You may hear other descriptions of what sound is, but without air, you'll hear nothing. Sound is a wave in its purest form. These waves ride on air particles and spread out in all directions. A great way to imagine sound is to think of a ripple of water in a still pond or a wave in the ocean. Dropping an object into a still pond will produce circular waves that emanate from the center and travel out equally in all directions. An acoustic sound wave spreads through the air that it vibrates. Your acoustic guitar, a speaker, or any other instrument you can think of simply vibrates the surrounding air. This is how you are able to hear sound. In places where there is no sound, such as outer space, there are no audible sounds because space lacks air to transmit the waves.

Sound as Waves

Acoustic sound is represented as a periodic wave. A periodic wave is such that it oscillates back and forth a set number of times per second. The number of times it repeats per second is called its frequency. The frequency is also how you determine the pitch of any note. Frequency is measured in hertz, named after the scientist Heinrich Hertz, who discovered that frequency was a factor of how many times a wave cycles in a second. Figure 2.1 is a representation of a very simple sound.

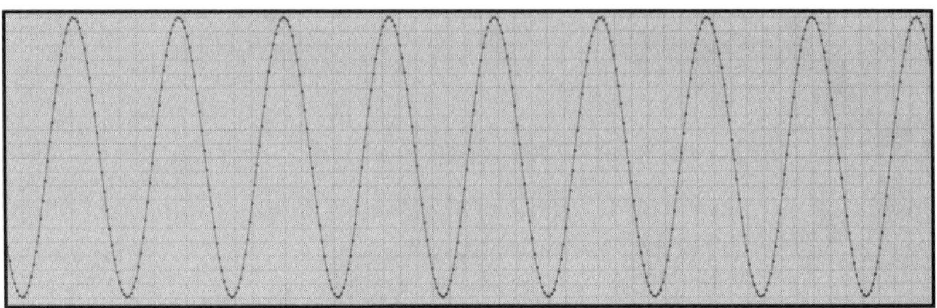

Figure 2.1
A simple sound wave.

What you are looking at may be familiar to you from eighth grade math class—this is a simple sine wave. You can see that the wave oscillates above and below the midline. The frequency of this sound is 1 hertz (Hz). A 1 Hz sound repeats exactly once per second. For example, 1 Hz would be a sound that you could feel as a rumble, but you could not hear it, because it's simply too low for your ears to hear.

THE RANGE OF HEARING

Human beings can hear sounds as low as 20 Hz and as high as 20 kHz (20,000 Hz). As you get older, you lose the ability to hear very high sounds, so for most people, their top frequencies are between 17 and 18 kilohertz (kHz).

As these waves travel through the air at different speeds and frequencies, we hear music. This is the very basic principle of acoustic sound. It's a relatively simple concept to understand. Now let's talk about sound when transmitted as an electrical signal.

FREQUENCY RELATIONS

When talking about frequencies, as we are going to do often in this book, there is one important concept to understand right way. The lower the number of hertz, the lower the sound we hear. The higher the number of Hz or KHz, the higher the pitch of the sound. Makes sense, right?

Sound as Electricity

The majority of guitar players who utilize digital technology in some way are playing electric guitars. Our discussion about sound waves moving through the air is about how acoustic sources are transmitted. In our case, this is how our amplifier speakers transmit the sound. However, this leaves us with another question: What's coming out of the wire from the guitar? It certainly isn't air! On any electric instrument, the sound is converted to electricity. On an electric guitar, this is done by magnetic pickups that convert the sound waves into an A/C current. Amazingly enough, electricity and sound waves have a lot in common. Both are periodic repeating waves. Both have frequency. The difference is that a sound wave is a compression of air molecules. Acoustic sounds rely on a medium to transmit them, such as earth, air, or water.

Electricity is voltage, also called current. What's even cooler to understand is that no matter what you are looking at, whether it's an acoustic wave of a 1 Hz sound or an electric current of a 1 Hz sound, they will look exactly the same as they do in Figure 2.1.

> **AC/DC**
>
> Electricity comes in two forms: alternating current or A/C, and direct current or DC. Batteries are a great example of DC current. The power in your house is A/C. The electricity produced by your guitar's pickup is also A/C.

Analog Processing

Now that we have our bearings about how sound behaves, let's talk about every guitarist's favorite subject: effects processing. Examples of effects processing are the following:

- Distortion
- Reverb
- Chorus
- Delay
- Flange
- Phaser
- Wah-wah

For the longest time, if you wanted to affect your sound, you needed to invest in pedals. A pedal was simply an electrical device that took your guitar's signal and mucked with it somehow. These pedals were completely analog—they worked with the electricity your guitar outputted and affected the sound in some way. You sent the end result to an amplifier, and you got a different sound. Figure 2.2 shows a common effects pedal, the Boss DS-1 distortion pedal.

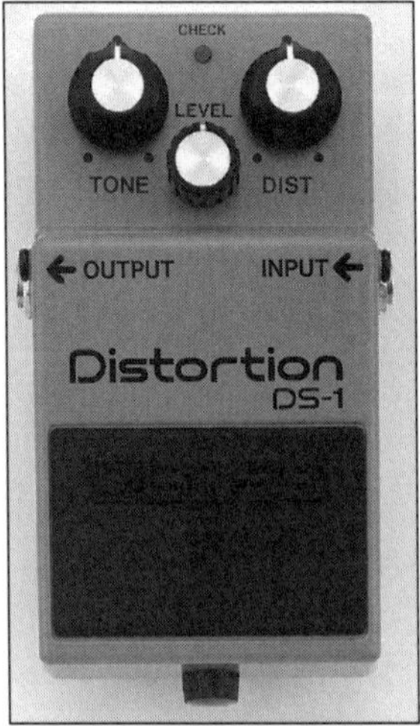

Figure 2.2
A popular stompbox effects pedal: The BOSS DS-1 distortion pedal.

One of the cool things about pedals was that they were relatively small and light, and you chain many different effects together to produce long, complicated chains of sound processors. However, there were several negative sides to this approach, as follows:

- The pedals took time to set up and interconnect.
- The controls had to be manually adjusted; for example, you had to bend down and turn a knob to change a sound.
- The quality of the sound when attaching many pedals often degraded your signal because of the added noise that came with using so many devices at once. Gain was also a huge issue when using pedals. Both contributed to sonic degradation.

Over time, individual pedals grew into "multi-effect" pedals, which were units that combined many pedals into one. Figure 2.3 shows a DigiTech floor effects unit.

Figure 2.3
A multi-effect floor unit.

While these units were very convenient, they weren't always durable. Many of the single pedals were cased in steel. Conversely, the multi-effect units were often plastic, yet durability was still an issue. This is not true for all units, but big changes were right around the corner.

Digital Sound

Sometime in the 1980s, a revolution occurred. Digital sound became a reality. Instead of electricity transmitting sound over cables, computers were able to translate audio signals into highly accurate code that could be processed and manipulated. The pitfall of analog sound was that it could suffer from many issues, including magnetic interference, impedance changes, impurities in the cable, noise—you name it, it could be an issue. Digital rarely suffered from any of these issues.

Digital sound works on the principle of binary code. Every piece of digital information is represented by either a 0 or a 1. Even this book, which was typed on a computer, is nothing more than a complex string of 0's and 1's to the machine. Amazingly, the combinations of 0's and 1's are limitless in long sequences, and data can be stored this way. At first, digital information was used for word processing, documents, databases, and such. For music, digital sound meant that a device called an analog-to-digital converter or A/D converter took the traditional waveform and converted it into bits of information.

The technology surrounding digital audio was in its infancy in the early 1980s. The CD was just becoming standard, and yet many audio engineers disapproved of the new digital sound as being "harsh" and "cold." Digital processing products suffered from the same issues of harsh, cold sound quality at first, and some still do. The A/D converter is based on three main factors, which we will go into in more depth later on: sample rate (how many times per second the sound is scanned), bit depth (how many possible levels of dynamics/volume can be recorded), and word length (how many pieces of digital information can be processed at one time). The combination of these three key factors is what makes digital audio sink or swim. As time went on, all three of the factors improved and better sound quality resulted. Digital signal processing was born from these basic elements. The beauty of DSP is that once your sound was converted into binary code, it could be manipulated in complicated ways that traditional electronics could not be—or so they said.

The quality of the conversion process from analog to digital is crucial in the accurate representation of the sound. In the early days, the technology was new, and to put it mildly, digital audio left a lot to be desired. Still, many people forged on because of its distinct advantages.

Digital technology had a few major benefits that many, many guitar players jumped on. Instead of chaining one analog pedal after another, the processing was done digitally inside of the digital processor. This meant that you could have an unlimited number of effects chained together in unlimited ways, each with completely different settings. Using a simple MIDI foot pedal, you could change your sound dramatically from song to song. This was a boon to many guitar players. These digital processors came not in the shape of pedals or floor units, but as "rack units."

RACKS

A rack was a standard way for equipment to be physically connected together. On either side of the rack casing were rails that contained threaded screw holes. The rack processors were screwed permanently into the housing for easy transport and security. Each rack "space" measured 19 inches in width and 1 3/4 inches tall. Rack processors could occupy more than one space, and many did.

Rack Processors

By the mid-1980s, everyone and his mother had a rack setup. Figure 2.4 shows a single rack processor, and Figure 2.5 shows multiple items in a rack case.

Figure 2.4
Single rack processor.

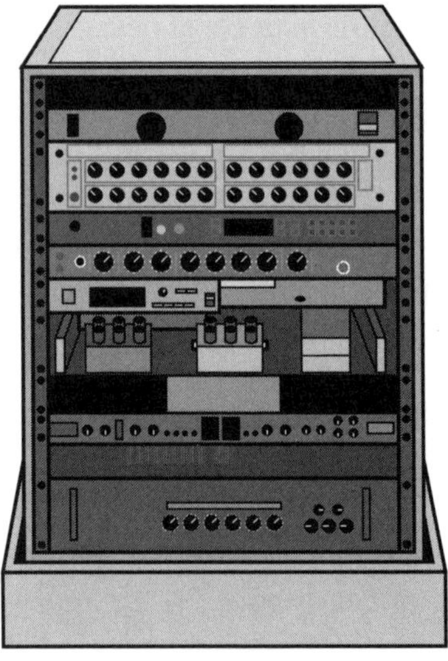

Figure 2.5
A full-blown rack setup.

Back then, rack setups got very complicated. Many players had dedicated units for each effect—a reverb rack, a separate delay, a distortion processor, a chorus unit, and so on. Getting all of these to work together was a chore. The whole idea was to have control over the sound from a foot pedal, but as the racks grew larger, it became harder to handle them. Programming your setup to work as expected became an art in itself. It wasn't uncommon for touring professionals to have techs that specifically tweaked and worked on their rack setups. Another problem had occurred: these racks became mammoth units themselves. Many players had six feet of vertical rack space in enclosures that weighed hundreds of pounds. Not exactly the kind of thing you took from bar to bar. But then again, everything in the '80s was big—big hair, big amps, big arenas.

To be fair, you can't just blame the poor guitarist. This was the way the market was, and when he went shopping for the next "killer" setup, this is what was displayed in the local store.

All of this "bigger is better," "no, digital is better" conversation led to some very important questions. First, how did it make you sound? Many players soon realized that their new and very expensive tone wasn't as hot as they had imagined. What we have to remember is that DSP was done by a computer chip. What could your home computer do in the late '80s? Mine couldn't do much more than type a paper and play Minesweeper. This was the limitation: The resolution and power of the DSP algorithms (the formulas responsible for your sound) did not yield results that sounded as good as the analog units they were replacing. In other cases, to get the pristine sound, you had to spend a considerable amount of money. Many musicians found that after years of lugging around all the gear, it simply wasn't worth it. All of these factors led to the decline of the big rack guitar rigs.

WHERE HAVE ALL THE RACKS GONE?

Rack processors are still alive and kicking today! You will find the majority of them in recording studios and live sound applications. Some players still use rack mount processing gear for guitar, but it's more common in the studio.

During the early 1990s, the invasion of grunge music, exemplified by Seattle-based trio Nirvana, was seen as the end of the overblown guitar setups. Less became more, and guitar players took a step back in technology and a step forward in sound quality. Remember, that was 15 years ago. Things will change again.

Tube Amps

The tube amplifier has been a staple for guitar players since the guitar was first amplified. When electric guitars were becoming popular in the 1950s, they were powered by a set of vacuum tubes. At that point in history, almost everything had tubes in it: TVs, radios, and most electronics. The tube was responsible for amplifying the signal that came through the amp. Tubes are made of glass and are actually very fragile. Figure 2.6 shows what a vacuum tube looks like.

Regardless of the fragility of the tubes and their tendency to wear out with use, they were the technology of the time, so guitar players grew up with that sound. Tube amplifiers did and do have a certain vibe to them. Eventually, the rest of the world stopped using vacuum tubes, which were

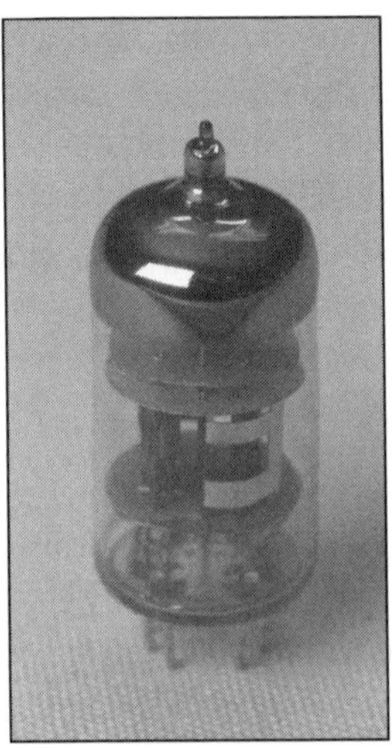

Figure 2.6
A dual triode vacuum tube.

expensive, large, and required great heat dissipation. The transistor was the replacement for vacuum tubes, which led to the general shrinking-down of electronic gear. Transistors were small, very cheap, and had a much longer life. The rest of the electronics world went to transistors, except, of course, the guitar players. Since we are creatures of habit, we kept on using our vacuum tube amps.

> **TUBE LOYALTY**
> It's not hard to understand why guitarists still favor tube amps. The classic musicians we all know and love, Zeppelin, Hendrix, etc., used tube amps, and frankly, who could argue with their sound?

Power Tubes and Preamp Tubes

Inside of your modern tube guitar amplifier, you will find two different types of tubes: power tubes and preamp tubes. The power tubes are responsible for amplifying your signal. The preamp tubes are much more important, though, because they are responsible for the tone and color of your sound; that is, the distortion sounds. An example of a common preamp tube is the 12AX7 tube (12AX7 is simply its part number). These tubes alter your sound and create distortion that, after all these years of technological advancement, still cannot be matched (at least for some people). Again, many guitarists came back to tube amps because they really did still sound better than anything else you could buy, whether digital or not. Digital simply was not ready for prime time.

The Nature of Distortion

Distortion, dirt, grit, whatever you call it, was an accident. Vacuum tubes were meant to cleanly amplify a signal so that it was simply louder. If you pushed a tube too hard, you got what was considered the worst possible thing—distortion. In the audio world, distortion was an ugly, horrible sound. Leave it to guitar players to take an awful sound and fall in love with it.

When these guitarists drove the amps too loud, the tubes began to distort and created a fuzzy sound. The louder the amps were, the more fuzz. This fuzz turned into a sustaining sound and became the signature tone that we all know and love. It was not uncommon to take your Marshall amp and turn every control to 10, or 11 if you're Nigel Tufnel, to get the sound you wanted. What began as a mistake became the guitarists' signature. As time went on, amplifier manufacturers added circuits inside of the amps to increase the distortion, even at lower levels. No longer was it necessary to blow your ears out to get the sound you wanted. But one simple fact remained: Tube amps sounded better when pushed as hard as possible. This was not very practical for home use. It was time to check out the transistor and see if it had any advantages.

Transistor/Solid State Amps

At the same time that TVs and other electronic equipment were transitioning from vacuum tubes to transistors, so were many guitar amplifiers. They were cheaper and less fragile, and unlike vacuum tubes, they didn't need to be cranked all the way up to get a distorted sound. These amplifiers were also called solid-state amplifiers. They started showing up around the 1970s. Many guitar players took issue with the sound of solid-state amps. Vacuum tubes impart a particular sound on your guitar's signal. It's very hard to describe exactly what it is in simple terms, but it can be stated generally as a pleasing sound. If you must know, tubes have a natural compression factor and emphasize the second-order harmonics—this all makes for a good sound.

Solid-state amps had one thing going for them—they could be pushed very loud without distorting at all. This was a good thing for jazz and country players who found distortion a less than desirable effect. One of the most famous solid-state amps was what the Roland JC-120 called their "Jazz Chorus." This amp, pictured in Figure 2.7, is still very popular and manufactured today.

For many players, transistor amps lacked a high-quality distortion sound because the distortion was based not on a vacuum tube being overdriven, but on an integrated circuit that was responsible for emulating the distortion circuit. It seemed that no matter what anyone tried, whether it was digital DSP, solid-state amps, or anything else, nothing quite sounded like the tone you could achieve with a tube amp.

Figure 2.7
Roland JC-120 solid-state amp.

> **TUBE USE**
> Vacuum tubes are only used in guitar amplifiers and certain audiophile amplifiers for music. Otherwise, the vacuum has been defunct for almost 30 years. If it weren't for the guitarists' "old habits" dying hard, vacuum tubes might be gone forever.

Transistor amps are generally found in the less expensive models. As the price goes up, you encounter vacuum tube amps. But hey, isn't this book about digital guitar? Yes, it most certainly is. But remember that a lot of this is history and ceremony. It's only very recently that things have changed over to the digital side in a way that is viable and sounds incredible.

The Birth of Digital Modeling

The next major step in technology was the advent of digital modeling, which is a specialized form of DSP. Digital modeling became possible simply because the computers of the day were fast enough to finally handle the complicated math involved with digital modeling. When it comes down to it, any kind of audio on a computer system is nothing more than math.

The Long Road to Modeling Amps

To fully explain digital modeling, we need to explore in a bit more detail what makes an amplifier sound the way it does. Every single wire, every single tube, and every variation in the power transformers—literally every possible variable in an amplifier—contributes to the sound of that particular amp. Even the smallest detail can have a tremendous effect on the final sound.

An amplifier is a complicated piece of machinery with many circuits, resistors, transformers, and other complex variables. The number of variables in a single amplifier explains why every attempt to sound like a tube amp had failed; there were simply too many variables. Couple this with human error. Imagine that you have the killer Marshall Plexi amp. It literally sounds better than any other amp you've ever heard. Maybe it sounds that way because one small aspect of the amp was wired incorrectly, or the hand-wound transformer was wound just a few more times, and this contributed to the unique sound of your amp. Now imagine how many sought-after amps there are out there. Start to see the variables here? It was impossible for anyone to replicate all of those factors together. The result was that in the early days of DSP, there were very boring sounds, based on generic models of amps. Here is where digital modeling changed the playing field.

NOT JUST MUSIC

Digital modeling does not just refer to audio technology. Architects use it to realize buildings in digital forms, and science uses digital modeling extensively to run experiments that are either unsafe or extremely difficult to perform in the real world.

Digital Modeling to the Rescue

What digital modeling was able to do was to analyze with a computer every path that your signal took through the amplifier and exactly how that signal changed, based on the different factors. For example, they could make models of every different position of the treble knob and how that affected the overall sound and the circuitry of the amplifier. They also were able to model how the tubes themselves reacted under different conditions, different levels of amplification, and even different brands of tubes. There were literally thousands of variables at play here! Digital modeling was able to create virtual models of the amps in software that replicated exactly what happened inside of a good tube amp. These virtual models could be manipulated in ways that traditional DSP could not. But like any digital process, it was only as good as the technology at the time. Factors such as A/D conversion and sample rate word length contributed to the sound, and because the technology was in its infancy at the time, the sound wasn't as mature and refined as most players had hoped.

In 1996, Line6 unveiled what they had been working on so diligently—pioneering digital modeling work. They had been analyzing all the components of great amps and what made them sound so good by creating software models of not just one type of amp, but many different kinds of amps. In 1996, the AxSys 212 was released, which was the first digital modeling amp. Figure 2.8 shows the Line6 AxSys digital modeling amp.

Figure 2.8
The Line6 AxSys 212 digital modeling amplifier.

The Line6 AxSys 212 was revolutionary for many reasons. The first was that many of the tube purists finally stood up and listened to a sound that they recognized. While the AxSys 212 wasn't perfect, it was light years ahead of what had come before, and for many, it was the first truly viable alternative to tube amps. The other reason that the Line6 was so cool was that it contained models of many different types of amps. Embedded inside the amp were models of Marshall, Fender, Vox, Mesa Boogie, and other amps. Not only could you carry one amplifier and get the sounds of all your favorite amps, but they reacted similarly to the amps they were modeling. Also included were a variety of effects that you could turn on and off in stompbox style, via a foot pedal called the Floor Board. Figure 2.9 shows the extensive foot pedal.

Figure 2.9
Line6 Floor Board foot controller.

In addition to controlling the preset changes, turning effects on and off, the Floor Board also had a built-in tuner and a Wah-wah pedal. This was 1996, ten years ago. Chapter 3, "Digital Modeling Amps," will go into all of the currently produced modeling units that work either as amps or as effects units based on amp models. Again, since this is technologically based, Line6 further developed products and amplifiers that took advantage of the advances in computer technology. As good as the AxSys 212 sounded, the amps that came after it sounded even better.

They released a digital modeler without an amplifier, and you supplied the amp. The Line6-POD was an immediate success. It was small, portable, and sounded better than most digitally based products that had come before it. It also allowed guitar players to record directly into multitrack tape recorders or early computer workstations (DAWs). Of course, Line 6 might have been the first, but they certainly weren't the only players in the game. Today, digital modeling is a staple on many current amplifiers. Now that you have an understanding of this technology, when we get to Chapter 3, you will be able to appreciate just what goes into making all this happen.

MIDI/Synth Guitar

Since we are talking about the history of guitar processing, we have to talk about MIDI guitar. MIDI guitar will occupy its own large section of this book, but the early MIDI guitars were not MIDI guitars at all. They were analog synthesizers driven by special guitars that converted their analog audio signal to a synthesized signal. In 1977, the first analog guitar synth was manufactured—the ARP Avatar. For keyboard players, the invention of the analog synthesizer was an immediate revolution. Groups like Yes, ELP, Pink Floyd, The Who, and many others made the sound of an analog keyboard synth famous. Guitar players never want to be left out of the party. We wanted all those neat sounds! Thus, the analog guitar synth was born.

ARP was one of the first to the party, but other manufacturers quickly joined in. One manufacturer joined the party and never left, and that was Roland. There were many different models of analog guitar synths that Roland produced. The sounds produced by these units were anything but guitar-like. Many guitar players, such as Robert Fripp, Andy Summers, and Pat Metheny, experimented with analog guitar synth, but it never really caught on in the mainstream market.

PAT METHENY

Think you've never heard an analog guitar synthesizer? Simply listen to any Pat Metheny recording. The exotic, horn-like sound Pat uses to solo with is his trusty old Roland GR-300 analog guitar synth. This unit came out in 1978, and despite advancements in technology and sound, Pat continues to use this synth on all his recordings and performances. Unfortunately for the rest of us, no one can use it without sounding like a blatant rip-off of Pat Metheny.

Keyboard synthesizers eventually utilized digital technology over analog technology, and there was a changing of the guard. One of the benefits of synthesizers going digital was that now it was possible to control the keyboards from an outside source (a computer). The Musical Instrument Digital Interface, MIDI for short, was born in 1983, appearing on a sequential circuits keyboard. For keyboard players, MIDI opened up a whole world of interconnectivity and power. Again, the guitar world wanted in on the action. Around the same time, Roland came out with the first MIDI guitar, the GR-700. Coupling a special guitar equipped with a hex pickup (a pickup that was capable of sending each string to its own channel) to a digital floor unit, the first MIDI guitar was born.

The Complexity of a MIDI Guitar

Keyboard synthesizers, whether analog or digital, have it very easy: You press a key and complete an electric circuit. There is virtually no lag in processing, and since each key has its own unique circuit, the system works well. A keyboard may be the ultimate digital interface because of this simple fact. A guitar, on the other hand, is a whole other story.

With analog synths, the guitar sent an audio signal that was fed to an analog wave processor. There was no need to know what note was being played, because the synth simply converted the voltage of the string to a sound. When guitar synth went digital, the game changed. Now, the note had to be identified. On a keyboard, this was a simple switch. On a guitar synth, the processor had to listen to the note and figure out what pitch you were playing and then send out a MIDI signal. This was called pitch-to-MIDI conversion. It was a complicated process that took time. Guitar players were used to instant sound, and with the early MIDI systems, there was some major latency. The amount of time it took to figure out what note was being played depended on the pitch. The processor usually had to listen to a few full cycles of the note before it could make a decision about what note you were playing. Higher notes have higher frequencies and cycle faster, so it took less time for higher notes to convert. Lower notes and their slower cycles took longer to convert.

Just how long are we talking here? Well, it wasn't minutes, but there was lag that you could feel. It felt like you were in some sort of quicksand; you'd play and expect to hear it instantly, but the note came afterwards. This made playing precisely very difficult. Also, the early units suffered from a high degree of errant notes. As the years went on, Roland and other companies took advantage of technology and produced newer units that improved the tracking, but for many players it was never good enough. Many simply wrote off the technology altogether. That was then, this is now. We will cover the "now" later in the book.

Building a Better Mousetrap

Since pitch-to-MIDI had some obvious flaws, several designers attempted to build a better mousetrap: a MIDI guitar system that did not require pitch detection. There were a few designs. The Synthaxe, which retailed at about $20,000, actually worked like a dream. It had a wired fingerboard and could sense where you pressed. It had strings so that you could feel at home playing the guitar, but they had nothing to do with the MIDI stream, which was all based on where you pressed. There were triggers for your picking hand that would send velocity information. This system was fast and amazingly accurate. Its two best known proponents were Allan Holdsworth and Futureman from Bela Fleck and the Flecktones. Unfortunately, at over $20K a unit, they didn't last long. The company went defunct. Too bad, because they were almost perfect. On the negative side, they were very, very heavy (read: caused back problems).

Other companies made their own attempts at skirting around the pitch-to-MIDI issue. Another company produced the Stepp controller, another wired fret controller. Casio had their DG-20, which looked like a toy at the time, but did much of what the Synthaxe did at a fraction of the price. There was one other notable attempt: The Ztar, by Starr Labs. This is the only synth controller that is still around. We are going to talk about the Ztar in Chapter 14, "Mixing Strategies for Guitar," in greater detail.

What is amazing is how many different companies jumped on the MIDI bandwagon at the time. Guitars from Gibson, Fender, Yamaha, Casio, Korg, and others were all producing synth guitars. Just about all of these went the way of the wind. Only two stand-alone pitch-to-MIDI systems exist now, Roland and Terratec, and only one alternative controller, the Starr Labs Ztar. The Brian Moore iGuitar.USB is the only model in existence now that converts to MIDI inside of the guitar, alleviating the need for an external processor. One guitar, one cable, total control.

3 Digital Modeling Amps

In the last chapter, we went over much of the history of digital modeling and why it has become such a relevant and important technology today. Digital modeling has extended far beyond its original incarnations. At first, the idea of modeling a vacuum tube's characteristics seemed like science fiction. Now, not only do we have amplifier modeling, but we can also model the guitars themselves. Imagine grabbing a guitar with no pickups, dialing in the sound of a Stratocaster, and, with the flip of a dial, changing it to a Gibson L5 hollow-body guitar. As far out as this sounds, we have reached this point where the fusion of technology and music has enhanced our music rather than getting in the way. Now we are going to investigate the current state-of-the-art units.

Digital Modeling Amplifiers

In 1996, Line6, a virtually unknown company, introduced the AxSys 212 (pictured in Figure 3.1) and started a revolution.

For the first time, guitar players could model the sounds of various amplifiers in a super-realistic fashion. One amp actually contained models of some of the most popular amplifiers in the world. This one amp had Marshall sounds, Fender sounds, Mesa Boogie sounds, Vox sounds—you name it, it had it. It also had high-quality effects. Technology marched on, and while Line6 continued to improve their designs, other companies entered the fold. Johnson amplification introduced a competing amplifier shortly after the Line6 AxSys appeared. Figure 3.2 shows the first Johnson modeling amplifier, which is the Millennium.

Figure 3.1
The AxSys 212: The world's first digital modeling amplifier.

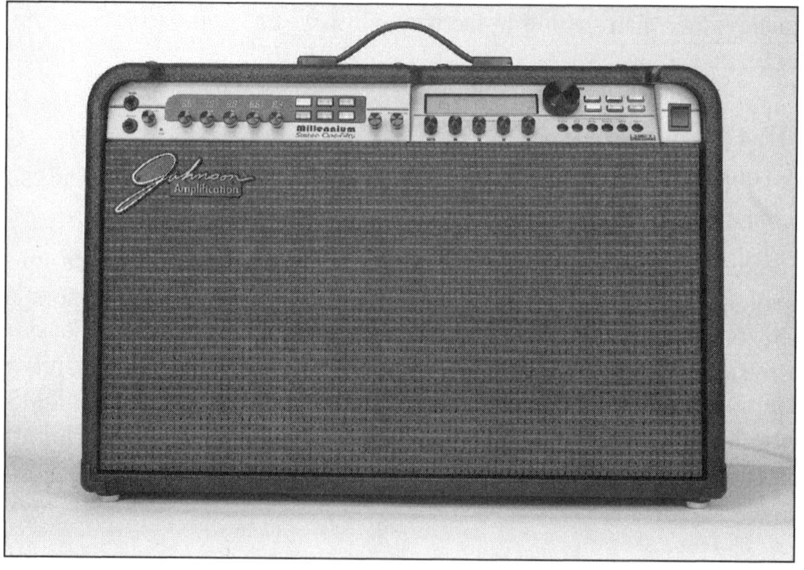

Figure 3.2
The Johnson Millennium.

Let's talk about Line6 first, as they started this whole game.

Line6

As I've said, Line6 was the first out of the gate, and their flagship, AxSys 212, was really good. A few years later they released the Flextone series, which sounded even better than the AxSys 212. The Flextone amps have gone through three incarnations and are now in production as the Flextone III (see Figure 3.3). With each new Flextone incarnation, the models have become more accurate, better-sounding, and more real.

Figure 3.3
The Line6 Flextone III.

> **MODELING FUTURE**
> One of the best parts about modeling technology is that it is tied so closely to computer processing. As computers become faster and are able to handle more complicated calculations, the quality and features of the modeling amps will continue to improve. The current crop of amps is so good that I can barely tell what's real and what's virtual. History has shown that it's only going to get better; at this point, I'm not sure what could possibly be better. But I will surely take it when it comes along.

During the Flextone's run, Line6 introduced the Spyder series, now available as the expanded Spyder II, a budget-minded amp that packs an impressive punch. You get fewer amp models and fewer effects than the Flextone series, but the sound is nothing short of remarkable for the price. The Spyder II, pictured in Figure 3.4, is still in production.

Figure 3.4
The Line6 Spyder II.

Line6 really got serious with the Vetta series of amplifiers, now produced in its second series, the Vetta II.

The Line6 Vetta II

In 2002, Line6 introduced its most advanced amplifier yet, the Vetta II. It features advanced modeling and a few bells and whistles not found anywhere else. Let's take a closer look at this amplifier and see what makes it state-of-the-art. The Vetta II, pictured in Figures 3.5 and 3.6, is available as either a combo amp (an amp with speakers) or as just the head itself (you supply the cabinet).

Figure 3.5
The Line6 Vetta II combo.

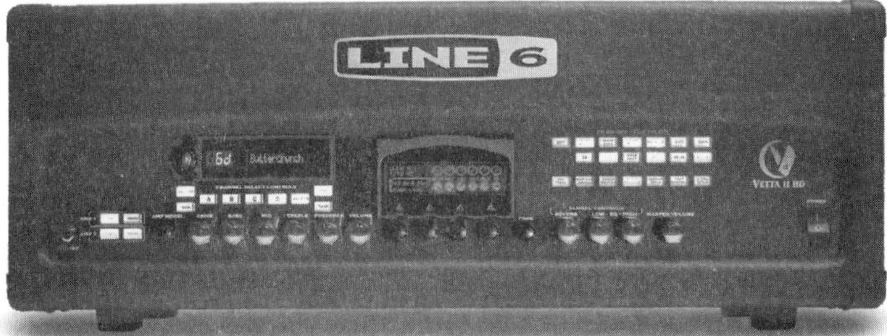

Figure 3.6
The Line6 Vetta head.

The Amps

How many amps would you like to carry around if you had a roadie and money was no object? I'd start with maybe a Fender Twin for my clean sounds, a Marshall Plexi for some crunchy sounds, and a Mesa Boogie for my lead sounds. Of course, if the situation arose, it would be nice to have a Vox amp around for the more British sounds. Heck, since we're going all out, I'd like one of those super-expensive Bogner amps everyone raves about. OK, the price tag would equal nearly $35,000, not to mention the upkeep of these vintage amps. This is probably not going to happen to you or me. Here is where digital modeling becomes so cool. The Vetta II includes 74, that's right, 74 different amp models within one amp. Without listing every amp they modeled, here is a brief rundown of the brands of amps they studied:

1. Marshall
2. Fender
3. Vox
4. Mesa Boogie
5. Hiwatt
6. Supro
7. Soldano
8. Silvertone
9. Matchless
10. Peavey
11. Roland
12. Gibson
13. Gretsch
14. ENGL
15. Conford
16. Diezel
17. Budda
18. Bogner

Since there are 18 types of amps modeled, how do we get to 74 amp models total? Simple, each of the companies listed above made several famous amps, each of which had its own signature sound. So among the 18 brands listed above, different models were studied and replicated. It's a pretty amazing list of sounds in one amplifier. Digital modeling allows you to be prepared for any tone that you might need, but what about effects?

Two Are Better Than One

Many artists carry more than one amplifier to a gig. This is because certain amps excel at certain sounds and are weak at other things. One of the amazing things about the Vetta II is that you can have two amp models active at the same time. Since the combo version has two speakers, you can control the panning of each of the amps. You literally can have one amp coming out of your right speaker and a totally different one coming out of the left speaker. By using the external jacks, you can have the amps routed to different speaker cabinets at different parts of the stage. As you can see from the built-in LCD display shown in Figure 3.7, there are two amps active, each with its own settings.

Figure 3.7
Multiple amps at once on the Vetta II.

Optionally, you can layer the two amps on top of one another and send them through the same set of speakers, creating a tone that would be impossible in the real world.

Effects

Of course, no amp setup would be complete without some effects, either in pedal form or rack processor form. The Vetta II includes a plethora of effects to choose from. Here is a list of the types of effects found in the unit:

1. Distortion Stompboxes
2. Modulation Stompboxes (Chorus, Flanger, Tremolo)
3. Delay Stompboxes
4. Dynamic Stompboxes (Compressors)
5. Filter Stompboxes (Synthetic Effects)
6. Amplifier Modeled Tremolo
7. Noise Gates and Compressors
8. Graphic Equalizers
9. Pitch Shifting Units
10. Reverb Units

In each of these categories, there are multiple modeled units. In the distortion section alone, eight classic effects were modeled. Adding up all the effects types together brings us to an impressive 110 different types of effects built into the amp. Again, these are not just generic algorithms, but computer-generated models of the original units. So now we have loads of amps and loads of effects.

Setting Up Effects

To set up the Stompbox effects, you can choose from any three Stompbox effects to use in each preset. These effects can be in any order you choose. Like a real stompbox, these are in the signal chain before they hit the amp, just like you would have in real life. You can have certain effects on one amp and other effects on the other amp. The routing is done from the convenient LCD screen. Figure 3.8 shows the visual routing of the Stompbox effects.

Figure 3.8
Effects routing on the Vetta II.

Stompbox effects are simply one type of effect you can tweak within the amp. Inline effects (which are the same as stompbox effects), such as Tremolo, Gate, Compression, and EQ, are available as separate effects. Inline effects are inserted sequentially into your sound chain. The Tremolo, Gate, and Compression occur before your virtual stompboxes, while the EQ happens after the cabinet/mic section (more on that later).

Post Effects

A Post effect is something that you blend into your sound. This is the opposite of an Inline effect, like a stompbox pedal, in which your sound is completely processed by the effect. Examples of Post effects are Reverb, Chorus, Delay, Pitch Shifting, and Modulation. Effects like these traditionally would be placed through your amplifier's effects loop. In the Vetta II, this is all done virtually through the interface. One of the amazing things is that not only can you change the order of your Post effects on the fly, but you can also choose if the effects are run in series or parallel for the greatest amount of control.

> **SERIES VS. PARALLEL**
> Series effects run one after another. That means that the affected output of one effect runs into the input of the next, and so on. Series effects are like old Christmas lights; when one bulb breaks, the whole chain goes dark. A parallel chain allows each effect to have a separate path to the audio, without having to run into each other. This is like the new Christmas lights in that when one bulb breaks, the chain stays on.

Control

All of these options are only useful if you have control over the amp during live use. This is certainly an issue for any amp/effects unit that has great depth and complexity. In the case of the Vetta II, Line6 has a few solutions for controlling different aspects of your amp. The most basic and recognized solution is a foot controller. This is nothing new in the guitar world. Foot controllers have been around for many years, even during the "big hair, big rack system" days!

Foot Control

At the most basic level, you can control the Vetta II with the FBV4 controller, shown in Figure 3.9.

Figure 3.9
The Line6 FBV4 foot controller.

The FBV4 is a basic preset change controller, allowing you to access any four sounds within any current bank of sounds with your foot. You can also use any of the four foot-selected buttons to "tap tempo" any effect that is based on time, such as delay or speaker rotation. This is the entry-level control pedal. However, with an amp like this, you're going to want some more control. Next up in line and size is the FBV Shortboard, as seen in Figure 3.10.

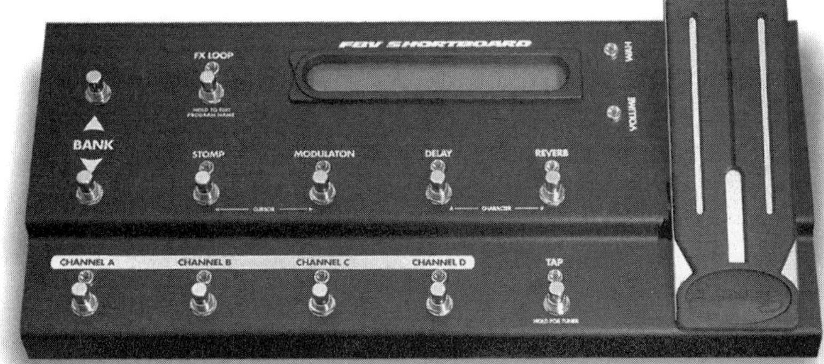

Figure 3.10
The Line6 FBV Shortboard foot controller.

As you can see from Figure 3.10, the Shortboard controller instantly raises your ability to do more with your feet. The first difference you will notice is the inclusion of more switches. The Shortboard controller not only allows you to select four presets, but unlike the FBV4, you can switch bands with the bank up and bank down buttons. This gives you unlimited access to any of the presets you've designed in the unit. Thankfully, an LED readout strip is also provided to give you the name of the preset you are currently using. Handy.

Above the strip of preset change buttons is a bank of buttons for controlling the individual effects inside of the Vetta's presets. These buttons, when activated by holding down the Hold to Start Program Mode, turn into individual on/off buttons for Stomp, Modulation, Reverb, and Delay. These buttons mimic the good old days of individual pedals, where you could turn effects on and off simply by clicking. The same holds true for the Shortboard. You have your convenient Tap Tempo button for setting up the time-based delay or modulation effects with your feet.

The last feature on the Shortboard is the pedal on the far-right side. This is called an expression pedal, and by default it is set up to function as either a Wah-wah or a volume pedal. You can select which one it is by simply rocking your foot all the way forward to the top position. By doing so, you can select either the Wah-wah or volume pedal option. Conveniently, there is an LED indicator on the unit itself that shows you which is active, either Wah-wah or volume.

But it doesn't stop there! The expression pedal can be assigned in the amp's editing screens to control more than just Wah-wah and volume. You can have it set wet/dry mix for effects, delay time, and almost any effect that has variable parameters. If one pedal isn't enough for you, there is a jack on the Shortboard that allows for a second Expression pedal (sold optionally), and you can set up that Expression pedal for any function you need.

If the Shortboard isn't enough for you, and you need to have the biggest, most powerful controller out there, then you need the FBV controller, as seen in Figure 3.11.

Figure 3.11
The full FBV controller.

As you can see, this is a more massive control surface. You can also see why the Shortboard is called short; this thing is huge! The massively expanded pedal gives you control over almost every possible control on the amp, all with your feet. However, you can still choose four presets at once and navigate up and down the banks using the bank select feature. A new feature called Favorite Channel is added via a button, so that you can call up your favorite sound, no matter what bank you are in. This is a very handy feature. The stompbox-style buttons have been greatly expanded to control the following controls:

- Amp 1 On/Off
- Amp 2 On/Off
- Reverb On/Off
- Tremolo On/Off
- Modulation On/Off

- Delay On/Off
- Stompbox 1, 2, 3 On/Off
- Tap Tempo

These extensive functions tweak your sound in any way you need, whether live or in the studio. Like the Shortboard controller, an LED readout reflects the patch on which you are working. On the far-right side, you have two Expression controllers that can be set to Wah-wah or volume, or via the amp's setup menus can control other aspects, such as reverb mix, tremolo speed, distortion saturation—a huge list of functions.

OTHER GOODIES

In addition to all of the functions on the Vetta II's floor control, they have added a tuner to the pedal, making it very convenient to tune onstage. There is also an option to turn on and off the external effects loop on the back of the amp, allowing you to use your favorite hardware effects alongside the Vetta II's internal effects.

As you can see, you have a great deal of control over your sound with the range of pedals offered by Line6.

MIDI Control

The back panel of the Vetta II and many of Line6's other amps supply you with MIDI input and output jacks, which control many of the functions of the Vetta II via traditional MIDI messages. While the FBV wins in terms of the number of functions you can control, with MIDI, you are able to change any of the presets on the amp remotely from a computer or any other source capable of transmitting MIDI messages. You can also control Wah-wah, volume, and any of the pedal functions on the Vetta II from MIDI.

When would this be desirable? If you are using the amp in a studio setup with a sequencer application like Pro Tools or Logic, you could send messages from the application at specific times to change sounds and modulate the sounds along with your music. You could do this remotely, without having to use your feet at all. This may be the *only* way to pull off difficult passages that require frequent changes in sounds that need to be synched with a prerecorded track or tracks.

ARE YOU A MIDIOT?

Don't know much about MIDI? Don't worry, I didn't either until the computer became a fixture in my music studio. For the lowdown on what MIDI is and what it can do for you, consult Chapter 15, "MIDI Guitar." There I'll explain all about the MIDI language and how you can use it to the best of your ability.

Other Options

Believe it or not, there is a bit more to talk about on this amp. Since this book is about the marriage of guitars and computers, it would make sense that modern amps would have more options for interconnecting with computers. The Vetta II has a digital output section that consists of S/PDIF and AES/EBU output connectors that are capable of delivering 24-bit/96 kHz digital signals to your computer for the purest tone transfer possible. The other connection is for the Variax guitar, also made by Line6. We are going to cover the Variax in the next chapter, and I will talk about how cool this particular connection really is.

VARIWHAT?

The Variax is a modeling guitar. Just like amps can model other amps, the Variax models the sound of guitars. The Variax and the Vetta II are made to work together in a very unique way.

Other Amps

We have spent a good deal of time looking at the offerings from Line6, which provided a nice sample of what is available technologically. However, they are not the only company to produce amplifiers that utilize digital modeling technology. I'm not going to go into intense detail on each amp, nor is it possible to cover *every* amp that is made. However, I will give you a well-informed idea of what's out there.

Fender Cyber Series

Fender Musical Instrument Company, long known for its famous guitars and workhorse amps, has entered the modeling fray with the Cyber series of amplifiers. Their first foray was the Cyber-Twin, now in its second version, the Cyber-Twin SE (Second Edition), which can be seen in Figure 3.12.

What makes the Cyber-Twin a bit different from the other modeling amps is that even though it uses DSP modeling technology for its amp models, it still utilizes a tube preamp with two 12AX7 tubes to add warmth to the sound before it is processed. Like you would expect, it has a full complement of amp choices (all modeled from Fender's line of historically important amps). It also boasts a full range of effects: LCD preset display, MIDI control, and digital outputs for easy computer connectivity. If you are a fan of the Fender sound, you may dig this amp. On a separate geek note, the knobs on this amp are motorized, which means that after you select a preset, the knobs magically move to their new positions. So you can always tell what the amp is doing without having to squint at an LCD menu, or worse yet, having to guess like you do with amps that *don't* have motorized knobs.

Figure 3.12
The Fender Cyber-Twin SE.
Fender® and Cyber-Twin® are trademarks owned by Fender Musical Instruments Corporation and are used herein with express written permission. All rights reserved.

Fender has also expanded its digital line to include the Cyber-Champ and the Cyber-Deluxe. Both the Cyber-Deluxe and Cyber-Champ have a complement of modeled amps and effects, just not as extensive as the Cyber-Twin. The Cyber-Twin SE remains Fender's flagship DSP amplifier.

Fender is now utilizing effects in DSP on other amps, such as the Dyna-Touch III amps, but DSP effects are nothing new. Amp modeling on the Cyber-Twin SE is new.

DSP EFFECTS

Expect to see DSP effects on many amplifiers in the coming years. DSP is an industry buzzword these days. Many amps will now include Reverb, Chorus, Delay, and other effects, all built into the amplifier via DSP.

Vox Valvetronix Series

Vox is a legendary name in tube amps. From the Beatles to Queen, their signature sound defined the music of the British Invasion for years. Now Vox is riding the wave of the future and has entered the world of digital modeling with their Valvetronix series of amplifiers, pictured in Figure 3.13.

Like many of the modeling amps available on the market, the Vox is a combination of modeled amps and effects. Since each company has its own proprietary way of sampling guitar sound, each company yields different results. Vox has made some incredible tube amps, so they know

Figure 3.13
The Vox Valvetronix digital modeling amp's top control view.

exactly how to brew legendary sound and have unrestricted access to their own designs and engineering, something that the other modeling companies don't always get. Couple this with a partnership with Korg (which distributes Vox amps), and you have the Vox Valvetronix amps. Korg has lent its modeling technology and years of DSP knowledge to the project, and the entire Valvetronix line is a collaboration between Korg and Vox. Also, like the Fender Cyber-Twin, the Valvetronix makes use of a 12AX7 tube as part of their digital amplifier. Vox has a proprietary technology called *Valve Reactor*, which makes use of a tube in its power section to accurately model the response of a vacuum tube in the signal chain. This hybrid of digital and analog technology is something we may see more of in the future. This fusion of the old and the new is certainly worth an audition.

Roland VGA

Riding on the wave of success that Roland had with the VG floor processors, Roland introduced the VGA series of amplifiers, pictured in Figure 3.14.

Figure 3.14
The Roland VGA digital modeling system.

These amplifiers did more than just about any other modeling style of amp. Of course, this came with a price. In the case of the VGA series, it required the use of the GK divided pickup to reach the amp's full potential. Later incarnations of the VGA series allowed for amp-only modeling using a standard quarter-inch guitar jack, but the full power of the amplifier was not reached doing this. The power of this amp was the combination of the GK divided pickup and the amplifier's ability to model more than just "amp sounds."

The VGA was more than just an amp modeler. It modeled guitars and synthesizer effects as well. For example, you plugged in your guitar (equipped with the GK synth pickup), and not only did the amp model different classic amplifier and effects sounds, but it was also able to model the very sounds of the guitars we all know and love so much. The VGA is no longer in production, but the technology that spawned it, the VG-88, is still alive and well, and I'll discuss it later in this chapter.

Digital Modeling Processors

The digital modeling amps were the first wave in this exciting new technology. As unbelievable as they were, not everyone wanted or needed a new amp. The next logical step/jump would be to remove the amplifier altogether and put the modeling technology into a small box that you could either plug into a preexisting amplifier or simply record directly into a recording session. While there have been floor-based processors that offered distortion and other effects integrated into one unit, none of them were based on the new computer-aided digital modeling that changed many guitarists' opinions of gear that didn't have tubes in it. The first successful modeling processor was the Line6 POD. Let's explore the POD.

Line6 POD

The Line6 POD, introduced in 1998, looked more like an oversized red kidney bean than a piece of musical gear (see Figure 3.15).

The POD was essentially the modeling section of the Flextone amplifier, without the amplifier. It offered the same amp models and effects in a compact, affordable package. It also added guitar speaker cabinet emulation for a more realistic direct-recording sound. The POD was a popular item, and many studio and recording guitarists employed the POD as something of a "Swiss army knife" of amps and sounds.

The POD was upgraded to Version 2, which added more amp models and updated modeling technology by means of a new chip implanted in the unit. The POD was also introduced in a Pro model, occupying two rack spaces. The POD Pro added such important features as digital outputs for higher-quality computer and recording connections (see Figure 3.16).

Figure 3.15
The original Line6 POD.

Figure 3.16
The POD Pro.

As with all technology, things improve, and as the parallel line of amplifiers improved, so did the PODs. The current version is the PODxt, which is pictured in Figure 3.17.

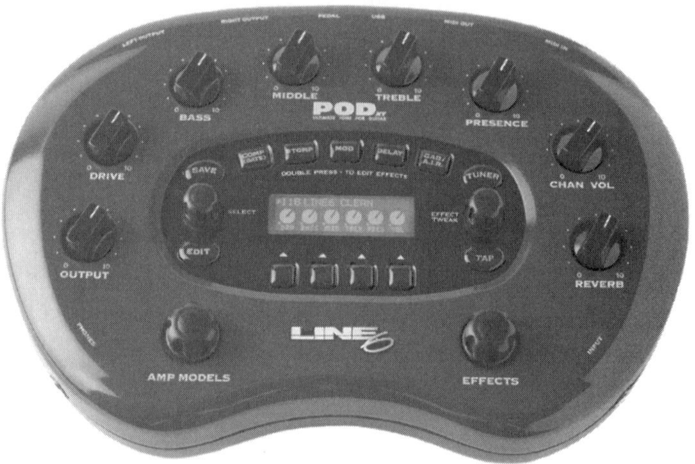

Figure 3.17
The PODxt.

The PODxt boasts a bunch of neat new features that make it a very appealing choice. Here are some of the features of the PODxt:

- 36 amp models based on the VETTA II
- 24 different speaker cabinet models
- 4 modeled microphones with speaker axis placement options
- 50 stompbox effects
- USB digital input/output
- MIDI control

Two features are significant with the release of the PODxt. The first is the USB output, which allows the PODxt to connect directly to the computer without needing an audio interface. You can route your audio signal from the POD to your computer, directly into the recording application of your choice. This is a boon for the guitarist who has no need for other inputs and outputs.

The other feature that has been introduced with the xt, and also with the Vetta II, is the ability to purchase model packs. These are downloadable banks of newly modeled amplifiers, cabinets, and effects. This allows for further expansion.

The PODxt is also available in a Pro version, as seen in Figure 3.18.

Figure 3.18
The POD XT Pro.

The Pro model adds digital outputs at a 96 kHz sample rate for high-quality digital transfer to your recording setup. Just like the original POD Pro, the PODxt PRO is also a rack-mountable piece. It's perfect for a recording studio to keep in their rack and allow any guitarist to plug into for great direct sound.

Control

As with any guitar system, foot control is a must! You can't bend down and tweak the presets as you go. Fortunately, Line6 enables the POD series to connect with the same floor controllers as the Vetta II, specifically the FBV, the Shortboard, and the FBV4, giving you complete control over preset changes and effects settings. With the FBV and Shortboard, you also gain the option of using the Expression pedals for Wah-wah and volume, and you can also see the preset name you are using.

> **NO AMP?**
> With the floor units we are talking about, is it possible to survive without an amp? If you play live and do a lot of recording, you can simply plug the line level outputs of any of the devices into the house PA or the mixing board. It's becoming possible to work without an amp. The only downside to playing live is that you are at the mercy of the house's PA system and the sound man they employ—which can be great or really bad.

In order to build a better mousetrap, Line6 recently introduced the PODxt LIVE, pictured in Figure 3.19, which combines a PODxt with a full floor controller for the ultimate in sound and flexibility.

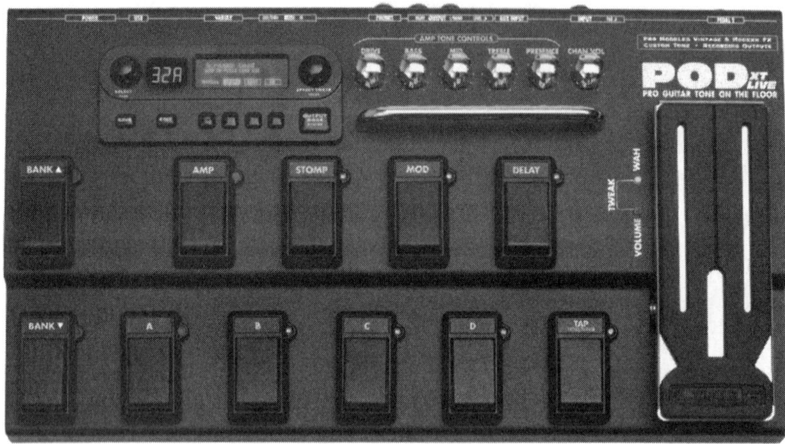

Figure 3.19
The PODxt LIVE.

The PODxt Live boasts a number of high-end features that make it the most complete system that isn't the Vetta II. Here are some of the features of the PODxt LIVE:

- 36 amps based on the Vetta II
- 80+ stompbox effects
- 24 guitar cabinet models
- 4 modeled microphones with speaker axis positioning
- Input for the Variaxe modeling guitar
- USB digital outs
- Dedicated switches for stompboxes

All in all, you get a pretty cool package. Now, how about the editing? All of the PODs have knobs and small LCD screens for accessing and manipulating the presets. Surely, there must be a better way to edit your parameters! Of course, there is.

Computer-based Editing

One of the neat things that you can do with the computer now is to edit the parameters of your hardware effects unit if the manufacturer writes an editor program. Line6 has developed a special piece of software called *Line6 Edit*, which allows you to edit any of the parameters of your patches using a computer. Through MIDI or USB connections (depending on which model you have), not only can you edit with a mouse and a screen and upload your changes to your amp or POD, but you can also back up your precious sounds onto the computer. This is great if you ever run into trouble and your memory is erased. It's always good to have a backup. Here is a shot of the editing software in action. Figure 3.20 shows the computer editing software for the Vetta II amp, while Figure 3.21 shows the editing software that comes with the PODxt.

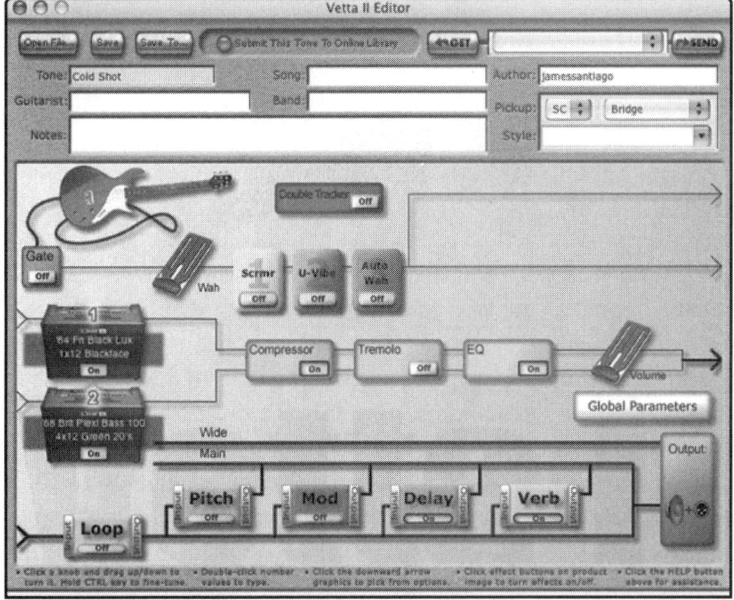

Figure 3.20
Computer editing software for the Vetta II.

As you can see from the above images, not only is it easier to work this way, but it also gives you a much clearer representation of exactly what these products are capable of doing. This type of software is not exclusive to Line6, as we will see when investigating other units of this type, because computer control is becoming a standard feature. Think about it, what would you rather do: Stare at a small screen and push a few buttons, or create your dream sounds in a virtual visual

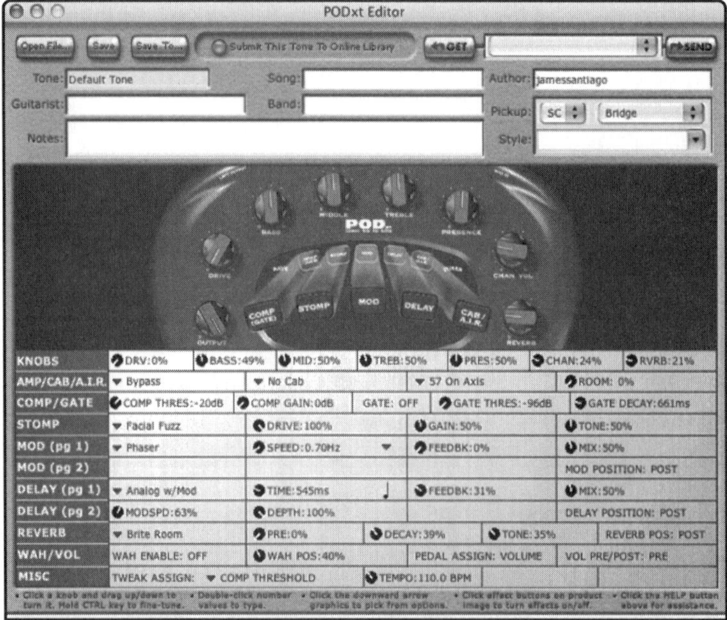

Figure 3.21
Computer editing software for the PODxt.

environment? The ability to back up presets makes the software a must, even if you don't ever plan on editing with your computer.

Behringer

Behringer is no stranger to the music world. They make just about anything you could ever want for any musical situation. Behringer gained popularity with its low-cost mixers and studio equipment. It was only a matter of time until Behringer entered the modeling arena. Their first foray into guitar modeling was the V-AMP (virtual amplifier). The guitar-shaped modeling processor boasted an impressive list of modeled amps, effects, and cabinet simulation. Now, the V-AMP is in its second incarnation, the V-AMP 2, which expands on the original V-AMP. It's hard not to draw parallels to the POD series, or any other modeling processor, in that they basically do the same thing. They use digital modeling technology to allow a guitarist to re-create the sounds of amps and effects in a convenient package. Each company has its own particular computer algorithms (formulas) for the DSP involved, so while the units may resemble each other, each one has its own signature sound. It's up to you to investigate all your options if you're thinking of purchasing any digital modeler.

The V-AMP 2 ships in two versions: the V-AMP 2 and the V-AMP 2 Pro. The V-AMP 2, shown in Figure 3.22, is designed to be a portable unit you can take with you from gig to gig or to the recording studio.

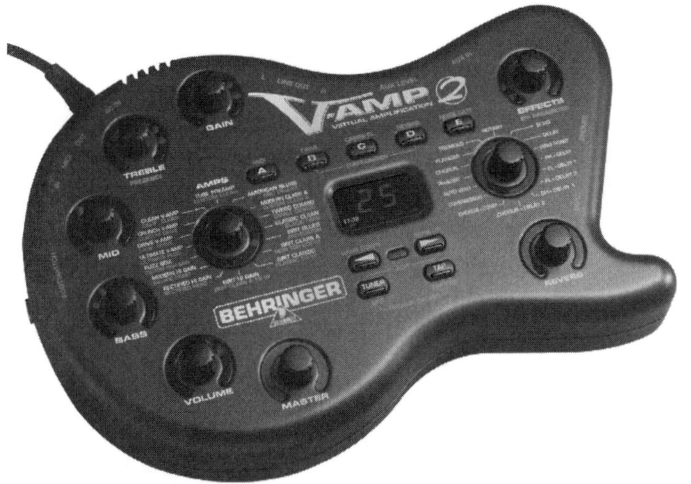

Figure 3.22
The Behringer V-AMP 2.

The V-AMP 2 boasts 32 different amplifiers, 15 speaker simulators, and a plethora of 24-bit effects to fulfill any sonic need. It supports MIDI control, either for use with Behringer's own FCB1010 floor controller, as shown in Figure 3.23, or any MIDI-capable control pedal, allowing you to change presets on the fly while you play.

Figure 3.23
The Behringer FCB1010 MIDI foot control.

The MIDI jacks also serve a few other important purposes. Behringer has an archive of presets made by professionals and users alike on its Web site. You can browse through thousands of readymade presets to suit any style. Once you've chosen one, you can send the data from your computer though MIDI directly into the V- AMP 2. The MIDI support also allows any of the functions on the unit to be controlled via a computer. In practical terms, you can have your computer change and automate any of the parameters of your V-AMP automatically. Here is an example in this note.

> **MIDI CONTROL TIP**
>
> To better understand why MIDI support is so vital to the digital modeling processors, let's set up an example. You are recording a guitar part. During the process of recording your song, aspects of your sound change. Maybe you add delay for the intro and take it away for the verse. When it comes time to take your solo, you want to change to a lead-type sound. Traditionally, you would have to record these as separate audio events, on separate tracks, all at different times. If you're recording with a computer, you can set up a MIDI control track that, at specific times, will change your tone for you. As the track progresses, all the changes will happen instantly, thanks to MIDI control. I'll get into the nuts and bolts of working like this in Chapter 17, "Virtual Instruments." For now, just know that it's possible.

DigiTech GNX4

DigiTech has a long, distinguished history in the guitar world. They are a long-time maker of stompbox-style guitar pedals, and they also manufacture digital floor and rack mount effects processors.

Their current top-of-the-line floor modeling processor is the GNX4, shown in Figure 3.25, which is one of the most comprehensive packages on the market.

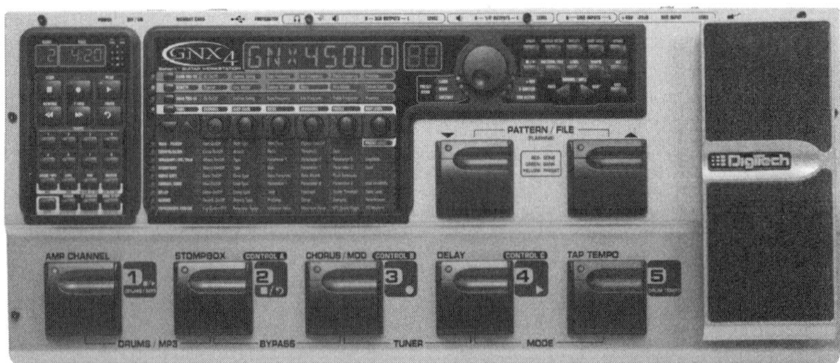

Figure 3.25
The DigiTech GNX4.

In one floor-mounted unit, DigiTech has managed to squeeze in the following:

- A multi-modeling guitar processor
- An onboard 8-track recording studio (no computer needed)
- A general MIDI drum machine
- An MP3 player
- Guitar, line level, and microphone inputs
- Balanced and unbalanced inputs and outputs

- A 4-channel 24-bit audio interface via USB to your computer
- Included software for computer recording

Let's start by talking about the unit itself and its connections, before we get into what it can do.

Physical Layout and Connections

Physically, the GNX4 is a sturdy pedal. It is made of steel and weighs somewhere between "not heavy, but not light." It reassures you that you can stomp on it, and it can take it. Figure 3.26 shows the top view, which I'll break into sections to explain the functions.

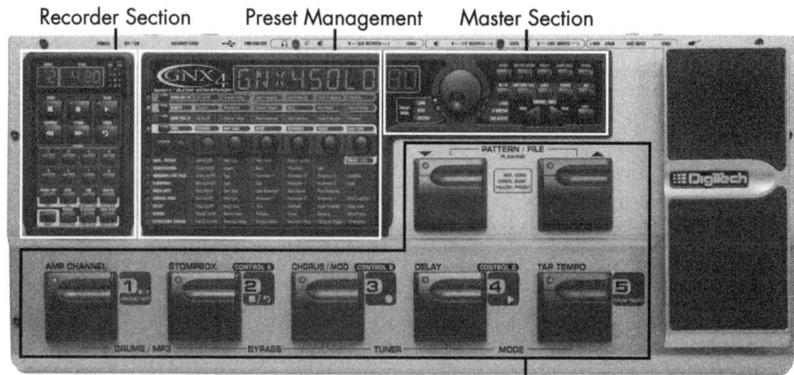

Figure 3.26
The GNX4 top view.

The top panel is broken up into four main sections, which are detailed here.

Foot Control

The first section is the foot control section of the unit (see Figure 3.27).

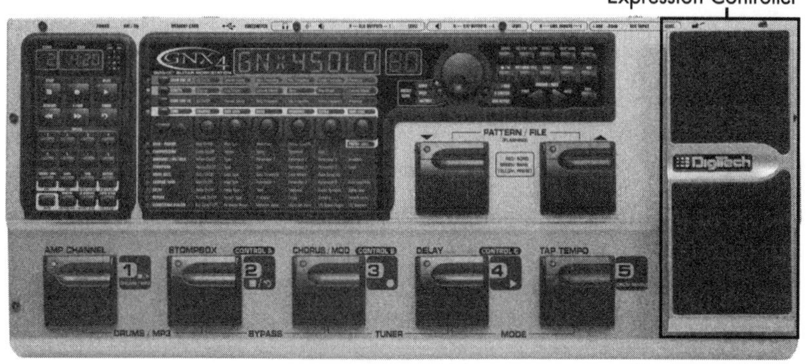

Figure 3.27
GNX4 foot control.

The foot control section consists of seven foot switches and one expression pedal. The foot switches are multipurpose. Their functions can range from a simple preset switch to turning effects on and off, starting and stopping the recorder, turning on the tuner—a myriad of functions. Their actual functions are dependent on which feature of the GNX4 you are currently in. The Expression pedal, like most expression pedals, controls a variable controller, such as volume, wet/dry mix, or any effects parameters that can be controlled in real time. This behavior of the expression can be programmed differently from patch to patch. As we explore the different features of the unit, I will comment on what the foot switches do.

Recorder Section

The GNX4 also serves as a standalone eight-track audio recorder. It captures its data onto a compact flash card (the same ones used in cameras) that is inserted into the rear of the unit. This is great for catching inspiration as you practice because recording is never more than a foot press away. The recording section has its own real estate on the face of the unit, as seen in Figure 3.28. The onboard recorder records internally to WAV files, but can play back .MP3 tracks for play-alongs.

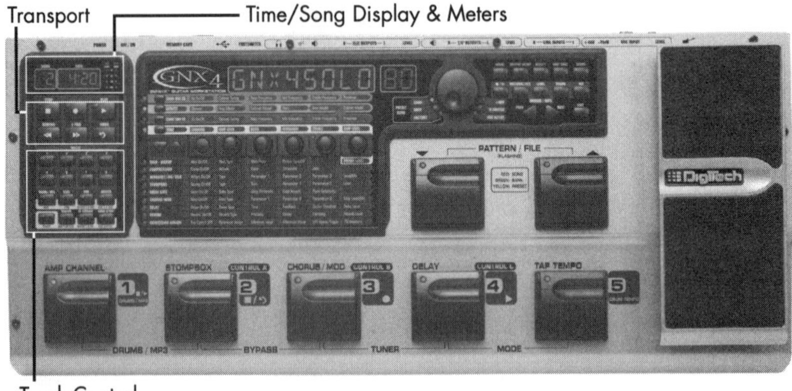

Figure 3.28
The GNX4's recorder section.

The recorder section is composed of 22 buttons and two LED screens. The buttons control the normal transport (stop, play, record, rewind, etc.), while the other buttons select the track you are recording on, help to set level and pan, and control the drum machine.

The LED screens provide access to the song number (you can store multiple songs on one compact flash card) and the current time of the tracks. Along with the recorder section, the seven footswitches serve new purposes when in Record mode—hands-free control of the recorder's functions. Figure 3.29 shows what the footswitches are responsible for in Record mode.

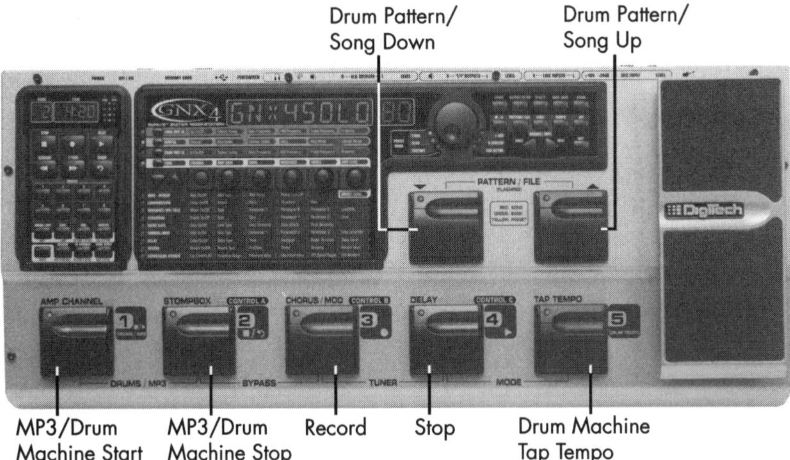

Figure 3.29
Record mode foot switch functions.

There are some advanced functions for which you will need to use the smaller hand-operated buttons, but the freedom to stop and start your recordings with your feet means that you will never miss a beat.

> **RECORDING TIME**
> Just how many songs can you record into the GNX4? Well, this depends on a few things. First, how many tracks are you utilizing in your recording? The more tracks, the more room you're going to take up. Also, the length of your songs will be dictated by your available space. Most importantly, the capacity of the compact flash card will really govern this. If you plan to use the GNX4 as a main recording station, get the biggest-capacity compact flash cards you can find, possibly a few of them. The GNX4 will accept up to a 2 gigabyte flash card, which holds 6 hours, 24 track minutes of WAV files that you can divide as you need between any of the 8 tracks. Divided equally among 8 tracks, a 2 gigabyte card will provide you with 48 minutes on each track.

Preset Management

Dead center on the GNX4 is the heart of the unit: the preset management section, as shown in Figure 3.30.

This section allows you to choose and edit any aspect of a preset, which can include the modeled guitar pickups, amps, effects, EQ, reverb, amplifier type, and cabinet type. Through a myriad of LED lights, buttons, rotary controls, and LED displays, you can program patches as you see fit.

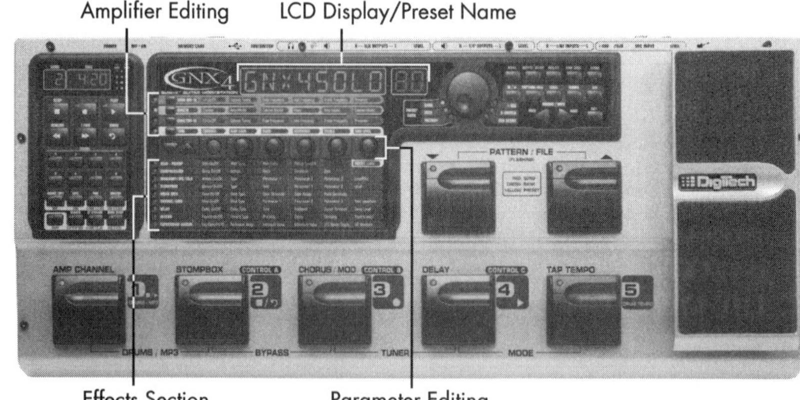

Figure 3.30
GNX4 preset management.

Master Section

The last section of the GNX4's top housing, shown in Figure 3.31, is basically a master section, allowing you to access utility features of the unit, switch between user and factory presets and the compact flash slots, and even audition drum loops. A jog/shuttle wheel enables you to rapidly change patches in this section.

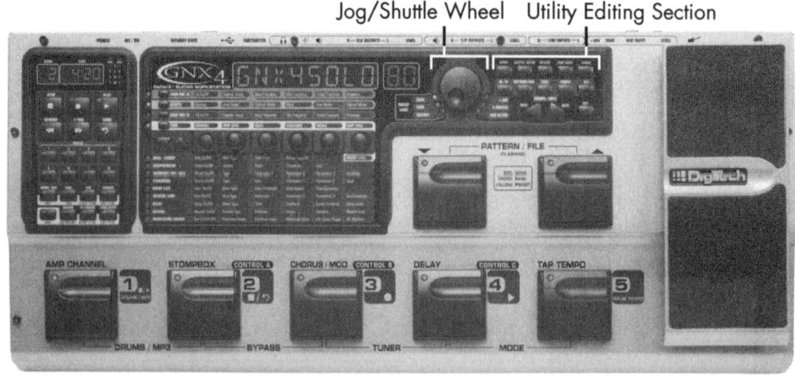

Figure 3.31
The GNX4 master section.

Rear Panel Connections

The rear of the GNX4 gives you access to all your inputs and outputs. It's where the unit "happens." Figure 3.32 is a shot of the rear unit.

Let's go over the connections from left to right according to the figure.

1. **Guitar Input**: Plug your guitar in here.
2. **Microphone Input**: With controls for microphone level, phantom power, and a -20dB pad for louder sources.

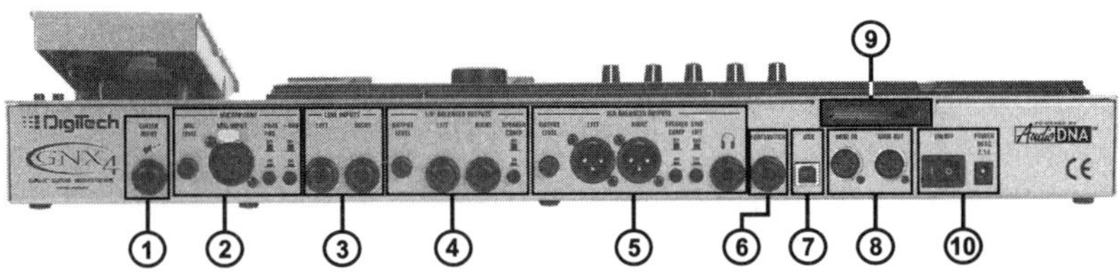

Figure 3.32
GNX4 rear connections.

3. **Line Inputs**: Left and right mono inputs for line level sources, such as keyboards and other line level devices.
4. **Quarter-inch Balanced Outputs**: Left and right balanced outputs with level control and speaker compensation switch (for connections to full-range speaker systems, not guitar amps).
5. **XLR Balanced Outputs**: Left and right balanced outputs with level control, speaker compensation (as above), and a ground lift to reverse hum/noise from ground loops.
6. **Foot switch**: Insert for the optional GNXFC foot control, providing extra access to the onboard recording functions of the GNX4.
7. **USB Connection**: Stream four channels of 24-bit audio to your computer and edit patches with the included X-Edit software.
8. **MIDI In/Out**: Connect external MIDI controllers for further control of the parameters in real time. Also, control other MIDI devices with the GNX4 or functions and parameters for computer recording/editing.
9. **Compact Flash**: Storage medium for the onboard recorder using Type I Compact Flash Cards.
10. **On/Off Switch**: I have no idea what this one does.

Modeling and Effects

The GNX4 has all the standard models you would expect—amplifier models, cabinet models/simulation—but it adds a new feature not found in other units, which is pickup modeling. With pickup modeling, you can take your single-coil Strat and make it sound like it has a humbucker in there.

PICKUP MODELING

Pickup modeling isn't new per se. The Roland VG series did pickup modeling, but it did so through a special pickup. The GNX4 does this with any traditional guitar on the market. It certainly yields a tone change, but my Brian Moore Les Paul-style guitar didn't magically sound like a '61 Fender. It was effective in varying my sound, though, and that's worth something.

Modeled Amps

The modeled amps are a list of everyone's favorite tube amps and a few other surprises. The GNX4 breaks its amp modeling into a few categories: Direct (Direct Box), Guitar Amps, Acoustic Guitar, Bass Amps, and a User Amp. More on this in a minute.

The Direct Box doesn't require too much explanation; this is meant to bypass the amplifier section altogether.

In the Guitar Amp section, there are 15 modeled amps to choose from, and they are as follows:

- '65 Twin Reverb
- Matchless DC30
- Dual Rectifier
- Mark II C
- '57 Tweed Deluxe
- AC30 Top Boost
- Clean Tube Combo
- '78 Master Volume
- Crunchy Tube Combo
- High Gain Tubes
- Blues Tube Tone
- JCM9000
- High Gain Fuzz Distortion
- Bassman Amp
- HiWatt 50 Watt Stack

Of course, the above list just contains the models the amps are based on.

The next type of amp is an Acoustic Guitar modeler of a flattop acoustic guitar. Selecting this model will transform your traditional electric guitar into an acoustic-type guitar. Will it make your solid-body sound like an old Martin? No, but onstage it will give you the desired effect. It's got that sparkle that an acoustic has. It's quite a neat feature.

For the bass players in the house, or for the guitar player who likes the sounds of bass amps (the Fender Bassman was a bass amp first and was adopted by guitar players), the GNX4 models 10 popular bass amps. Here they are:

- Ampeg SVT
- Ashdown ABM-C410H

- Trace-Elliot Commando
- Sunn 200S
- ’69 Ampeg SVT Classic
- Ampeg B15
- SWR Basic Black
- Fender Dual Showman
- Mesa Boogie Bass 400+
- Hartke Model 2000

The last type of amp is a user-made amp called a HyperModel. How does a user make an amp? Well, in the GNX4, you are able to load up two amps at once. Using a feature called warping, you are able to blend the characteristics of two amps together. When you save one of these Frankenstein warped amps, it’s a HyperModel. You may use a saved HyperModel as one of your amplifiers. The warp feature can yield some very interesting results. I had fun with this feature. I made some amps that can’t and probably shouldn’t be combined. If you’re looking to make a truly original sound, this might be the feature for you.

Cabinet Modeling

Cabinet modeling is a prime feature of the GNX4. The unit allows you to select any two amps in any preset. Either of the amps can have its own different cabinets. You can use any of the 22 cabinets listed below (23 if you count bypassing speakers for a direct sound). Each of the cabinets tries to re-create the natural EQ and sound characteristics of famous cabinets, from huge 4×12 stacks to small 1×12 combo amps. The cabinets are taken from famous guitar and bass speaker cabinets. Here are your choices:

- Direct (No Cabinet Modeling)
- American 2×12
- British 4×12
- Vintage 30 4×12
- British 2×12
- American 1×12
- Blonde 2×12
- Fane 4×12
- Greenback 4×12
- Boutique 4×12
- Bassman 4×10

- '65 Tweed 1×12
- Pro 1×15
- Ampeg Portaflex
- Ashdown 4×12 w/Tweeter
- Sunn 200S 2×15
- Acoustic 360
- Hartke 1×15
- SWR Basic Black
- Ampeg 8×10
- Ashdown ABM 410
- SWR Goliath
- Hartke 4×10

In addition to just being able to choose any of the cabinets, you can further edit the tuning of the cabinets, changing the main resonant frequencies. These can help to further tweak and fine-tune the sound of the amps and cabinets together. You can even save some of your custom tune cabinets for later use in other presets.

Effects

Sorry, the GNX4 has no effects. No, just kidding! It has a great selection of effects. Some of these effects are stompbox style, in that they appear before the virtual amp (such as Wah-wah and Stompbox distortion), while others are placed after the amp in a virtual effects loop (such as Delay and Reverb).

Here is the full listing of effects that the GNX4 can generate. There are eight different types of effects that can be used in any one preset. Within the eight effect types, there are multiple choices, such as different stompboxes or different Wah-wah pedals. Here is a list of the effects available:

- Wah-wah/Pickup: Wah-wah modeling or pickup modeling
- Compression
- Whammy/IPS/Talk: The famous DigiTech Whammy pedal, Intelligent Pitch Shift (IPS) (pitch shifting based on diatonic musical keys), and a talk box emulator
- Stompbox: Classic distortion pedals (10 to choose from)
- Noise Gate
- Chorus/Modulation: Chorus, Flanger, Phaser, Tremolo, Vibrato, Rotary Speaker, AutoYa (an Auto Wah-wah), YaYa (Wah-wah and Flanger combination), Synthtalk (a talking guitar), Envelope Filter (a type of Auto Wah-wah), Detune (a doubling effect), and a Pitch Shifter

- Delay
- Reverb

One of each of the eight effects categories can be active within the patch. Editing is simply done on the face of the unit, or through the X-Edit software that tweaks your patches on the computer—more on that later. The Expression pedal can be assigned to a myriad of functions, and the stompbox-style buttons on the face of the unit can be assigned dynamically to turn effects on or off or tap tempo for any of the time-based effects. All of this is easily done from within the editing features on the unit.

> **MANUAL LOOK**
>
> If you'd like to find out more about any of the products we have talked about in this book, many of the companies involved have full product manuals available for free download so you can get a full idea of what's possible. I certainly can't go into every detail here, but the manuals will give you a very good idea.

Onboard Recording

One of the unique features of the GNX4 is the capability to record up to eight tracks directly into the unit. Through the use of a Compact Flash card, you can easily record over six hours of track time on a 2 gigabyte card. This is great for capturing those moments of inspiration as they happen. You can use the GNX4 as a full-featured recorder, making this more of a workstation than just a guitar modeler pedal. Couple this with microphone inputs and two additional line level sources, and you can create full-featured demos right within the unit.

The recording functions are accessed from the recording panel, as seen in Figure 3.33.

Figure 3.33
Recording section.

From this panel, you can control stop, start, rewind, and undo features. You can also assign which of the eight tracks you are working on, monitor your levels through the level meter on the right side, change pan, and many other features. Through the USB connection, you can stream your creations to the computer for further work and creation, using the supplied software DigiTech ships with the GNX4 (Pro Tracks Plus for the PC and Bias Deck SE for Mac).

You can even create JamMan-style loops with the GNX4 and quantize them to play back seamlessly together! Very cool.

MIDI Drum Machine and MP3 Player

The GNX4 has two very neat features: drums and MP3 playback. Drum loops are not unique to the GNX4, but the quality of the loops is very high. These are great for practicing with to help you work on feel and timing. There are a total of 110 different drum files and five standard metronome sounds to work with. The drum grooves can be used to practice with. You can even use them in the recording section of the unit as a great background.

The best news is that these drum sounds are not audio loops, but they are driven by MIDI files. This means that you can supplement the loops in the unit by adding MIDI files to the compact flash card. There are many royalty-free MIDI drum loops that you can use with the GNX4. Since MIDI files are very small and Compact Flash cards are large and cheap now, it's possible to store thousands of extra drum sounds. The GNX4 comes with eight different drum kits, each with its own unique sampled sounds. You will find sounds ranging from brushed jazz to techno! There are a ton to choose from here. Even cooler is that the tempo of the drum loops can be changed on the fly by simply tapping the tempo with your toe on the unit. Since this isn't an audio loop, the drum sounds can play back at any speed, without degradation of sound as the tempo reaches extremes (either slow or fast).

The other option is to load the Compact Flash card with MP3 files that you can play along with on the unit. These may be backing tracks you've purchased or loops you have loaded from third-party sources. Bottom line—if it's audio in MP3 format, you can use it on the GNX4!

USB Interface

Another nice feature of the GNX4 is the ability to use the unit as a 24-bit recording interface. Using a USB 1.1 cable connected to your Mac or PC, you are able to stream four channels of audio to the computer. The four channels are Guitar, Microphone, and Line Level 1 + 2. The MIDI ports on the rear of the unit can be used in the computer recording environment. The GNX4 ships with recording software for PC and Mac to get you started, but it uses standard ASIO and CoreAudio drivers on the PC and Mac. So if you already own another recording package, the GNX4 will fit right into your current setup. One simple USB cable takes care of everything. If you're looking for a device that can function without a computer while at the same time fulfilling the needs of an audio interface, the GNX4 deserves a look.

Additional Features

There are two more things to mention about the GNX4 before we move on. The first is the patch editing software, X-Edit. The GNX4 crams a lot of information into a relatively small package. I find editing on the unit easy enough, but computer control is always easier when given the choice. Thankfully, that's exactly what the X-Edit software does. It allows you to edit patches graphically and send them via the USB cable back to the unit. I have always found that working with patch editor software is much faster than working on any unit, no matter how well designed it is! Figures 3.34 and 3.35 show the X-Edit software in use. It's very easy to visualize your patches and even create those cool warped amps, creating HyperAmps of your very own.

Figure 3.34
X-Edit, view one.

Figure 3.35
X-Edit, view two.

The last feature is cooperation between guitar magazines (*Guitar World* and *Guitar One*) and DigiTech. Most guitar magazines feature transcriptions of songs, so this is nothing new. What is new is that along with the transcriptions are links to the presets for your DigiTech GNX4. This allows you to re-create the tones of the songs you are learning. You can download these files, and many other users' submitted presets, and load them in through the USB cable. This is great for the student guitarist and anyone seeking to learn how to make the tones they know and love. A little patch reconstruction goes a long way.

M-Audio Black Box

At NAMM 2005, M-Audio launched the Black Box, a collaboration between M-Audio and legendary music instrument designer Rodger Linn. The Black Box is joining the ranks of the new breed of guitar modeling processors that do more than just model. M-Audio has added a few new twists that make the Black Box pretty unique. Figure 3.36 shows you what the Black Box looks like.

Figure 3.36
The M-Audio Black Box.

The unit is comparable in size to the Line6 POD, and both are small enough for easy portability. As previously, the Black Box has a few tricks up its sleeves. Let's discuss the highlights of the Black Box:

- 12 amp models
- 43 effects
- Effects are beat synchable via MIDI
- Separate beat-synched delay
- A 99-pattern drum machine
- 200 presets (100 user-defined)
- USB connection allows the Black Box to be a direct digital audio interface to the computer

- Microphone input
- Support for external expression pedals
- Digital output
- Multifunction rotary encoders for control of effects and amp parameters
- Large LCD display for displaying the different parameters

The face of the Black Box has a user-friendly layout with knobs and buttons that access all of its main features. Figure 3.37 is an overview of the top panel and all of its control options.

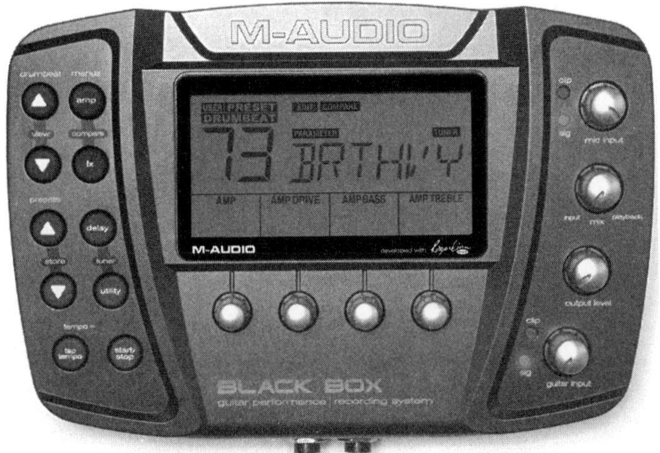

Figure 3.37
A closer view of the Black Box's top panel.

Amps

The Black Box has a myriad of amps and effects to create your signature sound. The modeled amplifier section gives you a selection of 12 well-known amplifiers to help you start building your own tone. The amplifiers that M-Audio based their models on are as follows:

- Fender Bassman
- Fender Deluxe
- Fender Twin
- Vox AC-30
- Marshall JTM-45
- Marshall Plexi
- Marshall JCM-2000

- Hiwatt DR-103
- Soldano SLO-100
- Mesa Boogie Maverick
- Mesa Boogie Dual Rectifier
- Bogner Ubershall

The Black Box allows you to select any one of the 12 amps as your sound source. Selecting an amplifier, via the Amp button on the left side of the unit, changes the front LCD panel to enable you to edit the parameters of the amp, or even reselect a new amp.

When in Amp mode, the face of the Black Box's lower screen is devoted to the amps. The lower third of the display shows amp type, the amount of distortion, and tone settings, as shown in Figure 3.38.

Figure 3.38
The Black Box amp editing functions.

Unlike other units, cabinet selection is done for you. As you select the different amplifier models, each model has an associated cabinet that is modeled with the amp. You can't mix and match like you can on other units. This is not necessarily a bad thing at all. The amps are represented with their usual cabinets and speakers, so you'll hear the sound you are used to hearing in regards to the particular amp you have selected. What you can't do is "go Frankenstein" and combine amps and speakers in unusual ways. Never fear, there is still lots more to explore with the Black Box.

Effects

The Black Box comes equipped with 43 different effects. Without going into all the gory details about exactly what is contained in the unit, let's give you a brief overview. Everything you expect to appear is going to be there: Tremolo, Flanger, Chorus, Wah-wah, Talk Box, and Delay. Those are the standard effects you would expect to find. However, the Black Box has a few surprises, including filters, tremolo sequences, filter sequences, arpeggiators, and MIDI effects. The last group of surprises is made possible because of the Black Box's ability to tempo sync. Of course, when this is not available, you can use the Tap Tempo button on the Black Box and establish your own tempo.

TEMPO SYNC

Tempo synching is really cool, but don't just take my word for it. Effects like Tremolo, Delay, Arpeggiators, and Filters can work just fine without knowing the speed of your song. However, when you give them this additional information, effects are able to sync, (short for synchronize) to the tempo of your song. The tremolo will operate at the same speed as your song so that everything lines up. Any effects that are based on time are greatly enhanced when they are able to sync to a host tempo. Computer plug-ins have the ability to do this easily, but it's very cool to have the same power with a piece of hardware.

The effects section shares its screen real estate with the amplifier section—the bottom half of the LCD screen. When you press the FX button shown in Figure 3.39, the bottom half of the screen changes to reflect some new choices.

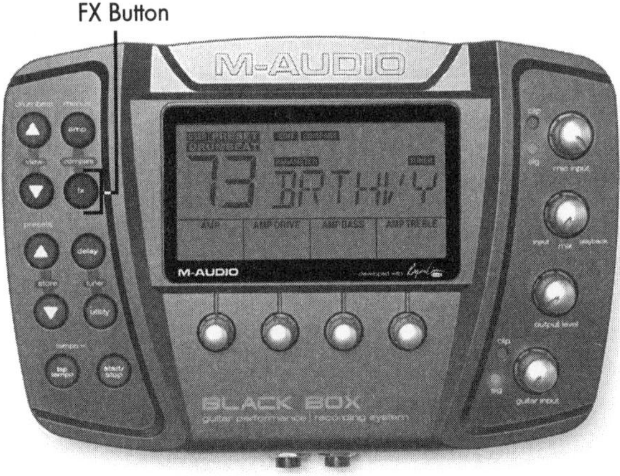

Figure 3.39
The FX button to enter Effects Editing mode.

After you enter the Effects mode, the bottom screen changes to what's shown in Figure 3.40.

The screen and its corresponding rotary knobs allow you to choose an effect, tweak its speed or frequency (depending on the effect), change its key or depth (again depending on the effect chosen), and lastly, change the wet/dry mix of that effect.

One effect can be chosen for each preset in conjunction with one amp. Delay is considered a different effect and has its own editing screen. So, in truth, you can have two effects going at

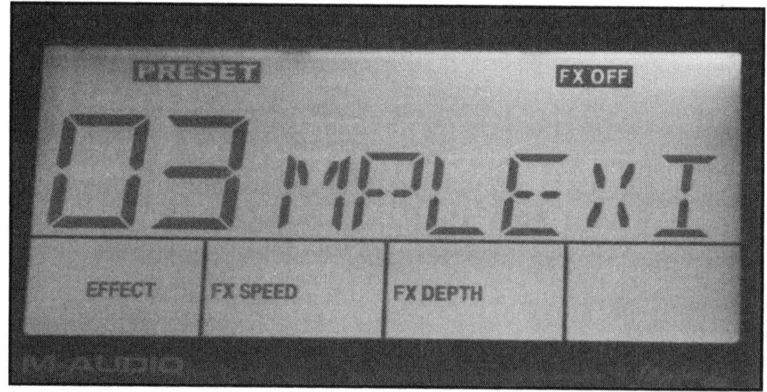

Figure 3.40
Effects Editing screen.

once. When you're accessing the Delay screen, the bottom third of the LCD display changes once again, allowing you to work on delay-specific changes. When in Delay mode, the parameters you can adjust are Delay Time, Delay Repeats, Delay Volume, and Drums to Delay/Input. The four rotary knobs control these aspects of the Delay effect. The one that needs some explaining is the last feature: Drums to Delay. This allows you to mix the prerecorded drum tracks through the delay processor. Delay is another effect that works very well when synched to tempo.

THE EDGE OF TEMPO SYNC

For a great example of tempo-synched delay, pull out any U2 album. Their guitarist, The Edge, makes frequent use of time-based delay effects. When used properly, they can be very musical.

The tempo synchronization happens one of two ways. The first way is when using the included drum grooves built into the unit. This is the next area we will explore. The second way is when you use the Black Box in conjunction with the computer, which we will explore in just a bit.

Drum Grooves

The Black Box has an onboard battery (pun intended) of drum tracks built into the unit. There are 99 to choose from, in varying styles and tempos to suit any practice purpose. These drum tracks probably won't make it to your next record, but when you practice, these backgrounds do the trick and help you imagine what the final product will sound like. The tempos of the loops are set, so you can't change that in the unit, but within the 99 drum grooves, there are many tempo variations to choose from. You could also think of the drum grooves as a very glorified metronome. This could be a valuable practice tool for you, and in many ways, it's a more musical way to keep time than to listen to the perpetual beep of a metronome.

The drum grooves have tempo information embedded within them as metadata. As you play with a drum groove on, all your tempo-synched effects (Delay, plus one other of your choice) will sync right up to the tempo of the drum loop. This is a very, very neat idea, one currently not found elsewhere.

Interfacing the Black Box

Let's take a look at the different connections and interfaces on the Black Box. Figure 3.41 shows the rear panel of the unit.

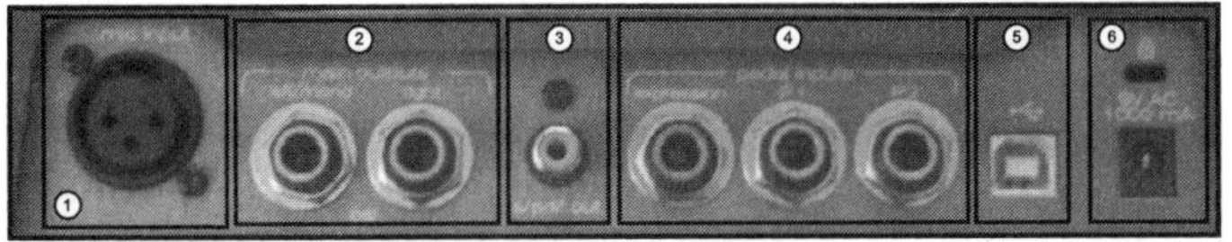

Figure 3.41
The Black Box rear panel.

From left to right, let's look at all the connections and their functions.

1. XLR Mic Input
2. Balanced Stereo Outputs
3. S/PDIF Digital Output
4. Expression and Switch Pedals
5. USB Connection
6. Power Connection

The XLR microphone input is a very nice feature. It hooks up to a microphone, so you can sing along while you play. It is also handy when you're using the Black Box as an interface to your computer, because the microphone input will carry on its own channel. For the price of an amp modeler, you also get a capable audio interface, complete with microphone inputs! The level of the microphone signal is controlled from a dial on the face of the Black Box.

THE PHANTOM

The XLR input on the Black Box is for microphones that *do not* require phantom power. We will explore this later in greater detail, but this input is intended for dynamic vocal microphones. If you plug in a microphone that requires phantom power, such as a condenser microphone, you will get no sound.

The output section is fairly self-explanatory, so we will jump to the digital output beside it. The Black Box is equipped with a S/PDIF digital output. If you intend to record with your Black Box, and your recording interface or equipment will accept a S/PDIF connection, this will give you the highest possible sound quality.

At the rear of the Black Box are three ports for optional external pedals. Of the three inputs, one is used for expression, which means that it can change a value in real time, such as volume, delay rate, or any other variable in the unit. Exactly what the expression pedal is controlling is something you can easily set up in the software of the Black Box on a per-patch basis. The other two pedals are for switch pedals. You may use these to turn effects on and off or start and stop drum tracks. There are a myriad of functions that you can assign from the Black Box. Foot control is something that is exceedingly important to guitar players, and it's nice to see that this option is available on just about every unit we are talking about.

USB Connection

The USB cable allows the Black Box to turn into an audio interface, sending guitar and microphone (if you choose to use it) down a single cable to your computer. The beauty of this particular setup is that the USB connection that M-Audio chooses to use is class compliant. Class compliant means that you don't need to load a driver on your computer for the device to function as an audio interface. It's also cross-platform, so it functions the same way on both Mac and PC, which is something that is so important these days. While many professional musicians use Macs, PCs still enjoy the largest part of the market share.

M-Audio does offer you separate drivers that expand the functionality of the Black Box. Through the drivers, you can access features such as processing the XLR microphone input and the tempo sync, which I'll get to in just a minute. The class compliance is great for plug-and-play, but to get the most of the unit, install the drivers.

Tempo Sync Via USB

If you are using your Black Box with your computer's sequencer (or even the included version of Ableton's Live), the USB cable also serves as a conduit for tempo synching of effects on the Black Box. This means that whatever tempo your host program is working at will be received by the Black Box through its USB cable tempo, synching any of the effects on the Black Box. For integration in a computer studio, this is a very hip feature. Using tempo changes on your computer, you can manipulate some wild sounds out of the Black Box, especially when using delay, filtering, and arpeggiators.

Everything Else

The back panel leaves us with quite a complete connection set. Of note is the security cable. Laptop owners will be familiar with the Kensington security locks found on almost every laptop in production. M-Audio very nicely added a security port so you can secure your Black Box on stage, without fear of it growing thieves' legs and walking away.

The very front of the Black Box, pictured in Figure 3.42, gives you a place to plug in your guitar and a port for stereo headphones, so you can practice in peace and quiet.

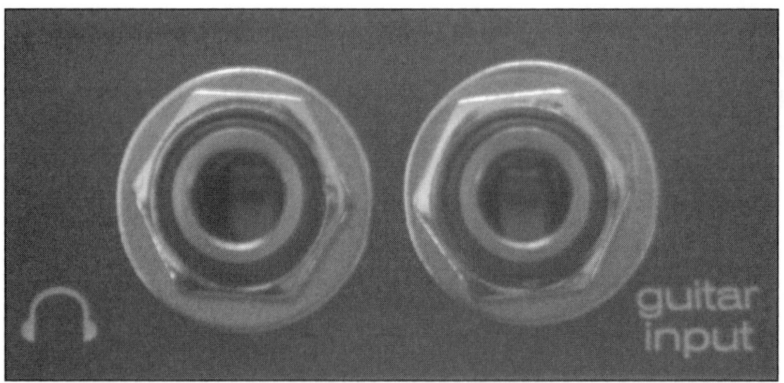

Figure 3.42
The Black Box's front panel.

Roland VG Series

The Roland VG series may be the first true modeling guitar processor that arrived on the market. What's even more amazing is that it has undergone three revisions in its 10-year (so far) history. In the electronics world, 10 years is an eternity—maybe they got it right the first time? So, if this thing is so revolutionary, then why did I wait so long in this chapter to tell you about it? Well, there are always good reasons for these things, so read on.

The first unit was the VG-8, which was upgraded to an expanded version. The major upgrade came with the introduction of the VG-88, which is now in its second version, the VG-88v2, Roland's powerhouse modeling unit. The VG-88 is a floor-mounted box with pedals and buttons, and on the surface it looks a lot like other guitar effects processors. The VG-88 can be seen in all its glory in Figure 3.43.

Figure 3.43
The Roland VG-88.

Under the hood, this is a whole different animal. Roland has developed its own modeling technology called COSM (*Composite Object Sound Modeling*). Roland's modeling technology allows accurate modeling of amps, effects, and even guitars and synths. What? Come again now? Guitar *and* synth modeling? How is this possible on an ordinary floor unit? Well, there was a reason we kept this one for later in the chapter.

A Very Different Interface

The VG-88 in many ways is still ahead of its time because it's able to model guitars and do some other very unique things. The reason it does this, and more importantly, the way it does this may be the reason that every guitarist in the world doesn't have one. The VG-88 requires a special pickup to be installed/affixed to your guitar. The pickup is special in that it has a separate pickup for each string and sends the signals down a very large cable, known as a 13-pin cable, because it has, well, 13 pins inside of it. The pickup is known as their divided pickup, currently available as the GK-3 pickup shown in Figure 3.44.

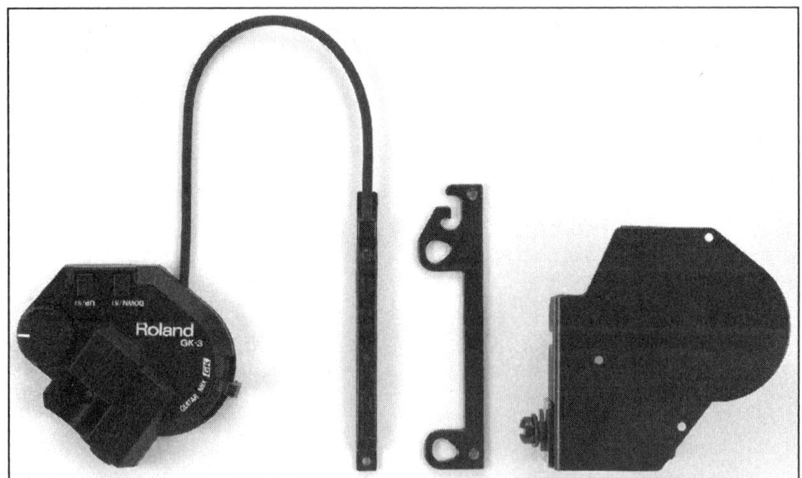

Figure 3.44
The Roland GK-3 divided pickup.

The GK pickup is installed either temporarily with double-sided tape or permanently with screws into the slot between your bridge and your bridge pickup. It's a small, thin pickup that is fairly unobtrusive. The pickup then feeds a junction box of sorts that houses the connector for the 13-pin cable. This junction box sits on the edge of the top of your guitar. Fellow guitar synthesizer users may recognize the pickup as the same one you use for guitar synthesis (covered later in the book). For optimal results, the GK pickup needs to be permanently attached to your guitar with screws so that the height and angle can be accurately controlled.

For many, permanent modifications of their existing guitars made this a no-no. Companies such as Brian Moore, Godin, and Fender offered guitars with 13-pin outputs built into the instruments, so you wouldn't have to mess with your precious instruments. The reason you didn't have to mess with your guitars was that Brian Moore and Godin used a different MIDI pickup, manufactured by RMC, and this pickup is built into the guitar. While it's a different pickup and reacts *much* faster that the Roland, it still uses Roland's 13-pin connector for its output, so you can interface with anything compatible with the 13-pin standard. Again, for some, getting a new guitar wasn't for them. For those forward-looking enough to try this, there were rewards to be reaped.

The Benefits of Division

The VG-88 *required* the use of its special divided pickup that sent each string down its own channel to the VG-88. The reason it did this was because the VG-88 had a few tricks up its sleeves. It was able to process each string differently. The "Divided Effects" and "Divided Tunings" sidebars will clarify just what you can do with the VG-88 that you can't do just about anywhere else.

DIVIDED EFFECTS

Since the GK pickup sends each string on its own channel/wire, the VG-88 is able to process each string individually. This means, for practical purposes, that you could assign different effects to different strings. Imagine distortion on the lower three strings and clean chorused sound on the upper three strings, within the same patch. Play your power chords and then grab some clean chords up top. This list goes on and on, only limited by your imagination. Without the divided GK pickup, this would not be possible. What's even more amazing is that you could do this in 1996.

DIVIDED TUNINGS

Probably the coolest thing on the VG-88, the thing that blew my mind when I first saw it, was the capability to access alternate tunings within the unit without actually having to retune your strings. Since the GK pickup feeds each string separately, it's not too hard to pitch-shift each string into a different spot. With the push of a button, your regularly tuned guitar is suddenly in DADGAD tuning. Another press, and you go to a completely different tuning. This is a wild idea because you keep your guitar in regular tuning and the output is transformed. This is all possible because of the 13-pin pickup technology.

The pitch shifting wasn't limited strictly to alternate tunings. Bass guitar, 12-string guitar, and any combination of offsets were possible with the VG-88. Even folk legend Joni Mitchell uses a VG-88 to manage her extensive collection of alternate tunings. Before this technology, she toured with about 20 guitars—one to facilitate each of her special tunings. With the advent of the VG-88, she simply programmed in her tunings and used the guitar modeling to provide her acoustic sound via an electric guitar outfitted with a GK pickup. When a tuning changed, a press of a button was all that was needed for Joni to switch to any of her special tunings.

Normal and Not So Normal Sounds

To start with, the VG-88 has many of the sounds that you would expect from a modeling guitar processor. You could emulate tons of classical amplifiers, countless cabinets models, and multiple microphone emulations. All the normal effects such as Reverb, Delay, Chorus, Wah-wah, etc. were found on the unit. These are all cool, and at the time they were a revolution by themselves, but there were even wilder things inside of this unit that to this day still aren't matched.

The guitar modeling is one such thing. Let's say that you attach the GK pickup to a standard Stratocaster type guitar and plug into the VG-88. A solid-body guitar strung with .009 gauge strings, for that matter. It's entirely possible that the sound coming out of the unit was that of a hollow-body guitar, a 12-string acoustic, a nylon-string acoustic guitar, or even a sitar! All of these sounds from a lowly ol' Strat with .009 gauge strings. This was all due to the GK pickup.

GK

Even though the thought of adding a new pickup to their guitars turned many players off, those who did were able to access the unique characteristics that the GK pickup allowed, such as alternate tunings, guitar modeling, and even synthesized sounds.

WITHOUT A PICKUP

The VG-88 has been upgraded to version 2, which added many new features. The most notable feature is the ability for a standard guitar without the GK pickup to access the modeled amps and effects. This is certainly a nice feature, but the real power of the unit is harnessed when using the GK pickup (alternative tunings, synth effects, different effects per string, and guitar modeling). Still, it's nice to know that you can use the unit either way.

The VG-88 was the first unit to model guitars and their unique characteristics, and it did an amazing job at that. This was a revolution in itself, and Roland engineers easily could have stopped there, and they would have had a completely unique box, still unrivaled today. They did not stop there, but instead added one more feature that really set the VG-88 apart from the rest. One of the things that we mentioned early on was that the GK pickup was the same unit used in Roland's guitar-to-MIDI synthesizers. It would be very cool if they were able to add some synthesized sounds to the unit, since the main drawback to MIDI guitar was the time it took to convert from pitch to MIDI. Roland got around this by not converting to MIDI at all. Using a technique called HRM (*Harmonic Restructure Modeling*), they were able to manipulate the basic signal of the guitar into synthetic sounds that included organs, brasses, wave type synths, and much more. This greatly expanded the palette of sounds for the traditional guitar player, including synthetic effects that were not feasible or useable for many guitar players.

FRETLESS?

One of the coolest and possibly unmatched features of the VG-88 is its ability to "de-fret" any guitar and give you access to the sound of a fretless guitar, even though your guitar has frets! This is a wild sound that has to be heard to be believed.

Control

On the face of the VG-88, you will find a row of buttons for changing presets sequentially, and Bank Up and Down buttons for accessing other presets stored in banks. The VG-88 can hold a large number of presets inside of the unit. You will also notice in Figure 3.45 that the unit features an expression pedal.

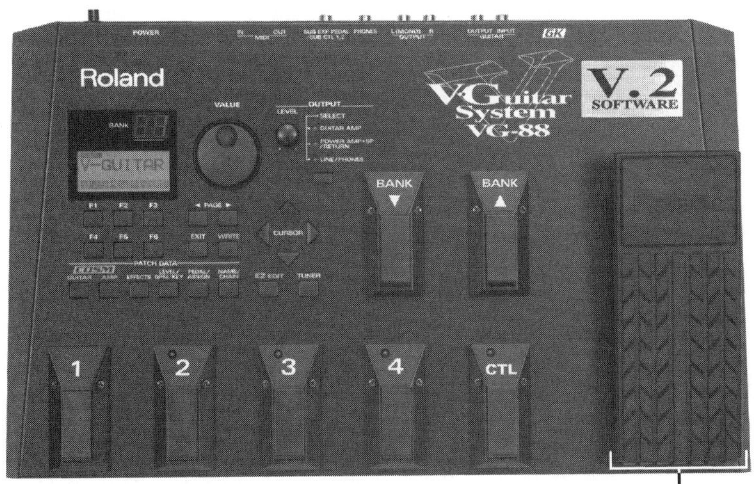

Figure 3.45
VG-88 expression controller.

Like most expression controllers we have dealt with, this expression controller can be assigned to different functions on the unit, such as delay parameters and, most popularly, the Wah-wah pedal. A second optional expression controller can be added and connected to the rear of the unit. The functions of any of the expression controllers (depending how many you have hooked up) can be assigned via the software interface on the front of the unit. An LCD display, rotary wheel, and bank of buttons control and program the aspects of the VG-88 directly on the face of the unit. The version 2 upgrade added the capability of remote control and editing of the VG-88 via SYSEX.

SYSEX?

SYSEX is short for system exclusive messages. It is a way for devices to communicate data back and forth. In the case of the VG-88, using SYSEX through the MIDI port allows patch exchange through the computer. Thanks to some very crafty users, a few visual patch editors/librarian applications have been devised to allow you to back up your presets, add new ones, and edit existing patches from the comfort of your mouse and keyboard. If you own a VG-88, hop on over to www.vg-8.com, which is a meeting place for VG owners to share patches. You can find helpful information, as well as links to the patch editors we discussed previously.

OK. That's a lot of info. We need to learn to make all this technology create music for us. Would you care to dance? Read on.

4 Digital Modeling Guitars

What digital modeling means for guitars is that one single guitar can model and emulate the sounds of other guitars—making it a bit of a guitar chameleon. This is now possible without an extra processor like the VG-88. All of these models are built into the guitars themselves. Not surprisingly, it was Line6 that started it. In 2002, Line6 launched the Variax guitar, the world's first digital modeling guitar.

The Variax Electric

The Variax debuted at NAMM 2002, and as you can see in Figure 4.1, it doesn't look like much.

The first thing you notice is its apparent lack of pickups on the body of the guitar, which is possibly its most unusual feature. The instrument itself looks rather stark—just a body, neck, bridge, and a few control knobs. Under the surface is advanced circuitry that performs some magic.

Regarding the pickups, there is in fact a pickup on the guitar, just not the traditional magnetic pickups you are used to seeing. The pickup is actually built right into the bridge of the guitar. The pickup uses six individual piezo elements to pick up the guitar's signal.

PIEZO

Piezo pickups have been used in guitars for a number of years now. A piezo is a special crystal that produces current when pressure is applied to it. Piezo pickups are most commonly used for amplifying acoustic guitars. Their pickups are mounted under the bridge saddle, and the vibrations are passed along to an amplifier. Since this technology doesn't really harness much of the acoustic nature of the guitar, electric guitar manufacturers have been using piezo elements in the bridges of their guitars to give ordinary electric guitars an acoustic sound. In the case of the Variax, the piezo is used simply to get six individual signals into its internal processor. As you will see later in this book, piezo has a few other neat uses as well, one of them directly relating to significant advancements in MIDI guitar tracking technology.

Figure 4.1
The Line6 Variax guitar.

Variax Controls

The Variax is currently available in various models that differ only in their aesthetic qualities. Each Variax has the same "guts" as any of the other guitars in the series. Upgrading the higher-priced models will get you better tuners, a tremolo bridge, and a nicer finished-wood guitar. The modeling is identical in all the guitars.

As for the controls, each of the guitars has three rotary controls and a five-way switch. Two of the controls are simply volume and tone knobs like you would find on any guitar. The third knob is the "magic" knob. The third knob is what allows you to select the different guitar models and change your sound from a clean Strat to a chunky Les Paul with the turn of a knob. Figure 4.2 shows the control knobs on the Variax guitar.

Figure 4.2
The Line6 Variax guitar's control layout. Notice that the last knob is a stepped black knob that has guitar models listed on the outside so you know which guitar you are accessing.

The magic knob, as I call it, is actually called the model select knob by Line6. It is a rotary knob with 12 positions to represent the 10 preset modeled guitars and two spots to save your custom guitar. The guitars modeled in the first 10 spots of the model select knob are as follows:

1. T-Model (Telecaster)
2. Spank (Stratocaster)
3. Lester (Les Paul)
4. Special (various Gibson models: Les Paul Special, Les Paul Jr., Firebird)
5. R-Billy (Gretsch Solid and Hollowbody guitars—think Brian Setzler)
6. Chime (Rickenbackers)
7. Semi (Semi-hollow 335s and Casino models)
8. Jazzbox (175 and Super 400 models)
9. Acoustic (Martin, Guild, and Gibson acoustics)
10. Reso (Resonator guitars, banjos, sitars, and other odd guitars)

The listing of the 10 types of guitars does not equal the total number of guitars in the unit. The Variax models 25 different guitars, for example. So how do we go from a 10-position rotary switch to 25 guitars? We use that handy five-way switch on the guitar, which is the key to this. In each of the modeling categories, the five-way switch selects individual guitar models. The T-Model, for example, is a position on the rotary knob, but the switch accesses different variants of that model. So you have 12 positions on the dial (ten for the pre-built custom guitars and two for your own storage), you dial any one in, and the five-way switch gives you five variants of that model. Positions one and four give you neck and bridge pickups from a 1960 Telecaster Custom, while positions three and five give you two different pickup combinations from a 1968 Thinline Telecaster. Position two gives you a custom-modified '68 Tele with special wiring. The model selector knob simply gives you the broad category, while the five-way selector selects from the different models within the guitar. It's the combination of the rotary controller and the five-way switch that will give you full access to the 25 modeled guitars inside of the Variax.

MODELED VOLUME AND TONE

Regarding the ordinary-looking volume and tone knobs, there's some magic there as well! For each of the modeled guitars, the volume and tone knobs are also modeled after the original units. Because every guitar's circuitry is different, just using a generic volume and tone knob would not accurately represent the particular guitar being used. For example, if you are accessing a Strat sound, the tone knob traditionally uses a 250 kHz tone knob, which would sound very different than a Les Paul's 500 kHz tone knob. These aspects have been modeled into the sound, so when you select a new guitar, the volume and tone knobs react just as they would on the original guitar. This brings a further level of realism to the instrument.

Custom Banks

The Variax's model selector knob has 12 positions, and we have only detailed 10 of them. This is because the remaining two positions are available for saving custom instruments. Rather than feverishly flipping the controls around, Line6 enables you to save your most-used guitars in these two custom positions, with a different guitar on each of the five-way switches' selector knobs. This way, you can set up all the guitar models you want to use for quick recall during a gig.

Programming into the custom banks is easy. First, you navigate to the sound you want to save. Then you simply pull the selector knob up to start the process of saving, select which position of the five-way switch you want this sound to be saved to, and rotate the knob to either custom one or custom two. Then press the model select knob down to save your preset. You can set up the custom guitars in all 10 slots of your two custom (user-savable) knob positions. You can change this whenever you need to—this is not set in stone.

Variax Connections

Figure 4.3 shows the output section on the Variax 700 model guitar.

When you turn the Variax on its side, you gain access to its output configuration. The first connection you come across is no real surprise: a standard quarter-inch mono guitar cable. If you want to plug in and play with your existing amp, just go ahead and wail like normal. The second connection is a special connection that will allow you to do some really amazing

Figure 4.3
The Line6 Variax guitar's connections.

things, such as directly connect the Variax to your computer for additional tone shaping options. You can also connect to other Line6 products, such as the Vetta amps or the Floorboard foot controllers. This connection is done through a CAT-5 Ethernet cable—the same one used for Internet connections. This makes the cable very easy to replace if lost or damaged.

Power

The Variax needs battery power to run under normal operation. There are situations that don't require battery power, and you'll learn about those shortly. For now, if you want to run your Variax, you have a few options. The first is to supply 6 AA batteries in the battery compartment of the guitar. A fresh set of batteries will give you about 12 hours of continuous use. Can you say "rechargeable batteries"?

SAVE POWER

If you plan to run the Variax from its batteries, there is something you should know. The batteries are only tapped when you plug the quarter-inch cable in. If you are in the habit of leaving your cable in all the time, you're going to personally fund Duracell. When you aren't using the instrument, unplug the guitar to conserve battery life.

Line6 also equips you with an emergency option. If your AA batteries are drained, you can remove the battery compartment and stick in a regular 9-volt battery for about two hours of use. This won't get you through every situation, but it's nice to know you have that option. Plus, since most tuners and stompbox effects run on 9-volt batteries, it shouldn't be too hard to find one. If you haven't already started to do this, keep lots of extra batteries in your gig bag. You *never* know what's going to happen.

Power Plus

If the thought of relying on batteries scares you, you are afforded another option to power your Variax. Line6 has included a XPS footswitch/power box with your Variax. Figure 4.4 shows the XPS.

The XPS serves a few functions. The first is as a permanent power solution. You can plug an AC wall charger into the wall and connect it to the XPS. If you then connect a balanced cable (tip-ring-sleeve) from the XPS to the Variax, the guitar will receive its power without the need for batteries. This is a great way to save a bundle on batteries.

Figure 4.4
The Line6 XPS footswitch/power box.

The XPS also serves another important purpose: it's an A/B direct box. The standard Variax serves two main purposes. One is to emulate electric guitars. The other is to emulate acoustic guitar tones. Electric guitar signals are perfectly suited for electric guitar amplifiers, but an electric guitar amplifier is not what an audio person would call "full-range." Most guitar amps don't reach into the higher frequencies. When dealing with acoustic guitar models, there are elements of the sound in those higher frequencies that contribute to the realism of the model. If you were to simply plug your Variax into any old electric guitar amp and play an acoustic guitar model, you might say to yourself, "This doesn't sound like an acoustic guitar at all." That is due to the amp, not the Variax. To remedy this, the XPS is also equipped with a balanced XLR connector that you can connect to a full-range speaker, a mixing board/PA system, or directly to your computer for recording purposes. A small footswitch on the XPS allows you to switch back and forth between the regular guitar output and the balanced acoustic output. Did I also mention that the balanced output is line-level, meaning that the XPS can interface with your line-level computer gear? Very neat.

Digital Connection

The last connector on the Variax is the digital connector. This allows your Variax to interface with a few Line6 products digitally. The Vetta II, PODxt, PODXt Live, and Line6's workbench USB interface all accept this special digital connection. The wire it uses is actually a standard CAT-5 Ethernet cable that we all use in home networking. This is handy if you ever lose the cable. Just run to any home office supply store and grab a new cable. Pretty smart.

The Workbench

Definitely the most amazing feature of the Variax series of guitars is the Workbench software. We are going to take a detailed look at the software, since it enables you to do things that aren't physically possible in the real world. It is one of the most revolutionary pieces of software to hit the market in quite a long time.

Workbench is a combination of software and hardware. On the hardware side, Workbench supplies you with a small USB interface that connects the digital output from your Variax and converts its information into data for your PC or Mac.

As a piece of software, Workbench is exactly what its moniker describes: it's a virtual workshop for building guitars in the virtual world that you can play with your hands. The workshop software allows you to combine different guitar bodies, different wood types, and different pickup placements to make guitars that you've always wondered about. What would a Les Paul sound like if it was hollow with a Strat neck and single coil pickups? This is what Workbench allows you to do—make guitars in your own virtual Frankenstein lab and save them back to the real guitar.

Let's take a closer look at what the software allows you to do. Figure 4.5 shows what one of my preset guitars looks like.

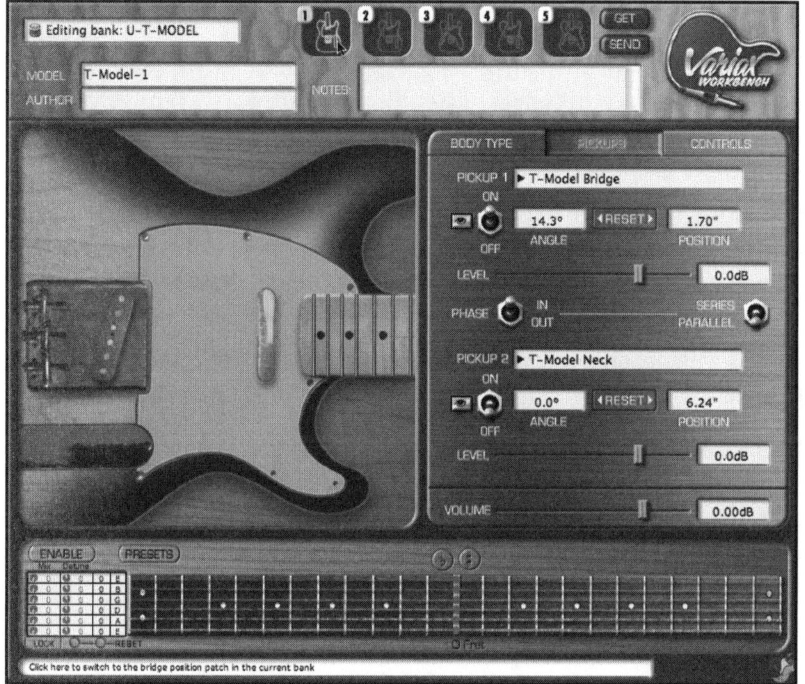

Figure 4.5
Workbench T-model.

For fun, what would it sound like if you kept the model the same, but changed the body from a solid body to a hollow body? First, enter the Body Type editing screen and choose a hollow-body model. Figure 4.6 shows what happens when you cross the two.

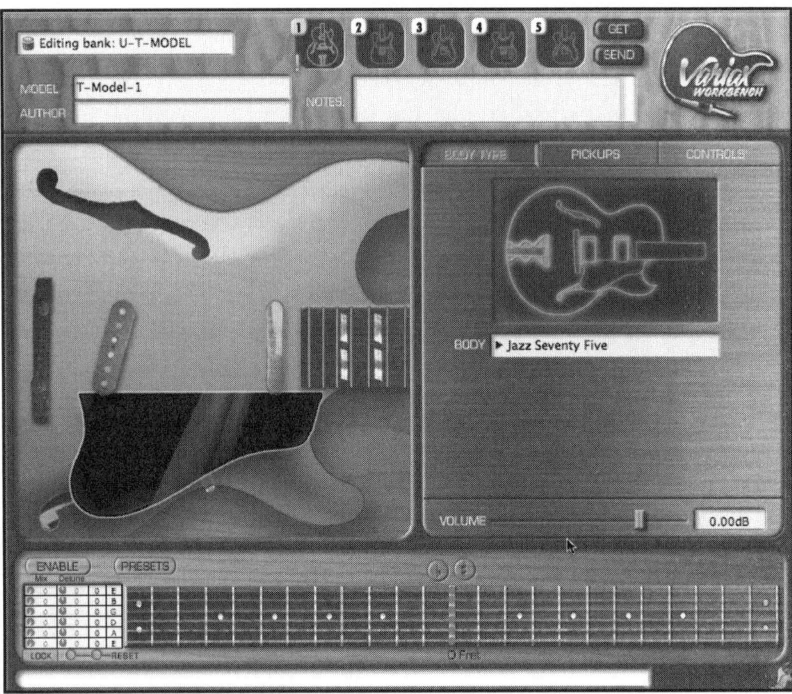

Figure 4.6
Adding a hollow body.

Now for some real fun. Let's not only change the pickups themselves, but also let's move their positions and angles to some unorthodox spots. This guitar would simply never exist in the real world. Figure 4.7 shows us what it might look like if it did.

As if we hadn't done enough, you can even change the types of volume and tone knobs, the impedance values, and the type of capacitor used on the tone knob. Figure 4.8 shows you yet another step in the evolution of our super-ax.

Last, but not least, Workbench allows you to change the tuning of the guitar's models. This happens digitally, inside of the Variax, but without Workbench, you aren't able to access this. If you use alternate tunings often, or even if you're just going from E to Eb tuning, imagine being able to program presets with different tunings without ever having to reach around for a knob!

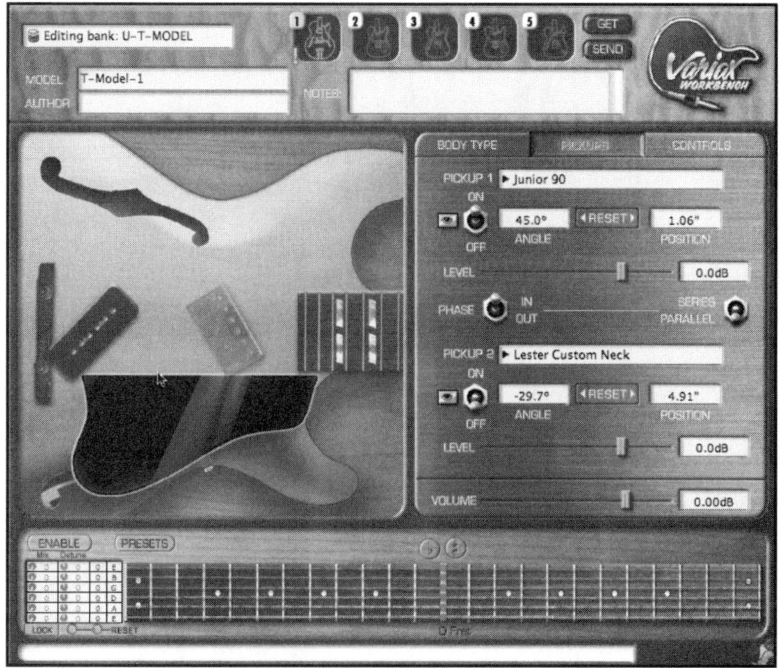

Figure 4.7
Tweaking the pickups.

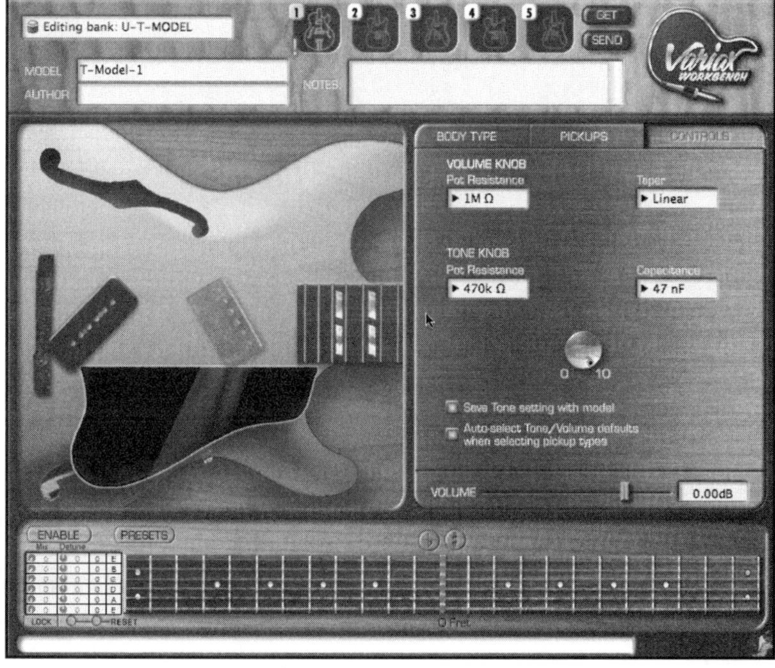

Figure 4.8
Control knob tweaking.

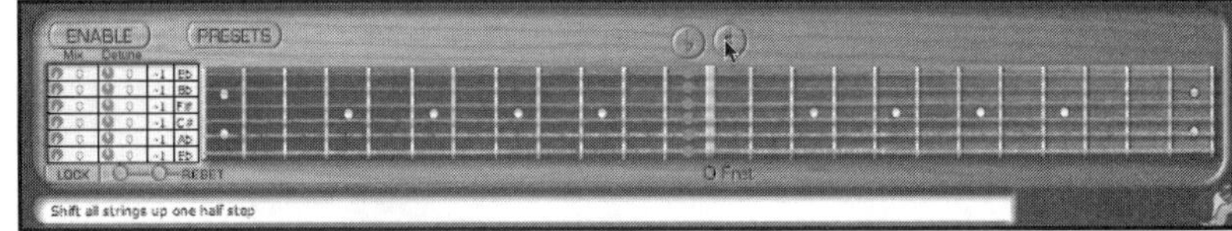

Figure 4.9
The tuning window.

The Variax and Other Line6 Products

The Variax's digital output connects you to the Workbench software and creates some cool guitars. It also has another purpose: It allows you to connect to other Line6 products, such as the Vetta II and the PODxt Live, for the ultimate meeting of the minds.

When you digitally connect the Variax to either the Vetta II or the PODxt Live, something really cool happens. The Vetta or the POD takes control of the guitar choice for you when you switch presets. Imagine that you are playing on a patch made to emulate the vintage tones of Stevie Ray Vaughn. SRV's rig consisted of a Strat guitar playing through a few vintage amps with some effect pedals in line. When you have the Variax digitally connected and you select a patch like this, regardless of where the model select knob is, the Vetta II or the PODxt Live will switch your Variax to the appropriate guitar model for you. This is the ultimate in tone control! Not to mention that you can change guitar models with your feet from the floor control units. Line6 will surely continue to innovate and allow the digital connection to do more. But for now, the ability to make a preset change the amplifier type, modeled guitar, effects, microphone, cabinet, etc., is wild and revolutionary to say the least.

The Variax Acoustic

It certainly had to happen. First, we had a modeling electric guitar, which included a *few* acoustic guitar models. So it was time for an acoustic guitar that modeled other acoustic guitars. The Line6 Variax Acoustic was born from this idea. The acoustic version of the Variax, pictured in Figure 4.10, is a bit different from the original Variax because on the surface it resembles a thin-body acoustic guitar.

Just like the original Variax, the bridge of the guitar contains special piezo saddles that feed into the electronics of the guitar that provided the modeling. It's also worth mentioning that the Variax acoustic will function as a normal acoustic guitar when not plugged in. Also a nice feature!

Guitar Models and Controls

All Variax models share some common traits. The bridge system is common to all the Variax models, as is the rotary selector knob. On the Variax electric, additional volume, tone, and five-way switches are provided to access different tonal varieties in the instrument. The Variax acoustic has the same rotary knob, although it is positioned in a totally different spot than on the Variax electric guitar. All the controls for the Variax acoustic are on the side of the guitar near

Figure 4.10
The Line6 Variax acoustic guitar.

where the neck joins the body. This is consistent with how other acoustic guitar manufacturers place their controls. A player coming from using a traditional amplified acoustic guitar will feel right at home with the locations of the controls.

As for the controls, as you can see in Figure 4.11, in addition to the rotary selector, there are three long throw sliders that control various functions of the guitar. We will explore these sliders as the instrument utilizes them.

Figure 4.11
The Variax acoustics control layout.

The rotary control knob gives you access to the modeled acoustic instruments inside of the Variax. Here is a listing of the 16 instruments that Line6 studied when modeling the Variax acoustic guitar:

- 1941 Martin 5-17
- 1946 Martin 000-28
- 1960 Martin D-21
- 1954 Gibson J-45
- 1951 Gibson SJ-200
- 1933 Selmer Maccaferri
- 1951 D'Angelico New Yorker Jazz Acoustic
- 1958 Manuel Velazquez Classical Guitar
- 1973 Guild F412
- 1934 Stella Auditorium
- 1933 National Reso-Phonic "O" Style Resonator Guitar
- 1937 Dobro Model 27
- Gibson Mastertone Banjo
- Mandola (a tenor mandolin)
- Japanese Samisen
- Indian Sitar

That's quite a collection of guitars. It would certainly take considerable time and expense just to collect and find working examples of those historic instruments. With the turn of a knob, you can dial in models of all of them.

The three long throw sliders are multifunction, in that they can do more than just their basic designated purpose. Let's go over the basics of these three sliders. Figure 4.12 shows an illustrated view of the control panel with the sliders named.

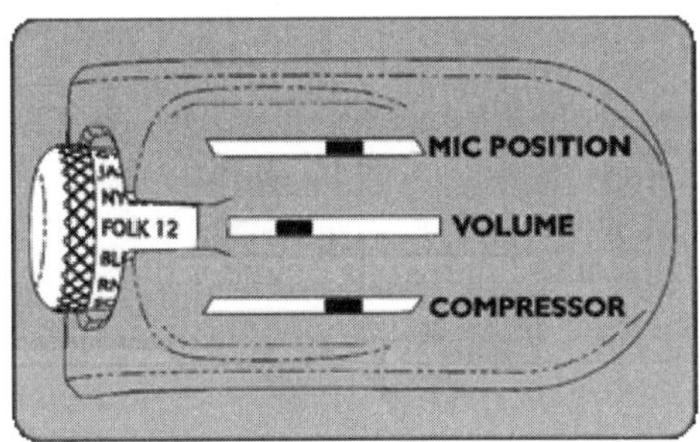

Figure 4.12
The Line6 Variax acoustic controls.

The Three Slider Controls

The topmost slider is the volume control. Anyone want to venture a guess as to what that control does? Basically, when the club owner yells that you're too loud, slide this one down.

Under the volume slider is the microphone position slider. This allows you to move the position of the modeled microphone in relation to the sound hole of the guitar. As you slide the control towards the physical sound hole of the guitar, you are placing the microphone closer to the virtual sound hole. I know that sounds a bit confusing. Basically, this is mimicking what you would encounter in the studio when placing a microphone on an acoustic guitar. The closer the micro-phone is to the guitar's sound hole, the more lower-frequency content you capture with the micro-phone. This gives the feeling of a bassier and more full-bodied guitar. This effect is partly due to the fact that you are closer to the wood, but also due to something called the proximity effect.

PROXIMITY

The proximity effect is a simple side effect when placing any microphone (except an omnidirectional microphone) close to a sound source. The closer the microphone is to the sound hole, the more that the low frequencies get boosted. When you get *really* close to the source, the low frequencies may boost in an undesirable way. This is the nature of how microphones work at close distances. If you position the mic correctly, you can add the feeling of body to an instrument that may not sound all that fat.

As you move the mic slider away from the sound hole, you pull the microphone away, and you hear more of the higher-frequency content and more of the snap of the strings. This is a very cool control that allows you to subtly shape the sound of each of the instruments. One more note: For instruments that don't have a sound hole, the slider simply moves the microphone closer to or farther from the instrument, either adding to its bass response or accentuating the higher frequencies.

The last slider is the compressor control. Compression is a studio tool that limits the dynamic range of a signal. I will go into compression in greater detail when we discuss mixing the guitar using plug-ins. On the Variax acoustic, the compressor control smoothes out the volume level of your playing. Typically, a compressor would have many different controls, such as threshold, ratio, attack, and release. The Variax takes care of this for you. You can dial in no compression for a totally acoustic sound, or engage some compression to smooth out the dynamic range of the signal coming out of the guitar.

These are the default jobs for the three slider controls. As stated previously, these are multi-function controls. Let's explore what else they can do.

Alternate Tunings

Acoustic guitar players love to play in alternate tunings besides the standard E A D G B E tuning that everyone is taught. The complexity of this is that you have to retune the guitar every time you want to stray to a new tuning. Players who employ alternate tunings frequently often have multiple guitars, each one dedicated to a particular tuning. That's nice if you have 10 guitars. For the rest of us, we have a few options. You could simply retune your guitar, that's certainly possible. Another option is to use the VG-88 (mentioned earlier in the chapter) and use its instant tuning feature. That's another choice, but we are in the Variax section of this chapter.

It just so happens that the Variax acoustic has an advanced alternate tuning feature. Simply press the model select knob down twice. It will flash red and green, letting you know that you are now in alternate tuning mode. The microphone position slider now becomes the alternate tuning selector. You can slide it through eight preset tunings.

Here are the preset tunings:

- Open E
- Open A
- Open D
- Low G
- High G
- DADGAD
- DROP D
- E & A octave tuning

Simply sliding the microphone position slider up and down while the Variax is in alternate tuning mode gives you instant access to those eight tunings.

> **INSTANT TUNE**
> No doubt about it, being able to flick a switch and retune your guitar is wild. There are a few things you should keep in mind. First, the strings don't actually move or physically retune. This is done inside the guitar and sent out the cable. This means that your amp will play your sound in one tuning, but the actual guitar will still sound like it's in normal tuning. To get around this, you will need to turn the amp up or wear headphones to block out the acoustic sound. Also, keep in mind that this is a retuner, not a tuner. So make sure the original strings are in tune to start with, or your alternate tunings will sound really, really bad.

Look at Figure 4.13 to see how the tunings are accessed.

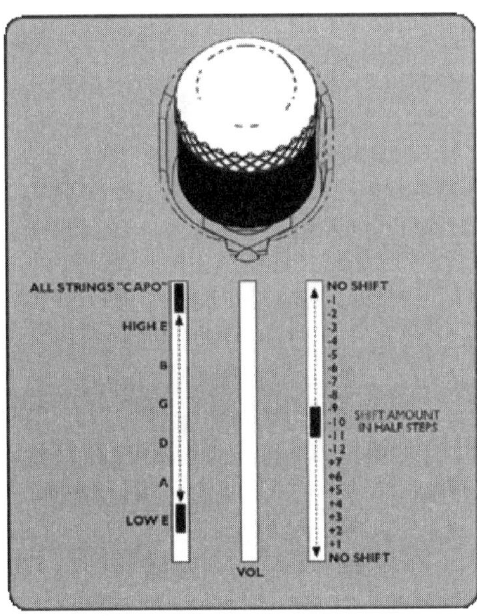

Figure 4.13
Selecting alternate tunings on the Variax acoustic.

In addition to the preset tunings, the Variax acoustic has a few more tricks up its sleeves.

Virtual Capo and Custom Tuning

Preset tunings are great and certainly very handy, but what if you want to invent your own tunings or even put on a virtual capo? This can also be done!

In the same alternate tuning mode (press the model select knob down twice), the compression slider takes on a new role—it allows you to select any individual string, or all the strings for a capo effect, and retune them to your heart's delight. The microphone position slider now controls how many half-steps up or down each string, or all the strings, are moved. Look at the layout of the custom-tuning mode in Figure 4.14.

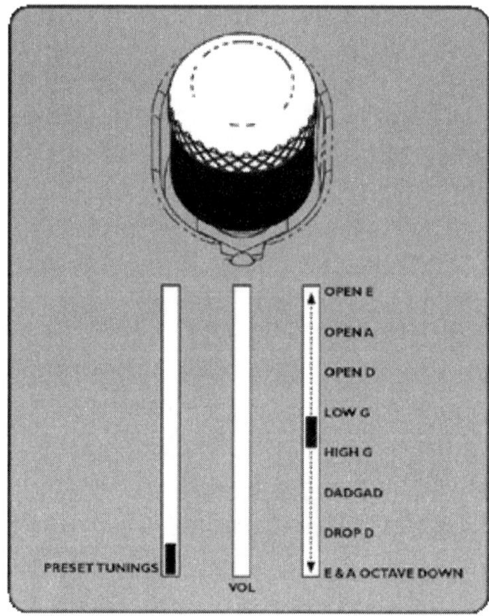

Figure 4.14
The custom-tuning mode.

Using the custom tuning and capo modes, you can put the Variax into any custom tuning you want and store the tunings in any of the positions on the model select knob. That means that you can have a Martin in one tuning and a Gibson in a different tuning. You simply save the tuning along with the model and any other modifications that you make to the instrument, such as compression and microphone placement. This makes creating the ultimate guitar set as easy as turning a knob! Welcome to the future.

Outputs and Power

The outputs of the Variax acoustic are basically identical to the electric Variax models. There is a balanced XLR output on the guitar, which is standard with amplified acoustic guitars. You will also find the same digital output as on the other Variax models, allowing for future expandability through the Workbench software, which will support the Variax acoustic by the time this book gets to you. Power consumption is the same because it runs either on batteries or by plugging into the floor junction box, which is AC-powered. In just about every respect, the output sections on the Variax models are identical.

The Age of Computers and Interfaces

There is no doubt that we live in the age of computers. Email and the Internet permeate just about every aspect of today's society. For musicians, it's clear that the computer is a fixture in today's home studio. The computer is also a hotbed of activity for music-tech advancements. Even in the world of keyboards, we are seeing less and less innovation in keyboard hardware and more and more innovation in virtual instrument plug-ins. We are starting to see the same paradigm shift in the guitar world that the keyboard world saw only five or six short years ago. Sure, tube amps are still made and so are analog keyboards. But the convenience of the computer's power over a guitar signal is just too overwhelming to ignore. Now that we are sold on the idea of using a computer, we need to know how to get the computer set up for use with a guitar. Since many guitarists are new to this emerging field, we're going to go into a lot of detail on the computer and its parts; this is something you really have to know. This chapter will teach you the following:

- What computer you will need.
- What CPU speed really means.
- How bus speed affects your computer.
- What RAM means and how much you'll need.
- How large a hard disk you will need.
- How to get your guitar's signal into the computer using an audio interface.
- The differences between PCI, USB, and Firewire interfaces.
- What latency is and how it will affect your performance.
- Understanding impedance.
- Direct boxes and when to use them.
- Monitoring setups.

- Understanding electromagnetic interference in your setup.
- How to optimally set up your computer for audio.

Computer Setups

Now that we have arrived at the section on computers—the heart of the digital guitar universe—we need to discuss the different parts of the computer and how they will affect your overall experience. The computer is one of the most complicated machines we use on a daily basis, and when all of its parts work together, you are able to utilize its amazing power. Like any great machine, if one part is weak or not performing up to snuff, the whole chain will suffer as a result. Understanding which computer is right for you will require us to look at all the common elements of any computer and explain their functions. Since we are focusing on audio, we will also discuss which sections are critical for audio. Cutting-edge technology needs cutting-edge computers. Simply calling up Dell and telling them, "I like music," doesn't necessarily mean that you will get a computer that will suit you. Let's start by going through all the major parts of the computer one by one, so that you will understand how best to harness their power for your music.

The Central Processing Unit

The central processing unit has many names. Some call it the CPU, others say Pentium, Athlon, or G5. No matter what you call it, no other part of the computer is as close in function to the human brain as the CPU. The CPU is the basic computational brain of the computer. Its ability to crunch numbers and do math problems is what makes it special. Even though you plan on plugging your guitar directly into your computer and making music, as the computer sees it, audio is nothing more than a complicated set of math problems. The CPU won't hear a single note you play. What it will do is compute the digital information needed to fuel your sequencer and your effects plug-ins.

Surfing the Internet and checking your email place a fairly small processing load on the CPU. It's just not that challenging a task to read a Web page. However, manipulation of audio data is one of the most complicated tasks a computer can do. Other complex tasks are film and video editing and graphics work. All three of these areas require a fast, capable CPU because of the nature of real-time processing. Real-time processing is exactly what it sounds like—processing data in real time as the computer works. Each task a computer does is analogous to a complex math problem. That's exactly what a plug-in, or intensive process, does to a machine—it makes it think. The opposite of real-time processing, offline processing, eases the load on your CPU, but for modern music applications, real-time processing is needed and expected. One of the ways that you can quantify the speed of a computer is by measuring the speed at which it's able to handle data.

One of the ways that the speed of your CPU is measured is based on the number of processing cycles it is able to execute in one second. The term used to measure this cycle is named after the great inventor Heinrich Hertz.

HATS OFF TO HERTZ

The term *hertz*, which is abbreviated as Hz, is a term used to measure the frequency of a repeating event. One hertz means one "something" per second. A simple analogy for hertz is that a clock ticks at a frequency of 1 Hz. Hertz is a multifaceted term in this book. I am using it to measure the frequency of the CPU's master clock signal, which basically equates to the speed of the chip. What is interesting is that I will reuse the term hertz when I discuss audio later in the book. Audio waves are also periodic repeating waves, and I express them in hertz as well. Our discussion of equalization will utilize hertz as well, because the hertz in that case will denote the frequency of the EQ.

The early computers had their clock speeds measured in megahertz. Ten years ago, your computer may have shipped with a 50 MHz processor. This number meant that it could perform 50 million cycles of computing power a second. When it's put in those terms, it seems like a huge number. But nowadays, computer speeds are measured in gigahertz, which means *billions* of computing cycles a second.

The general rule of thumb used to be that the higher the clock speed in gigahertz or GHz, the faster the computer you were going to have. This is not always true because the differences between CPU manufacturers make this a more difficult task to quantify in numbers. The old "Mac versus PC" talk was a lively debate that focused on the speed of one machine versus another. Let's talk very briefly about the speed debate that's been going on for far too long, and how things have finally changed for the better.

For the longest time, basically up until a few years ago, CPU speed in hertz, more recently in GHz (gigahertz), meant everything. There was a point in time when you could judge CPUs simply by looking at the numbers. This is no longer the rule anymore. There are two basic CPU types used for consumer computers: x86-based and PowerPC-based. There are other types of processors, but for the kinds of computers musicians use, it comes down to x86 and Power PC.

Intel and AMD currently make the x86 family of processors, while Freescale and IBM make the PowerPC chips. Until mid-2005, x86 ran Windows and Linux, and PowerPC was the Macintosh chip of choice (and could run Linux, too). In mid-2005, Apple announced that it was moving to x86 processors, made by Intel. This means that by the time you read this, the old Mac vs. PC debate will be a matter of which operating system you'd rather run, since the new Macs will be capable of booting OSX and Windows.

When it comes to CPU speed, you simply can't look at numbers anymore. Even between manufacturers in the same family, for example, Intel vs. AMD, the raw score in GHz will not clearly equate speed and performance. The same was true of the move from Motorola-based G4 chips to the IBM-based G5 chips. The last G4 chip in a PowerMac was rated at 1.42 Ghz, and the IBM-based G5s debuted at 1.6, 1.8, and 2.0 Ghz. Was the G5 only .18 GHz faster? No, the architecture of the new G5 chips had significantly changed. The way that the chip handled data had been reworked, and the new chips were *much* faster.

These days, the speed of the chip is taking a back seat to other factors. We have just moved through a major transition—well, actually two major transitions. The first is the move from 32-bit computing to 64-bit. The shift of the chips' architectures from 32-bit to 64-bit and the corresponding switch of the operating systems' and programs' ability to utilize the new power are leading us to chips that do more at roughly the same "paper speed."

The second shift is the efficiency of the chips that are manufactured now. Elements like performance per watt are now the better benchmarks to look at. How well does the chip operate at low voltages? The higher the voltage, the higher the heat, which is a terrible thing for computers. Heat is the number one component killer. The new breed of laptop chips are making great use of lower voltages for increased performance and less heat (no more burning your legs on a hot laptop). The other part of efficiency is the move towards multi-core chips. A core is simply a second subchip that is able to handle data. So if a chip has two cores, it's able to handle twice the data of a single-core chip. You essentially get two for one. This is the future of computing: multi-cores. We are starting to see multi-core chips appear, and they will no doubt be the de facto standard shortly.

All of this must be leading you to ask: "How do I know what the best system is for me?" It's getting harder to equate all of this simply by looking at specs. The MHz war is winding down, and Apple has gone to Intel. Hopefully, this will level the playing field and make things easier on us as consumers. Certainly, the multi-core evolution is one to watch carefully. Something that takes up the space of a single chip while doing the job of three is a no-brainer.

Bus Speed

Bus speed is another crucial factor in the overall speed of a computer. A bus is simply a pipeline of information in the computer. The bus interconnects different parts of the computer and allows data to flow between them. The "Bus Explained" sidebar offers an analogy that may help you understand the importance of a bus.

> **BUS EXPLAINED**
>
> Think of a bus like you would think of a highway. If you have a fast bus, you have many lanes, and a great number of cars can speed down the highway at fast speeds. In cities where there are many cars (bits of information), like Los Angeles, the highways have five or more lanes to allow the large amount of traffic (data) to flow. On country roads, when you have few cars, one lane will do.

The speed of the bus is crucial, as it has the primary job of interconnecting the CPU to the rest of the computer. Currently, the speed of the bus is measured in hertz–megahertz. If we relate the highway analogy to a bus, we can draw this simple conclusion: No matter how fast your CPU (car) is, if the bus is slow (road is small, congested), then you're not going to get anywhere. The speed of the bus is a crucial factor in picking a system. You will see bus speeds advertised in the literature you read when shopping for a computer. A higher number is always better. Since digital audio is a very demanding process for any computer, having an ample bus is crucial to your experience. A slow bus speed can result in fewer tracks, fewer effects, and overall system sluggishness. Figure 5.1 is a diagram of the relationship between the computer's bus and the CPU.

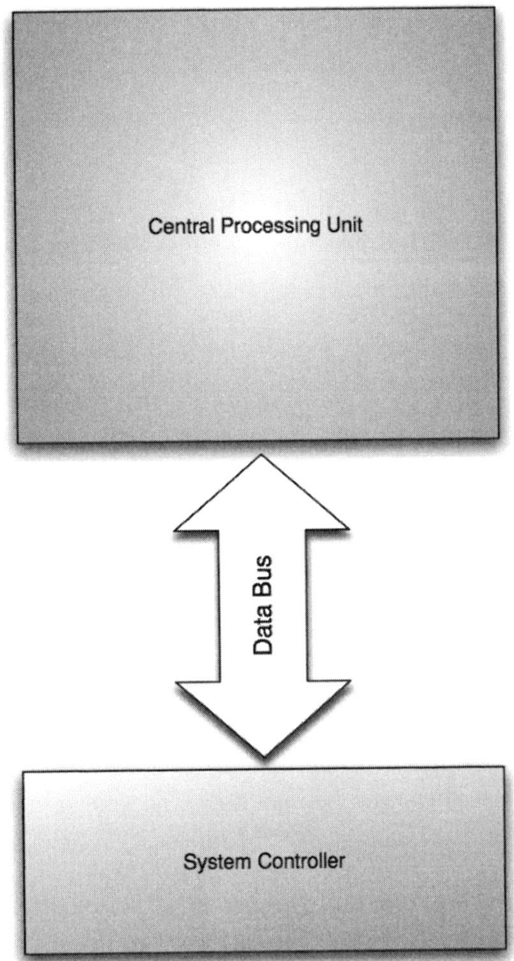

Figure 5.1
Bus and CPU data flow.

Computer Memory and Storage

The two most common storage types on your computer are temporary storage (RAM) and permanent storage (hard disks). Both serve a crucial and specialized role in the overall performance of your computer. Let's start with RAM, which is short for Random Access Memory.

Random Access Memory (RAM)

As your computer works, it is constantly calling upon information. The rate at which it can call upon information from a hard disk is relatively slow in computer terms. When the computer needs to store and access data rapidly, it uses a special set of chips called Random Access Memory, or RAM for short. RAM chips are lightning-fast and hold data for quick and easy retrieval by the CPU. In terms of architecture, RAM is one of the components that the bus we discussed earlier connects to the CPU. There are a few critical things that you need to understand about RAM:

- RAM comes in different speeds.
- RAM comes in different storage sizes.
- RAM is one of the easiest computer upgrades that a user can do.
- RAM is volatile memory and is erased when you power the machine off.

RAM Speed

Like the other components we have talked about, RAM comes in different speeds. The important thing to know regarding RAM speed is that it is tied to your particular computer. Simply put, your computer will come from the factory with a certain speed of RAM; you can't simply add faster RAM to speed up your machine without changing the motherboard, which is an option not available to Mac owners. If you are thinking about RAM speed, it's a decision to make at the time of your computer purchase. The speed of the RAM is expressed in MHz (megahertz), and faster RAM is another component in a powerful computer system. However, this is not really the most important aspect of RAM. Fast is fine, but the amount of RAM that you have is the more crucial aspect in the long run.

RAM Storage Size

Put quite simply, the more RAM you have, the better. Your computer is constantly calling upon information that it needs in the blink of an eye. RAM is the space allocated for this ultra-fast storage. On a normal computer, a decent amount of RAM will do, as basic computing use does not call for extreme RAM usage. On a digital audio computer, RAM quantity is a crucial aspect. Not only do your audio programs and guitar effects rely on RAM, but if you go the route of MIDI guitar and utilize sampling, most samplers place their samples in RAM for playback, so a generous amount of RAM is needed. Oftentimes, your software of choice will have stringent requirements for RAM size, and you should always make sure to meet or exceed the minimum values suggested by the manufacturer. A safe choice would be to double the amount of RAM that your software calls for.

RAM Upgrades

Adding more RAM is one of the easiest ways to speed up a computer and help it perform faster. It's also one of the few things that you can do yourself on most computers. It's possible to upgrade the CPU over time, and many PC-based musicians do upgrade the components inside their computers, including the CPU/motherboard for increased performance. The Mac is much harder to upgrade in this way, due to Apple's tight control over parts supply. (You can upgrade the G4s in the older PowerMac desktops, but most users do not and opt to buy new computers. This is also largely due to the fact that upgrade options are limited to your current Mac motherboard, which is something that the PC folks can swap out and the Mac folks can't.)

RAM is something that you can easily upgrade yourself. RAM is sold as silicon chips called DIMMS. Installation varies from one computer manufacturer to another, but it is usually a quick and simple procedure that only involves unplugging the machine, removing the case, and setting the chips into their allocated spaces.

RAM FACTORS

As we discussed previously, RAM comes in different shapes, sizes, and speeds. Each computer uses a specific type and size of RAM. While many computers use the same RAM, there are still many choices on the market that require an informed choice. Simply running to your local computer store will leave you confused, as there are many variables involved. When in doubt, contact your computer manufacturer and find out exactly what specifications you need to know. In many cases, the computer manufacturer will sell you the RAM directly, eliminating the possibility of purchasing the wrong chip and possibly damaging your system.

RAM Volatility

One last thing to understand about RAM is that it is considered volatile or non-permanent storage. RAM stores data on electrically charged chips, but it has no way of permanently writing the information there. As soon as you turn your computer off, the information stored in the RAM chips is lost forever.

For permanent storage, computers use hard disks to archive and access data between system shutdowns. Hard disks, contrary to popular belief, do not hold their data forever. After 10 years or so, you need to move the data to a new drive. With the speed of technology, this is rarely an issue, since most of us don't own anything in our computer setups that is 10 years old.

Hard Drives

Computers use hard disks to store data permanently. They are called "hard" because unlike the floppy disks from the old days, hard disks use metal platters that are magnetized to store information. For an audio computer, the hard disk is an extremely crucial part of your setup. Selecting the correct drive for your machine is important. When stored on disk, digital audio can be very large, so selecting an adequate-sized drive is important. If you are mixing many tracks of guitar and other music, the speed at which the drive can access data will either help you or slow you down. Drives comes in several different varieties; some are better for music, some worse. Drives can be mounted inside the computer, or they can be external drives. As you can see, there are a lot of variables. Let's talk about the aspects that affect our ability to create music on the computer.

Hard Drive Size

When audio is digitally stored on a hard disk, it is written into audio files that can be read and played back by your computer. Audio files are complex, and the size of each file can be very large. At a minimum, each minute of audio takes up five megabytes. With higher sample rates, the amount of storage space needed will increase.

> **SAMPLING RATE EXPLAINED**
>
> Sampling rate refers to how many times the audio wave form is looked at (or sampled) as it is converted to digital. When audio manufacturers talk about higher sample rates, the effect is that of a high-definition TV. Higher sample rates get a better look at the audio before it's converted into digital information, resulting in a clearer and sharper audio signal. The only drawback to higher sample rates is that they take up more space on your hard disk.

The technology behind making hard drives larger is constantly improving. My first computer had an 8-megabyte hard drive, and this was only 10 years ago. Today, you can get drives that measure in the *gigabyte* range. As for how large your drive should be, if you are planning on recording and archiving your music, you'll need a large drive. Since the ceiling of drive storage is ever-expanding, get the most drive you can afford. As you'll read shortly, if you run out of room, you have other options.

Hard Drive Interfaces

Hard drives connect to the computer through a physical interface—usually a flat-ribbon cable. Since this is usually concealed within the computer, you may not be aware of it. There are three main interfaces for internal hard drives: IDE, SATA, and SCSI.

IDE has been the most common drive interface and the one that ships with most stock computers. IDE drives are easy to find and come in large storage capacities. SCSI drives are a different story. SCSI drives are usually *much* faster than their IDE counterparts. As you will learn, drive speed is an important variable for audio computers. SCSI has a few points to consider. First, SCSI drives aren't as large as their IDE counterparts. They are more expensive, and usually much more so. Also, SCSI drives require that your computer have a SCSI controller card to attach the drive to. Most computers don't ship with that option, so you'll have to buy a card to place inside the machine.

A newer option is SATA, or Serial ATA, hard drives. SATA is another data interface and is becoming common on newer computers. It is emerging as the successor to IDE drives. SATA yields faster data transfer and one other key factor, which is longer cable runs. (IDE was limited to a short cable.) This allows SATA drives to exist as external drives (eSATA) that can operate at speeds up to 5x faster than current USB and Firewire disks.

AN EASY UPGRADE

While most computers ship with a single hard drive installed inside, there is often room for additional drives. Check with your computer manufacturer to see if you can add an additional drive. Just like RAM upgrades, adding a second internal hard drive is about as complicated as hooking up a TV set to a cable wire.

Hard Drive Speed

Second to the storage size of a drive, its speed is the next crucial factor. Hard drive speed is measured in two ways. First is the speed of the rotation of the disk. A hard disk is composed of a small metal disk that spins around while a small magnetic arm reads the data from the drive. Figure 5.2 shows what the innards of a hard disk look like.

Figure 5.2
A hard disk drive.
Photograph of the Seagate Barracuda 7200.8 400GB Serial ATA drive is used by permission of Seagate Technology.

The faster that your disk spins, the faster it can retrieve and stream data to your system. We measure the speed of the spin in revolutions per minute, or RPM—just like your car's engine. The higher the number of RPMs, the more tracks and samples you'll be able to play back at once, and the higher the number, the better. Currently, 4,200 RPM is on the slower side, and 10,000 RPM is among the fastest discs you can get. If you are custom-configuring a computer for purchase, ask about the speed of the drive. You can usually opt for a faster drive for a slight upgrade in price. The difference in performance is worth the slight expense.

The other speed variable is seek time. Seek time is an average measurement of how long it takes from the instant you ask the drive to find a piece of information until it seeks and finds it. This number is measured in milliseconds (ms), and the lower the number, the better for you. Anything lower than 10ms average seek time should be sufficient. Remember, faster equals a lower number of milliseconds!

In the end, the two things you need to look for when buying a hard drive are a fast rotation speed (a high RMP number) and a fast seek time (a low number in milliseconds).

Internal versus External Storage

Up until a few short years ago, hard drives resided only inside your computer. There were options for external storage, but they often were as big as the computers themselves. The thought of taking large amounts of data from place to place was more fiction that fact. Nowadays, external hard drives allow us not only to add additional storage to our computers, but to do so without ever cracking the computer open. This is the perfect solution for the mechanically impaired among us. External hard drives also allow us to take our large amounts of data to other computers with ease. External drives come in two varieties: USB and Firewire.

USB 1.1 and USB 2.0

USB drives exist in two varieties: USB 1.1 and USB 2.0. USB 1.1 has been around longer and boasts a relatively slow transfer speed to the computer. The slower speed makes it perfect for keyboards and mice, but not great for hard drives that need to push a lot of data at a fast rate. USB 2.0 was introduced a few years ago and boasts a *much* faster interface, suitable for hard drives. The majority of computers shipping today include at least one USB 2.0 port. Figure 5.3 is what a USB cable looks like.

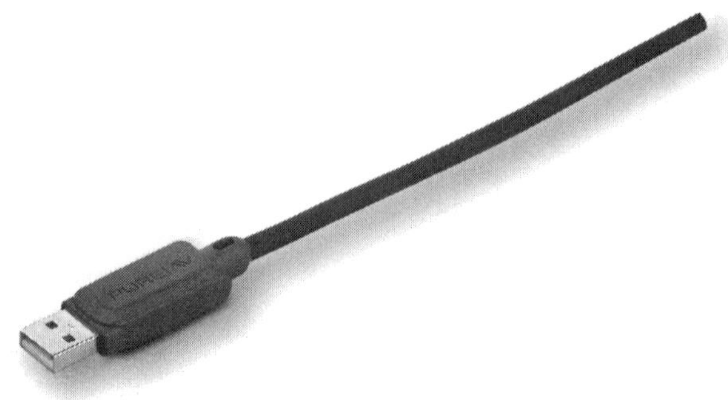

Figure 5.3
A USB cable.

WHICH IS WHICH?

USB 1.1 and USB 2.0 ports look identical on your computer, so it's easy to get confused as to what you have. If you currently own a machine, you can look up its specifications by calling the manufacturer.

If you own a computer that has only a USB 1.1 port, and you'd like to add an external hard drive, you can easily do so on both laptops and desktop computers by simply adding an additional USB 2.0 card (PCI for desktop computers and PCMCIA for laptops). This way you'll be able to add a fast, high-capacity drive to your existing setup. USB hard drives are a great way to add additional space to laptops that don't have the luxury of space for additional internal drives. For desktop computers, an external drive will cost you slightly more, but it will more than make up for it by sheer convenience and portability.

Firewire

Firewire is another external port used for connecting all sorts of peripherals to your computer. It was originally implemented by Apple computer as a high-speed transfer protocol for devices such as cameras and hard disks that need to move large amounts of data quickly. It comes on just about every Apple made since the late 1990s. Figure 5.4 shows what a Firewire cable looks like.

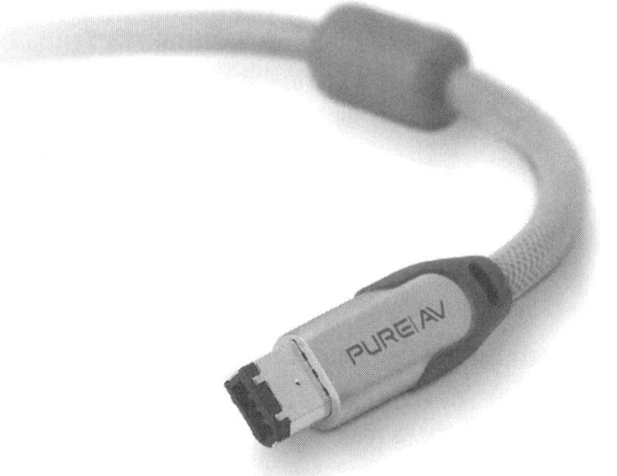

Figure 5.4
Firewire cable and port.

Historically, Firewire had the speed advantage. While USB 1.1 was trotting along, Firewire was moving data extremely quickly. The only caveat about Firewire is that it isn't standard equipment on Windows-based computers. All modern Macs have Firewire, but not all PCs do. Just like USB 2.0, you can add Firewire ports to your laptop or desktop computer by using expansion cards. Speedwise, Firewire and USB 2.0 are almost neck and neck (400 MB for Firewire and 480 MB for USB 2.0), so neither is better or worse for you.

Just as USB got a second, faster incarnation, Firewire got its second coming: Firewire 800. Firewire 800 boasts an 800 MB transfer speed, twice that of the original Firewire and much faster than USB 2.0. The future will tell if Firewire 800 becomes a long-term usable standard. Unlike USB 2.0, Firewire 800 uses a completely different cable and port, so devices are not backward-compatible like USB 1.1 and 2.0 are with each other. If you use a Mac, Firewire is a great choice because it's built-in. However, if you are planning on taking your hard drive from place to place, USB may be a smarter adoption because practically every computer made now supports USB 2.0, i.e., both Macs and PCs.

Bus Power

One of the nice features of both USB and Firewire is bus power. Bus power is simply a method by which peripherals plugged into the USB or Firewire bus can draw their power from the computer. For us digital guitarists and musicians, this means that the possibility exists for completely battery-free use of certain interfaces, as the computers take care of the power.

For bus power to work, two things have to happen. First, the computer must be able to supply it. All built-in USB ports on Macs and PCs deliver bus power. Firewire on Macs does, but Firewire on PCs (called IEE 1394) does not. This is because the Mac version of Firewire uses a 6-pin interface and the PC uses a 4-pin one (the extra two on the Mac provide power).

The second aspect is that the interface itself must be able to run on the current passed through the bus. Many devices are bus-powered, but some devices require external AC power, because the power that runs through USB and Firewire may not be enough to power the device. If bus powering is important to you, check with the manufacturer to make sure that the device is compatible. Bus powering is great if you want a truly mobile setup.

For PC users who have 4-pin Firewire ports that do not give power and would like to utilize a bus-powered Firewire device, use a PCMCIA Firewire card. That will provide 6-pin ports and the bus power that you need.

Multiple Drives

One of the greatest performance tips for running a reliable, fast audio computer is to have a second drive to store your work on. You can, of course, use only one drive, but when you ask a single hard drive to hold your operating system, music programs, and music files, you give that one disk a lot of work. You can dramatically increase your performance and track count by simply adding a second hard drive, internal or external, and keeping your audio files and samples on the second drive. By doing this, you will divide the load between multiple drives. If you couple this with an extremely fast second audio drive, you will have an extremely capable system. Using a dedicated drive for audio is a trick used by all professional studios.

Having a second drive also gives you a touch more security. By keeping your valuable audio files and projects on a separate disk from your operating system, you give yourself an extra layer of protection if your main system drive crashes or is attacked by a malicious computer virus. If you use an external drive for this task, you can share your work between multiple computers so that your data is always within reach. This is becoming more and more important, with the average musician owning both a desktop and a laptop computer.

Guitar to Computer Communication

Now that we've gone over the nitty-gritty details of the inner workings of a computer, it's time to discuss the specifics of how the guitar and the computer interact and everything you need to know to get the most out of your setup. The previous information will serve you in every aspect of computer recording, whether you're using a guitar or not. The following information directly deals with how the computer and the guitar communicate.

Audio Interfaces

Now that you have a rock-solid computer setup, and you understand the parts that go into putting together a solid music computer, you have to get your guitar connected to the computer. While we will spend some time in this book talking about how to throw a nice microphone in front of your Marshall amplifier, the main technology here is happening virtually inside of your computer, so talking about microphones and amps isn't as important as simply routing your dry guitar signal into the computer. To do so, you will need a computer-recording interface.

Simply put, the job of an interface is to take the analog signal from your guitar and convert it to digital information that the computer software can interpret and work with. This is called analog to digital conversion, or A/D conversion for short. Once the software has done its magic, the digital sound is sent back to the interface and is converted back from digital to analog, so you can hear what's going on.

Interfaces come in many sizes, prices, and connection types, and with many features. Lots of different companies make audio interfaces for use with a computer. Let's talk about the different types of interfaces out there so that you can select the best one for you.

Connection Type

Interfaces are mainly classified by the method that they use to connect with the computer. When we discussed hard drives a few pages ago, we talked about Firewire and USB as connection types for drives. Audio interfaces make use of those as well. There are two more interfaces to talk about—PCI and PCMCIA. Let's talk about each type separately.

PCI Interfaces

PCI, which stands for peripheral component interconnect, is a card that plugs directly into your computer's motherboard. This type of interface has been around for a long time and is still popular today. Because it sits inside the computer, this interface is only applicable to desktop computers. PCI interfaces usually have a small bundle of wires that extend out of the back of the computer in order for you to make your connections. Figure 5.5 shows what a PCI audio card looks like.

Figure 5.5
A PCI audio interface.

On the plus side, a PCI interface can be obtained for a relatively low cost and is very stable and reliable. The only negative about it is that you can't easily take it from computer to computer. It's fine if you have one desktop computer and never go anywhere with it. These days, with laptop computers becoming such powerhouses, selecting an interface that is suitable for use with a desktop *and* a laptop computer is becoming important.

PCMCIA Interfaces

When laptops first appeared on the market, the only way to get audio in and out of a laptop computer was to use a PCMCIA card. A PCMCIA card is a thin, narrow card that slides into the side of your laptop computer (if you have the slot for it) and enables laptop musicians to place high-quality audio on their computers. Figure 5.6 shows what a PCMCIA card looks like.

Just like the PCI cards, because of their relatively small size, the audio connections on PCMCIA cards are bundles of wires that protrude from the end of the card. Manufacturers refer to this as a breakout box. If you have a laptop, a PCMCIA card is a viable option for an audio interface. The reality is that in the last few years, USB and Firewire have become more prevalent in the market, and there are more options for your laptop if you look at Firewire or USB. Just like PCI, PCMCIA cards only work with a laptop computer.

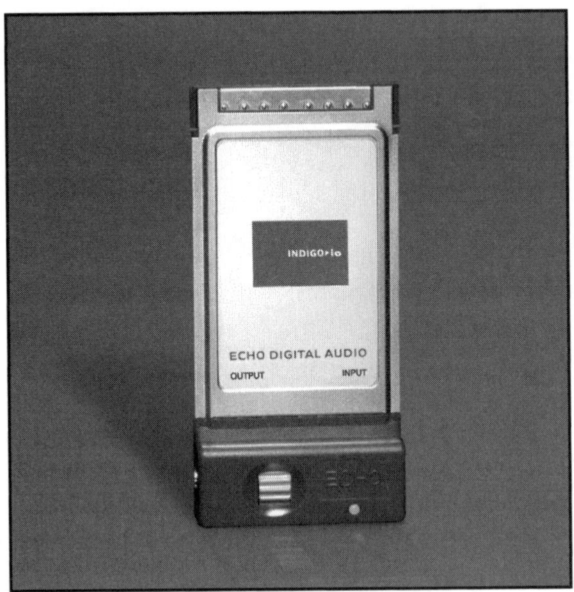

Figure 5.6
A PCMCIA interface.

USB Interfaces

USB audio interfaces were the first interfaces that were suitable for both laptops and desktop computers. This heralded a revolution in computer music-making: portability. USB interfaces started out using the USB 1.1 specification, which at the time was the state of the art. USB 1.1's greatest limitation was the amount of data that it could stream over its cable to and from the computer. More data means more tracks. USB 1.1 wasn't a particularly speedy interface, and the early USB audio interfaces only allowed a few simultaneous inputs and outputs to your computer. They had a chameleon like ability to work with any computer, but PCI cards had more options and speed, which resulted in more tracks. However, for many musicians, the limited input and output design was fine, since many USB interfaces were low-cost and allowed project studios to pop up all over the world using the home computer as a base. With the invention of USB 2.0 and its larger data throughput, USB audio interfaces were able to handle many simultaneous inputs and outputs, and, in general, handle larger tasks (see Figure 5.7).

USB interfaces may include the following input and output options:

- Preamplified microphone inputs
- Line-level inputs
- Digital input and outputs
- Multiple outputs
- MIDI inputs and outputs

Figure 5.7
A USB audio interface.

As you can see, USB provides a fairly complete solution of inputs and outputs. If some of the bulleted terms above seemed confusing to you, have no fear, because I will define all those terms in the rest of this chapter. If you are working between a laptop and a desktop and need an audio interface that will work with both, USB is a great way to go. For many Mac laptop users, it's the only option these days, because PCMCIA isn't standard on every Mac laptop. (Every PC laptop does have PCMCIA.) You'll be extremely hard-pressed to find a laptop that does not include a USB port! Currently, every Apple laptop ships with at least two USB ports, and popular laptops running Windows ship with at least two and usually more. USB ports can be multiplied by simply buying a hub, which acts like a power strip of sorts, essentially splitting the port into more ports. This is a great option for laptops that don't ship with enough ports.

Firewire Interfaces

Back in the early days of USB 1.1, many musicians became frustrated with the limitations of early USB interfaces. The speed limitation directly equated to fewer tracks and lesser performance across the board. Those musicians had another option: Firewire. Firewire was originally invented by Apple computer as a high-speed laptop and desktop connection for audio and video devices. Even though this technology was originally implemented by Apple, it was a standard interface that other manufacturers used, so it was not exclusive to Apple computers. One of the most significant differences between USB 1.1 and Firewire was the speed of the interface. USB 1.1 topped out a transfer rate of 12 megabytes per second. On the other hand, Firewire was able to stream up to 400 megabytes per second. That meant Firewire was able to pump over 33 times the amount of data down its cable. This equated to more tracks, more inputs and outputs, and greater performance across the board. Firewire audio interfaces, like USB interfaces, could be utilized by desktops and laptop computers, making them a very attractive choice for a wider section of musicians. Figure 5.8 is a picture of a popular MOTU Traveler Firewire interface.

Firewire interfaces boasted similar specifications to USB interfaces. The only difference was that whatever inputs and outputs USB had, Firewire had many more of them. A popular interface, the MOTU 828, first introduced in 1997 (which in computer terms is a long time ago), boasted eight analog inputs, eight analog outputs, two digital inputs and outputs, and eight additional ADAT connections. This was a generous supply of inputs and outputs, suitable for any studio.

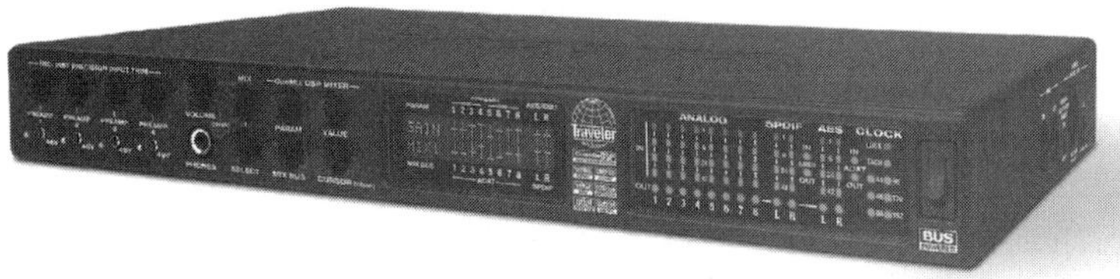

Figure 5.8
A Firewire audio interface—the MOTU Traveler.

Firewire interfaces have remained popular because they've allowed for a flexible computer studio interface, suitable for laptops and desktops.

The only caveat about Firewire interfaces is that not every computer comes with a Firewire port standard. Apple computers do (they invented the thing), but not all Windows computers do. For desktop computers, you can easily add a Firewire PCI card (see Figure 5.9).

Figure 5.9
A PCI Firewire card interface—the M-Audio Audiophile.

THE NEED FOR SPEED.

While Firewire may appear to be faster and more useful to the computer musician, USB 2.0 boasts a transfer speed that is slightly faster than Firewire 400. If your computer does not boast Firewire connectivity, USB 2.0 and the new crop of USB 2.0 interfaces will meet your needs nicely.

Input Types

No matter what interface you ultimately end up choosing, we should talk about the different types of connections offered on the interfaces, so that you can hook in with little trouble.

1/4 Inch Connections

Since this book is aimed at guitarists, this should be a no-brainer for you. The guitar cable you have been using your whole life is a quarter-inch cable. Many audio interfaces use these connections for inputs and outputs.

> **PLUG AND PLAY?**
>
> Just because an interface has a quarter-inch input does not mean that you can simply plug your guitar in and start recording. The section titled "The Guitar's Signal" will explain all about the guitar's signal and what you'll need to record with it.

Quarter-inch connections come in two varieties: balanced and unbalanced. Unbalanced is the most common quarter-inch cable and is the one you are currently using for your guitar. Balanced connectors are used mainly for connecting computer monitor speakers to audio interfaces and interconnecting professional-quality audio gear. For the guitarist, unbalanced connections are the way we work.

RCA Connections

RCA is another standard cable for connecting audio gear together. RCA is a smaller cable and connector, and you will find it on some of the smaller interfaces sold. The quarter-inch connector is more common and useful to the guitarist, but if your interface supports RCA, you can simply purchase a converter that will transform your unbalanced guitar cable into an RCA cable. Since the guitar is an unbalanced signal, converting it to RCA will have no affect on your signal quality. Figure 5.10 is what an RCA cable looks like.

Figure 5.10
An RCA audio cable.

RCA connections are unbalanced like guitar cables and almost always come in pairs of two cables molded together. You may recognize RCA cables from your home stereo connections or TV hookups; RCA is a common cable in these scenarios.

XLR Connections

XLR cables are commonly used as microphone cables. You may not have even realized that they had another name besides "microphone cables." XLR cables are always balanced, and while they are commonly used for microphones, there are some situations when a guitarist will use this connection. Many acoustic guitars with piezo or microphone systems will use an XLR connection. The Line6 Variax guitar uses an XLR connection as well.

If you play primarily acoustic guitar and don't feel the need to drill holes in your guitar for electronic systems, such as internally mounted microphones or piezo systems, you'll most likely be using an external microphone to record your acoustic guitar. In these cases, an XLR connection is a must. Also, you don't have to just plug your guitar straight into the computer. Many times, recording electric guitars involves placing a microphone directly in front of a speaker. Since this is still a viable way to record guitar into the computer, XLR is an important connection to have on your interface.

Digital Connections

All of the connections we have discussed so far have been analog connections, meaning that they transmit electrical signals back and forth based on periodic waves. Digital cables and connections do exist and are used in music studios. Some of the digital modeling gear, such as the Line6 POD series and others, has digital outputs. Digital connections come in two basic flavors: optical and wired. Let's talk about the wired connections, because the optical ones aren't currently in use for guitar products.

> **OPTICAL CONNECTIONS**
>
> If you're wondering who uses optical connections, CD players, DVD players, and digital cable boxes output audio via a fiber optic cable called a *TOSLink cable*. In the recording world, the most common optical cable is the ADAT interface. ADAT optical is a multi-channel cable that was created for streaming eight tracks from an ADAT (a digital tape recorder) to a computer. These days, ADAT connections are a common way to expand your inputs and outputs. Many companies produce interfaces based on the ADAT optical spec, allowing you to add more connectivity to your studio.

These are the two kinds of wired digital audio connectors you commonly find on audio interfaces. By wired, we mean that it's an actual metal wire that transmits the signals, as opposed to the fiber optic cables used in TOSLink and ADAT connections.

S/PDIF is a digital connection that uses standard RCA cables for streaming digital information to and from a computer interface. This is by far the most common interface on the market for digital signals.

AES/EBU uses XLR microphone cables to send digital signals back and forth. This is still used in studios and is a common digital connection format, but for the purposes of this book, its use in the guitar world is limited. It's still nice to know about it, since your audio education will not be limited to just guitars. There's a whole world out there!

Does Your Audio Interface Need MIDI Connections?

What about MIDI? Well, it depends on you. If you are into exploring the world of MIDI guitar, you will want a MIDI connection on your interface. The truth is that when you buy an interface, you are buying it for more than strictly recording guitar. MIDI continues to be an important standard for keyboard and guitar controllers. Since an interface is an investment, you'll probably want to get as complete a connection scheme as possible. The good news is that most interfaces include at least one MIDI input and output. If you buy an interface without it, don't sweat. You can add a USB MIDI interface for about $30.

Latency

Latency is no small thing. The root of the word latency is "late," not necessarily something you associate with guitar. That is, unless you're talking about the typical guitarist's inability to show up on time, but that's another matter. Here is the bottom line on latency: everything has it. For example, pick up your guitar right now and pluck a string. Do you think that you heard the string at the exact microsecond you hit it? No, there is an extremely small delay as the sound travels to your ears. In the case of a traditional guitar amplifier, it takes a very short time for the signal to pass down your guitar's cable and out of the speaker to your ear. Everything has some sort of delay, but most things are so quick that you can't sense them.

When you interface a guitar with a computer, latency becomes a very important factor. It takes a certain amount of time for your signal to be converted from analog to digital, time for the signal to be processed on the computer, and time for it to be converted back to analog again on the way out. The time it takes to do so is called latency. As we said, everything has some sort of latency. For the early adopters of digital guitar technology, latency was a big deal, because if you tried to play through one of the new guitar amp simulator plug-ins and your setup wasn't optimized to deal with latency, it felt like there was a considerable delay from the time you played a note until you actually heard it. If you've never experienced this, it's a bit disorienting, almost like walking through a fog. Latency can make it hard to record parts onto a computer and keep accurate time with a click track or drum track/loop. Latency is largely controlled through the speed of the machine and settings in your software of choice. To combat this, interface manufacturers have a workaround called zero latency or direct monitoring.

> **TDM**
>
> Pro Tools Time Division Multiplex system (or TDM) has one distinct advantage over other systems—extremely low latency. On a Pro Tools TDM system, the latency is so small that it is not an issue. This is because TDM systems use special DSP cards to handle the processing, in contrast to host-based programs that utilize the CPU for all processing. In fact, the first amp modeler was Line6's Amp Farm, which debuted on and still only runs on a TDM system.

Direct Monitoring

Hardware interface manufacturers have devised a very smart way around latency by beating it at its own game. Signal latency (which is an issue for anyone who plans to record anything on a computer) is based on the amount of time it takes the signal to get in and out of your computer. Other factors can affect this amount of time, but the general thought is that it just physically takes time to get to and from the computer. What the hardware interface manufacturers have done is cut the computer out of the loop, and they allow you to monitor your signal before it gets to the computer, with virtually no latency. MOTU's interfaces use a technology called Cuemix that allows you to mix many signals together with zero latency. Figure 5.11 is a shot of the software mixer for the MOTU 828 Firewire interface.

Figure 5.11
MOTU's latency-busting Cuemix software.

There are pros and cons to this approach. The pro is that there is no delay at all; the sound is immediate. The con is that by cutting the computer out of the equation, you lose the sound that the computer is giving you. For example, if you are plugging into a guitar effects plug-in, such as Guitar Rig or another plug-in, and you enact the direct monitoring option, you won't hear the sound of the virtual amp. All you'll hear is a clean, dry signal.

Direct monitoring wasn't invented just for guitarists, but for general recording latency incurred by any instrument. The good news is that fast computers, fast interfaces, and correct software settings can bring your latency down to such a small number (under 6 ms) that you will hardly feel it at all. The computer will feel just like a physical amp or effects box. For the times when razor-edge accuracy is a must, you can always monitor with zero latency. Your monitoring will have no effect on the sound that hits the computer. As soon as you're done recording and you play back, you will hear the correct sound that you wanted in the first place.

Selecting the Right Interface for You

Think there are enough variables and options for you to think about now? USB or Firewire, how many inputs and outputs, latency options, and other concerns are all part of your decision-making process. Here is a list of things to think about when purchasing an interface:

1. Pick an interface that will grow with your needs—this includes the number of inputs and outputs.
2. Direct monitoring is a great feature for guitar players to have.
3. MIDI, of some sort, is extremely handy in this day and age.
4. Digital connections—you may not need them today, but you may want them tomorrow.
5. Make sure it's compatible with your computer's operating system!
6. Check the Web sites and forums, and ask questions about which interface will work best for you. There are so many to choose from now, and a little advice goes a long way.
7. Make sure it comes with at least one or two microphone preamplifiers. You'll need this to record an acoustic guitar or direct electric guitar signals.

The Guitar's Signal

The guitar is a more complicated piece of electronics than you might think. For the longest time, we have simply plugged a quarter-inch cable into the output jack of our favorite ax and plugged into an amp for instant gratification. The truth is that the guitar is a fairly amazing piece of technology.

Many people think that the cable that connects the amplifier to the guitar "powers" the guitar in some subtle way. This is not true at all—the guitar makes its own signal through *induction.* Electric guitars are equipped with magnetic pickups. The magnetic pickups are composed of magnets with copper wire wrapped around them. If you can hearken back to ninth-grade physics, do you remember what happened when your teacher wrapped a magnet with wire and then waved a steel nail in front of it? Waving the steel nail by the magnet produced a current through induction. This is the same way that a guitar makes its own power. The pickups are like the magnets with wires wrapped around them, and the guitar strings are like the nail. By playing the strings, a small amount of electricity is created. This electricity is sent down a cable into an amplifier, which does simply that: it amplifies the signal—greatly! The guitar makes a very, very, very small amount of current. This current is barely enough to make a Radio Shack voltmeter do much of anything.

When you plug into an amplifier, there is a hidden preamplifier that boosts your signal up to an acceptable level that the power amp can amplify. Without the preamplifier, the amp would be useless. One of the things you'll learn is how to plug your guitar directly into a computer interface. To get an adequate signal into the computer, you are going to need a preamplifier.

Preamplification

Many computer interfaces feature microphone preamplifiers. This is because microphones work with the same principle as guitars, in that they induce current to make power. Instead of a string, microphones have membranes that are coated with a metallic substance that moves in front of its magnet. In any case, the principles behind microphones and guitars are the same. To plug a bare, direct guitar into a computer, you are going to need to preamplify the signal. There's no way around it, because your signal will be too weak without going through some sort of preamplification.

Thankfully, most if not all computer recording interfaces feature some sort of preamplification. You can simply plug your guitar's quarter-inch cable into the preamplifier input (which is usually labeled Mic/Guitar) and adjust the Gain knob to bring your guitar's signal to the proper strength. Figure 5.12 shows you where to plug into a standard interface.

Figure 5.12
A preamplified guitar input.

To say that you always need preamplification is a lie; there are a few cases where you don't need to worry about this. The first is if you are using an external guitar processing box, such as a Line6 POD, a Behringer V-AMP, or anything like those devices. The outputs of those devices are said to be line level. Line level requires no preamplification because devices such as the POD and V-AMP have preamplifiers built directly into them and feature a direct out, meaning that you can plug the devices directly in to them. Nor would you need a preamplified input if you already have an external preamplifier—either a guitar preamp or a microphone preamp that functions as a D.I. box for your guitar.

Let's define one important term that relates to all electronic devices, and specifically to guitar: impedance.

Impedance

Impedance is one of the main reasons that you can't just plug a guitar into a recording source without amplifying it. A guitar is described as a high-impedance device or HiZ (Z is the scientific shorthand for impedance). Impedance is simply a measure of a device's ability to resist the flow of electricity and is measured in ohms. Impedance comes from the root "to impede," which means "to stop." When a device is high-impedance or HiZ, that device resists the flow of electricity greatly, resulting in a very weak signal. This is why the guitar has such a weak signal; it's a very high-impedance device.

> **UNDERSTANDING IMPEDANCE**
>
> If you're having a hard time understanding impedance, here is an analogy that will help you understand it better: Impedance is like a traffic jam. A stalled car or two makes it almost impossible for the other cars to move along at high speed. A high-impedance source has many traffic jams along its circuit path, lowering the overall output. On the same road, a low-impedance device has open lanes in all directions, so the electricity flows just like cars on the Long Island Expressway at 5 p.m. on Friday. (That was a terrible joke that I hope you never have to experience firsthand!)

Because of the popularity of direct recording with guitar these days, many manufacturers have supplied inputs on their interfaces that automatically adjust for the guitar's high impedance. These inputs are labeled HiZ inputs, meaning that they are suited for devices that have high impedance, such as a guitar.

Direct Boxes

If you've ever played live, you've probably seen a direct box in your travels. A direct box is a simple device that takes a signal with high impedance and converts it to a signal with low impedance. These are popular with live sound engineers who plug guitars and basses into mixing boards. They are also important to the guitar recording buff. You may use mixers as interfaces to your computer hardware. If you opt to do this, a direct box will be needed unless your mixer has specific HiZ inputs.

Many of the computer interfaces that feature a guitar/mic input, which is multipurpose for use with either a microphone or a guitar, often have a direct box (or some equivalent) built into the interface.

> **DIRECT BOXES FOR NOISE**
>
> Another great feature of direct boxes is that they have the ability to perform a ground lift. If your guitar is buzzing and making other unsavory noises because of poor grounding or other electrical anomalies in your studio, a direct box may save the day.

Miking Your Amp versus Direct Recording

I have focused a lot of our discussion on direct recording as the main way to get your guitar signal into the computer. This isn't the only way. The future of guitar technology doesn't mean that you have to abandon your amp. You may simply want to record your amp as-is. Maybe you already have a modeling amp like a Line6 Vetta II and want to record its sound into the computer. Or you might want to use the computer to add effects to your amp's sound. Embracing new technology does not mean throwing the old gear away. If you have a great amp, you may want to capture the sound of that amp with a microphone and place it as an audio track in your computer's sequencer of choice.

If you do choose to go direct, you get some different options that we will explore in the next chapters on software tools. I'll cover recording your guitar in great detail in Chapter 11, "DSP Systems: UAD and Powercore." Either way you go, you need to get your sound into the computer.

Monitoring

All of these fancy interfaces are no good without being able to hear what you are working on. To work in a computerized setup, you will need speakers to play back the audio. These special speakers are called monitors and should not be confused with your computer screen, also called a monitor. From now on, we'll just call your computer's screen a "display," leaving the moniker "monitor" for audio speakers.

Monitoring is achieved in one of two ways. The first is by use of a pair of speakers to reproduce left and right channels independently. The second way is to use headphones. Let's talk about each.

Monitor Speakers

Monitor speakers are a pair of audio speakers that are designed specifically for recording and mixing music. They are different from the typical home audio speaker that you would buy for your stereo system. Monitor speakers are designed specifically to have an equal response across the entire frequency spectrum and reproduce exactly what you give them. This is not the way that most home theater speakers are designed. They accentuate different frequencies to enhance your viewing of TV and sports. This is not the way you want speakers in your musical environment to act. Just like a properly calibrated TV set, you want to hear what's really there, in terms of frequencies.

Monitors, like the ones shown in Figure 5.13, come either with internal amplifiers (powered) or without amplifiers (passive). Passive monitors require separate amplifiers to power the signal you feed them. Active monitors are the most common you find in the marketplace now, and are certainly the most convenient for many studios.

What should you look for in a set of monitor speakers? You don't look for anything. You must hear them first. Take a CD that you know very well to the store with you. Compare all the models in your price range using the same CD and the same track. Listen to how each different brand and type of monitor affects the sound in a different way. Monitors are an investment, and to truly get the most out of your investment, you want to get to know how yours sound intimately, so don't skimp in selecting them! This is a crucial part of your listening chain.

Figure 5.13
A pair of stereo monitor speakers.

> **MONITORS VS. GUITAR SPEAKERS**
> The typical guitar amplifier has a single woofer speaker. This speaker reproduces the low range of the guitar well, but since the guitar does not produce a great deal of high-frequency content, there is no need for a separate high-frequency speaker. Monitor speakers combine a woofer and a high-frequency driver, because monitors are expected to re-create a full range of frequencies accurately. You will most likely hear more when you listen back to your guitar on monitor speakers than you will from a traditional guitar amplifier.

Headphone Monitoring

The other way to monitor your music is through a pair of high-quality headphones designed for audio. iPod ear buds simply won't do; you'll need headphones specifically designed for this sort of thing. Just like the monitor speakers above, a good pair of headphones should have a flat frequency response and sound exactly like the source they are playing back. There are many brands at many price ranges to choose from. Visit your local music retailer and hear them using source material you're familiar with. Most stores will have a display area where you can listen to the popular models.

Headphones have their good and bad points. They are small and relatively cheap when compared to monitor speakers. They also allow you to work late at night and not bother your dog sleeping on the floor next to you. Some of their bad points are that headphones are extremely close to your ears and can give you a different impression of your sound than monitor speakers do. Sound typically interacts with its environment by reflecting off and absorbing into surfaces. What you hear is the result of the environment you work in. Using headphones, or "cans" as they are also called, cuts out this factor and can affect what you hear. Headphones are essential to any studio, so get a good pair. It's just not recommended to use them to monitor everything all the time. Headphones are a great way to get a second opinion on a particular mix that you're working on with monitor speakers. Oh, and as a precautionary note, headphones sit so close to your ears that it's very easy to damage your hearing by monitoring at unsafe levels. Make sure that you are smart about protecting your ears, because you only get one pair.

Electromagnetic Interference

Guitar is *very* susceptible to interference from other electrical and magnetic sources. Just ask anyone who's played a Fender Stratocaster on the first click, and they will tell you all about noise. In the typical home studio, there are a great number of things that can interfere with the guitar's clean signal. Guitar is especially sensitive to electromagnetic interference. You can pick this up from your monitor speakers, nearby TVs, studio equipment, and even fluorescent lighting.

Many monitor speakers are already shielded, meaning that they contain their own interference by use of internal shielding. One of the most common culprits is a tube monitor, also called a CRT monitor. Unlike the sleek modern LCD displays we see so often, CRT monitors let off a good bit of electrical interference. If you are sitting directly in front of a screen like that with your guitar in hand, you may notice some fuzz and interference in your sound. If this is the case, you're simply going to have to find another place to sit. Many times, simply moving out of the way, even a few degrees in the other direction, will be enough to curb the noise. Cell phones can be a huge problem as well. I've heard many a cell signal through a guitar's pickup right into an amp or computer! Certain guitars are more prone to interference than others. This may be due to how your guitar is set up. A direct box may cut down on some of the noise by use of a ground lift switch. It it's really a problem, you might want to take your guitar to a technician, because you may have a wire loose!

Getting the Most from Your Computer System

To end this mammoth section, I'm going to give you a few tips to streamline your system and help it run as well as possible. Of course, I will address Mac and Windows separately, since each system handles data and optimization differently. Don't overlook these little tweaks! Audio systems require different strategies for performance than typical computers.

Mac-Specific Tips

On the Mac side, specifically OSX, there are a few things you can keep in mind. Here is a list of things to do. First, create a user account just for audio programs. Since OSX allows you to create multiple user accounts, it's great to have a clean account just for audio with no other items clogging your computer. Try not to be on the Internet when you are using your audio programs, because they consume processor cycles.

OSX has a tricky way of making you think that you've quit a program, when you haven't actually quit it. Here is how you can tell for sure. Call up your dock if you have it hidden; if not, just look at the bottom of your screen. Applications that are running have a small black arrow under them, like the ones in Figure 5.14.

Figure 5.14
OSX dock showing running applications.

It's possible for an application to look like it's off, but the black arrow says that it's on and consuming power.

UNIX Permissions

OSX is built on a foundation of UNIX, which uses a very special and complicated set of permissions for each file on your hard disk. The permissions basically tell each file who has permission to access them. It's possible to have these permissions messed up. If you suddenly lose the ability to read one of your important application files, you could be in real trouble! OSX provides you with a disk utility that takes care of this. Simply go to your utilities folder (inside of your main applications folder) and launch the Disc Utility, as seen in Figure 5.15.

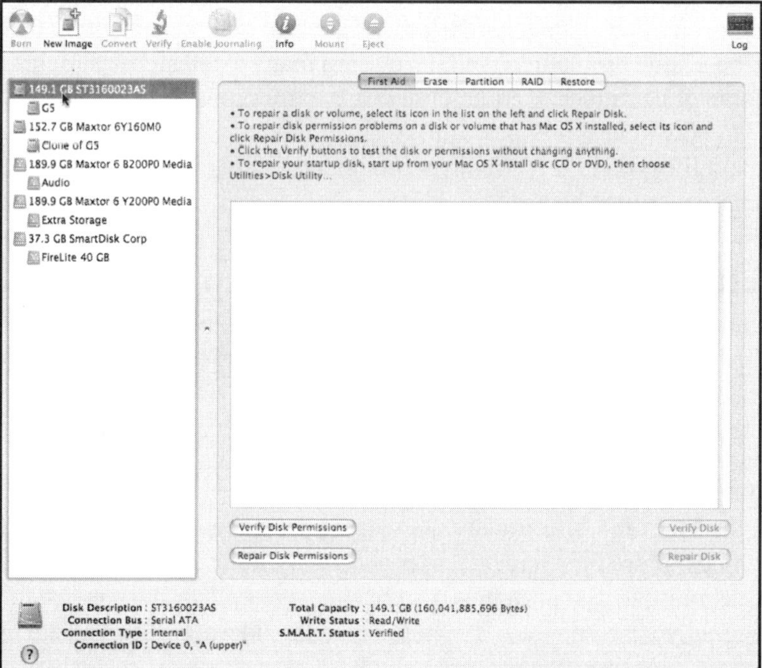

Figure 5.15
Disc Utility.

Select your main hard drive (the one that holds your applications) and select it on the left side. You will then see the Repair Disc Permissions button on the lower-left side. Click this and let it run (it may take a bit to finish). Do this once a month to ensure smooth performance. Always run it after you have installed or reinstalled major software, including system updates from Apple.

Laptop-Only Tips

Laptops run on batteries. Battery life depends on what the computer is doing and how active the CPU is. On an Apple laptop, there is a system preference for CPU activity. Simply launch your System Preferences, either by pulling down the Apple (top-left corner of your screen) or going to your utilities folder (inside of applications) and launching System Preferences.

After you launch that, you'll gain access to a whole bunch of features. The one you want to narrow in on is the Energy Saver, shown in Figure 5.16.

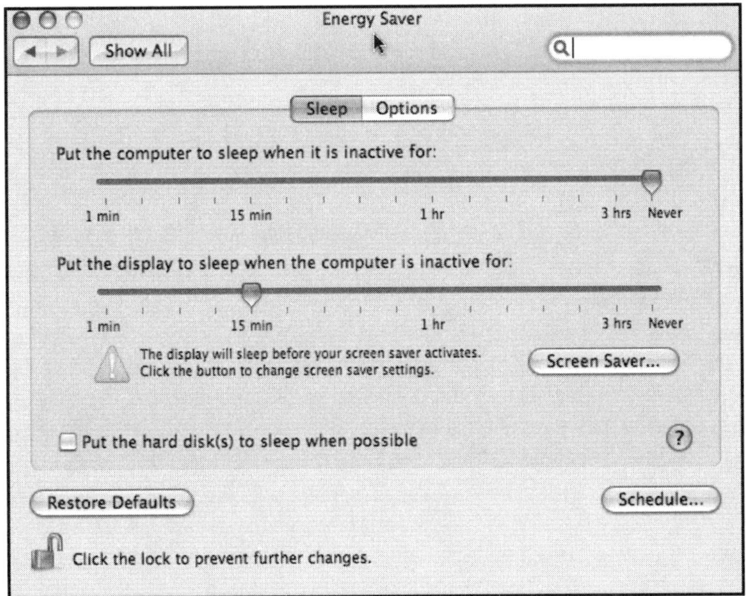

Figure 5.16
Energy Saver.

In the Energy Saver window, you'll see three tabs: Sleep, Schedule, and Options. Click on Options to bring up this screen (see Figure 5.17).

If you're on a laptop, you should see Processor Performance. This simple menu item lets you set if the computer should run at full or reduced speed. Reduced speed may be okay for writing email, and could eke out a few extra minutes of battery life, but it will make your CPU less effective. Make sure it's set to Highest, like Figure 5.18 shows. This will ensure the highest level of performance.

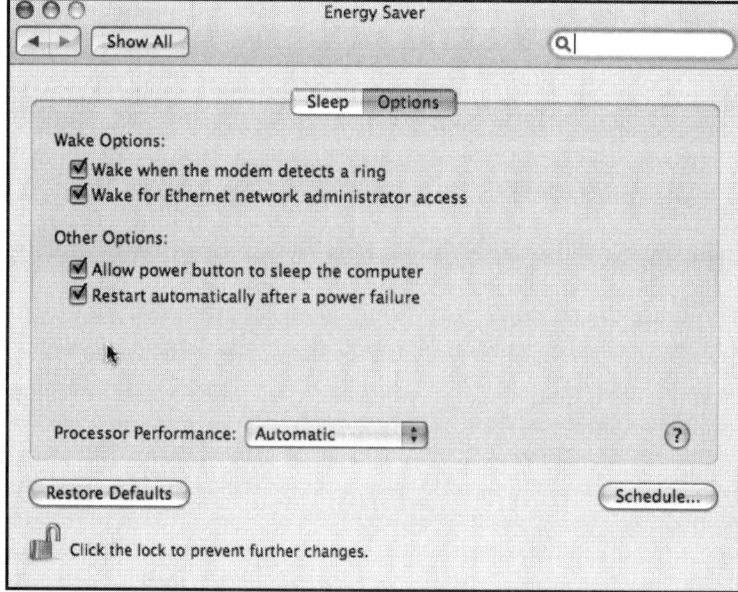

Figure 5.17
Energy Saver options.

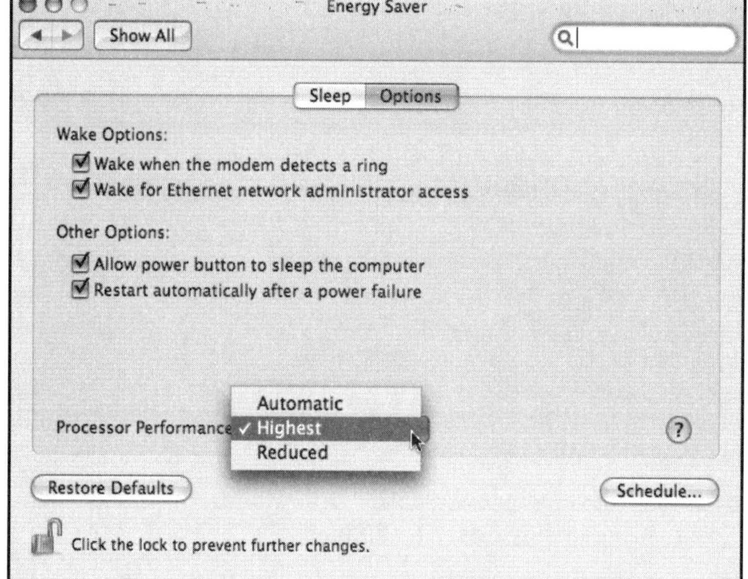

Figure 5.18
Setting your processor performance.

Windows-Specific Tips

Windows XP comes out of the box set up pretty well for audio. As long as you have followed the chapter so far and bought the right system, you should be okay. However, there are a few tweaks you need to know about to really make your system utilize its full potential.

The Joy of the Internet

The Internet is one of the most important facets in our lives—whether we want it to be or not! In the world of Windows, being online has its issues. Hackers have taken great pride in messing up our computers with spyware, adware, viruses, and other obnoxious programs, with the sole purpose of making our lives difficult. To combat this, most of us employ a fairly sophisticated set of tools to safeguard our computers. Anti-viral programs run all the time. Other programs, such as firewalls, keep our computers from being attacked. While these programs safeguard your computer and are necessary, they also take up valuable resources because they run in the background all the time, constantly watching. This can decrease your audio performance.

What to do about this? Honestly, if you are running a serious audio computer, take it off the Internet. Yup, that's right, unplug the cable or turn off your wireless connection. This way, you won't need all the safeguard programs hogging your CPU, plus your data will be safer. Most professional studios *never* take their audio computers online. If you must do so, create a second account for audio, and when working in that account, deactivate the Internet. On the audio account, don't start up any of the protective programs. When you need to switch back to non-audio mode, log into the normal account and reinstitute the Internet connection, and you should be good to go.

Graphics Performance

Windows XP was a considerable graphical makeover from the previous versions of Windows. As we have found out, pretty graphics have a cause-and-effect relationship with the performance of your machine. All those glossy buttons and rounded corners take CPU cycles to compute and redraw. Thankfully, Windows allows you to turn off these features for maximum CPU efficiency. Amazingly, following these simple steps for Windows XP will make a considerable difference in how your system reacts graphically. Everything will seem snappier.

First, on your desktop, locate My Computer. Right-click it to bring up its menu of options, as seen in Figure 5.19.

In the corresponding menu that pops up, choose Properties. Selecting this will bring you to the computer Properties screen, as seen in Figure 5.20.

Figure 5.19
Right-click My Computer for options.

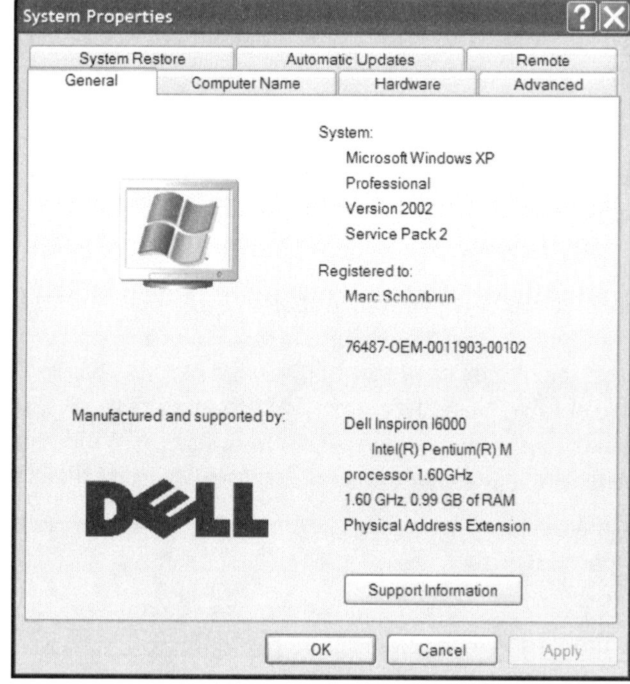

Figure 5.20
Your computer's properties.

In addition to displaying some basic information about your computer system, there are several tabs across the top of the screen. Locate the Advanced tab and click it. Figure 5.21 shows the results of your action.

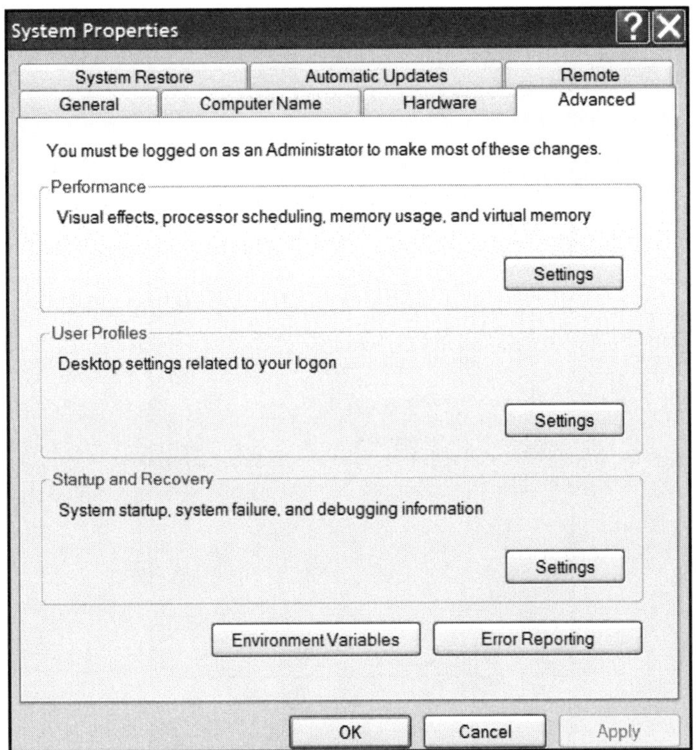

Figure 5.21
The Advanced tab.

In the Advanced window, Performance is the first category and has a button for Settings. Click that button, and you will be taken to the dialog box shown in Figure 5.22.

This dialog controls many of the visual effects that Windows applies to make XP look a bit sexier. There are a few preset buttons you can select. By default, Windows will manage this for you. You want to select Adjust for Best Performance by clicking the circle next to the phrase Adjust for Best Performance, as seen in Figure 5.23.

Once you have selected that option, you need to click the Apply button to make it happen. Windows will take a few minutes to think about the changes, and when it's done, your windows will now look like Figure 5.24.

You'll notice that the windows have lost their smoothness, and the buttons are rather bland. Basically, it looks a lot like Windows 98. That's just fine with me. Take a few minutes to open and close some windows, and notice how much faster and more responsive things are. Test your audio applications and enjoy the increased performance.

Believe it or not, following these simple pieces of advice will help your Windows machine perform at its best.

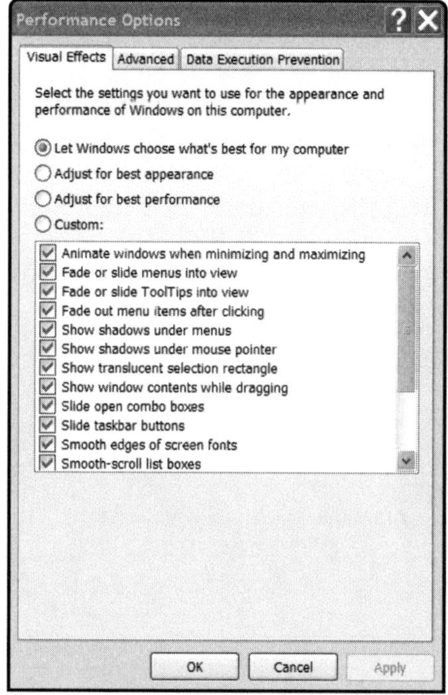

Figure 5.22
Performance Options.

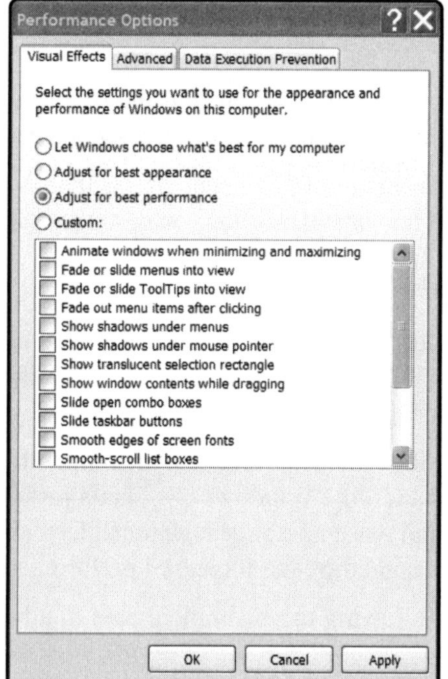

Figure 5.23
Adjusting for best performance.

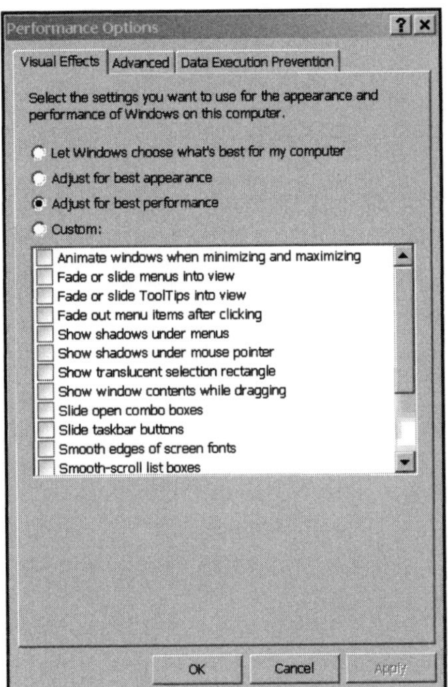

Figure 5.24
The result of better visual performance.

6 First Tools: The History of Modeling Plug-ins

Even in its short history, guitar amplifier modeling has undergone a major evolution since the first professional level amp modeler, Line6's Amp Farm, was introduced in 1998. The purpose of this chapter is to look back at some of the pivotal plug-ins that got us to where we are now.

Line6: Amp Farm

In 1998, Line6, a small company that produced digital amplifiers, debuted Amp Farm, a plug-in for Pro Tools TDM systems. You may know Line6 now, as they have grown to be a major player in the guitar industry, but you may not know about Amp Farm. There is a simple reason for this—it runs only on Pro Tools TDM systems, and few of us own those systems.

Without going into too much detail, Digidesign's Pro Tools TDM system is a combination of software and hardware that many professional studios use to make recordings. What is special about Pro Tools is the hardware portion of the system. Special DSP cards do all of the effects processing, and your CPU is left to do other things. This is not the only advantage of a TDM system. The big kicker here is that since the audio does not need to be transferred out of the DSP cards into the computer and back again, Pro Tools TDM systems offer audio processing with near-zero latency. This simple fact made Pro Tools TDM the most viable platform for Amp Farm.

Almost eight years later, Amp Farm is still around and kicking. Amp Farm remains a very popular plug-in for studios and professionals because of its highly realistic sound, even though there are now other TDM amp simulators. Amp Farm models a dozen amps, various cabinets, and several different microphones in its compact and efficient interface. Its simple design and high sound quality made it popular and keep it that way, even in the face of the very hot competition in the modeling market. Figure 6.1 shows what Amp Farm looks like in operation.

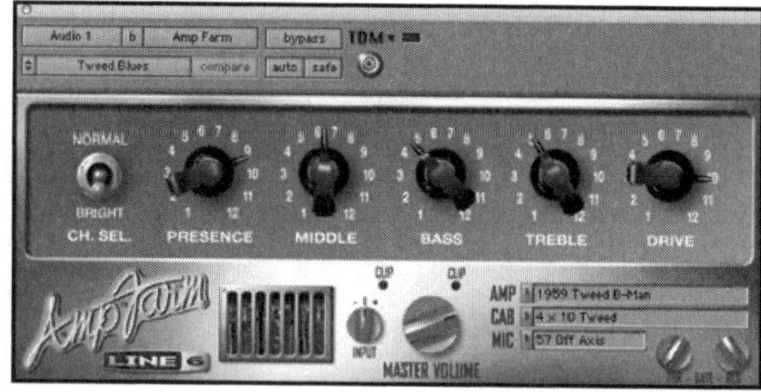

Figure 6.1
Line6's Amp Farm.

Bomb Factory: SansAmp

A year after the introduction of Amp Farm, Bomb Factory, a small software plug-in company, released SansAmp for Pro Tools. Bomb Factory had become a popular name for Pro Tools users because it accurately modeled several well known compressors and vintage hardware units and brought them to the Pro Tools TDM platform. The SansAmp PSA-1 plug was a re-creation of the Tech 21 hardware device of the same name. The SansAmp plug-in was an important step because it did one thing that Amp Farm could not do: it ran on the less expensive edition of Pro Tools, Pro Tools LE. This enabled many more users to get a taste of what amp modeling could do for them. The move to native systems meant that latency was going to be an issue, unlike the TDM world, but nevertheless, users reveled in the fact that this technology was finally available to the masses.

Now, SansAmp is only going to appeal to you if you liked the original hardware unit. The thing about Bomb Factory's plug-ins was that they sounded pretty much exactly like the hardware they were modeling, give or take an inch. I was personally never a fan of the original SansAmp unit, so a re-creation didn't do much for me, but lots of guitarists love the sound of the original SansAmp. The PSA-1 is still going strong. Bomb Factory sold its assets to Digidesign, which now markets and sells the plug-in that is still much beloved in the TDM world. Figure 6.2 shows the efficiency of the PSA-1's layout.

Steinberg: Warp

In 2002, Steinberg, already well known for its popular sequencer Cubase, joined the amp modeling game by releasing Warp, a VST plug-in that ran on both Mac and PC. Using the VST standard allowed any user whose host sequencer of choice used the VST plug-in to use Warp.

Warp was a collaboration between Steinberg and Hughes & Kettner amplifiers. Warp used Hughes & Kettner's DSM technology from their hardware digital amplifiers in plug-in form. The plug-in boasted three modeled amplifiers: a Jazz Chorus, a Plexi, and a Rectified amp. As for speaker modeling, add three cabinets: a combo and two 4x12s (American and British), and you round out Warp's main feature set.

Figure 6.2
The Bomb Factory PSA-1 SansAmp plug-in.

Unfortunately, any non-TDM guitar processor was going to experience latency. Latency was a factor of which sound card you chose and how fast your computer was. In 2002, we were just at the cusp of getting latency under control by using the right sound card and a powerful enough machine in a native system. With the right combination, you could get a workable sound, but unfortunately for Steinberg, Warp didn't catch on and was discontinued shortly thereafter. Figure 6.3 shows Warp's Spartan interface in action.

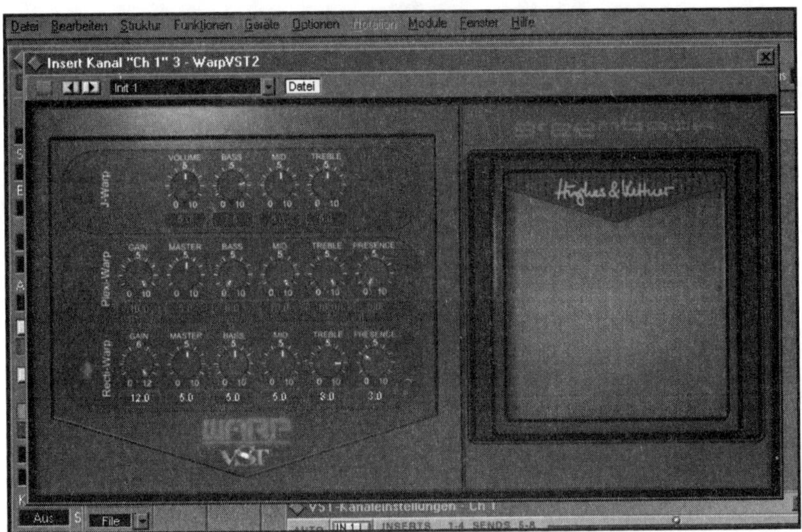

Figure 6.3
Steinberg's Warp.

IK Multimedia's: Amplitube

Also in 2002, IK Multimedia, an unknown Italian software developer, came out with Amplitube, a guitar modeler first for Pro Tools, and later for the other major native formats. It also had one other edge—it was the most realistic and complete modeler to date that almost every guitar player could get his hands on.

Amplitube soon became a standard plug-in because of an increased set of features and the most realistic sound to date for a native computer system. It simply expanded on what had come before and added more amps, more effects, and a more realistic sonic experience.

The plug-in was broken into three sections. The first section took care of the basic amp modeling, EQ modeling, microphone selection and distance, cabinet selection, and even an integrated tremolo effect on the main page. All of this was squeezed into the well-designed interface shown in Figure 6.4

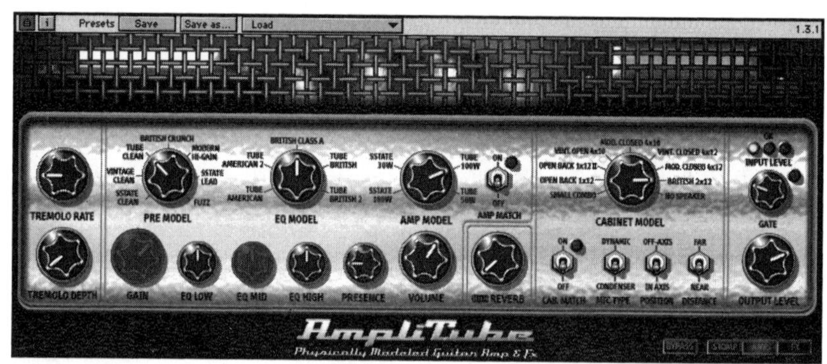

Figure 6.4
Amplitube's main view.

In the lower-right corner of the plug-in, we have tabs for accessing the other two sections of the plug-in: the Stomp and FX sections. Amplitube uses a single window interface that you can change to access the other sections.

The Stomp tab brings us to Figure 6.5. The Stomp page is a collection of virtual stompboxes that you can access from within Amplitube. IK gives you a Wah-wah, delay, chorus, flanger, and an overdrive pedal. Each pedal can be automated on and off, and its settings can also be automated. The nice selection of stompbox-style effects adds to the breadth of what Amplitube can offer.

The last section of the plug-in is the FX section, which gives you access to a high-quality stereo delay, a fully parametric EQ for more minute control of your sound, and a lush stereo reverb. Figure 6.6 shows the FX page in all its glory.

Figure 6.5
Amplitube's Stomp view.

Figure 6.6
Amplitube's FX page.

Amplitube is widely distributed in lite editions, along with many software and sequencer packages, and it also has a live version, a stand-alone version meant for live use.

Version 1 of the software was current from 2002–2005. At Winter NAMM 2006, IK announced the release of a second version of Amplitube. The specifications have already been posted, and Amplitube 2 boasts an impressive collection of new amps, flexibility, and sonic power. This will surely be a contender.

Now that we have talked about how we got here, let's talk about the current state of the art in guitar modeling plug-ins. It is indeed time to dance once again.

7 Proprietary Guitar Processing Software

As we progress through this book, we will be talking about plug-in solutions that you can use in your current computer-based recording setup. However, several DAW applications also have guitar amplifier modelers included with their packages. Apple's GarageBand, Logic Express, and Logic Pro are good examples of software that comes with guitar processors built in, which handle amp modeling and all that good stuff you usually pay extra for. The proprietary nature of these applications comes into play when you realize that the plug-ins are locked inside the program and can only be used within that host. Nevertheless, if you are a current user of these systems, you already have a guitar processor to work with—you may not even know that you have this!

GarageBand

In January 2004, during one of Steve Jobs' typical "larger than life" onstage product announcements, Apple introduced something truly extraordinary: GarageBand. This is a free recording studio application for the Apple Macintosh—that's right—free. Anyone who's purchased a new Macintosh that shipped from the factory after January 2004 receives GarageBand along with the rest of the iLife suite of applications. I know many Mac users who still don't know that they have a free recording application hidden inside their application folder. GarageBand touts many things: multitrack recording (up to eight with Garageband 2.0), onboard virtual instruments, built-in loops, and built-in effects. One of the built-in effects is a fairly comprehensive guitar amp simulator.

When I watched the keynote address given by Apple's CEO Jobs and watched John Mayer plug in and play his guitar though GarageBand, I thought it sounded quite nice. I was also sure they had some very expensive gear behind those black curtains making everything sound so good. I was skeptical to say the least! I mean, how good could a free recording application be?

My copy arrived a few weeks later—total shock is an understatement. This program was beyond usable; I actually really liked the amp simulations! Now, GarageBand as an application has a lot to it, and if you're interested in getting the most out of it, you should check out *GarageBand Ignite*, also available from Course Technology. But I digress... Let's talk about the guitar technology built into GarageBand.

GarageBand deals with two kinds of instruments: real instruments and software instruments. A real instrument is analogous to any typical audio track, be it a guitar track, a vocal—we're talking about something that you record as an audio file with either a microphone or a direct connection. Software instruments are also called virtual instruments by other companies, and they encompass instruments that respond to MIDI input and create sounds virtually, inside of your computer. For example, with a MIDI keyboard or MIDI guitar, you could trigger a trumpet or piano from a software instrument. In terms of guitar modeling, we are definitely talking about real instruments.

Launching GarageBand

When you start up GarageBand, you see its default screen, shown in Figure 7.1.

Figure 7.1
The default GarageBand screen.

Just about every installation of GarageBand I've ever used starts up with a single premade track: the Piano track. If you need to add a new track, you can do so in one of two ways. The first is by using a key command (Command+Option+N), and the second is by locating the Track pull-down menu across the top menu bar and selecting New Track. Either way you come to this (key commands are always faster), you will end up with something like Figure 7.2.

This window has a few elements to notice. Across the top, there are two major categories: real instruments and software instruments. Right now, my screen is set for software instruments, which

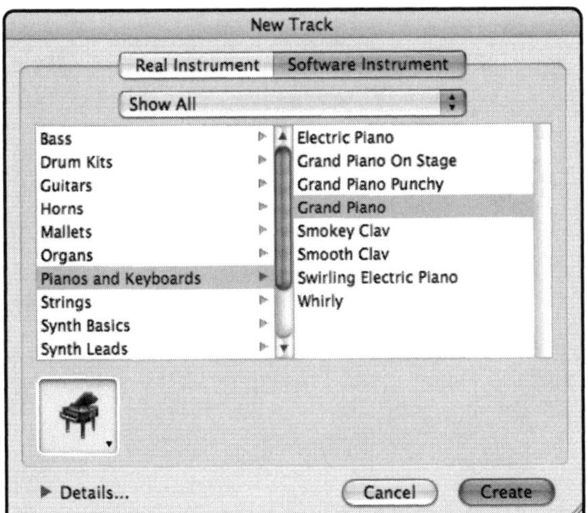

Figure 7.2
Adding a new track.

is wrong for our purposes. We need to switch it to Real Instrument. Doing so will change the selections in the menu spaces below, as seen in Figure 7.3

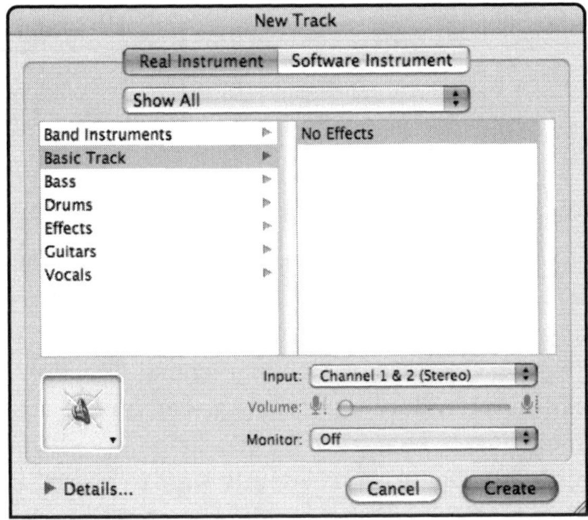

Figure 7.3
Real instrument choices.

The list of real instrument choices reads as one would expect. You need to select Guitars. Doing so will bring up a list of presets for guitars, as seen in Figure 7.4.

On the right pane, you'll see a bunch of premade presets. These are the ones that Apple supplies you with out of the box. Before you get too far into preset management and so on, let's start simpler. There is a very important part of this screen that you need to look at. In Figure 7.5, I

Figure 7.4
Guitar choices.

show the most critical aspect of getting a guitar sound in GarageBand—the I/O panel, which is where you set up what your inputs are and how you will monitor them. Without this set up correctly, you won't hear anything.

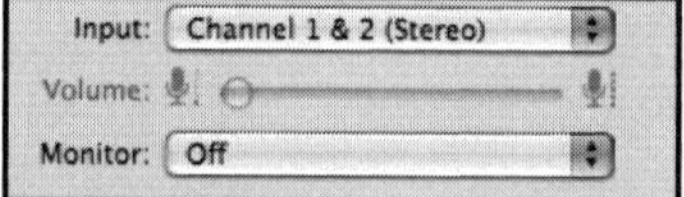

Figure 7.5
Setting up inputs/outputs and monitoring.

Under Input, you need to make sure that you select the correct input for your chosen audio interface. In my case, I'm plugged into Channel 1 (Mono) and need to change it to reflect that. Depending on which interface you have, you may have *many* choices to deal with. Just make sure that you know where your guitar is plugged in. The Volume control under the Input selection is used for internal microphones and won't affect you if you are plugging directly in. For now, you can just skip it. Below that is the Monitor button. This one is just a bit more important, because it's setting up whether or not you want to hear the affected sound through your speakers or headphones. In the case of an amplifier simulator, you certainly want to hear what you're doing. In this case, toggle the monitoring selection to On. Figure 7.6 shows the end result of my tweaks in order to get my guitar sounding right.

If all goes well, you should hear your guitar through your Mac. Now you can select the preset you like and hear the amps. Let's just choose Classic Rock to get started so we're all on the same page. Once you've highlighted that, click the Create button, and a new track will be made for you.

Figure 7.6
Inputs/outputs and monitoring successfully set up.

LATE

Latency is something you will have to deal with in some form or another constantly throughout this book. In the case of GarageBand and the example we just set up, you may have a bit of lag from the time you play the guitar to the time you hear the affected sound. This is your latency. Rather than dealing with latency *just* in GarageBand, since this affects us all, let's talk about how to deal with this on a global scale.

Latency is measured in buffers, which are expressed in numbers of milliseconds. A lower buffer will allow you to play with less latency, but it will increase the pressure on your CPU, decreasing your power to do other things. A higher buffer will free your CPU for other tasks, but will delay your signal considerably. Here is a quick rule of thumb: Track with a low buffer and mix with a high one. Since many interfaces offer near-zero latency monitoring, you can get away with higher buffers in your software and still feel "in time."

After you've created this track, not only can you play guitar now, but you'll also notice a Classic Rock track has been added for you, as seen in Figure 7.7.

By adding a track this way, you haven't been able to glance at what kinds of choices GarageBand gives you for amp modeling and effects. Since you want to learn this, I'll show you how to edit the sounds.

To start with, simply double-click on the track name, Classic Rock. Doing so brings up the Track Info dialog box (see Figure 7.8).

Now, you might look at this box and say, "Hey, I already saw this when I created the track!" If you said this, you're right. This time, you are going to access some more parameters. I want to

Figure 7.7
Your new track, Classic Rock, is added to GarageBand.

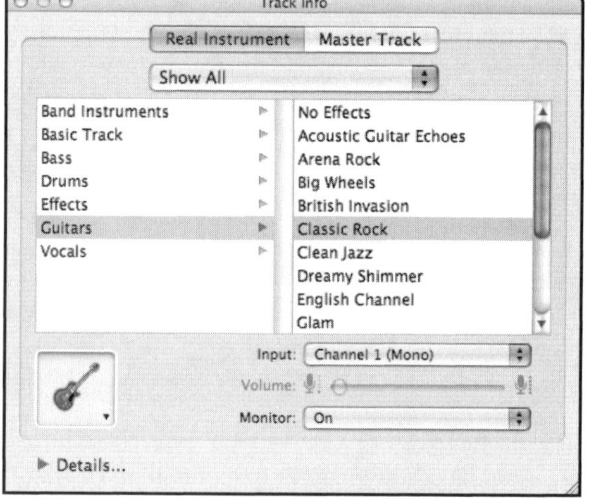

Figure 7.8
The Track Info dialog.

direct your attention to the bottom-left corner of the track info screen, where it says Details with a small arrow facing to the right, as illustrated in Figure 7.9.

Figure 7.9
Track details.

I dare you to click it! It's one of the boxes where you click on the arrow, and it magically rotates around and exposes a whole bunch of info. Aren't you glad you took my dare? The result of exposing the new details parameters is shown in Figure 7.10.

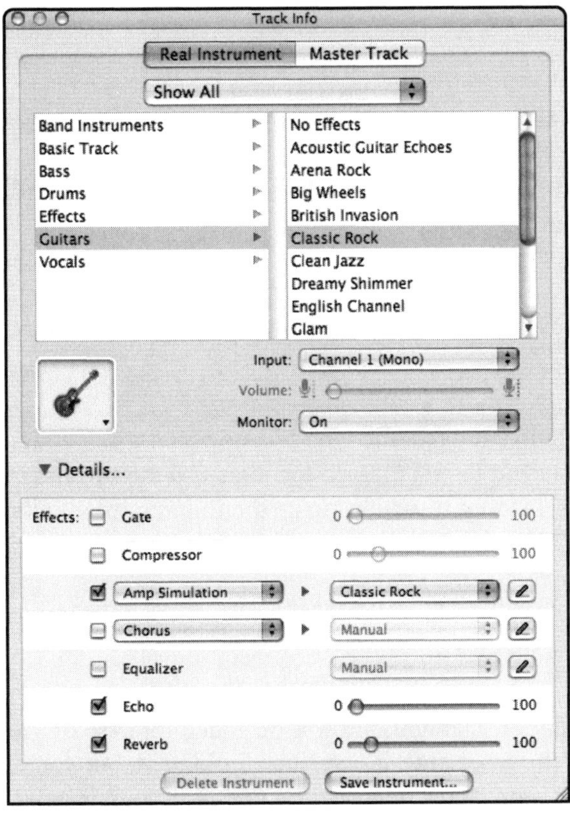

Figure 7.10
Additional track details.

Okay, now we're getting somewhere. Remember that GarageBand, while it may blow away your first tape-based four-track machine, isn't Pro Tools—there are only a fixed number of things you can do. In this particular preset, you see a fixed number of choices. Every real instrument has a Gate, Compressor, EQ, Echo (Delay), and Reverb. Garageband is also fully compliant with audio unit plug-ins, so in addition to the fixed choices you see, you can add any two audio units to GarageBand. You can turn them on by checking their checkboxes to the left of their names, as seen in Figure 7.11.

In this particular preset, only the Echo and Reverb are on (along with the amp simulator). The effects are very simple to operate. Once they are checked, you use the slider to the far right to mix in the effect. You can make your own changes and click the Save Instrument button to save this preset for later use.

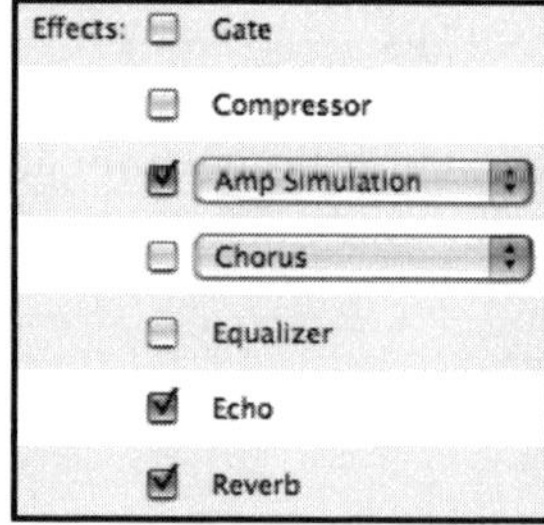

Figure 7.11
Activating effects.

Now, let's get to the amp simulation. Figure 7.12 shows the selection for your current amp simulator, along with the name of the preset.

Figure 7.12
The current amp simulation.

If you want to go into the amp simulation and edit the type of amp you are using along with the traditional EQ and gain settings, you need to enter the editor. This is done by clicking on the small pencil, as shown in Figure 7.13. Doing so will bring up the full amplifier editing display, as seen in Figure 7.14.

Figure 7.13
The editing pencil.

There it is, in all its magnificent splendor! GarageBand was designed for ease of use, so these menus aren't beautiful like some of the other plug-ins we'll be looking at, but you do have everything you need to set up a good amp. Most importantly, the thing sounds good, so who cares how it looks.

All joking aside, you get quite a bit of control here. Here's what you get to edit in the Amp Simulation pane (from top to bottom):

- Preset selection
- Amp model
- Pre Gain = Amount of distortion/dirt in your sound. This control drives the virtual tube preamp section.
- Low = Low-band EQ
- Mid = Mid-band EQ
- High = High-band EQ

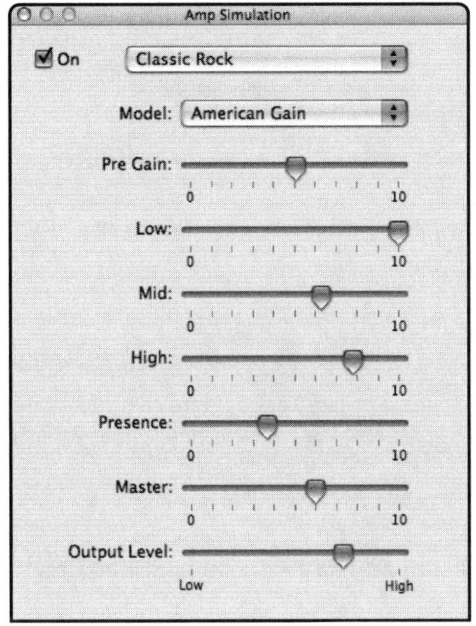

Figure 7.14
Full amp settings.

- Presence = A particular EQ centered on 5 kHz (can be anywhere from 4–6 kHz). Tends to bring your signal forward without overly affecting the tone too much.
- Master = The master gain
- Output Level = Final output level

To set up your amp, simply adjust the sliders until you get the sound you are looking for.

The Amps

With GarageBand, you can select from six different amplifiers. When you are editing the amp simulation, as seen in Figure 7.14, there is a selection for choosing the type of amp model you want to use. Figure 7.15 shows this section highlighted for you.

Figure 7.15
Your chosen amp model.

If you toggle this menu, you will reveal all the choices for amp models. Figure 7.16 shows you all the models you can choose from.

GarageBand bases its models on British and American amps. The British amps are modeled after Marshall and Vox, while the American amps are modeled after Fender and Mesa Boogie amps. In other words, you get six very different-sounding amplifiers right out of the box.

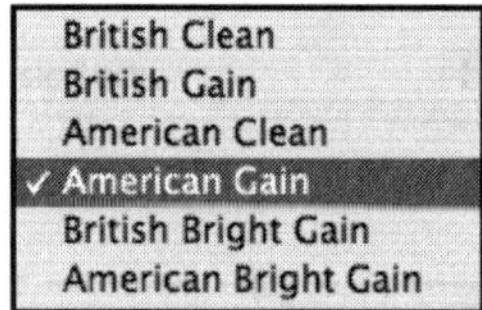

Figure 7.16
Your amp modeling choices.

One way you can extend the power of GarageBand is by using Jam Packs.

JAM!

Apple has released an add-on, Jam Packs, to augment the power of Garageband. Specifically, it adds more loops, software instruments, and in the case of Jam Pack 1, more amplifier presets. Each of the four Jam Packs has its own focus, and they are all very cool to have, but #1 adds guitar-specific features that the others don't.

If you end up adding Jam Pack #1, your list of amp presets will look like Figure 7.17.

Figure 7.17
New presets with the additional Jam Pack.

You don't actually gain any new amps, but you get many more presets that better utilize the six built-in amps. Several of the presets are quite good.

Well, that's about all we can cover about GarageBand for now. It's really a ton of fun and sounds great. For something that comes free with a new Macintosh, it's pretty unbelievable, to say the least. Even if you have an expensive system, you should still launch GarageBand to see what all the fuss is about. In this author's opinion, it is the most significant revolution in the home studio industry since the first Tascam Portastudio.

Now we get to look at GarageBand's older, more mature brothers: Logic Express and Logic Pro.

Logic Express

Logic is a very popular DAW application and has been around since the '80s (when it was called Notator). In 2002, Apple purchased Emagic GmbH, the company that wrote Logic. In 2004, Apple streamlined the Logic line into two parts: Logic Express is aimed at the consumer level, and Logic Pro is aimed at professional studios. (There were formerly three versions: Platinum, Gold, and Silver.) Let's look at Logic Express first.

Because Logic is designed to import GarageBand projects, its actual guitar modeling plug-in is exactly the same. Even though you gain more features in the Logic versions, everything is 100% backward-compatible.

Logic Express is a much different program than GarageBand, as Figure 7.18 will clearly illustrate.

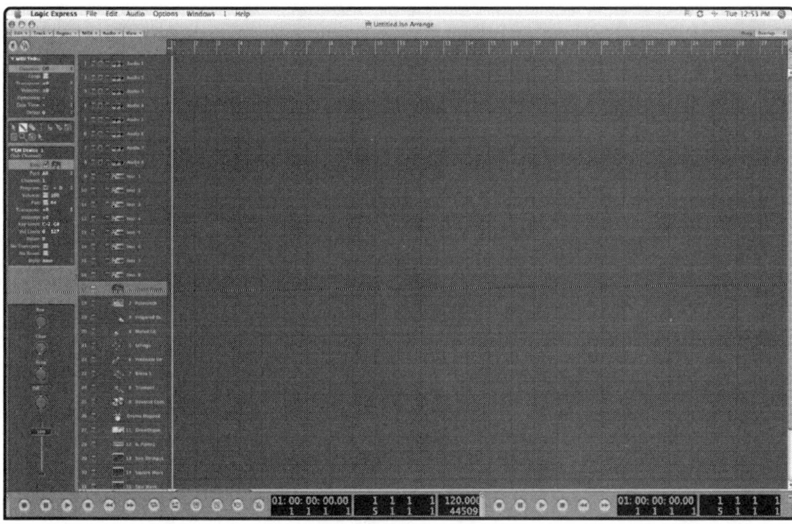

Figure 7.18
Logic Express.

Even though we have established that the amp simulations in GarageBand and Logic Express are the same, loading plug-ins in Logic Express is different, and we should take a second to look at how to get up and running.

Figure 7.18 shows Logic's Arrange Page. You can insert a plug-in here, but it's clearer to do it in the Track Mixer. To summon the Track Mixer, use the key command (Command+2), and Figure 7.19 will be your result.

Figure 7.19
Logic Express' Track Mixer.

From the Track Mixer, you can see an overview of your tracks. We're going to focus on Audio Track 1, as seen in Figure 7.20.

There's a lot to look at here, but this isn't a Logic Express book, so I'll get you into the plug-in as fast as possible. Logic uses inserts to apply effects. The inserts are clearly indicated in Figure 7.21—two inserts are visible right now, but more become visible as you add more effects.

To add an effect, you click and hold down any of the inserts. Doing so will bring up a menu. There are lots of subcategories, and you need to fish around to get there. The correct path to the Guitar Amp is Mono > Logic > Distortion > Guitar Amp. If you are using a stereo track, your path would be Stereo > Logic > Distortion > Guitar Amp. Another choice is to use a mono input and have Logic output in stereo. This is done with the use of mono/stereo plug-ins. The basic mono plug-in is seen in Figure 7.22.

Once you've done this, the Guitar Amp plug-in pops up looking almost exactly the same as it did in GarageBand. It's shown in Figure 7.23.

Besides being a bit more colorful (which you can't see because this book is black and white), the plug-in is the same.

Figure 7.20
Audio Track 1.

Figure 7.21
Effects inserts.

What's totally different is that in GarageBand, your signal path is preselected for you. In Logic Express (and Pro), you can now add insert effects before or after your amp simulator. The quality of the effects is the same as GarageBand; they share the same DSP code. Nice to know that Apple gives away such a robust effects solution with GarageBand! What is different in Logic Express is that you can change the order of effects, use bus effects, and perform other routing

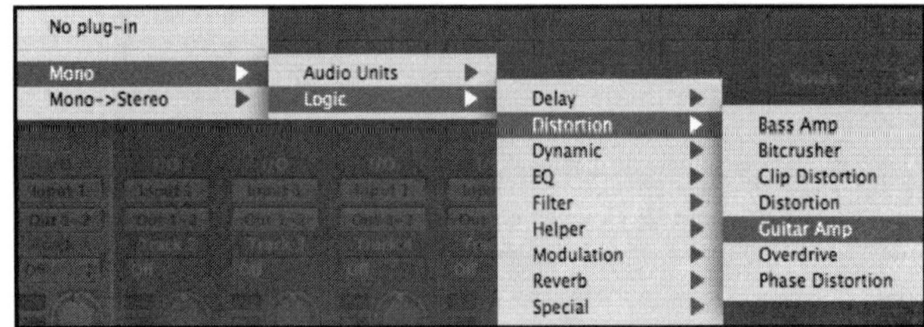

Figure 7.22
The path to Guitar Amp.

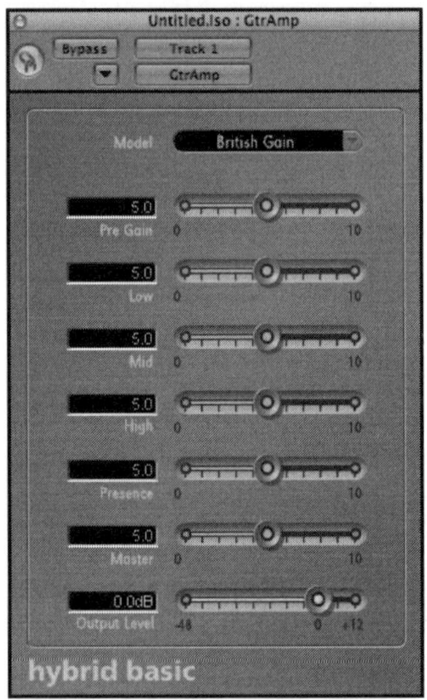

Figure 7.23
Logic's Guitar Amp plug-in.

schemes. Simply put, you can add a greater variety of effects this way, even if they use the same plug-ins as GarageBand. Figure 7.24 shows a track I set up with some delay, chorus, and the amp setup that I like.

Now, let's move on to the big daddy of the Logic Family: Logic Pro.

Logic Pro

Logic Pro is a considerable step up in features over Logic Express. We're only going to look at the Guitar Amp Pro plug-in now, but if you want to know more about Logic Pro, check out *Logic Pro 7 Power* by Orren Merton (also published by Course Technology).

If you load up a GarageBand song in Logic Pro, Logic Pro will open up the Guitar Amp Pro plug-in for you. In layout, Logic Express and Logic Pro share the same basic feel. Because of this, setting up the plug-in is exactly the same as it is in Express. Open the Track Mixer, select

Figure 7.24
My sample guitar track in Logic Express.

an insert on Audio Track 1, and navigate to the Guitar Amp Pro plug-in. The only difference is that this version of Guitar Amp is called "Pro." Well, that's not the only difference. Figure 7.25 shows the Guitar Amp Pro plug-in in action.

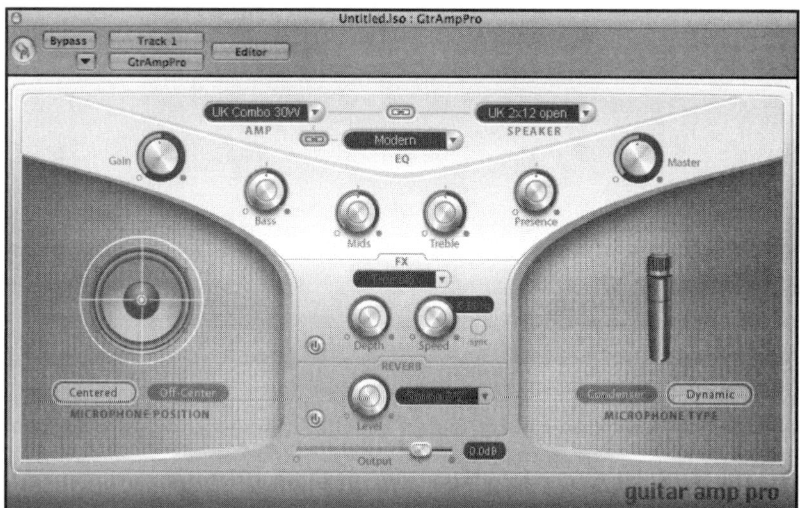

Figure 7.25
Guitar Amp Pro.

Okay, this one looks a tad more polished. There's also more you can do. Let's break down the plug-in into its sections. Figure 7.26 illustrates the different sections of the plug-in.

Now that we have the sections defined, let's look at them separately to see how they operate.

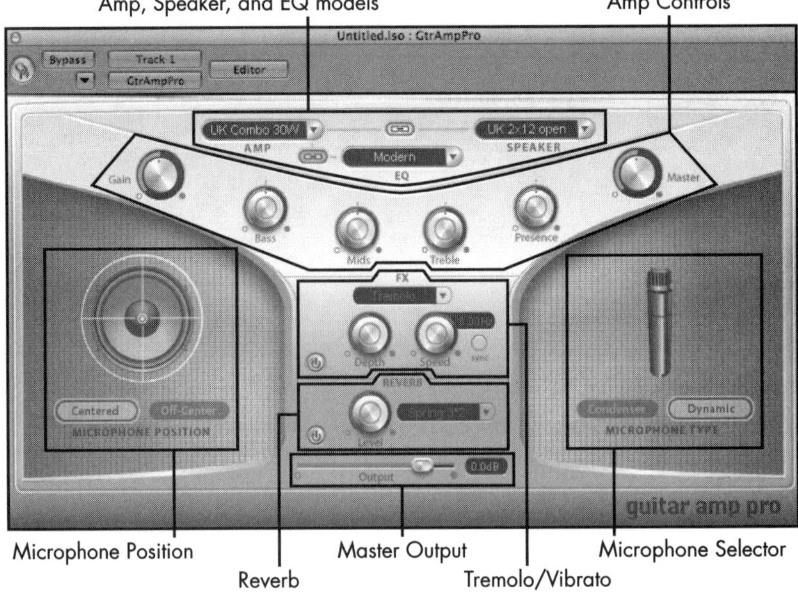

Figure 7.26
Guitar Amp Pro's interface defined.

Amp, Speaker, and EQ Models

At the top of the plug-in, you see three sections for selecting the type of amp model, speaker cabinet, and modeled EQ. EQ modeling is an interesting feature, because it mimics particular EQs from certain amps and allows you to use their EQ curves and response on other amps—something not possible in real life.

For the amps, you can toggle the amp menu by clicking on the down-facing arrow to list all the amps. Figure 7.27 shows the full listing of amps.

Figure 7.27
The available amps.

You can see a nice selection of amps here. One thing to notice is that the amps from GarageBand are still here. According to my contact at Apple, GarageBand compatibility was crucial, even in the $1,000 Logic Pro Application. Many folks are composing in GarageBand first and then going to Pro later, so full compatibility is essential. In the end, you are afforded a total of 11 amps to work with. The list is distinguished by American and British classics, even varying wattage from amp to amp, so you can emulate natural clipping at lower gains.

Next, on to the speaker section. This is a Pro-only feature, because GarageBand and Logic Express do not allow you to select your cabinets. This plug-in has 15 possible cabinets to pair with your 11 amps. Figure 7.28 shows the list of cabinets.

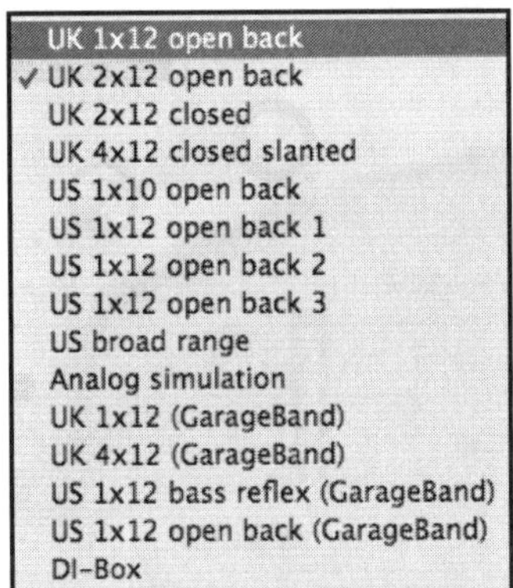

Figure 7.28
Available speaker cabinets.

The speaker cabinets run the gamut from open- and closed-back speakers to DI Boxes and even analog simulations. Each cabinet has its response modeled and can be paired with the amps for unique sound-shaping possibilities. You will also notice in Figure 7.28 that a few of the cabinets say "GarageBand."

HIDDEN CABS

GarageBand and Logic Express don't give you the capability to change amplifier cabinets separately, but that doesn't mean there isn't cabinet modeling going on. In GarageBand and Express, the cabinets are automatically matched to the default amplifier. In Pro, you can segregate these choices.

Now, time for the EQ. Each amplifier has its own way of providing EQ. This is due to differences in the circuit design and electrical components used. High EQ won't be the same for each amp—many of these factors contribute to the overall sound of the amp. Apple has modeled four different sets of EQs, as shown in Figure 7.29.

You can combine any amp with any EQ, and with any cabinet. The possibilities are numerous. Actually, according to my father, there are 660 possible combinations just by messing with amps, EQs, and cabinets. That's a lot.

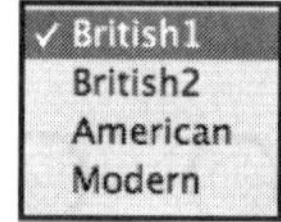

Figure 7.29
EQ curves.

Link Buttons

If 660 possible choices of amp, cabinet, and EQ seem a bit much to you, you will want to know about the Link buttons. In Figure 7.30, I have highlighted two buttons that serve as links.

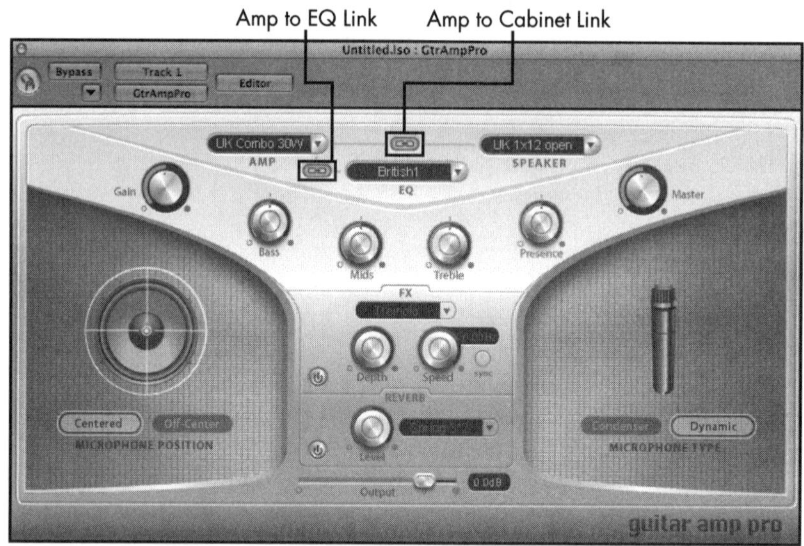

Figure 7.30
Parameter links

Now, what do these links do for you? Simply put, when Apple modeled one of the 11 amps, they modeled it along with a default cabinet. For example, a Fender Twin-type amp should have an open-back 2×12. Each amp has default choices for cabinets and EQs. There are two Link buttons. The button on the right in Figure 7.30 is an Amp to Cabinet Link. When this is engaged (it will glow yellow), any change you make to an amp will result in a corresponding change to a cabinet—a cabinet that is the default choice for that amplifier. The other link button identified in Figure 7.30 is the Amp to EQ link. When this is clicked, the amplifier will use the EQ curve associated with the amplifier when it was modeled. This way you can go for "bread and butter" sounds easily. You can click both Link buttons to make sure that your amp has the default cabinet and correct EQ. You can of course disengage the Link buttons and make an amp combination in any of the 660 possible ways you feel like.

Amplifier Controls

The amp controls are basically self-explanatory and mimic what you would find on any normal amplifier. So rather than going through each one, let's talk about the relationship of the controls to the EQ models listed in the previous section. When you change one of the four EQ curves, the controls won't change visually. What will happen is that the algorithms for each EQ control will change, based on the modeling of the amp selected. The controls are fixed and will not change; however, their behavior will change based on which amp and EQ model is chosen.

Tremolo and Vibrato

There are two built-in effects for this plug-in. The first is the Tremolo and Vibrato effect, shown in Figure 7.31.

Figure 7.31
Tremolo and Vibrato effect.

The first thing you have to do to access this effect is turn on the module. You do this by clicking the button shown in Figure 7.32.

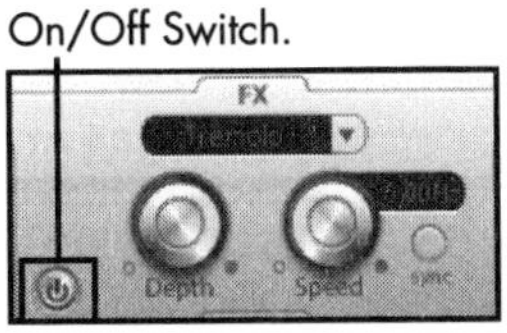

On/Off Switch.

Figure 7.32
Turning an effect on.

Once the effect is on, you can access the parameters, such as the depth and the speed of the effect. This effect is either a tremolo or a vibrato. In order to change which one you're using, you have to access the small arrow next to the word Tremolo and bring up the other choices. Figure 7.33 illustrates this.

Figure 7.33
Choosing tremolo or vibrato.

Tremolo is a rhythmic effect that chops the sound up, while vibrato is a change in the pitch modulation —also rhythmic. Since both effects are rhythmic in nature, you have a handy button that turns on sync, allowing you to tempo-sync either the tremolo or vibrato to Logic's host tempo. This is *really handy*.

Reverb

Just below the Tremolo and Vibrato effect is the all-important Reverb effect. This effect window shares the same on/off knob as the above unit, so make sure that you click that button and make it glow red before you call Apple asking why you can't hear any reverb. Once you turn this puppy on, the only controls you have are a level control (which is badly labeled in my opinion—it's really a wet/dry balance knob), but it sets how much reverb is in your signal. As for the type of reverb available, in Figure 7.34, you can see that Apple gives us three different kinds of spring reverb emulations to choose from.

Figure 7.34
Choosing a spring reverb type.

The three different springs represent three famous spring reverb modules commonly found inside amps. They will present varying degrees of color, depth, and reverb decay for your signal. A bit of experimentation will go a long way on this one.

Microphone Position

The bottom-right corner of the interface shows a lovely speaker with what appears to be a bull's-eye target on it. This is a microphone position selector. It offers two possible variations: on-axis (straight on) and off-axis (slightly off to the side). Figures 7.35 and 7.36 show both possibilities.

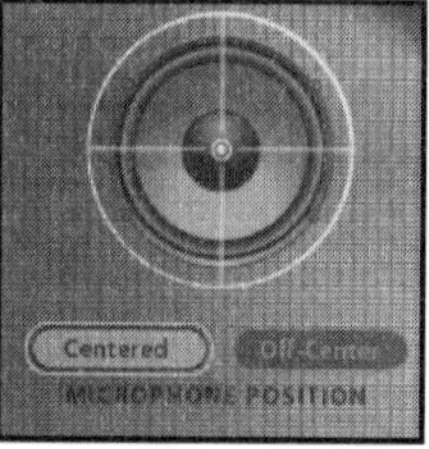

Figure 7.35
Microphone position on-axis.

Apple uses the terms Centered for on-axis and Off-Center for off-axis—they mean the same thing.

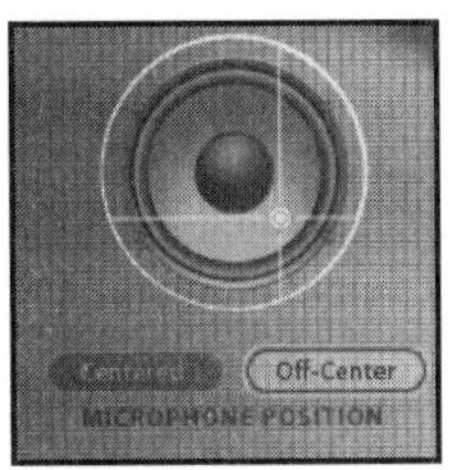

Figure 7.36
Microphone position off axis.

You can select the different microphone locations either by clicking the Centered or Off Center button or by clicking on the picture of the speaker. An on-axis sound will be very sharp, while moving the microphone off-axis will take away some of the high frequencies and smooth out the sound.

Microphone Selector

Within Guitar Amp Pro, Apple provides you with two different types of microphones to place in front of your virtual cabinet. You can use a condenser mic (which is clearly a Neumann) or a dynamic mic (which is clearly a SM57). Figure 7.37 shows the Microphone Selector window, where you can select your dynamic or condenser microphone.

Figure 7.37
Selecting your microphone.

Each microphone will have its own particular tonal sound to it. Couple this with the ability to place your microphone either on- or off-axis, and you get some nice sonic variety! As is the case with most of this plug- in, the elements are clearly laid out and quite easy to navigate. The myriad of options allows for some serious sound-shaping tools. Combine this with Logic Pro's myriad of included effects, and you have a potent, self-contained guitar system to be reckoned with—that is, if you use Logic Pro!

THE OTHERS

Apple's line of software tools (GarageBand, Logic Express, and Logic Pro) are the clearest examples of proprietary guitar amp simulations out there. This does not mean that other DAWs don't include some sort of distortion device with their systems.

> Digital Performer, Cubase, Nuendo, and others include some sort of distortion plug-in. These may get you through a session, but they are not meant to compete with the simulation-style plug-in we are seeing. The only other exception is Amplitube Lite/LE. This stripped-down version of IK Multimedia's popular Amplitube plug-in is coming bundled with an increasing number of DAW systems, such as Sonar and Pro Tools.

Now, let's look at some of the other solutions out there, namely ones that aren't proprietary. Let's see what you can use in any recording application of your choice. The dance continues…

8 Waves GTR System

In July 2005, Waves, a company well known for its studio-standard plug-in effects, took a bold step into a new market: the emerging guitar emulation market. At the 2005 NAMM summer session, Waves unveiled its GTR (Guitar Tool Rack) system. The system is one of a growing breed of systems that utilizes software and hardware in one package. Waves has teamed up with legendary guitar manufacturer Paul Reed Smith, who not only consulted on the project, but also lent his considerable vintage amp collection for modeling. Paul was also involved in the GTR Guitar Interface—the hardware portion of the GTR system.

The GTR System

At its heart, the Waves GTR system is a combination of software and hardware for your PC or Mac. It is available in two distinct versions. The first is the Native system, which runs on all native platforms. The other package is the TDM system, which runs only on Pro Tools' Time Division Multiplex (TDM) system. Both systems include a combination of software and hardware.

The GTR system is fully cross-platform-compliant, running happily on both Mac OS X and Windows systems. In order to run, GTR uses an iLok authorization scheme. iLok is one of a family of copy-protection hardware devices commonly referred to as *dongles*.

DONGLE?

What exactly is a dongle? Simply put, a dongle is a key to unlock your software. Unlike long serial numbers you need to enter, or challenge/response codes, dongles utilize a hardware key (usually in the form of a USB key) that activates the software. You can install the software in as many locations as you want, but it will only run if you have the dongle key attached to the machine. Some find it annoying to haul around keys from place to place because forgetting the key at home will render the software useless. Dongles are becoming very commonplace, though, and are used by such notable companies as

Apple (Logic Pro), Digidesign (Pro Tools and all TDM plug-ins), Steinberg (All products), and various other plug-in manufacturers that utilize iLok to store authorizations.

The beauty of iLok, as I see it, is that you never have to worry about reauthorizing software; you simply take your authorization with you on a key. iLok is also used by many other companies, and a single iLok key can hold as many authorizations as you want, so it's not like you need to haul 100 different keys around for all your iLok-protected software. Some users, no matter what you do, will feel that dongles are restrictive. I personally find them convenient, but to each his own.

Just as a note: The GTR system does not come with an iLok. You have to purchase one separately in order to run the program. Then again, you may already have one.

The Guitar Interface

As I said at the beginning of this chapter, the GTR system is a combination of software and hardware. Let's start with the hardware. Here is what it isn't: It isn't a computer interface. It does not have USB/Firewire or any other direct communication protocol to the computer. The Waves Guitar interface is a direct box with a few tricks. No matter how you slice this one, you will need an audio interface to get the audio into your computer. All the Waves box does is *optimize* your signal.

The guitar's signal is a complex one, and this is a topic that we are going to spend a bit of time talking about, as it comes up so often in this book. Guitar pickups put out a very high-impedance signal, and most recording interfaces rarely accommodate a guitar's signal very well. Many have tried to standardize the Hi-Z (high-impedance) signal; few have succeeded in making one that translates the sound of *every* guitar pickup well. The difference in output and impedance between a single-coil and a humbucker is noticeable. Waves and PRS set out to make an impendence transformer circuit in the interface that addressed this problem. The goal is to take the guitar's pickup signal into the interface and change it from high-impedance to line or microphone level at the back. A preamp knob allows you to dial in the correct amount of gain for your guitar. Also included is a handy ground lift switch, which may eliminate buzzes from your setup. Figure 8.1 shows the front panel of the guitar interface.

The front panel yields few surprises. A single guitar input jack and a rotary preamp knob are standard issue here. A three-light metering system shows your input signal at three stages: green—signal present, yellow—optimal signal, and red—signal overload. Also on the front panel are a low battery light (the device runs on two 9V batteries or optional AC power supply) and an on/off indicator. The box itself is compact, measuring only four inches wide, five inches deep, and under two inches tall, making it easy to move around.

Figure 8.1
The Waves guitar interface front panel.

The rear panel has much more to look at. Figure 8.2 shows the rear panel and its connections.

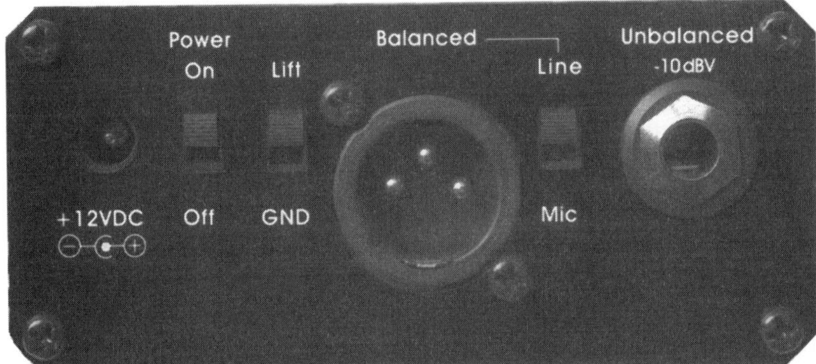

Figure 8.2
The Waves guitar interface rear panel.

From left to right, we start with the AC power input (if you choose to run off wall power) and the obvious power On/Off switch. Next to that is your ground lift. If you encounter buzzing through your system, engaging the lift may help quiet your system to a ground loop buzz.

STRAT BUZZ

Attention Strat owners: Your guitars will buzz on pickup positions one, three, and five because of how single-coil pickups work, and the Ground Lift switch won't do much for you in this regard. Positions two and four are hum-canceling, though.

Let's focus on the output choices for the guitar interface, as seen in Figure 8.3.

As you can see, the interface gives you many outputs to choose from. The Balanced connector should be used if your system accepts balanced signals. The switch between microphone and

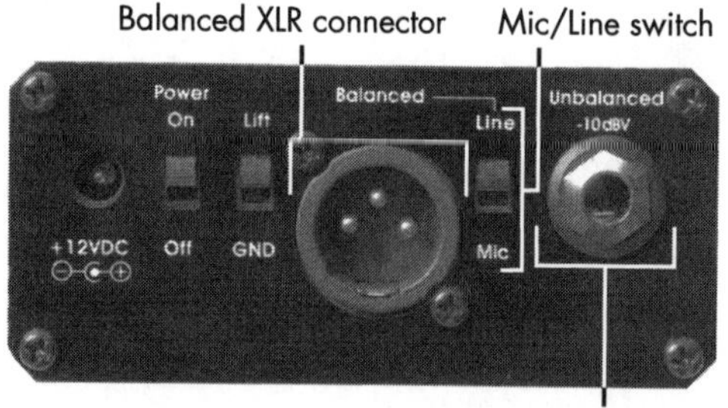

Figure 8.3
Output connections.

line level should be set depending on where you are plugging in. Microphone level and line level have different output values. If your interface has a line level input, this is the best place to interface, because the front panel's Gain knob takes care of your signal. Microphone level is going to be lower than line level, and may require additional gain, either at the front end of the system or on your computer's audio interface. Doing so can cause gain staging issues and unwanted distortion and noise. The other output is a basic, unbalanced quarter-inch connector. These are probably the most common plugs in an audio studio, and more often than not, this is the cable you will use in your setup.

That's it for the hardware portion of the GTR system. Waves designed the interface to match exactly a guitar's signal and typical frequency characteristics. Even though direct boxes serve a similar purpose, the special impedance-matching technology allows the guitar's signal to retain its full range of sound through all stages of level and distortion. (The kind of distortion we like, namely overdrive—something plugging directly into a board or interface may not let you do so as clearly.) In my own personal testing, I have found that there is some merit to this. My guitar sounded more "true," especially as I rolled my own volume knob down. Doing so enabled me to clean up the distorted signal while still regaining my original sound. The only other thing that has allowed me to do this thus far is using my own very expensive direct boxes and preamps—so it's nice to see a comparable direct box included.

The Software

Waves has broken the GTR software suite into two parts. The amp emulation resides as a separate plug-in from the effects processing. The purpose of this is probably to keep the screen of each plug-in to a reasonable size. My personal taste is that it would be great to have them both in one window, but that's just me. Waves has also included a nice tuner as another separate plug-in.

Waves GTR Amp

Waves breaks the amplifier modeling plug-in into further divisions: stereo and mono plug-ins. The stereo version has one amplifier and two cabinets. If you run your audio tracks in mono, you can choose a plug-in that only utilizes one speaker cabinet. Let's focus our time on the Stereo plug-in, which Waves calls Guitar Amp Stereo. Figure 8.4 shows a shot of the software in action.

Figure 8.4
The Waves GTR amp emulator.

Since you're getting familiar with what goes into guitar amp modeling, you should start to notice that the essentials are well covered in this interface. Selections for the type of amplifier, cabinets, and microphones dominate the layout of this plug-in. Let's take a closer look at the interface and call out what the different sections dom as pictured in Figure 8.5.

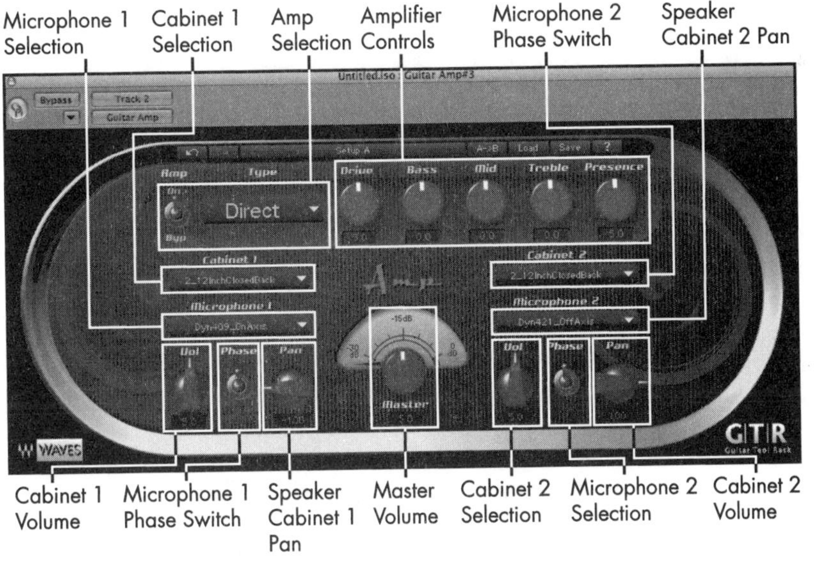

Figure 8.5
Guitar amp sections defined.

Now that we have this plug-in more or less defined, let's go ahead and break the sections down so you can look at what the plug-in offers.

The Amps

Within the plug-in, you can select one amplifier per instance. You can do so by clicking the arrow next to the amplifier name, revealing the full amp list, as seen in Figure 8.6. Doing so will bring up a list of the amplifiers that you can select.

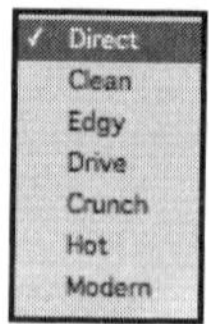

Figure 8.6
Selecting amplifiers.

The listing of amps is as follows:

- Direct = A direct box, no amplifier
- Clean = A clean amp, probably Fender Style
- Edgy = Bright but not terribly high-gain; sounds like an AC-30
- Drive = More grit, sounding like a British amp pushed a bit
- Crunch = Very chunky, sounding very American
- Hot = Smooth, bright, and high-gain
- Modern = Either a Soldano or a Mesa Boogie; tons of gain and very detailed when doing so

(Note: Waves did not divulge which amps were modeled, so I'm going to take my best guess as to what's modeled.)

Now, in all honesty, these descriptions don't help you all that much. However, I can say this much—with the seven amps listed, you are basically covered for any musical situation you might encounter.

After you've decided on an amplifier, you can adjust its controls just like you would on any amplifier. Next to the amplifier selection are the drive and EQ settings you'd expect to see, as shown in Figure 8.7.

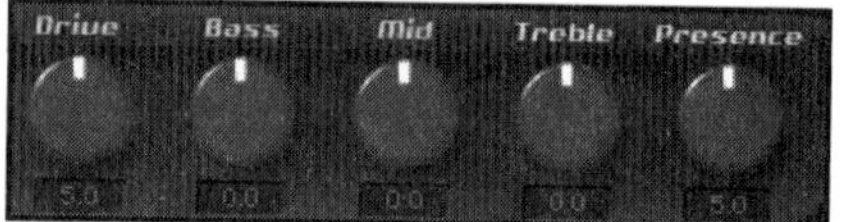

Figure 8.7
Controlling the amp's drive and tone.

Of course, all of these controls can be automated in your host sequencer of choice, allowing you a wealth of flexibility.

The Cabinets

With the exception of the mono-only version of the GTR plug-in, the Waves GTR system utilizes two different cabinets in your setup. This is done by selecting the cabinet pull-down menu (see Figure 8.8). Since the plug-in has two identical sections for creating and selecting cabinets, we will talk about one of them, and this information is simply duplicated for the second cabinet.

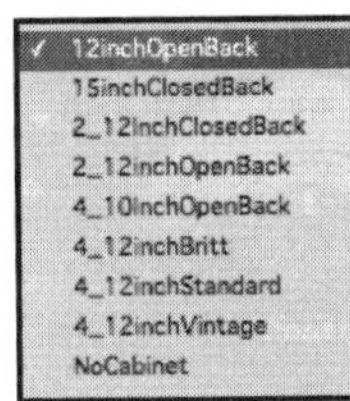

Figure 8.8
Selecting your cabinet.

As you can see, Waves gives you a nice selection (eight cabinets and the option to select No Cabinet). The cabinets vary from small combo-type speakers to large-scale 4×12 stacks. It's actually pretty amazing how much your sound changes when you flip to a new cabinet. Waves modeled their cabinets using a technology called convolution, which is fast becoming a standard high-tech way to model sounds in a highly realistic fashion.

CONVOLUTION

Convolution is a highly specialized mathematical process. It's only recently that music has utilized it. In a nutshell, convolution is a process in which the sound characteristics of an object are captured to a computer. In the case of modeling a cabinet, a frequency sweep is sent through the cabinet, and this sweep contains every frequency, from the lowest frequency the cabinet can reproduce to the highest. Highly accurate microphones capture the sound of the filter sweep. The filter sweep is a perfect signal; however, the way that the speakers re-create this sound is not perfect. Naturally, certain frequencies will be boosted and certain others will be attenuated. This "fingerprint" is what makes cabinet X sound different than cabinet Y.

Once the sweep has been recorded through the cabinet, a highly complicated piece of math occurs, and the amplifier is turned into a set of parameters that exits into a computer; this is called an *impulse* response. After this is complete, as complicated as it sounds, you basically get the fingerprint of what the cabinet you are modeling would do if it were fed any frequency, such as your guitar sound. You would get to hear what it sounded like if your guitar was going through a real Marshall stack, as realistically as possible.

For you, the guitar player, you get the most realistic idea about what it would sound like if you actually played through that cabinet. Convolution is used for more than just cabinet modeling; the most accurate

reverbs are based on convolution technology. Popular examples are Waves' own IR-1 and Altiverb. I know this sounds horribly complicated, but in the end you get highly realistic cabinet sounds, while a few geeks get to crunch the numbers for you.

Now that you have your cabinet selected, you need to place a microphone in front of the amp. As you probably know, the type of microphone and its placement in front of the cabinet will have a dramatic effect on the final sound of your recording. Because of this, microphone selection has become a staple of plug-ins of this type.

The Microphones and Other Settings

Once your amp is all set up, let's talk about the last bit of control you have over the amp, which is the microphone selection. If you toggle the microphone pull-down menu, you see the list of available choices, as seen in Figure 8.9.

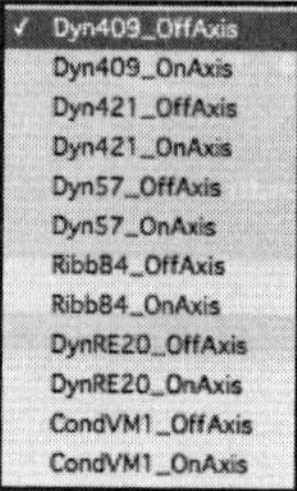

Figure 8.9
Microphone selections.

The microphones are also sampled using a convolution technology. As you can see from the list in Figure 8.9, Waves didn't try to hide these choices—the names have not been obscured to change the innocent! If you know your microphones, you will be keenly aware of the microphone choices allotted to you. If you're newer to microphones, the Shure SM-57 has been *the* stalwart staple microphone on guitar cabs for as far back as I can remember. While this may not be the best choice for guitar, it certainly is famous and popular.

Back to the microphone selections. Waves gives you three categories of microphones to choose from: Dynamic, Condenser, and Ribbon. Within each section are a few popular models to choose from. If you're new to this, you should be aware that the microphone is a large part of the sound you hear on records. Simply take an amp that you've built, change around the microphones, and listen to how much the sound changes. In this case, the microphone is acting like an EQ, imparting its sonic fingerprint on the final sound. Many of the microphones have the option to be on-or off-axis. Let's talk about what that means.

AXIS

The term "axis" refers to the orientation of the microphone in relation to the sound source it is picking up. A microphone is on-axis when its sound pattern (also referred to as a polar pattern) is directly facing the sound source. If we use the good old vocal microphone as an example, then on-axis is when the microphone is facing the speaker. Taking a microphone off-axis means changing its orientation somewhat so that it's not getting a direct hit, so to speak. The effect of this is a change in the sound that comes through the mic. Off-axis microphone placement typically rolls off many frequencies and is less edgy in general. With a real guitar cabinet, experimenting with the placement of a mic is crucial to getting the sound you want. While Waves doesn't give you the choice of moving the microphone to different locations on the speaker, it does give you the choice between on- and off-axis, which will result in a very different sound.

After you have decided on a proper microphone, you have a few other parameters to tweak before it's all said and done. Figure 8.10 shows you the last few buttons and knobs to play with.

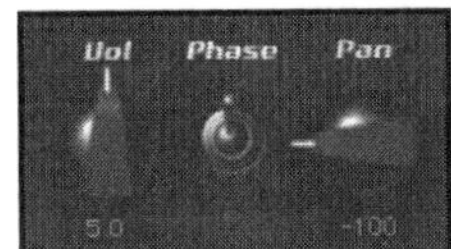

Figure 8.10
Cabinet volume, microphone phase, and cabinet pan.

The volume of your cabinet can be adjusted with a simple rotary knob. Cabinet volume may sound foreign to you, but remember that Waves is giving you two cabinets to work with, so you need to have a way to blend the two together. The cabinet pan sends the sound of your speaker to a real speaker (you know, when it actually stops being virtual) and pans it to taste. This also makes sense because not only do you have two speakers, but GTR is a stereo plug-in, and you have the entire left/right stereo field to work with. You can build up quite a huge sound by panning each cabinet hard to one side (each cabinet should have its own side) and cranking up the volume on both. You get a "wall of sound" effect this way.

The last control is a phase control, which allows you to flip the phase of the microphone picking up the sound. In phase versus out of phase also affects your final sound. Phase is included here because you have multiple amplifiers. Phase is a measure of time delay, but it takes a certain amount of time for a signal to reach a microphone. If you move the mic farther away, it takes longer to pick up. If those mics were mixed together, the sound would be out of phase, because the sound is getting to each mic at a different time, causing phase cancellation. Flipping or inverting the phase can sometimes alleviate some of these issues, but it can also change the sound of a single cabinet. Yes, yet another way to tweak your sound! Phase flipping is a common engineer's trick in the recording studio. Try it, you may like it.

The last thing we have to look at before we wrap up the amp modeling section is the master volume. Figure 8.11 shows the master volume and VU meter to assist you in setting the proper master output volume for your rig.

Figure 8.11
Master volume.

Now that we have gone through the amplifier modeling, it's time to look at the effects. Waves has provided a separate plug-in for dealing with the effects, called Waves Stomp. Let's take a tour of the other half of the GTR system.

Waves Stomp

Just as the amplifier plug-in had multiple versions (mono/stereo/one cabinet/two cabinets), the stompbox effect plug-in comes in three varieties, based on how many virtual pedals you want to load at once. There are separate plug-ins for two, four, and six pedals at once. Each of these is accessed from within a separate plug-in. You simply choose the right number of pedals based on the sound you want to create. On a personal note, I find myself choosing the six plug-in versions no matter what I do, even if I leave a few slots blank. Waves does allow you to upgrade to the larger versions without losing your work. Simply choose a larger version, and GTR automatically moves your work over to the new, larger plug-in. I guess Waves just wanted to give you the flexibility to choose. Choice is good.

When you load up the Stomp plug-in (in this case, the Stomp 6 Stereo), you are confronted with what's shown in Figure 8.12.

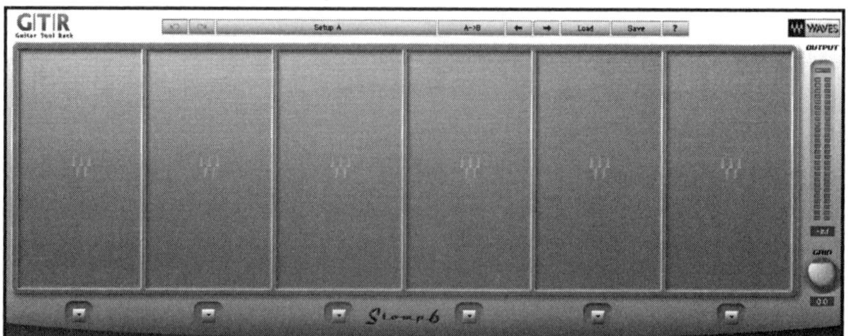

Figure 8.12
An empty six-slot virtual pedal board in Waves Stomp 6.

Figure 8.12 doesn't look like too much. You can see six empty slots where pedals will go. In order to load pedals, you need to look at the row of six buttons across the bottom of the plug-in, pictured in Figure 8.13.

Figure 8.13
Buttons for accessing the stompboxes.

Clicking any of the buttons calls up the list pictured in Figure 8.14.

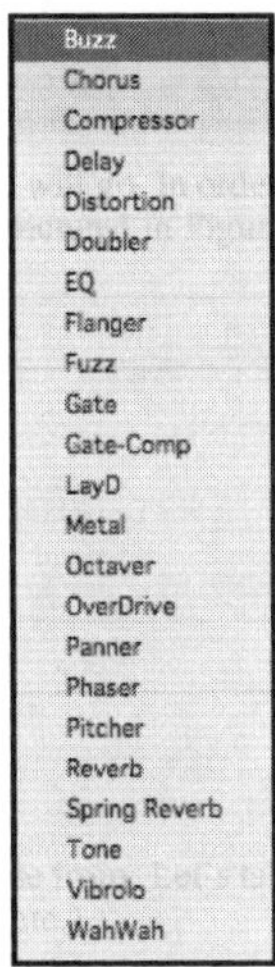

Figure 8.14
Available stompboxes.

As you can see from Figure 8.14, there are 23 available stompboxes to choose from. Let's take a look at what's available to you based on the categories they occupy (Distortion/Chorus, etc.):

- **Distortion Pedals**: Overdrive, Distortion, Fuzz, Buzz, and Metal. These all provide varying degrees of distortion and overdrive to suite your needs.
- **Modulation/Other Pedals**: Flanger, Vibrolo, Panner, Phaser, Octaver, Wah-wah, Chorus, Doubler, Delay, and Lay-D. Various ways to chorus, flange, pan, add vibrato, and octave effects.
- **Reverb: Reverb and Spring**: Two different types of reverb: a digital room emulator and an old-school spring reverb.
- **Dynamics**: Gate/Comp, Compressor and Gate. Compression and noise gating.
- **Filtering**: Tone and EQ. Three- and six-band equalizers.

The majority of the effects are adaptations of many of Waves' preexisting effects put in stompbox format. Certain effects, such as Wah-wah and the distortions, are models of preexisting units that Waves has not released previously.

Adding an effect is as simple as clicking one of the six buttons and choosing the pedal you want. Figure 8.15 shows a fully loaded pedal board.

Figure 8.15
A fully stocked Stomp.

As you can see, I've added an assortment of pedals. This is just an example. You can also add as many duplicate pedals as you'd like. Six distortion pedals in a row is possible!

One of the cool things you can do is simply rearrange the order of pedals by dragging them freely with the mouse. This way you can experiment with the order or processing in your setup. Simply click and drag to your desired location.

Control

In addition to the normal DAW-style automation most plug-ins give you, the GTR system is fully MIDI-aware. This means that you can control the parameters of any of your pedals through MIDI control. With a simple MIDI footswitch, you can have hands-free control of any of your stompboxes or amp selections in the other plug-in as well. To do so, right-click on any knob or on/off button to bring up a Learn button, as shown in Figure 8.16.

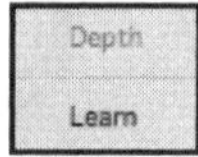

Figure 8.16
MIDI Learn button.

The Learn field shows you the parameter you are going to learn—in this case, Chorus Depth. Activating the Learn command will put the plug-in into a listening state, waiting for a MIDI control to come through. You simply rotate a rotary encoder or foot pedal, or tap on a foot pedal, and the GTR maps that control to the external MIDI device. This makes it very easy to emulate how a real guitar player works with his feet, and not with his hands on a mouse.

The last element is a master gain for all of the Stomp effects. It is found on the right side of the plug-in, as seen in Figure 8.17.

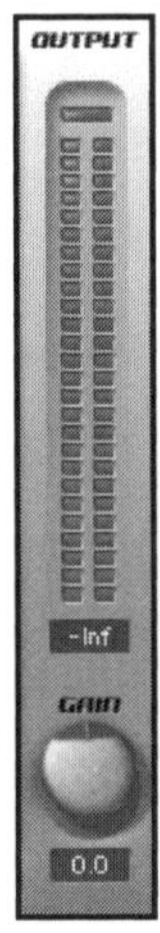

Figure 8.17
Master gain.

Even though many, if not all, of the individual pedals have some sort of gain control, this allows you to bring the combined level up or down to suit your own tastes.

Amazingly enough, that's pretty much all there is to the GTR system. It's simple to use and well organized enough to get your playing going in short order. There is one last thing I want to mention, since the bundle is broken up with two plug-ins.

THE ORDER

Since there are two plug-ins, one for the amps and cabinets and one for the stompboxes, it's vital that you get the order correct. In real life, your stompboxes are usually placed before the amplifier, not after it. The other option would be to place the effects in an effects loop and mix their signals together. In the virtual world, you should set up your amp the same way you would in real life.

In your sequencer of choice, you need to load the Stomp plug-in before the Amplifier plug-in in order to get the desired sounds. No one is stopping you from doing it the other way around, but it may not sound like you think it should, simply because of the order of processing. Again, try to treat the virtual amps just like real amps and configure them as you're used to doing. Also, remember that these plug-ins work as a team, so they need to be instantiated in the same track.

One last thing! Waves lets you demo this software online. You need to have an iLok to do so, but you can grab the software for a seven-day trial and put it through its paces. Granted, you won't have the hardware box, which is a pretty important part of the sound, but if you already have well recorded clean guitar tracks, you can get an excellent idea of what this plug-in can do. Check it out.

9 iZotope: Trash

With the variety of guitar distortion plug-ins available on the market, it's nice to see a generation of new distortion processors that try to take from the old and mix with the new. iZotope's Trash plug-in is just one of the new breed of hybrid processors that excels not only at vintage-type guitar distortion, but also at sound shaping that you can apply to other tracks, such as drums. Trash is available as a plug-in for both Mac and PC, so everyone can join in the fun. Trash tries to be less of a guitar modeler and more of a distortion processor with guitar-friendly features.

Talkin' Trash

Let's talk about the basic features of Trash and then break them down section by section to get an idea of what this processor is capable of doing. When you instantiate the plug-in, no matter which operating system you run, the first thing you run across is the main Trash screen, pictured in Figure 9.1.

Within this main screen, there are several visual elements that remain the same, no matter what subwindow you choose to activate. Across the bottom, you have the buttons that allow you to activate and edit the different nested screens within Trash. Figure 9.2 shows these six buttons.

Let's detail the basics of the buttons and cover them more thoroughly later:

- **Squash**: A full-featured compressor and noise gate with multiband compression capabilities.
- **Pre-Filter**: Equalization (filtering) of your signal before it hits the distortion stage. 36 sweepable filter types.
- **Trash**: Two stage distortion processes with multiband capabilities and 48 different types of distortion.

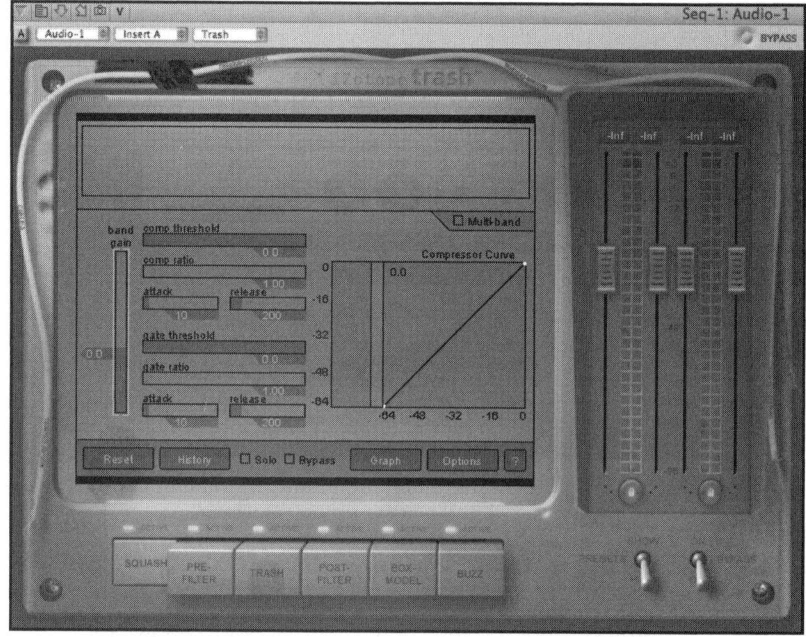

Figure 9.1
Trash's main screen.

Figure 9.2
Trash's navigation buttons: (Left to right) Squash, Pre-Filter, Trash, Post-Filter, Box-Model, and Buzz.

- **Post-Filter**: After-distortion modeling equalization (filtering) with multiband capabilities. 36 sweepable filter types.
- **Box-Model**: Speaker cabinet emulation with various microphone choices and 85 different cabinet choices.
- **Buzz**: Tape-style delay with selectable tape saturation and buzz.

MULTIWHAT?

In the above list, the term "multiband" has come up in several areas. Multiband refers to the ability of a plug-in or processor to separate the frequencies of your signal into different bands and affect them differently. For example, you could select the bottom frequencies of your guitar to receive a heavy distortion, and the higher frequencies would receive a smoother or different distortion. Multiband simply is the ability to process different ranges of sounds differently. With respect to Trash, multiband can refer not only to distortion, but also to filtering and compression.

Each of the modules in Figure 9.2 has a small green light and the word Active above its respective button. This is where you can engage or bypass any of Trash's modules.

Along the bottom-right edge are two flip switches, as seen in Figure 9.3.

Figure 9.3
The Presets switch (left) and the Bypass switch (right).

The Bypass switch bypasses the Trash effect. Most sequencers have their own way of bypassing effects, but it's nice to see this on the main screen of Trash. I like this because Trash encompasses a bunch of effects at once, and you may only want to bypass one effect. To the left of the Bypass switch is the Presets switch. Flipping this switch transforms the center section of Trash into a preset manager (see Figure 9.4).

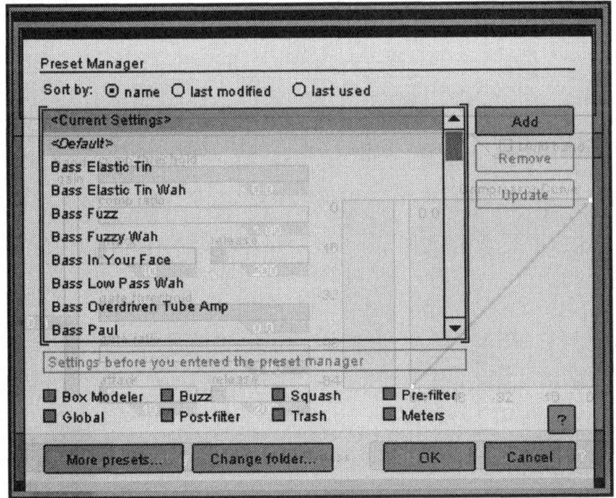

Figure 9.4
A quick flip of the Presets switch launches Trash's Preset Manager into the main window of the plug-in.

The Preset Manager can be instantiated at any time within Trash, no matter what other window you are editing. The Preset Manager window simply appears over the other windows you are editing. Actually, if you look very closely in Figure 9.4, you can see that there is a Content window in the background and the Preset Manager section has been superimposed on the foreground.

The Preset Manager is divided into two basic sections, as seen in Figure 9.5: the Preset list and the Modules checkbox.

The Preset list itself doesn't call for too much explanation. However, the whole design of the Preset Manager window reflects one basic design feature of Trash: It's more than a simple plug-in, it's a collection of effects. The Preset Manager window allows you to scroll through the included presets and activate them at any time.

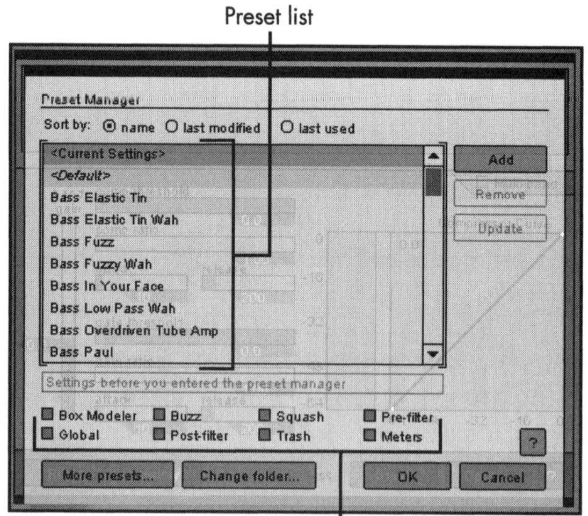

Figure 9.5
The Preset list and Modules selection.

MORE PRESETS

Are you a preset junkie? Most of us are! Thankfully, getting more presets is as easy as clicking the More Presets button within Trash's Preset Manager. Selecting More Presets will magically whisk you away to iZotope's Web site, where they have a collection of additional presets and user-made presets that you can download and use within Trash, all free of charge.

The second section of the Preset Manager window is the module selection section. A preset is more than just a sound, it is a snapshot of all the selected modules within Trash. One of the very cool things about the Preset Manager window is that it enables you to activate and deactivate modules from within a preset right there Manager. What this means for you is that you can save the distortion and cabinet type from an existing preset, disregarding the other modules saved within the preset. This feature allows you to take parts of presets you like and resave them using different names, allowing you to make fully custom presets or combining aspects from different presets into one preset.

Each of the modules has a checkbox, or rather a dark box, since selecting it doesn't show you a check mark. An unselected box remains light gray, while a selected box turns black. Figure 9.6 shows both selected and unselected modules in the Preset Manager window.

The last visual section to go over is the metering section, as shown in Figure 9.7.

The metering section is quite standard: The input signal is displayed on the left meter, and the output meter is on the right side. A pair of sliders (it's a pair because Trash is a stereo plug-in, regardless of the input type—mono/stereo) helps to control either the input or output level. The

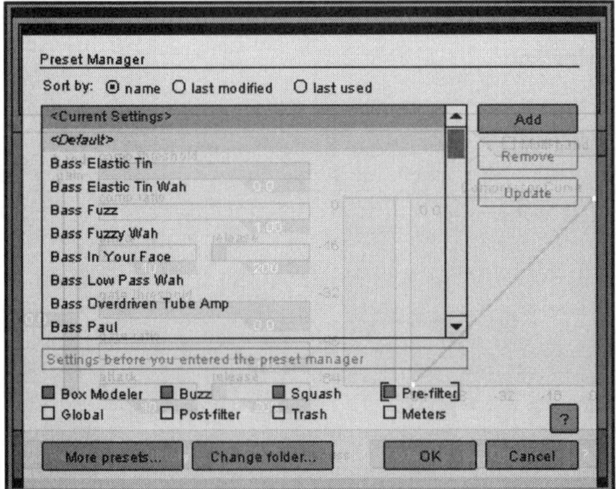

Figure 9.6
The top row of modules are all selected, while the bottom row are all deselected.

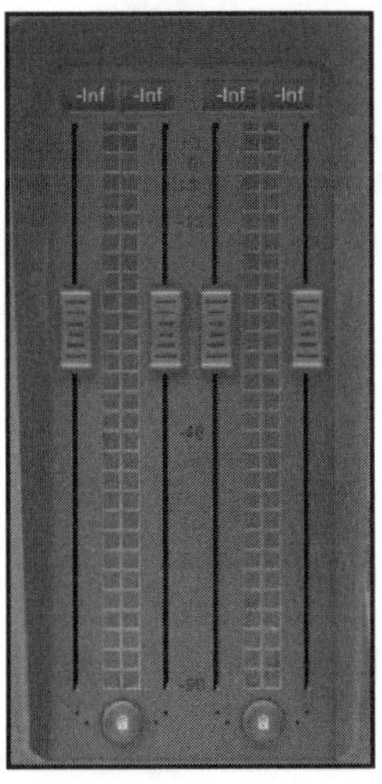

Figure 9.7
Trash's input/output metering section.

metering follows the basic tradition of "Green is good and red is bad" found on so many meters in audio products. As with any other plug-in or processor, you want to maximize your input level so that it does not clip or "hit the red." At the bottom of each meter is a clip indicator. If it's glowing red, that means you have clipped the signal at some point. You can reset this by clicking anywhere on the meter. The clip meter will display green if all is well!

In-depth Modules

We have gone through the basics of Trash's interface. Now let's get specific about each of the modules and its functions in more detail. Since the bottom panel of Trash's interface contains the modules, Squash, Pre-Filter, Trash, Post-Filter, Box-Model, and Buzz, in left-to-right order, we might as well cover them in that order too.

Squash—Compression

The first module to look at is the Squash module. This is a one-stop source for compression, multiband compression, and gating. Figure 9.8 shows the main display when the Squash button is engaged.

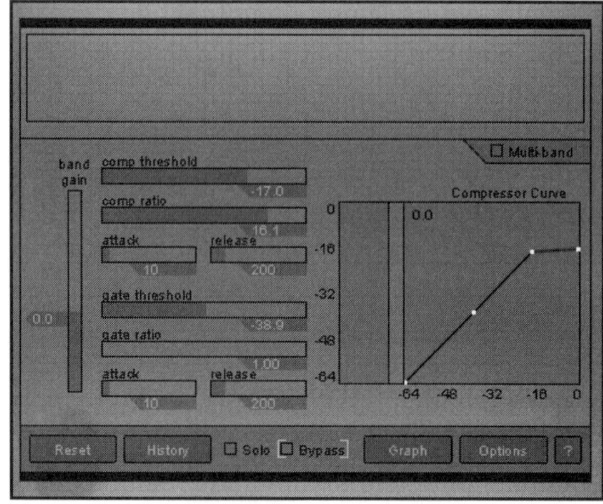

Figure 9.8
The Squash module's main window.

The last section of compression has to do with the Multiband compression settings allowed in Trash. Figure 9.9 shows the Squash window with the Multiband section highlighted.

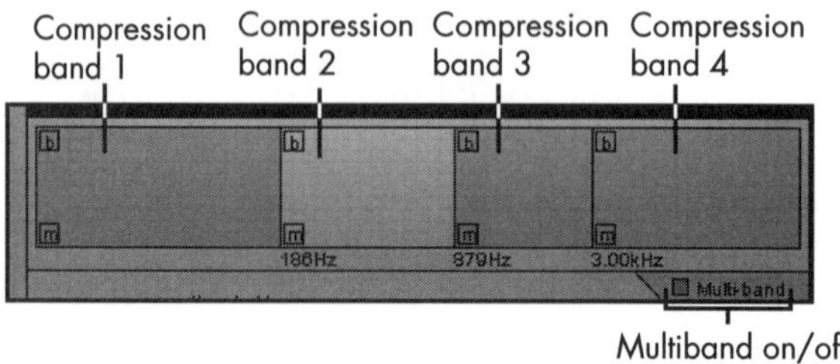

Figure 9.9
Multiband compression engaged.

There's actually quite a bit to look at in Figure 9.9.

Along the top of the window are four horizontal bands or blocks. These bands represent the "multi" in "multiband compression." Each of the bands corresponds to a different frequency band or range of frequencies. To set the range of any individual band of compression, each band has a vertical line at its edge, so simply grab it with your cursor (your cursor will turn into a hand) and move it left to right. You will notice right below that display is a numerical display signifying what frequency you have pulled the band to. By doing this, you are setting the range of each of the bands. Trash can display a maximum of four bands at once, although you don't need to use all four. Simply right-click on a band you want to remove and click Remove Band, as shown in Figure 9.10.

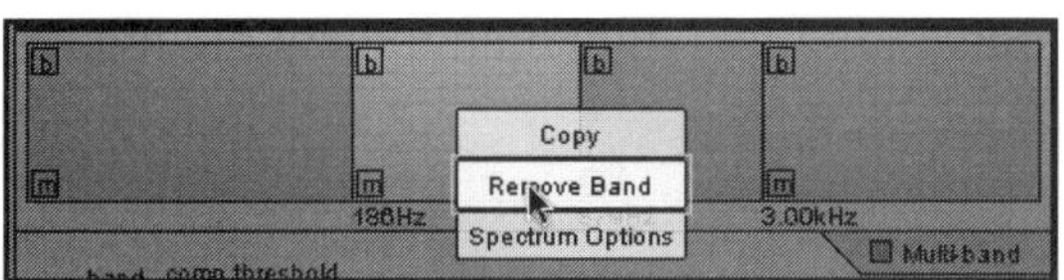

Figure 9.10
Removing an existing band.

Conversely, if displaying less than four bands, you can always add another band. To do so, right-click again and choose Insert Band (see Figure 9.11).

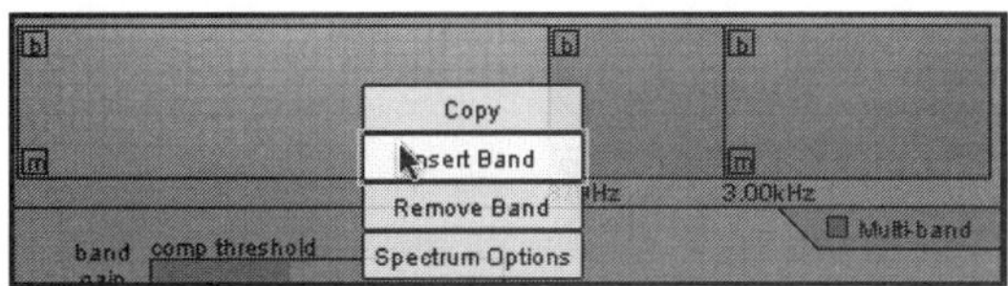

Figure 9.11
Adding a new band.

The last thing to see is that each of the bands has two small buttons, as shown in Figure 9.12. The buttons are labeled B and M for Bypass and Mute, respectively.

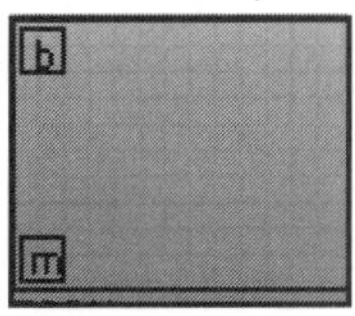

Figure 9.12
Bypass and Mute within the Multiband module.

Bypass will bypass the processing of that particular module, letting the unprocessed audio pass through. Muting will mute the entire module and all the sound that passes through. This is handy for working with one band only, by muting the other three bands.

You can solo a module, even though there is no S button, as you might expect. To solo a module: Alt+Click (same on Mac and PC) the M mute button, and the rest will be muted and that module will solo.

The last compression setting is the Band Gain, as shown in Figure 9.13.

Band Gain sets the level of each respective band of compression. Compression is an effect that reduces dynamic range. When working properly, compression will result in a loss of level. The

Figure 9.13
Compression Band Gain control.

band gain control makes up the gain lost by the compression effect. When you're using this in multiband mode, there will be different settings for each of the four modules enacted.

Squash—Gating

Gating, short for *noise gating,* has a very simple job. A noise gate sets a level where it closes the audio path. This is very handy for hiding noise, which is usually much quieter than a normal guitar's signal. Gating has the same controls as compression: Threshold to set where the gate enacts, Ratio for how hard it closes, Attack for how fast it closes, and Release for how slowly it reopens the signal. Setting this control is actually fairly simple. Start with the threshold. Let your guitar make noise, simply take your hands off it, let the background hum or noise come through (if any), and lower the threshold so that the gate closes. This should make sure that your signal stays quiet and clean when you're not playing. If you find that your playing is cut off abruptly, play with the Attack and Release controls to get a good, natural feel for the gate. You'll also notice that changes you make to the gate module are also represented in the compression curve, as seen in Figure 9.14.

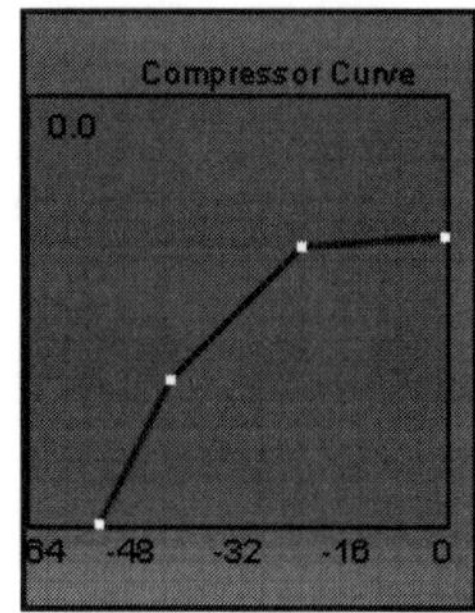

Figure 9.14
Compression curve with compression and gate visuals.

MULTI EVERYTHING

In all this talk about multiband stuff, you should mention that all of the multibands can have compression *and* gating specific to each frequency band. Talk about control.

Pre-Filter

The Pre-Filter module is an equalizer/filter that sculpts your sound before it hits the Trash (distortion) model. You can have three different bands of filtering in this module. Like most parts of this plug-in, there is more to Trash than just a simple filter. A filter point can represent a simple Bandpass filter, or more complex models, such as TalkBox emulations and different models of filter processes.

When you load up the pre-filter by selecting the Pre-Filter knob, you get the default screen shown in Figure 9.15.

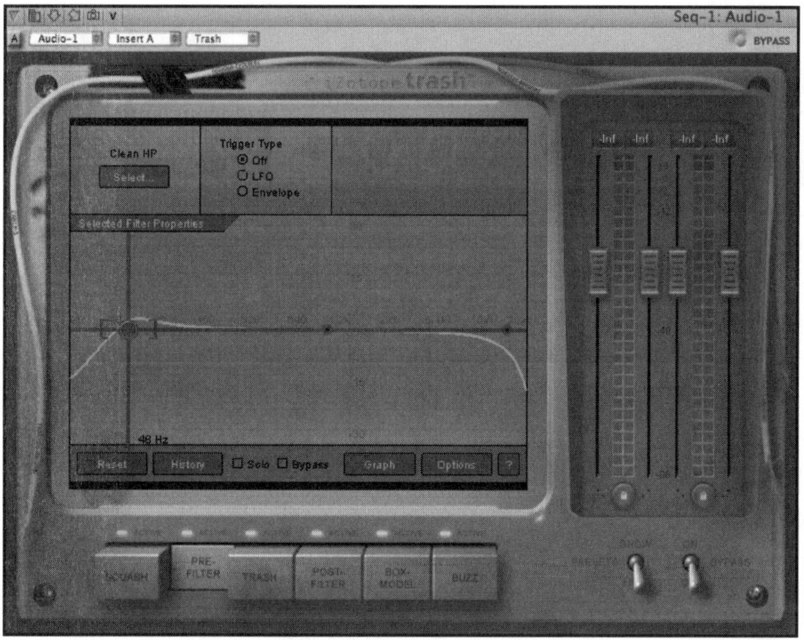

Figure 9.15
The default Pre-Filter screen.

In this window, you can see the three filter points as black dots across the frequency range. As with most graphical frequency range, you are looking at the pitch/frequency plotted on a horizontal axis, while the amount of filtering is shown by its vertical location.

Editing the parameters of any filter point is as simple as taking your mouse to one of the black filter points and moving it. As you move your first EQ band to the right, you change its point to a higher frequency. This is shown at the bottom of the screen, directly under the point, as a number expressed in Hz. To move your first point to 320 Hz, click and drag until the numerical display at the bottom of the graph reads 320, as shown in Figure 9.16.

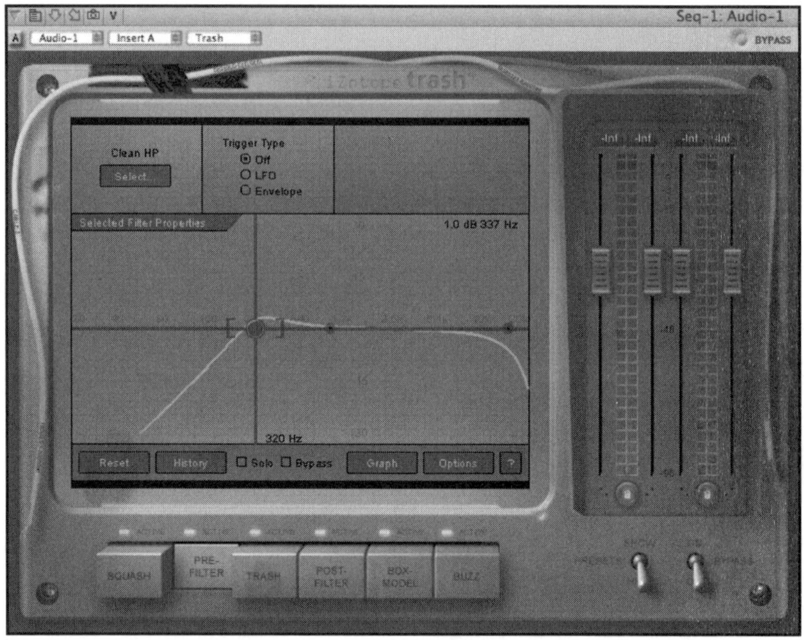

Figure 9.16
Setting an EQ point to a specific frequency by moving it horizontally to the desired point.

The type of filter you choose will affect the display of Trash's window. Your first point is a highpass filter—meaning that it is letting only the highs pass and cutting off the lows. If you change your first filter point to a different kind of filter, the display will look quite different. Let's change it to a bandpass filter, which is going to affect only a very specific frequency that you select.

There are two more unique things you can do within this filter window: LFO and Envelope control. Let's start with an LFO, which stands for Low Frequency Oscillator. An oscillator is a parameter that changes over a specific amount of time. LFOs traditionally are used on synthesizers to give a sort of vibrato effect. In this case, you are going to use the LFO to automatically sweep any of your filter points through a range of EQs. To do this, first select an EQ point; let's choose the second point. The top-left of the screen has a control for Trigger Type with three choices: Off, LFO, and Envelope. You are going to choose LFO, and Figure 9.17 shows the effect of your choice.

The LFO controls consist of two basic controls. The first is the Period control, which is the time it takes for the LFO to complete one full cycle. A faster period will create a faster filter sweep, and

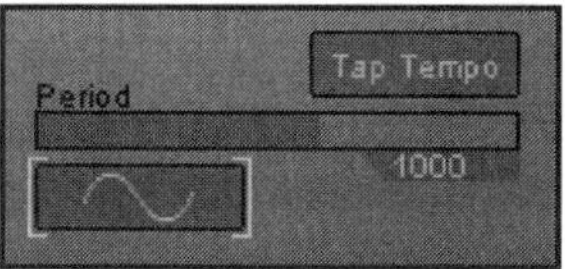

Figure 9.17
LFO controls.

a slower one will do the opposite. You can slide the slider from left to right to set the period, or you can use the Tap Tempo button to set the speed, based on the speed of two consecutive clicks.

As the LFO is put into effect, you're able to see the amount of sweep move across the screen from left to right, giving you instant visual feedback as to the amount of sweep and its speed. Figure 9.18 shows you the width of the filter sweep as a second "ghost" image is shown for the LFO.

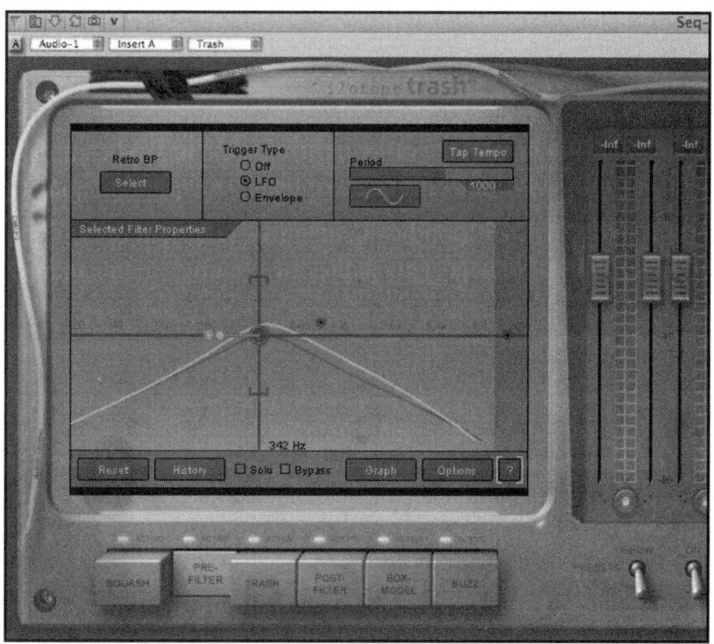

Figure 9.18
LFO in action.

Underneath the Period control is the box that changes the type of LFO in use. An LFO works by moving through a wave shape. The default selection is a sine wave, which moves smoothly from one extreme to another. Trash gives you six selections for the type of wave shape. These can range from sawtooth to squarewave and random step filters. Each different wave shape is going to change the way that your LFO automatically sweeps through the frequencies. The fun is that you can instantly hear the effects of your actions. Play around with these! Each of the three points can have its own individual LFO settings, so you can shape some very unusual sounds.

> **SYNTH GUITAR?**
> The addition of an LFO effect may be new for many guitarists. LFOs are traditionally found on synthesizers and not on guitar effects. That being said, the ability to automatically move an EQ point in time is an extremely cool way to shape your sound. If nothing more, it will give you, the digital guitarist, another sound-shaping tool in your arsenal. When all else fails, tweak, tweak, tweak!

The last control is the Envelope control. This also allows you to sweep a set of frequencies, but unlike the LFO, which was an automatic sweep, you can set this sweep to respond to the incoming audio, or the envelope of sound. In a basic form, you can have the sweep occur only if you play very softly, or loudly, based on how you set up the parameters. This is a very unique way to shape sound, and it allows you to make use of your natural dynamics to affect your filters. In the same upper-right window, you can activate the envelope by selecting its button. Once you do so, you get a list of variables (see Figure 9.19).

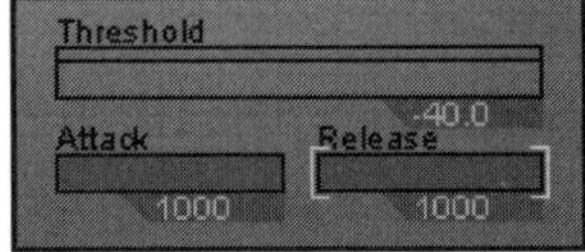

Figure 9.19
The Envelope controls.

The controls here may remind you of the controls for a compressor—they are in fact the same controls! Both a Compressor control and an Envelope control are going to respond to an incoming audio signal.

The Envelope control is a creative tool for sound shaping. By experimenting with it and the LFO controls, you can take the filter section of Trash to new levels. Three simple bands of EQ may not seem like much, but when you can also add LFO and Envelope shaping to each band, the filter section becomes much more robust and unique.

Trash

Since this plug-in is called Trash, you'd expect that the module called Trash would be fairly important. If you thought so, you'd be correct! The Trash module is the heart and soul of this plug-in, providing all the distortion. We guitar players do love our distortion, don't we? At its heart, the Trash module lets you add two different types of distortion at the same time and shape them to your taste. The distortions range from modeled distortions to some very lo-fi grit for unique sounds. The thing that makes Trash so cool is that you can work with it as a multiband processor, allowing you to add a different distortion device to a different range of frequencies, such as subtle distortion on the lower frequencies and more aggressive distortion on the higher frequencies. Let's take a look at Figure 9.20, which details the Trash window.

Figure 9.20
The Trash window.

Within the distortion algorithm selection, you find quite a long and distinguished list of the types of distortion you can apply. The list contains 48 different types of distortion that you can select. This list contains various emulations of popular devices, in addition to some unusual lo-fi and gritty effects. You can have any two distortions running at the same time by simply choosing the first and second tabs on the left side of the interface. This way you can blend two different distortions to make a desired "stew" of sounds.

The parameters you can set for each of the two distortions are fairly straightforward, but let's go through them. Figure 9.21 details the parameters you can adjust.

- **Input Gain**: This sets the incoming level into the distortion device. This is a crucial step, since most distortion is very dynamic and reacts to varying input levels while incurring different levels of saturation. Depending on how much prefiltering you have done, you may need to adjust your level up or down to avoid clipping.

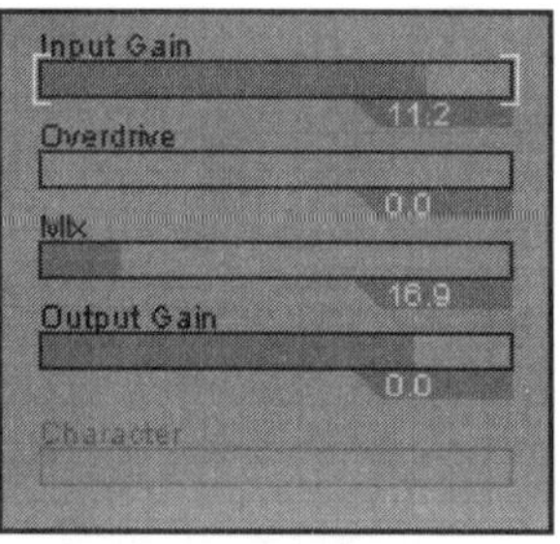

Figure 9.21
Adjustable distortion parameters.

- **Overdrive**: The amount of distortion or "dirt" in your signal.
- **Mix**: This allows you to mix the distortion in the first module with the distortion in the second module, blending the two distortions together.
- **Output Gain**: Different distortion modules have different output levels, and you may have to compensate for louder or quieter sources in order to balance your overall output signal.
- **Character**: Certain distortion modules access this control, which basically wrecks the sound more. This is not a global control, because only certain modules have it. If you can access it, it will turn itself on based on your selection.

The last aspect to talk about is the multiband operation of the Trash module. This is where I feel Trash is so unique. Each of the two distortion selections can operate with up to four different bands of frequency-specific processing. In this case, each of the two distortion sections can have four different distortions, allowing you eight different distortion algorithms at once, which are all frequency-dependant. Try that with an amp! Rather than falling into redundancy here, refer back to the section on the Squash module for more on the multiband concept.

In any of the four multibands for each distortion path, you can select a different algorithm and set all of its parameters differently. Figure 9.22 shows a setup with three multibands.

One of the neat things you can see in Figure 9.22 is that the waveform flows through each multiband, so you can get a visual cue as to what's happening. Also, just like the Squash module's multiband integration, you can mute and solo each of the multibands. The sum total of all this are some very hip ways to shape your guitar's signal. Trash really excels at distortion of all types, not just trying to re-create that 1962 Fender amp you never should have sold to your cousin. Trash does everything else.

Post-Filter

Ah, the Post-Filter! It filters the sound *after* it has been distorted. The main difference in the Post-Filter is that you only have two bands to work with. It is essentially designed to roll off the highs and lows to tame some of the aggressive frequency content you may add through the Trash module. Figure 9.23 shows the Post-Filter module.

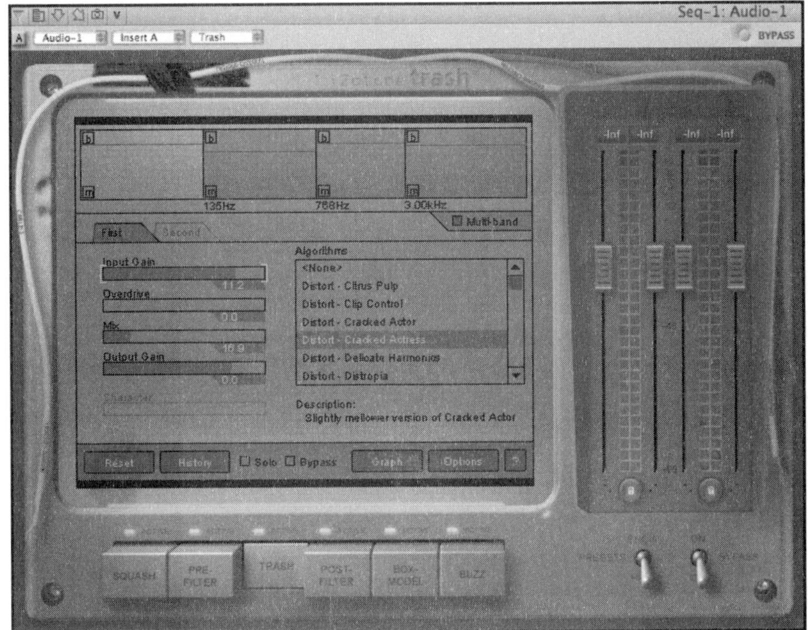

Figure 9.22
Multiband distortion in action.

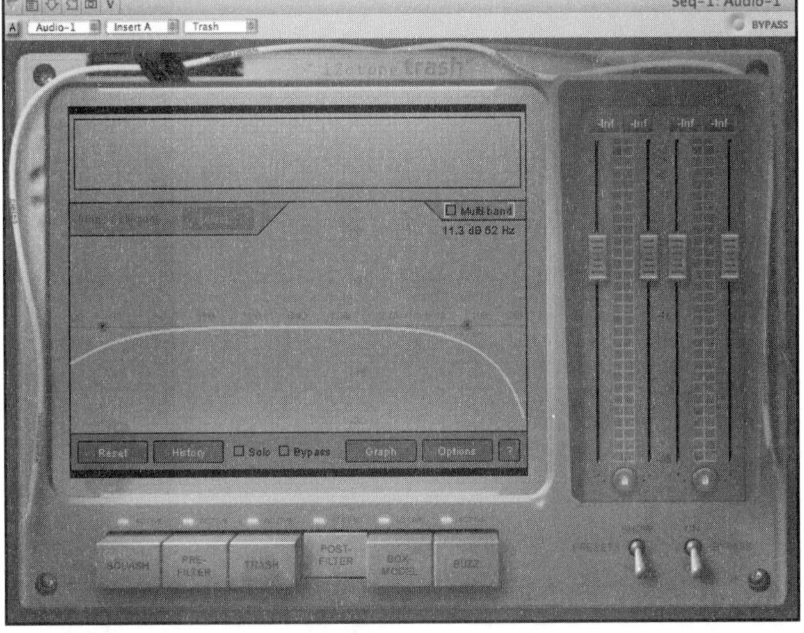

Figure 9.23
The Post-Filter module.

In many respects, the Pre- and Post-Filter modules are very similar. Let's talk about how they are different.

- The Pre-Filter has three bands; the Post-Filter only has two.
- The Pre-Filter has LFO and Envelope control; the Post-Filter does not.
- The Pre-Filter has no multiband operation; the Post-Filter does.

> **DO YOU NEED MULTIBAND?**
> Multiband processing is cool and all, but do you really need to use it? According to Mark Ethier of iZotope, the multiband aspect of the Post-Filter really only comes in handy if you are also using multiband distortion in the Trash module. If you aren't doing so, treat the Post-Filter as a simple high and low roll-off to control the harmonic content of your signal.

Other than the differences listed above, both filters follow the same visual way of setting up the EQ bands. The vertical sets boost and attenuation, while the horizontal sets the frequency to start rolling off.

Box Model

Next up in line is the Box Model, which is Trash's cabinet and microphone simulator/emulator. The full module is shown in Figure 9.24.

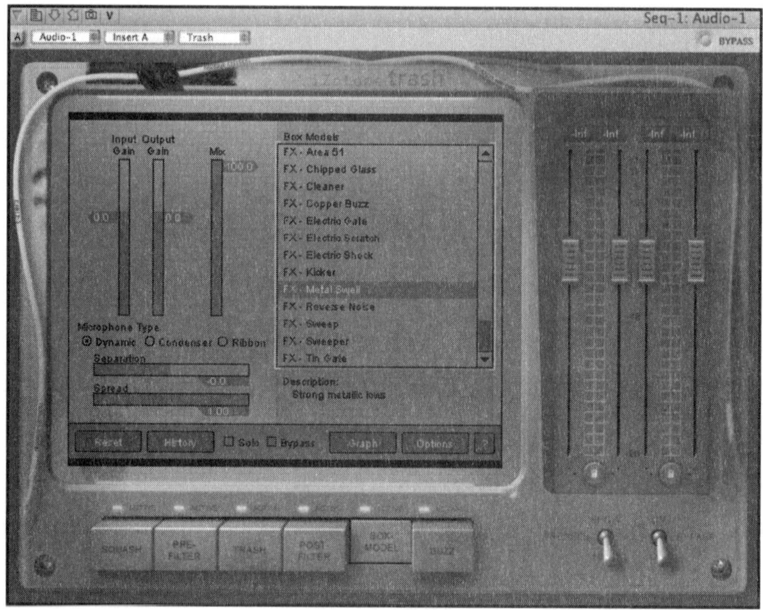

Figure 9.24
The Box Model screen.

On the right of the interface is a list of cabinet models. You can scroll through a list of 85 different models, as seen in Figure 9.25.

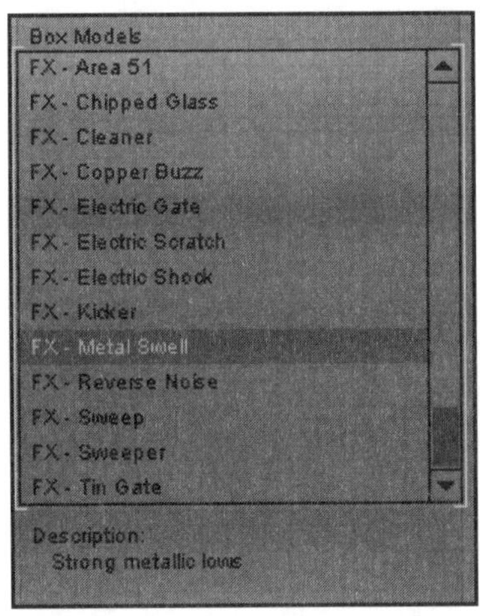

Figure 9.25
The Box Model selector.

What I like about Trash is that you get the standard 4×10 speaker cabinets that everyone else gives you, but you also run across some very random selections, such as Sheet Metal, Tin Can, and Cheap Radio.

The boxes are broken into three categories as you scroll through the list. The Amps category encompasses all the typical guitar-style cabinets you might want to emulate. The next category is Device, which models the sounds of such bizarre objects as cheap radios and rubber cones. I have to wonder what it's like to sample and emulate a rubber cone. I mean, they come in so many different sizes.

The last category is FX, which are models of random objects and synthetic models that may not exist in nature, such as Metal Swell and Chipped Glass. The Device and FX categories allow you to take sounds into an entirely new dimension, a dimension away from traditional cabinet modeling found in other plug-ins.

The left side of the Box Model, as seen in Figure 9.26, gives you the following controls:

- **Input Gain**: Sets how much level comes into the Box Model. Since the Box Model comes directly after the Trash module, which has its own output controls, you may not have to set this. On the other hand, you can get even more distortion by overloading the virtual cabinets this way.
- **Output Gain**: This is the output after all of the box modeling has occurred.

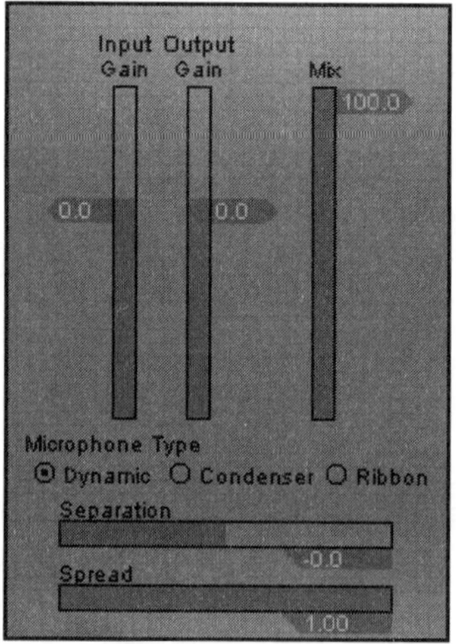

Figure 9.26
The addition Box Model controls.

- **Mix**: Since the box modeling is a very fancy EQ/effect, you can choose how much of the box sound you want imparted on your original signal. A level of 100 would let all of the sound through, while 50 would be a mix of one-half.
- **Microphone Type**: Trash has modeled the sound of a dynamic mic, a condenser mic, and a ribbon mic into the Box Model module. Regardless of which box you choose, selecting a different microphone will impart the characteristic sound of that microphone on your selected Box Model.
- **Separation**: In relation to the microphone models, by default, there are a pair of microphones in front of your virtual cabinet. These microphones are aligned in parallel together. The separation control moves one of the microphones closer to the box, causing a delay effect.
- **Spread**: This control *only* works if you have the separation control engaged in some way. If you do, the spread control lets you choose how far the microphones are from each other.

And there you have the Box Model!

Buzz

Ah, we now bring you to the last module in Trash: the Buzz module. This is a delay module with a "trashy" sound. (As if this plug-in wasn't trashy enough to begin with!) Figure 9.27 shows the Buzz window.

The Buzz module is broken up into a few elements. The first section to look at is the type of delay you are using, or the Buzz type. Here is a breakdown of the six different types of delays you can use, albeit one at a time.

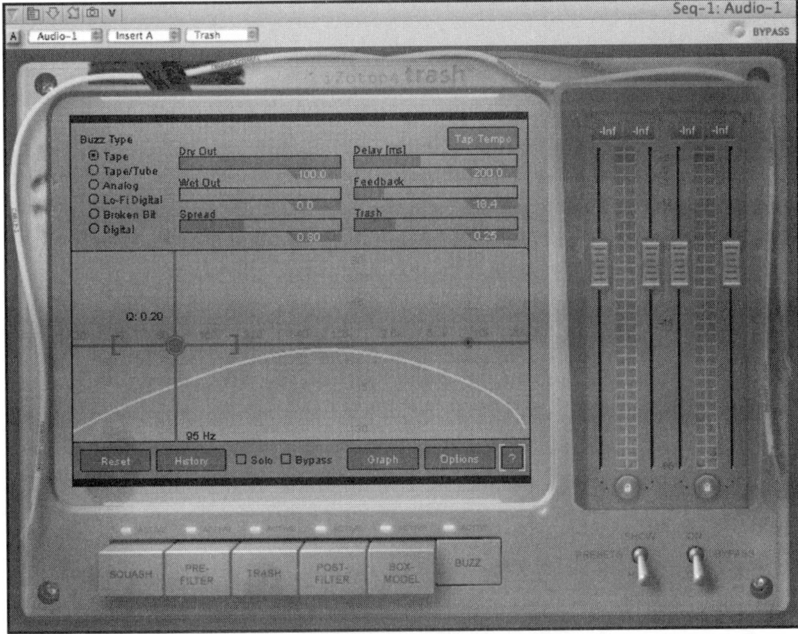

Figure 9.27
The Buzz module.

- **Tape**: A tape delay with saturation and flutter.
- **Tape/Tube**: Same as above, with the addition of tube saturation.
- **Analog**: A lo-fi delay that degrades the quality of your sound (in a good way).
- **Lo-Fi Digital**: Akin to the first digital-delay foot pedals.
- **Broken Bit**: A digital delay with a broken bit; the result is an infinite, odd feedback sound.
- **Digital**: Surprise, a *normal* clean, digital delay.

No matter which of the six delays you choose, there are common controls for each delay. Figure 9.28 shows those controls.

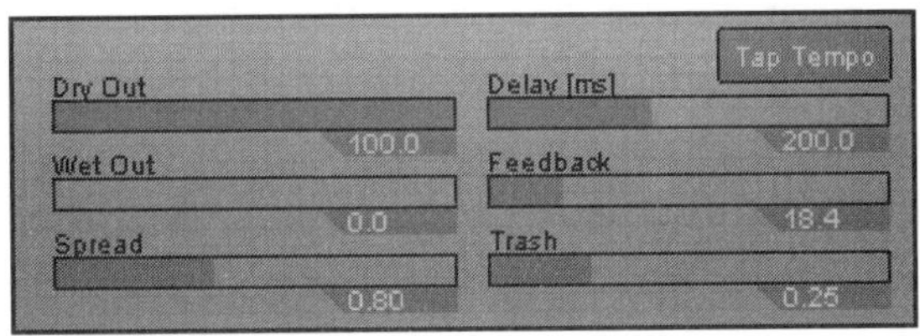

Figure 9.28
Delay controls.

Let's go over what the controls do to each delay that you select.

- **Tap Tempo**: Allows you to set the interval of your delay repeats with two mouse clicks.
- **Dry Out**: This is the strength of the dry, unaffected signal.
- **Wet Out**: This is the strength of the wet, affected signal.
- **Spread**: When using Trash as a stereo track, you can set the stereo spread from mono to extra-wide stereo.
- **Delay** (ms): This is the delay time, expressed in milliseconds.
- **Feedback**: This sets how loud the delays will be. Higher values will result in more audible delays as they repeat.
- **Trash**: Sets how trashy the final sound is. High values impart saturation and other trashy type effects (see a trend here?).

The last part to talk about is the bottom section of the Buzz window, which serves as yet another filter (see Figure 9.29).

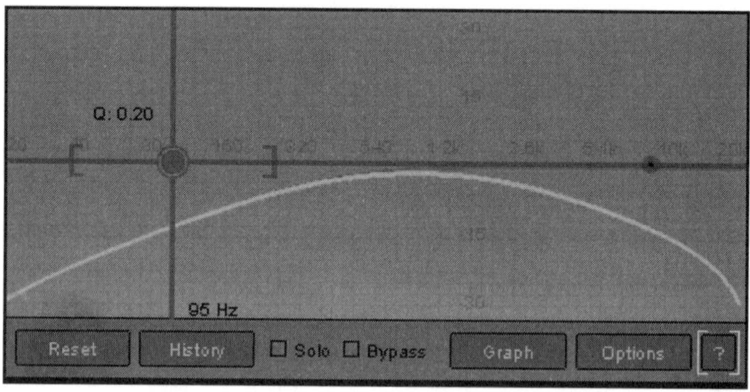

Figure 9.29
The Buzz filter.

The purpose of the filter here is to shape the sound of the affected signal, not the dry signal. Since this delay can impart many sonic disturbances and general "trash" to your sound, some shaping of the delay may be needed. This is your last line before the output, so it's your last chance to get the sound the way you want it.

The filter itself is a two-band filter that allows you to follow off the high and low end. It works exactly the same was as the Post-Filter module does.

And there you have it! Trash is a versatile and unusual distortion-shaping device. It has obvious uses for guitar and some sound-shaping uses for other sound sources, such as vocals, bass, and drums. It's definitely worth an audition.

10 Native Instruments: Guitar Rig

In March 2004, at the Musikmesse trade show in Germany, Native Instruments released Guitar Rig 1.0. Native Instruments has been one of the leaders in virtual synthesis technology, applying their DSP skills to a wide range of popular products such as B4, Reaktor, and Absynth. Until the release of Guitar Rig, Native Instruments was focused on synthesis technology—the release of Guitar Rig was their first foray into signal processing and their first step into the guitar market. Guitar Rig 1 was met with great success, and little more than a year later, a major upgrade was announced: Guitar Rig 2. Not only did Guitar Rig 2 expand its already successful list of features, but it added bass amplifiers, so now it might be subtitled "Guitar and Bass Rig."

REAL POWER

Guitar Rig is much more than *just* a plug-in. So much more, in fact, that Course Technology has released a book dedicated to Guitar Rig titled *Guitar Rig 2 Power*, written by Orren Merton. Considering that he has about 400 pages to cover Guitar Rig in detail, I will only give you the brief lay of the land here. Yes, the program really is big enough to get its own book! Here, you will get a clear idea of what Guitar Rig can do, but your ultimate resource for the program is Merton's book.

Guitar Rig is a cross-platform amp-modeling and effects application for Mac and PC. Guitar Rig, like all Native Instruments releases, supports all major plug-in formats (VST, AU, DXi, and RTAS), so you can work within your host of choice. Another nice feature is that Guitar Rig is a stand alone program that can run on its own without the need for a sequencer. This is a great feature for players who use Guitar Rig in a live setting.

Guitar Rig, as it was first introduced, was a combination of software and hardware. The plug-in took care of the modeling, the included Rig Kontrol foot pedal served as a DI interface to your sound card, and its buttons and expression controller allowed players to operate the software with their feet.

Out of all of the guitar modeling packages, I have personally chosen Guitar Rig as my program of choice. I find that its flexibility, intuitiveness, and impressive overall package allows Guitar Rig to stand above the competition. I have been fortunate enough to work with the developers/designers of Guitar Rig as a beta tester from its conception to the present. I have watched this program take shape and even had a few of my own ideas instituted into the program. Now, let's see what makes Guitar Rig tick.

The Rig Kontrol(s)

The first element that sets Guitar Rig apart is its included foot controller. There have been two major releases of Guitar Rig, and each one has included a new Rig Kontrol. The original, Rig Kontrol 1, as seen in Figure 10.1 was unique for many reasons.

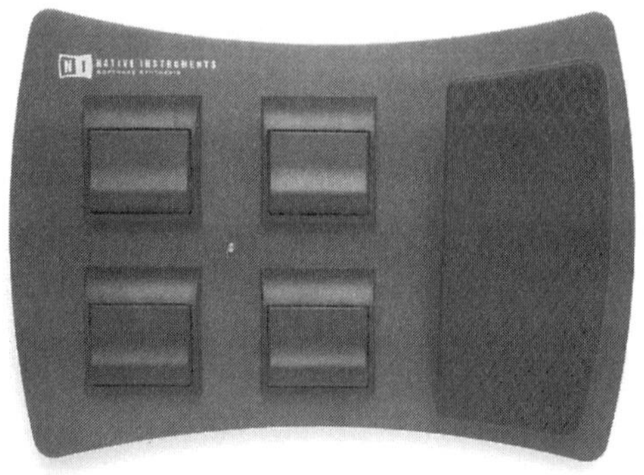

Figure 10.1
Rig Kontrol 1.

First, it served as a direct injection preamp for the guitar, bringing the guitar's Hi-Z (high impedance) signal up to line level. Secondly, it allowed the user to change presets and turn effects on and off, and it had an assignable-expression foot controller for controlling real-time changes, such as Wah-wah and volume pedal functions. What was unique about Rig Kontrol 1 was that it did all this without MIDI or USB/Firewire communications. The pedal interfaced directly with your computer's soundcard and required no drivers. The buttons on the Rig Kontrol simply sent control tones (high-pitched audio bursts for each pedal) that the Guitar Rig software could interpret. Because of this, the Rig Kontrol 1 was a stereo pedal—one cable carried the dry guitar signal, while the other cable carried the controller information. At the time, it was revolutionary, but the issue of "Which soundcard works best with Guitar Rig?" kept coming up, so Native Instruments decided to up the ante with Guitar Rig 2 and include the more capable Rig Kontrol 2, as seen in Figure 10.2.

Rig Kontrol 2 differs greatly from version 1, in that it's a USB 2.0 audio interface. A single USB cable carries power to the pedal and sends the audio information back and forth, all at extremely low latencies.

Figure 10.2
The new and improved Rig Kontrol 2.

Not only is Rig Kontrol 2 more rugged (housed in an aluminum enclosure—even the switches and pedal are steel now), but there are a total of seven switches on the face of the unit (six for preset change/effect on/off, and one under the expression pedal.) The top panel now has an LED readout showing preset number and signal levels. The input/output connection scheme has also received an overhaul. Figure 10.3 shows the rear panel on the Rig Kontrol 2.

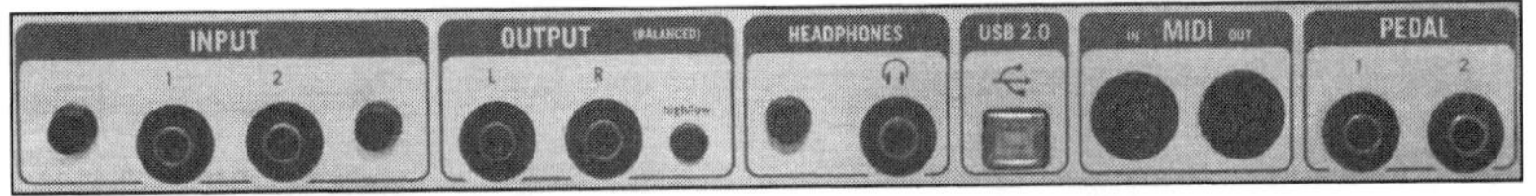

Figure 10.3
Rig Kontrol 2's rear connection panel.

You can see from the figure and its callouts that the rear panel has a great number of connections. There are inputs for two separate guitars, each with its own input level trim control, balanced stereo outputs, a full 1×1 MIDI interface, a headphone jack with level control for private practice/listening, and two additional expression controller inputs, giving you a total of three expression controllers to enable expressive control over your sound. The addition of the MIDI interface allows you to give you one of the many MIDI foot controllers on the market to give you even more control over Guitar Rig. A popular choice in this regard is the Behringer FCB1010, as seen in Figure 10.4.

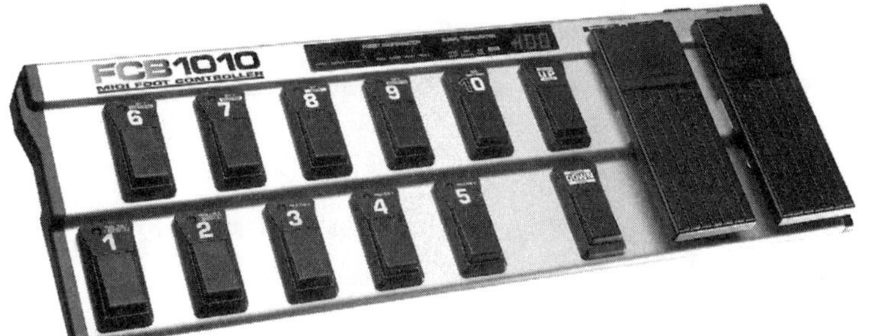

Figure 10.4
More tap dancing: The Behringer FCB1010 foot controller.

Rig Kontrol 2 not only serves as your interface, but also as your main control station, making it an excellent choice for both studio and live work. Its abundant connection scheme will harness the full power of the Guitar Rig software.

Okay, enough about the pedal. Let's get to the software—there's quite a bit to talk about.

The Interface

Without further ado, let's take a look at Guitar Rig 2 in action. Figure 10.5 shows Guitar Rig 2's interface.

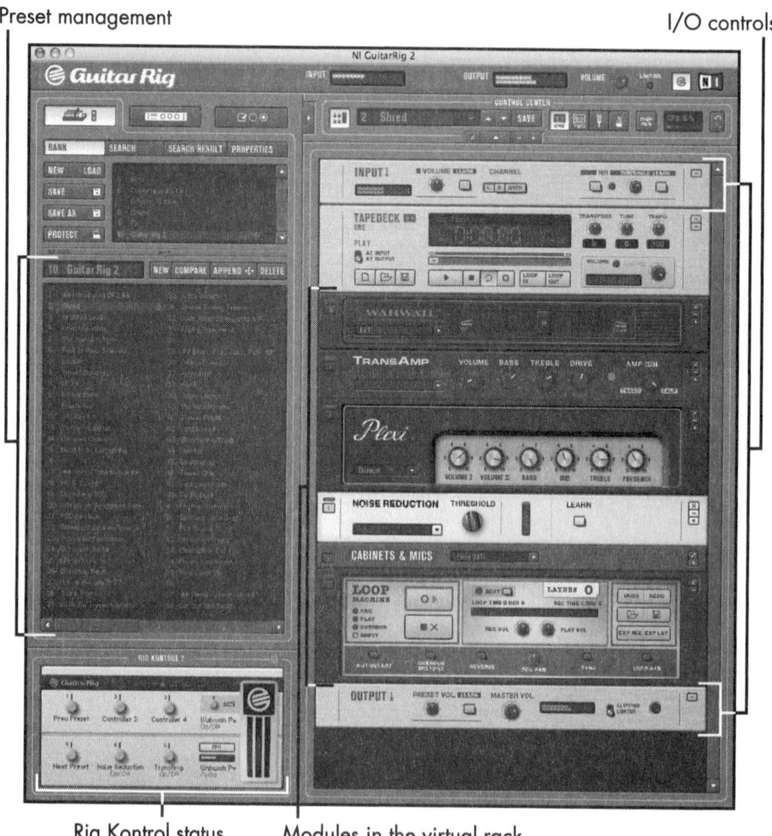

Figure 10.5
Interface overview.

Guitar Rig splits its interface into left and right panels. The left side allows you to select presets, grab modules for your rack, and set other system options. The right side is your virtual rack. Figure 10.5 features the preset management system in the left pane. Figure 10.6 shows

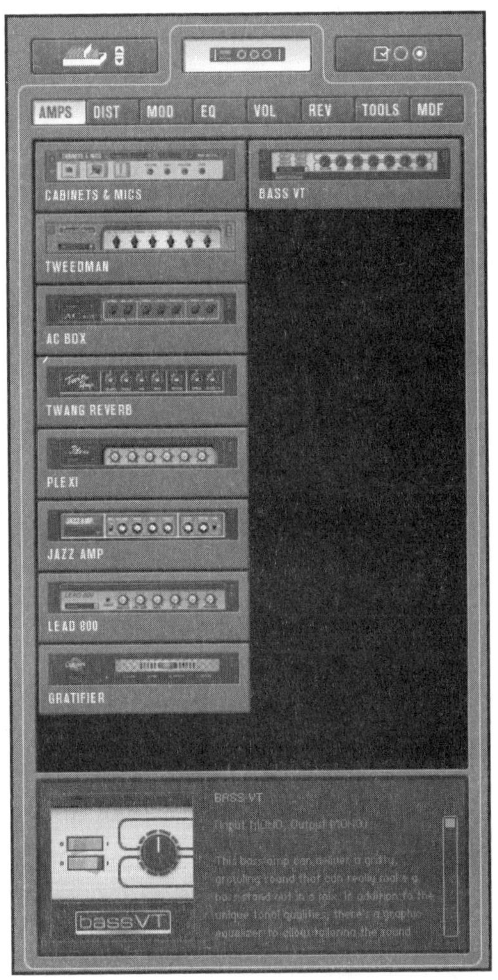

Figure 10.6
The module's view.

the module's interface where you can select the different modules that will make up your custom rig.

Across the top of the window are eight tabs for accessing the different categories of modules. In Figure 10.6, we showed you the amps. The Module view gives you an overview of the amps that you have to choose from. Clicking on any module will bring up more information about that module in the info pane below. Figure 10.7 shows some additional information on the Tweedman amp.

By choosing the different tabs shown in Figure 10.8, you can access all of the modules available to Guitar Rig.

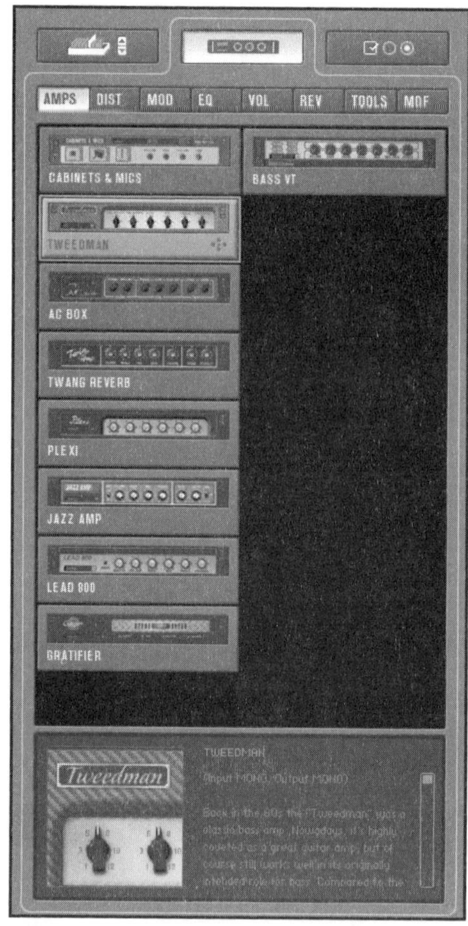

Figure 10.7
Tweedman information.

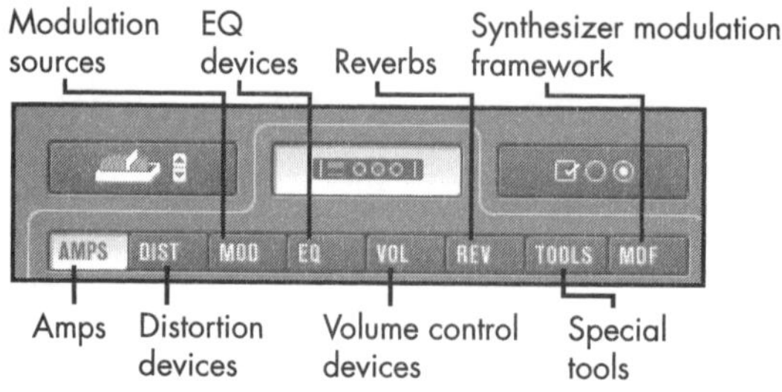

Figure 10.8
Module categories.

Adding components to your rig is as easy as dragging a module from the left module pane to the right side. For Figure 10.9, I started with an empty rig and added one amp, an EQ, and a Reverb, all by simply dragging and dropping the components into the right pane of Guitar Rig.

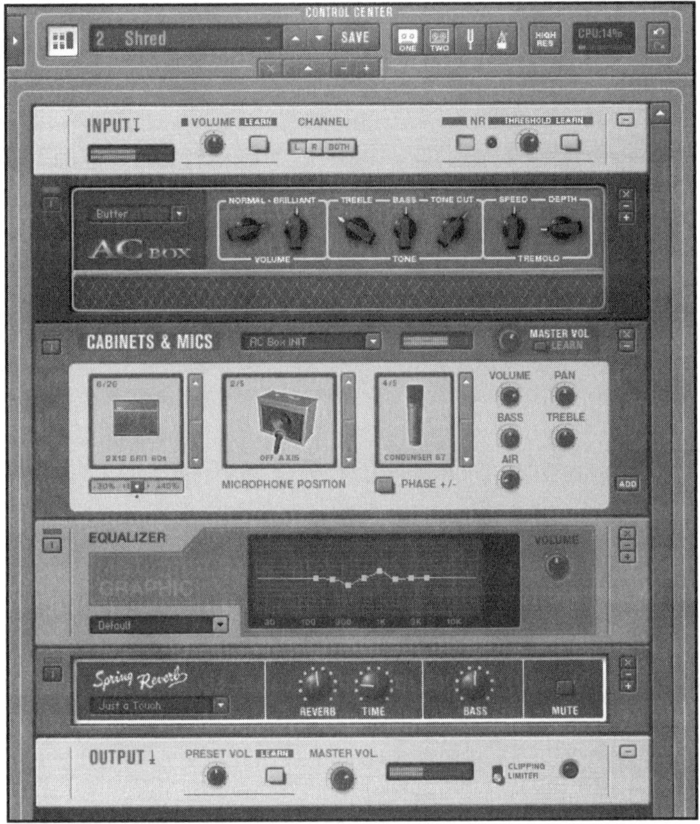

Figure 10.9
Building a simple rig.

Simply clicking and dragging is all it takes to build a rig. The placement of the components is not predetermined; you can specify precisely where you want your modules to appear and in which order. You can also move any module by clicking on it in your rack and dragging it to a new location.

On any individual module, there are a few buttons we need to identify. Figure 10.10 will detail these for you.

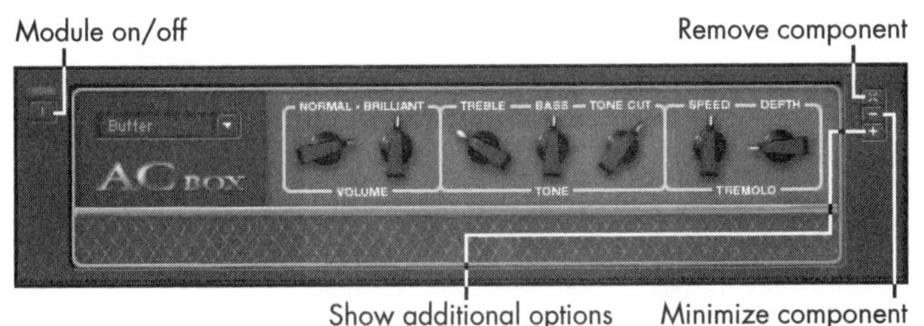

Figure 10.10
Component controls.

The on/off switch simply turns that module's processing effect, while the X removes the module completely from your rig. The – button minimizes the module to its absolute smallest visual state (great for long complicated rigs), while the + button (if present in the module) reveals additional controls for the module. In the case of the AC Box pictured in Figure 10.11, the additional controls revealed are extra ways to tweak the electrical nature of the amp. Tube bias, voltage sag, and even power supply frequency are options.

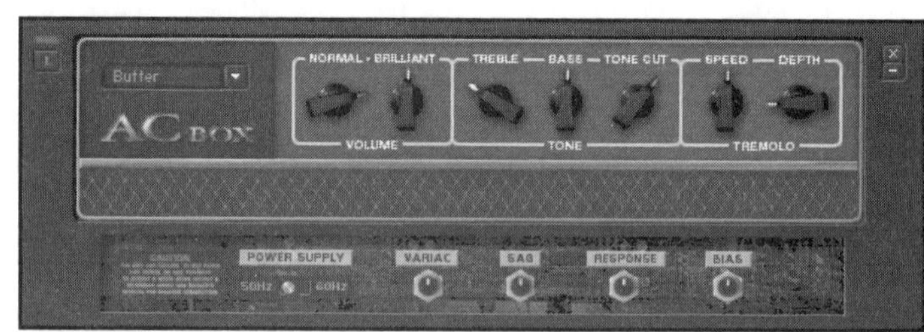

Figure 10.11
Additional parameters.

> **SEEK AND YE SHALL TWEAK**
> Almost every module in Guitar Rig has additional parameters that only become visible when you click the + button on the module's left side. Make sure when building your rigs that you explore the additional features of each module. This is one of the areas where Guitar Rig really shines—the amount of tweaking you can do to the sound through these extra parameters.

Now that we have given a very brief overview of the flow of Guitar Rig, let's take a look at all the modules available to us. We begin with the amps, cabinets, and microphones.

The Amps, Cabinets, and Mics

Guitar Rig does not disappoint with its selection of amps. A total of eight amps are available:

- **Tweedman**: A '60s bassman.
- **AC Box**: The venerable AC-30.
- **Twang Reverb**: A good ol' twin Reverb.
- **Plexi**: Everyone's favorite plexiglas-paneled amp.
- **Jazz Amp**: The amazing, clean JC-120.
- **Lead 800**: The sound of '80s metal, the JCM800 series.
- **Gratifier**: Dual rectifiers, anyone?
- **Bass VT**: At last a bass amp!

In Guitar Rig, when you drop in any amp, you automatically get a cabinet and a microphone added to your rig, based on the amp model you choose. We're going to talk about the cabinets and microphones in just a moment.

To get a look at our amps, we are going to drop all the amps into one long rig and show them in greater detail. The amp pane of the left side shows very small icons for each amp, so Figures 11.12 and 11.13 (I can't fit them all in one shot) show all of our amps in one rig. It's not exactly a practical rig, but it's visually compelling, to say the least.

Figure 10.12
Guitar Rig amps.

Part of the fun of Guitar Rig is that you can have multiple amps in the same rig. The only limitation is the amount of processing power your system has—Guitar Rig has no preset limit on the number of simultaneous modules.

Figure 10.13
More Guitar Rig amps.

Now that we've seen the amps, let's check out the cabinet and microphone sections.

When you load up an amp in Guitar Rig, there is always an associated cabinet that comes along with it. This module is aptly named the Cabinets & Mics. You can actually have a cabinet module without having an amp as well. Figure 10.14 shows the module in action.

Part of the fun of Guitar Rig is that you can have as many cabinets as you'd like. There are a total of 26 different amplifier cabinets, such as small 1×12 enclosures, modern and vintage stacks, bass enclosures, Leslie rotating speaker cabinets, and even a direct box. You could take a single amplifier and run it through 20 different cabinets if you wanted to! Under the cabinet selector, you can even change the virtual size of the cabinet to make it sound larger. There are further controls for Air (Early Reflection), Pan, Bass, Treble, Volume, and Distance (only visible when you have multiple cabinets together).

The microphone section lets you select your microphone and position it on the speaker.

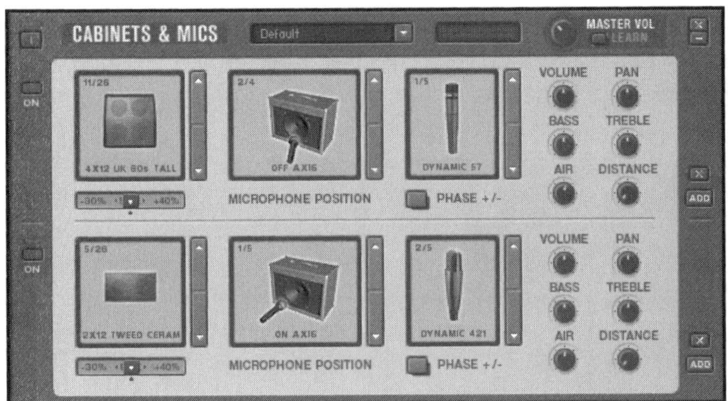

Figure 10.14
Cabinets & Mics.

CAB CHOICES

In Guitar Rig, the type of microphone available to you depends on what kind of cabinet you have selected. The guitar cabinets have guitar microphones, and the bass cabs have a different selection of microphones more suited to bass. Unfortunately, you cannot mix and match, because the cabinet modeling was done using convolution technology (previously described in Chapter 8, "Waves GTR System"). Each amp had to be modeled with each microphone at the varying positions, and not every cabinet was paired with each microphone. That being said, there are still plenty of choices for sound design.

On the guitar cabinets, there are five microphones to choose from, ranging from condensers to dynamic microphones, and you can place the microphones in either four or five different spots (on-axis, off-axis, edge, far, and back), depending on the cabinet chosen. This is because some amps have sealed backs instead of unsealed backs, and rear mic positioning is a possibility. The bass cabinets also have five microphones (although they are different microphones than the guitars use) and usually four choices for microphone position on the cabinet (the fifth choice is to mic the horn of the cabinet, if available).

The rotator cabinets are unique in that they have a predetermined microphone for each cabinet, although you can use any of the five microphone positions available to the guitar cabs.

As you can see, a lot of thought and design went into this module. By placing multiple cabinets and varying their positions and microphone placements, you can achieve a great deal of sonic variety in your rigs.

Distortion Devices

The amp's modules alone offer many guitar players enough distortion to suit their needs, but the distortion pedal refuses to go away! Many guitar players still love the sound of a

Tubescreamer before their favorite amp. With this in mind, Guitar Rig ships with 10 distortion devices that you can add to your rig to expand its sonic potential. Figures 10.15 and 10.16 show all of the distortion devices available for your rigs.

Figure 10.15
Distortion pedals 1.

Let's give you a rundown of the devices:

- **Fuzz Ace**: Jimi would approve of this fuzz.
- **Big Fuzz**: The ubiquitous "muff" sound.
- **Cat**: Not cat, rat (and not the '80s hair band either)!
- **Skreamer**: My favorite green distortion device.
- **Mezone**: Gobs and gobs of black death distortion.
- **Demon**: Truly possessed sounds.
- **TransAmp**: If you liked the SansAmp, you'll love the TransAmp!
- **Treble Booster**: A generic treble booster that can overdrive an otherwise clean amp or provide a bit of extra bite for your lead sounds.

Figure 10.16
Distortion pedals 2.

- **Distortion**: The distortion module provides a very basic overdrive-based distortion for guitar rig.
- **Gain Booster**: Tube amps react to the amount of incoming gain. The more juice you give an amp, the more saturated your sound gets. This simple, single-knobbed device puts more signal into the amp.

As with anything else in this program, you can chain as many devices as you feel like. The best part is that they never run out of batteries.

Next up—modulation!

Modulation Devices

A modulation device is anything that changes the sound over time. Chorus is a great example of a modulation device. Guitar Rig provides you with all the common modulation devices you could ever need. Figures 10.17 and 10.18 show the expanded view of all the modulation devices found in Guitar Rig 2.

Let's list the devices in more detail:

- **Tremolo**: Good old-fashioned tremolo!
- **Ensemble**: A rich and lush chorus device.
- **Chorus + Flanger**: Two for the price of one: chorus and flanging.

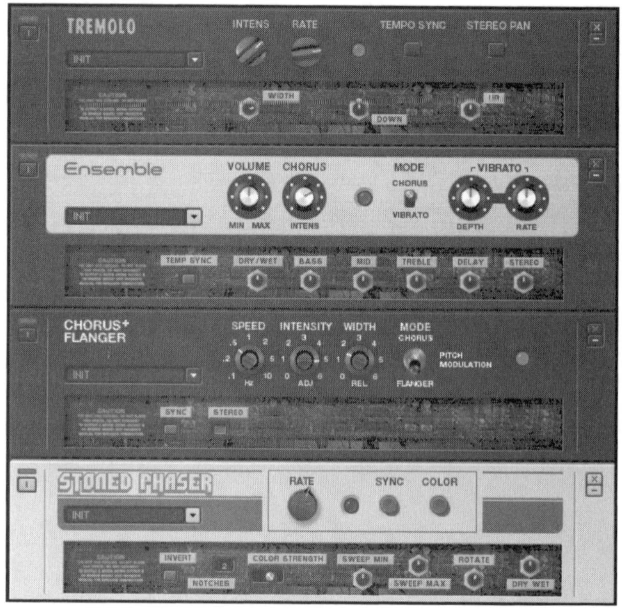

Figure 10.17
Modulation devices 1.

- **Stoned Phaser**: A tempo-synchable phaser for swirling sounds.
- **Rotator**: A Leslie rotating speaker direct from Native Instruments' B4 instrument.
- **Oktaver**: This pedal shifts your sound one and two octaves lower than the original. Great for bottom-dwelling and bass-stealing lines.
- **Pitch Pedal**: The hardware whammy pedal by DigiTech was a blast to use, and so is this one. Includes harmony, in addition to simple pitch-shifting up to two octaves up and down.

Figure 10.18
Modulation devices 2.

The next section of modules are EQ-based devices. Let's get funky with those.

EQ Modules

Our next section of modules is collectively called EQ modules. If you think that the definition of EQ is confined to Hi, Mid, and Low controls, you've got another thing coming! Effects like Wah-wah pedals and filters are all considered EQ devices, as they alter the frequency content of your sound. A picture is worth a thousand words, so Figures 10.19 and 10.20 show all of the EQ-based components.

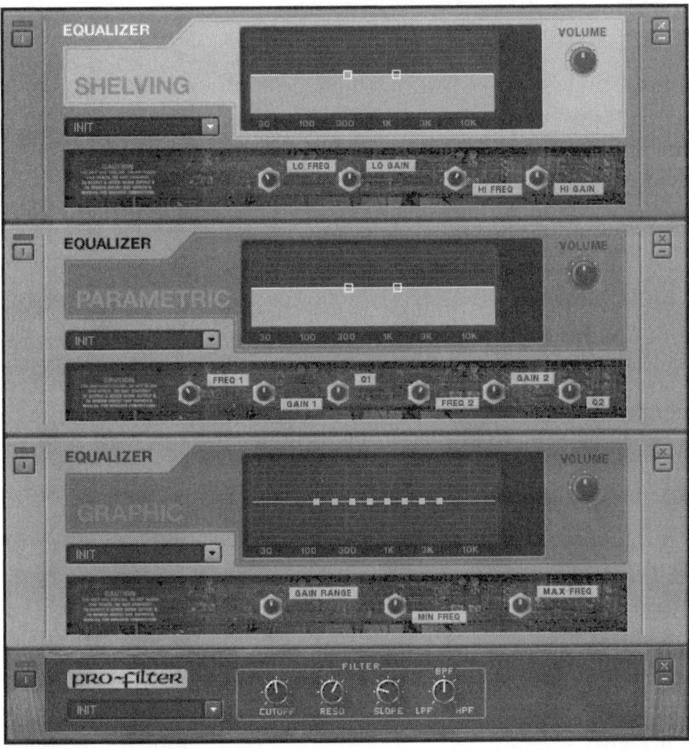

Figure 10.19
EQ modules 1.

Here are the modules listed in detail:

- **EQ Shelving**: This is a two-band EQ that boosts or attenuates a shelf of frequencies either below or above the set point. Great for rolling off low-end rumble and taming high frequencies.

Figure 10.20
EQ modules 2.

- **EQ Parametric**: A parametric EQ allows you to select two specific frequency bands and boost or attenuate just those bands. Using that "q" control, you can achieve a surgical cut of a specific frequency or widen the reach to other surrounding frequencies.
- **EQ Graphic**: A sophisticated eight-band EQ that allows you to graphically shape your sound using any of the eight preset bands.
- **Pro-Filter**: An analog filter derived from Native Instrument Pro-53, which is an emulation of the famous Sequential Circuits Prophet 5 synthesizer. If you like synth-style filtering, it doesn't get any better than this. (It's unusual for guitarists to have synthesizer-type filters in guitar setups, so this particular filter can yield some interesting results.)
- **Autofilter**: An auto Wah-wah filter that responds to the strength of your incoming picking signal. The harder you play, the more the auto Wah-wah responds. Great for porn soundtracks.
- **WahWah**: A good old-fashioned Wah-wah pedal, modeled after the famous Vox Wah-wah.
- **TalkWah**: A Wah-wah pedal that has been designed to emulate the frequency characteristics of the human mouth. You can get a bit of the old Frampton Comes Alive sound if you set this one right. If you're crazy, you can use this one to talk to yourself as well—really popular at psych wards.
- **CryWah**: If you favor the Crybaby over the Vox Wah-wah, this is the Wah-wah for you.

EQ TIP

The EQ modules can work well before or after the actual amplifier. The Wah-wahs really need to be placed before the amp for that authentic sound, while the other components can shape your signal before it hits the amp, or after amplification to shape your overall tone.

The Pro-Filter sounds good almost anywhere you stick it.

We are moving right along now. Next up are the volume components.

Volume Components

The next batch of modules operate on the volume in one way or another. These can be simple volume pedals, limiters, and compressors, or even noise reducers. Figure 10.21 shows all of the volume components lined up in a pretty little row.

Figure 10.21
Volume modules.

Let's take a closer look at our available volume module choices:

- **Volume Adjustment Pedal:** Place this before the amp, and you will vary the amount of signal that hits the amp, essentially replicating your guitar's volume knob with your foot. Place it at the end of your rig to have an *actual* full volume control!
- **Limiter**: A limiter is a very special compressor. You tell it what the absolute maximum signal can be, and anything that reaches that level is turned down. It's basically a brick wall for sound, useful for smoothing out peaks in your sound and raising the overall level. Don't set it too low, or it will squash the life out of your sound.
- **Noisegate**: A noisegate is simply a device that closes the signal path when the signal drops below a predetermined level. You set the noisegate with the threshold control low enough to cut out the background noise, while still allowing your natural signal and signal decay to stay intact.
- **Noise Reduction**: Noise reduction is an intelligent way to get rid of noise. Instead of a gate that simply closes off the lower ends of the dynamic range (where noise resides), the reducer actually looks for the sonic fingerprint of noise and eliminates it from your signal. This is great for getting rid of buzzes and other noises you don't want.
- **Stomp Compressor**: This is an emulation of a stompbox-style compressor that evens out the dynamic range of an input signal. The effect, when applied moderately, can smooth out your sound, and when pushed, it can supersaturate an amplifier with nothing but full-on, hot signal.
- **Tube Compressor**: Another compressor, but this one is modeled after a studio tube-style compressor. This yields a more polished, warmer sound than the Stomp Compressor.

Next up: Reverb effects!

Reverb

Reverbs, short for reverberations, are very short delays that emulate the effect of an amplifier playing in an actual room in which the sound is being absorbed by some walls, being reflected off other walls, and coming back to your ears. In Guitar Rig, reverb not only encompasses traditional reverbs, but also delays. Figure 10.22 details all four choices in the Reverb bank.

Let's take a look at the individual modules:

- **Spring Reverb**: Amp-style spring reverb.
- **Studio Reverb**: Digital-style reverb.
- **Quad Delay**: A four-tap delay with tap time features, also tempo-synchable.

Figure 10.22
Reverb/Delay modules.

- **Psychedelay**: A delay with a few neat features. The delay goes in reverse. You can even mute the direct signal and play backwards, while you play forwards. Tap tempo-enabled and tempo-synchable.

Golly gee, those are a lot of reverb and delay effects! But wait, there's more…

Special Tools

Within the next section of tools are a very special section of tools. Rather than show you screenshots of all of them, this section deserves a bit more attention because the features are quite revolutionary.

The first module is the Loop Machine. According to Native Instruments, the requests for a loop-style machine were overwhelming. Users asked, and the company listened. The Loop Machine is a component that allows you to record layered guitar loops on the fly, right from within Guitar Rig. Figure 10.23 shows the Loop Machine's interface.

The Loop Machine allows you to record a background track of chords and then solo over them. You can also keep layering guitar parts and build up elegant harmonies as solo parts. Since the buttons can be assigned to the Rig Kontrol (more on this later), you can do this all with your feet—you never have to miss a note. The Loop Machine can sync with your host tempo or the tempo of Guitar Rig's built-in metronome, ensuring that you are always in time with the beat.

Figure 10.23
The Loop Machine.

Any of the individual layers, or even a mix of the layers, can be exported as WAV files and used in your sequencer of choice. It's a great little sketchpad for ensuring that moments of inspiration aren't lost.

The next module is the Split module. Can you image being able to have two amps onstage, one for clean sounds and one for dirty sounds? Imagine that each amp has its own set of effects that is different from the other amp. Sure, you could just quickly switch presets, but what if you wanted to do this dynamically, in real time? What if you wanted to control your mix between the two setups? If any of this sounds cool to you, the Split module is for you. It's best to see it in action, so I can easily explain what you're looking at. Figure 10.24 is a simple two-amplifier split with basic effects.

Figure 10.24
The Split module in action.

Under Split A, you have a rig consisting of a Skreamer into a Tweedman, and under Split B, you have a rig with a Quad Delay and an AC Box amp. Below that is the Split Mix control. When this is assigned to the expression pedal of the Rig Kontrol, you simply switch between these completely separate rigs just by rocking your foot back and forth. You can press the pedal fully for a true split, or you can set the pedal anywhere in-between to get a mix of both sounds. Since Guitar Rig allows two inputs, you can use the Stereo Input L/R Split to run two guitars (or guitar and bass) through Guitar Rig, and each can have its own amp. Pretty neat.

In the same vein as the Split module is the Crossover Mix module. Instead of using a pedal to simply select two different rigs, the Crossover Split uses a frequency band to set which signal goes to which rig. That's right, you can use this module to send your low strings to one amp and your high strings to another.

Figure 10.25 shows the same setup from before, using a Crossover Split.

Figure 10.25
The Crossover Split module.

For a simple and practical example, imagine this: I simply want my power chording to have no reverb, through a very dirty amp, but when I go to solo, I'd like a sound with some delay and possibly a different amp's sound. Using the Crossover Split module, I can set up a low sound for my chording and a high sound for my solos, and if I set the frequency right (which takes some experimenting), I don't need to use a traditional split and do any work with my feet. The minute I cross over to the higher strings, my signal goes to the other sound. Like the original split mix, there is a Crossfader that you can assign to a foot controller if you wish. I believe that this module is one of the true gems of Guitar Rig and has to be heard to be believed.

Amazingly enough, we have one more section of modules to explore. Guitar Rig simply calls this section MDF, which stands for Modulation Framework.

Modifiers

A modifier is designed to modify your signal dynamically as you play. Traditional synthesizer players know this as modulation. Through the modifiers, you can add synthesis, like attacks and releases, note triggers and complex envelopes, to create sounds you've never heard before! It's a feature that only Guitar Rig has, and it allows for unbridled creativity.

First, let's take a look at all the modifier components, as shown in Figure 10.26.

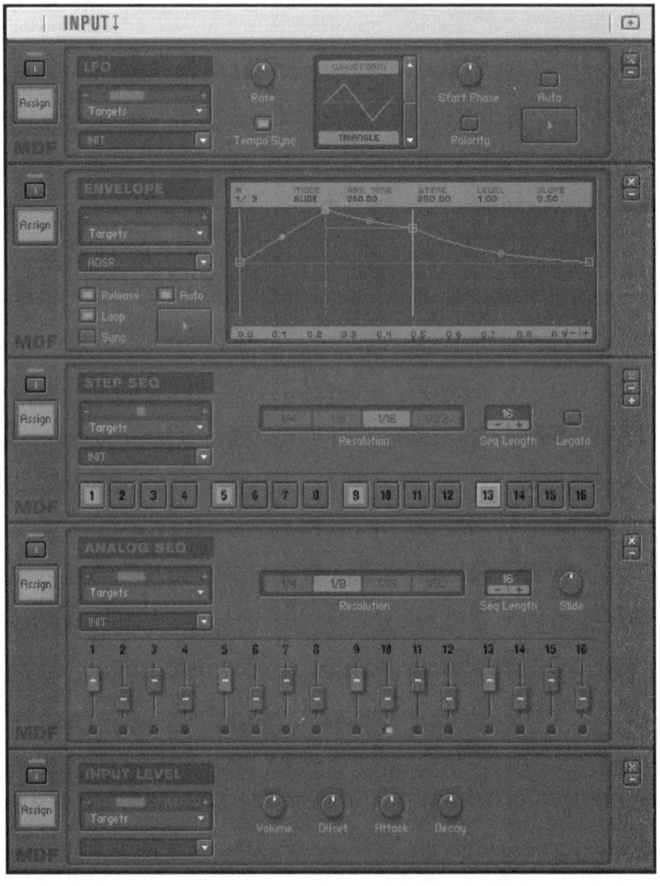

Figure 10.26
Modifiers!

Let's focus on one of the modules in depth, and if you are really intrigued in the power of what the modifiers can do, you need to read *Guitar Rig 2 Power!* by Orren Merton.

The module we will look at is the Input Level module. Simply, this module reacts to the force of your incoming signal and passes that information along to another source. This is the heart of modulation. Regardless of what the modulation source is, there is always a target—something is being changed as a result.

We are going to use the Input Level module to move the Gain control on our amp as you pick. The softer you pick, the lower the Gain knob rolls to; the harder you pick, the dirtier the signal gets. Look at Figure 10.27 to see how we did it.

Figure 10.27
Input modulation.

What I did was set up the Input Level modulator in front of an amp. On the left side of the modulator is a big button that says Assign. All I have to do is click and drag the Assign knob and drop it on any control I want to modulate. In this case, I dropped it on the normal Volume knob of the AC Box amp. This created a ghost knob image there, and as I play, this ghost knob image will move with the strength of my picking. I have now created an amp that dynamically responds to the strength of my picking.

I can also assign the same parameter to other effects, other amps, etc. Basically, if it has a control knob, it can be modulated this way. You can even have one modulator, such as my input signal modulator, mapped to several controls. It could turn up the gain and the brightness while changing delay depth, all at the same time.

Imagine the possibilities with this one modifier and multiply that by a factor of ten. The other modifiers are based on LFOs, Envelopes, and Step Sequencers. This is by far the most cutting-edge feature of Guitar Rig—something no one else has yet to offer. Not only can you create presets that live and breathe, but you can also make some unbelievably strange noises, too. (Some of you guys probably like that kinda stuff.)

Amazingly, that is the last series of modules you can add to Guitar Rig, and also amazingly, I'm not done yet! There are a few fixed components inside Guitar Rig that we need to list.

Fixed Components

Guitar Rig has several components that are fixed (always there). These include tapedecks, a tuner, and a metronome. You have the ability to hide them when not in use, but they are always "on" in some regard.

Figure 10.28 shows all the fixed components in view, with no other modules showing.

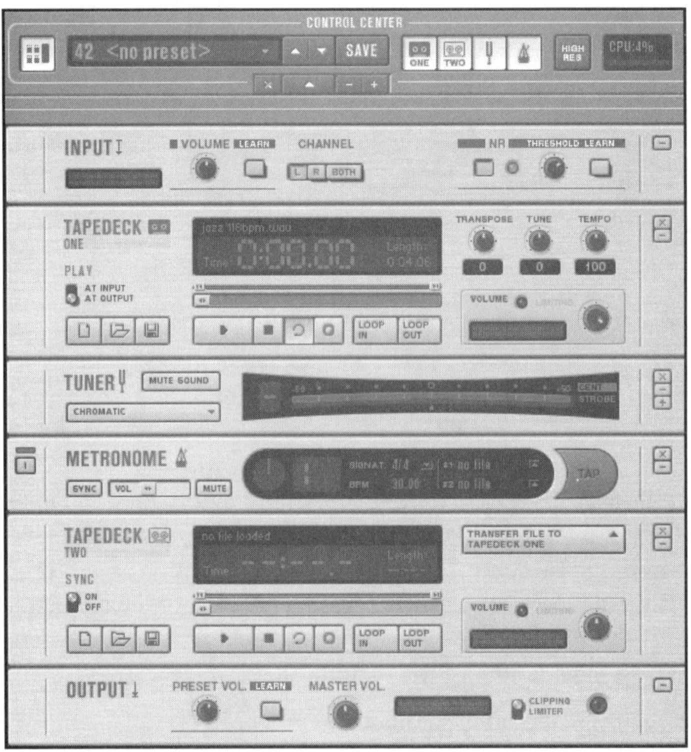

Figure 10.28
Fixed components.

Let's detail what the components are and what they do:

- **Input**: Here you set your input level, or simply have Guitar Rig learn a proper level for you. You can choose which channel your guitar is coming in on and initiate some noise reduction at the input stage, which can also be learned by Guitar Rig with the click of a button.
- **Tapedeck One**: This tapedeck plays back prerecorded tracks so you can play over them. You can also record into it, transpose, return, and time-stretch the tracks to fit your music. The recording feature has been far eclipsed by the new Loop Machine, but the playback feature is great for loading in drum loops or any song you want to jam over. Tapedeck One always appears at the beginning of your signal chain.
- **Tuner:** Everyone needs a good tuner. This one has preset tunings for guitar, bass, and common alternate tunings. You can switch between traditional cent tuning and the more advanced strobe mode for even finer control. Onstage, the Mute Sound button is handy for silent tuning in-between songs.
- **Metronome**: A good metronome is a great practice tool, and it's nice to see one included here. You can sync it to your host clock to make sure your licks are in time, or, out of host mode, you can set it to any tempo you feel like. It supports standard and odd time signatures, as well as loading in WAV sounds of the metronome beeps.
- **Tapedeck Two**: This tapedeck appears at the end of your rig and records the total output of your sound into a WAV file. You can load a file into the first tapedeck as a backing track, play through your rig, and record it all through the second tapedeck. You can then transfer the file back to the first tapedeck and start all over. Much of this functionality has been replaced by the Loop Machine module, but the tapedecks are very handy.
- **Output**: Your final sound levels. The program can learn a perfect preset volume with a single button click and adjust your master volume. You can also choose how to deal with signals that are too loud: either let them clip, or engage the built-in limiter to take care of the peaks.

The last thing to talk about is how to integrate the Rig Kontrol into the application to make the most of your feet.

Kontrol

The Rig Kontrol is a thing of beauty. You can finally control the parameters of your on-screen rigs with your feet. Setting up what the Rig Kontrol does in each preset couldn't be any easier. Guitar Rig employs a simple Learn functionality on every button, switch, and knob on the interface. This Learn functionality doesn't stop with the Rig Kontrols. You can learn any parameter through an attached MIDI controller as well.

To learn a control on the interface to the Rig Kontrol (or other MIDI device), you can either right-click on the control or Control+click on the Mac, which will bring up the menu shown in Figure 10.29.

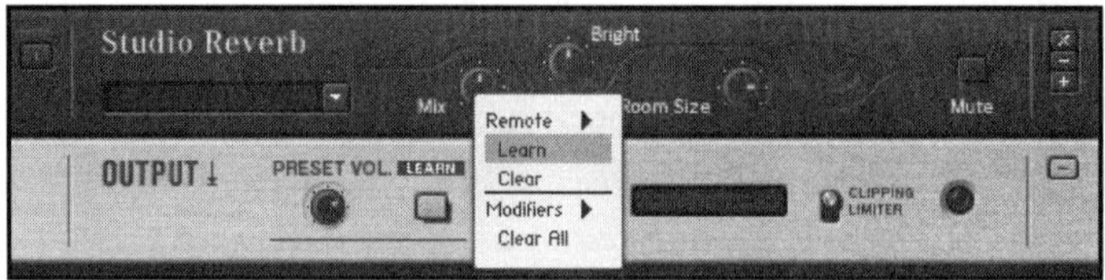

Figure 10.29
Controller Learn.

Once you select Learn, Guitar Rig simply waits for the next controller event to map automatically. You simply press the desired foot pedal or expression controller, and voilà, you are automatically mapped to that control.

Each preset can have its own set of learned commands. To view the state of how your Rig Kontrol is set up for each preset, you need to look at the lower-left corner of your Guitar Rig screen. You find a graphic of the Rig Kontrol showing what each controller is mapped to. Figure 10.30 shows an example of a fully mapped Rig Kontrol and its corresponding controls.

Figure 10.30
Your Rig Kontrol!

As you can see, each knob on the Rig Kontrol 2 is mapped to a different function. Elements like amplifier boost, LFO on/off, delay mute, and delay tap tempo are routed to the buttons on the face of the Rig Kontrol, while the expression controller takes are of the rotating speaker speed, and its footswitch turns the rotary effect on and off.

You can go through the factory presets, easily learn new commands for the buttons of your choice, and save them writing the presets. It really is that easy! You can have exactly the control you want, just the way you like it.

And that, my friend, is the 800-pound gorilla they call Guitar Rig. Next up in our odyssey is a look into the world of DSP card solutions.

11 DSP Systems: UAD and Powercore

In the world of native computer processing, the single most frustrating factor is running out of processing power for your system. Plug-ins require CPU power, and the more you run them, the less "oomph" you have for other tasks. Besides Pro Tools TDM systems, other solutions exist to add to the processing power of your system. Special DSP processor cards are available from Universal Audio and T.C. Electronic, which can extend the power of your system. Luckily for us, these DSP processors not only contain high-quality effects for mixing, but they also provide guitar amp simulators. The two systems we will be looking at are the UAD-1 card from Universal Audio and the Powercore system from T.C. Electronic.

Universal Audio UAD-1: Nigel

In 2000, Universal Audio introduced the UAD-1 Card, a PCI card that provided power for its own set of audio processing plug-ins. In the year 2000, computers were faster than ever before, but nothing like the speed we have now. Running loads of plug-ins, especially high-quality effects simultaneously, was a balancing act. With a single PCI card, UAD changed the rules of the game for users who relied on native solutions and couldn't afford the built-in power of a professional Pro Tools TDM system. UAD is a hardware and software solution. The card provides the DSP power to run only the plug-ins made by Universal Audio on the UAD card—you can't just run anything you want through the UAD card. Thankfully, Universal Audio has been making some of the best hardware audio processors in the business for a long time, and they know a thing or two about good sound. The plug-ins that come with UAD are a cross-section of reverbs, EQs, compressors, a guitar simulator, and other effects, which we will detail later in the book. Universal Audio makes hardware reproductions of two of the most sought-after compressors on the planet: the 1176 and the LA-2A. Studios consider these hardware compressors standard for darn good reason—because they sound incredible. Universal Audio has emulated its own hardware reproductions digitally on the UAD card. All this is well and good, but this is a guitar book, so we need to focus on the guitar side of things.

Nigel is UAD's guitar modeling solution, comically named after Nigel Tufnel, the guitarist in the immortal rock epic *This Is Spinal Tap*. Nigel is actually a combination of a bunch of different plug-ins grouped together with a guitar modeler in the middle. Let's take a look at the plug-in itself and talk about what you see in Figure 11.1.

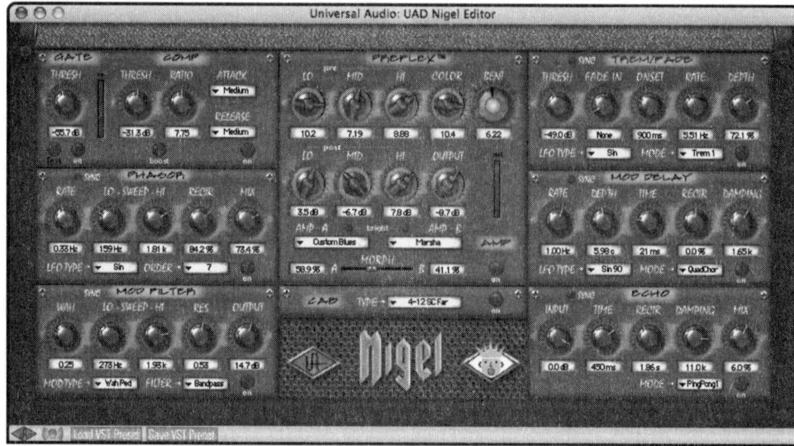

Figure 11.1
Nigel: An overview.

As you can see, there is quite a bit to look at. This single plug-in combines the following: Amp simulation, Tremolo, Mod Delay, Echo, Gate/Compression, Phasor, and Mod Filtering. We are going to focus on the Preflex and Cab sections of the plug-in, as seen in Figure 11.2, since they are specific to guitar modeling.

Figure 11.2
Preflex and Cab.

The Preflex module is where we work with the virtual amplifier—actually two in this case—and the Cab module allows us to select and emulate a speaker cabinet.

The Preflex Module

The Preflex module is broken down into a few visual sections. From high to low, you deal with preamp controls, postamp controls, amplifier selectors, and amplifier morph controls. Let's break down the plug-in piece by piece.

The first section of controls you encounter are the Pre modules, which control the sound of the virtual preamp (see Figure 11.3).

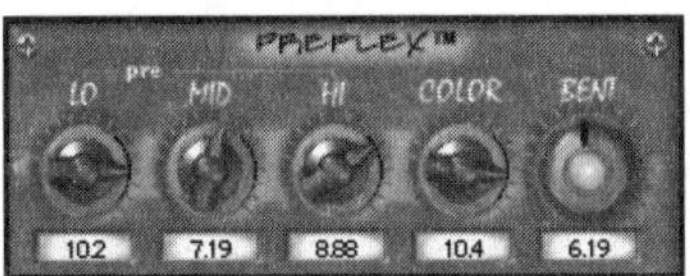

Figure 11.3
Nigel's Pre controls.

These controls shape the sound of the preamp section of the amplifier—these are most representative of the controls you would see on a real amp. A three-band EQ section of Lo, Mid, and Hi allows for rudimentary tweaking of your guitar's tone. The Color knob acts as a "super EQ" knob, changing several characteristics of the chosen amp at once. Since the documentation is a bit spotty about this knob, my guess is that it emulates different response curves on the tubes and the EQ section. Since the functionality is not fixed and changes from amp to amp, this knob falls into the realm of "Tweak and ye shall hear what it does." The next knob, Bent, has a definite purpose, which is gain. This is where you dial in your distortion! All of these controls affect your sound before the amplifier is engaged.

Below the Pre controls are a row of Post controls, as seen in Figure 11.4.

Figure 11.4
The Post controls.

We start with a row of Lo, Mid, and Hi EQs. These EQs differ from the Pre EQ controls in that they affect the signal after it has been amplified. You can use these to shape the character of the amp's overall sound, not just your guitar's signal when it hits the tubes. Next to the EQ is a simple output knob, which sets the overall loudness of the amp. A vertical level meter gives visual feedback on your overall level, so you can adjust it using the output knob to gain the desired level without clipping.

Next up, or actually down in this case, is the amplifier selector. In Nigel, you can run two amplifiers at once and morph between them. What's unique is that each amp shares the same Pre and Post controls above. This means that however you set up one amp, you set up the other as well. The trick is that each amp is different, and although the values are shared from amp to amp, their sounds will not be the same. The amps are chosen using a pull-down menu under Amp-A and Amp-B, as seen in Figure 11.5.

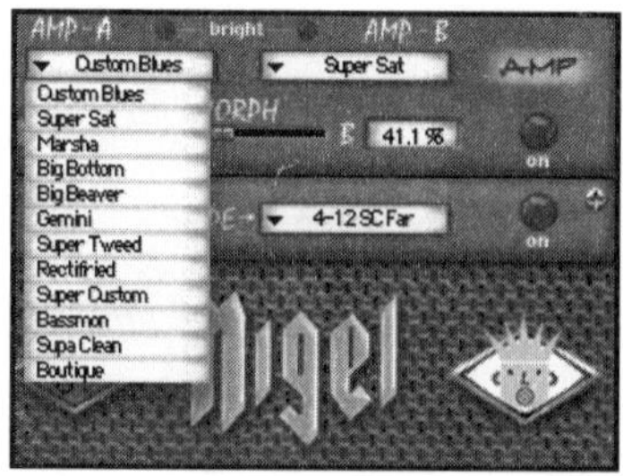

Figure 11.5
Selecting amplifier models.

There are a total of 12 amp models to choose from. The amps are as follows:

- **Rectified**: Modern/Hi gain.
- **Marsha**: Add a few L's, and you'll have it.
- **Bassmon**: American-style clean and mild overdrive.
- **Boutique**: Custom amps (read: expensive).
- **Custom Blues**: Lower-gain Blues drive.
- **Supa Clean**: A direct connection (no amp).
- **Supa Sat**: Heaps of gain.
- **Gemini**: A twin-style amp.
- **Big Beaver**: Stomp box pedal emulations.
- **Super Custom**: Another custom amp, with more gain than the Custom Blues model.
- **Big Bottom**: Use this for bass.
- **Super Tweed**: Small American-style amp, turned all the way up.

This list of amps can be selected in either the A or B slot. Once you've got those loaded up, you can use the Morph feature, shown in Figure 11.6, to mix the sounds between them.

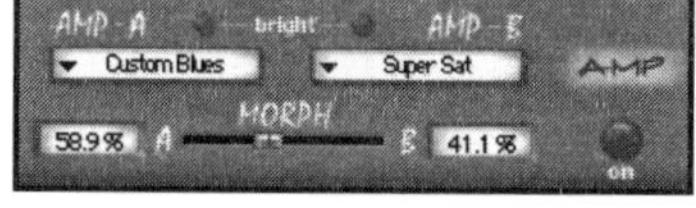

Figure 11.6
Morph your amps.

The last thing left to talk about with the amps is the bright switch, shown in Figure 11.7.

Figure 11.7
Bright switch.

Each amp has its own bright switch, which will glow red when engaged. This simply brings out the higher frequencies a bit more and, well, makes the amps brighter.

Now that you have the amps all loaded up, you need to get some cabinets paired with your amps.

The Cab Module

Every good amp needs a good cabinet, right? Well, this is where the Cab module comes in. This module is really simple. A single pull-down menu allows you to access 23 different cabinet models, as seen in Figure 11.8.

Figure 11.8
The Cab module with cabinet choices.

The venerable SM-57 was used to capture each cabinet at varying positions in relation to the speaker. On-axis, off-axis, edge, and far are all microphone placements used in the cabinet modeling process. As you would expect, a variety of cabinets were used with varying speaker sizes and microphone techniques. The list of 23 choices is a fixed set. You cannot choose your cab and vary the mic position; these are all fixed cabinet and microphone choices. Thankfully, 23 should be enough to get you through.

UAD Latency

One of the great things about the UAD card is that it allows you to run some very high-quality effects with almost no strain on your CPU. The only negative is that the UAD card incurs a fixed amount of latency when used. This is the nature of the beast when using this kind of PCI audio DSP card. Now, this is *not* all bad news. Most common host applications will compensate for the latency automatically when you play back, so you won't even notice it. In the case of Nigel, the latency you monitor with while playing live cannot be compensated for.

UAD has a fixed amount of latency that is exactly double that of your host application. This is because the audio has to make a round trip from your software into the card and then back again. If you set your host (Cubase, for example) for 256 samples of buffer latency, the UAD card will be 512 samples off (approximately 11 milliseconds at 44.1 kHz sample rate). Other applications, such as Logic, have their own internal process buffer that can result in even more samples of latency when using the UAD-1 card. This will only be heard when you are recording through the card in real time. The minute you go back to playback mode to hear what you've done, the latency compensation factor of Cubase will take care of this and line things right up. It's only when tracking that you will be a bit delayed. As for how much delay 11 milliseconds feels like, it can feel like the computer is lagging behind a bit. Audio interfaces that support lower latency rates, such as 128 samples, would reduce the latency to around 6 milliseconds, which is not enough to bother your timing. As the buffers get higher, it will feel like you're walking in a strobe light—nothing lines up.

As for the delay, some players simply deal with it, while some mute the sound from the plug-in and monitor the direct sound of the guitar another way (such as direct monitoring on a sound card). The issue with this is that you're not getting to hear Nigel until you play back. While recording, you get a dry, unaffected signal. Many players find that the sound of the amp has a direct result on the sound of their performance. Monitoring without the sound of the plug-in can be a negative thing, so latency must be dealt with in the most agreeable way. This is certainly my only beef with DSP cards. Not every one suffers from this, but UAD currently has a fixed delay of twice your host latency. Nevertheless, the card sounds rather good, and exceptions can be made with regards to latency.

UAD FOR GUITAR?

Should you buy a DSP card solution, such as UAD, just for the guitar processing? In my opinion, that would be a mistake. The UAD card offers useable guitar processing effects, but it really shines in every other respect. As a recording musician, you will be hard pressed to find better-sounding plug-ins than the UAD compressors, EQs, and reverbs. The fact that you get a guitar processor included with the rest of the plug-ins, and that these plug-ins don't take away from your CPU, is all gravy. All in all, it is one of my favorite tools to mix with, but Nigel, compared to the other guitar plug-ins on the market, isn't amazing in itself. It pales in comparison to Waves' and Native Instruments' offerings. What is amazing is that the UAD card continues to evolve, and new plug-ins are released for the card on a regular basis. Who knows, maybe Nigel will be replaced by something on the level of their EQs and compressors, which are about as top-notch as they come in the audio world. We can only hope! As I said, don't buy it just for Nigel.

UA Goodies

Recently, Universal Audio and Roland have teamed up to use the UAD platform to bring back a few of the most sought-after guitar effects in Roland's history: The CE-1 Chorus Ensemble and the SDD-320 Dimension D Chorus/Spatial enhancer. These two pieces of gear are long out of production, extremely sought-after, and *really* hard to find. Not only has UAD brought them back to life in virtual form, but they have done them true to the original! While these effects don't fall under amplifier modeling and might fit better in Chapter 14, "Mixing Strategies for Guitar," I want to mention them here because they are part of the UAD package and are of particular interest to guitar players. Figure 11.9 shows the CE-1, and Figure 11.10 shows the Dimension D in action.

Figure 11.9
Roland CE-1 Chorus Ensemble.

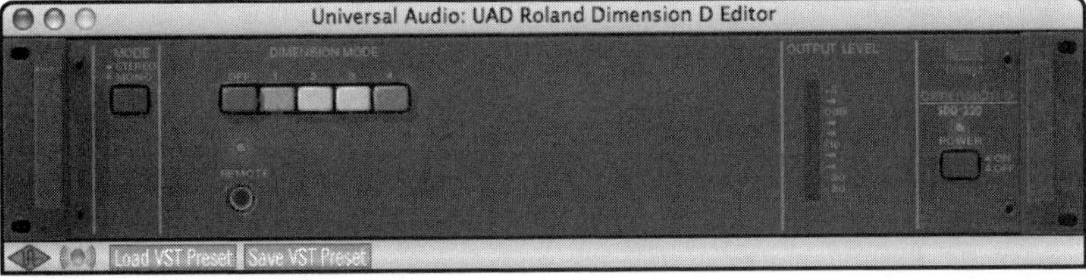

Figure 11.10
Roland Dimension D Editor.

T.C. Electronic Powercore

The Powercore system is a DSP system that is very similar to UAD. Both allow you to take strain off your computer by adding special DSP cards. Powercore is a bit different in two ways. First, Powercore is available as a PCI card for a desktop computer (just like UAD), but it is also available in two Firewire versions that run on desktops and laptops. (UAD could be run on a laptop, but that would require an expensive PCI-to-PCMCIA adapter.) Just like UAD, Powercore runs its own breed of plug-ins that are designed exclusively for the Powercore platform. Also similar to UAD, T.C. Electronic has reissued some of its classic signal processing equipment, especially their high-end reverbs and mastering processors, as optional plug-ins for the Powercore platform. The second difference is that other developers are able to port their plug-ins to the Powercore platform. Companies like Access, Sony, and Novation are allowing you to run their high-end plug-ins on the Powercore card! Besides Pro Tools TDM, this is currently the only DSP card solution that allows you to do that from third-party developers.

Luckily for us, Powercore includes some guitar modeling software. There are actually two different guitar modeling plug-ins for us to look at. The first Tubifex plug-in is included with all Powercore systems. There is also an optional TC Thirty plug-in that you'll learn about shortly.

Powercore: Tubifex

Included with all of the Powercore systems is the Tubifex plug-in, shown in Figure 11.11.

Figure 11.11
The Tubifex Editor screen.

Tubifex has a nice-looking interface, which I will break down into three main sections: the main amp controls, the tube section, and the noise/expander section.

HYBRID

Tubifex, like all of the Powercore plug-ins, can operate in an extremely low-latency mode. This is achieved by allowing the Powercore card to communicate directly with the computer at full blast when set to low latency mode. This will result in a more realistic experience, but will put more strain on your CPU. Even though Powercore was designed to take the burden off your CPU and offload it to the card, this technology allows you to handle latency easily when recording.

Tubifex is considered a hybrid plug-in because it uses parts of the Powercore DSP and your computer's CPU at all times.

Let's start with the main amp controls, as seen in Figure 11.12.

Figure 11.12
Tubifex main amp controls.

The Tubifex is designed to emulate a three-stage tube amplifier. What's unique about Tubifex is that you can actually adjust different parameters, such as tube voltage, to each of the three tubes independently of each other (more on this in a bit). Unlike a lot of the guitar modelers, Tubifex is not emulating many amps. It's emulating a '70s Marshall Super Lead.

If you look at Figure 11.12, you will see the main controls for the amp. Here is a list of their functions from left to right:

- **Trim**: This sets your input level into the amp.
- **Gain 1**: The amount of gain for the first tube. (You turn this on by clicking the button above the knob.)
- **Gain 2**: Gain for the second tube.
- **Lo, Mid, and Hi**: Your standard three-stage EQ, found on most every amp.
- **Gain 3**: Gain for the third tube. (This tube is after the EQ sections, while tubes one and two are before the EQ section.)
- **Master Out**: The overall level of the amplifier.
- **Speaker Pres**: Amount of high frequency "presence" in the speaker cone.

- **Speaker Dist**: Distance of the microphone to the speaker. You can choose close or 1 cm away.
- **Speaker Axis**: The orientation of the microphone's diaphragm to the center of the speaker, selectable by on-axis, medium axis, and off-axis.

Let's talk about the speaker modeling section (the last three controls). The speaker modeling in Tubifex is based on a single 2×12 Marshall speaker. You can't change the speaker type—it's a fixed model. The aspects that you can change are the distance and axis response of the microphone placed in front of the amplifier. The microphone is probably modeled after the SM57—big shock there.

Directly below the main row of controls, you have some other controls and one button in particular, which is the Expert button, as seen in Figure 11.13.

Figure 11.13
Expert mode.

Clicking this button will tweak the microcosmic aspects of the amplifier! When you activate Expert mode, you gain access to the tubes, as seen in Figure 11.14.

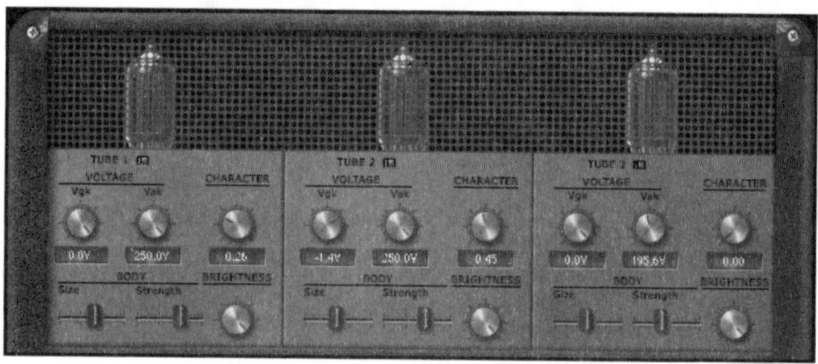

Figure 11.14
Expert tube settings.

In this section, you can control several aspects of the three preamp tubes. The tubes themselves can be activated, either from the top panel main controls or here in this lower pane.

Each tube has several controls that affect the voltage, bias, and tonality of the tubes. These controls can dramatically affect your sound, especially when mixing settings between the three tube stages.

Here are the controls and their explanations:

- **Vgk**: Grid to cathode potential. (This is a tube BIAS control.)
- **Vak**: Grid to anode potential. (This is the amount of voltage the tube receives.)
- **Character**: This affects the symmetry of the amplification. Turned to the left, you get more of a symmetrical sound, which is reminiscent of a power amp section. Turned to the right, you achieve an asymmetrical character, similar to how a preamp section responds.
- **Body (Size)**: This slider sets the amount of "girth" and low end in the tube's signal.
- **Body (Strength)**: The strength directly affects the size parameter. If the strength is slid to zero (all the way left), the size value will have no function. The size and strength sliders are closely tied.
- **Brightness**: This control attenuates the amount of high frequencies allowed through the tube stage. When turned all the way up, all frequencies are allowed to pass; as you turn it down, the upper shelf of frequencies become attenuated.

Each of the three tubes has identical controls, but can be set independently of each other. Remember that tubes one and two are pre EQ, while the third tube stage is after the EQ. Being able to change voltage and response to a tube like this is something you'd have a pretty hard time doing in the real world. But the results, once tweaked, are nothing short of amazing. I was really pretty impressed by the amount of tonal variation that I was able to impart on my sound.

The last section in Tubifex is a combination Noise Reduction and Expander section, (see Figure 11.15).

Figure 11.15
Noise Reduction and Expander.

The Noise Reduction is not just a gate-style reduction, but it is actually a noise print reducer, in that it listens to the noise and eliminates what it thinks or knows to be noise. This is very useful at high gain when things can become a bit noisy. The Learn button will allow Tubifex to listen to the noise, identify it, and filter it out. There are even stock Reduction presets that you can access from the left side of the interface. These provide basic settings—in real life, you are best learning your own particular noise.

The last section is the Expander. An Expander is a reverse compressor, in that all levels below the threshold will be reduced. The controls of the expander work as follows:

- **Threshold**: The amount of signal needed to engage the Expander, expressed in negative values.
- **Range**: Once the signal has reached the threshold, how much reduction will follow is set by the range parameter.
- **Attack**: After the signal reaches the threshold, how long until the Expander suppresses the signal?
- **Hold**: After it starts expanding, how long should it hold onto the signal? You can control that with this parameter.
- **Release**: After the signal has risen above the threshold, how long does the expander continue to suppress the signal?

And there you have the Tubifex! Next up is an optional plug-in for the Powercore platform: the TC Thirty.

Powercore: TC Thirty

One of the strengths of the Powercore platform is its ability to expand with additional plug-ins (not unlike UAD). T.C. Electronic's goal was to emulate the venerable Vox AC-30—not just *any* AC-30, but Brian May's (from Queen) amp with its custom treble booster.

The interface of TC Thirty is clean and simple with a single window showing you everything you need to see. Figure 11.16 shows the TC Thirty's main screen.

Figure 11.16
TC Thirty's main screen.

The amp itself is very easy to use. The controls work as follows:

- **Trim**: This allows you to set your input signal before it hits the preamp.
- **No Latency**: This mode, when enabled, cuts the latency down to a few milliseconds, but also raises your host CPU load. Only use this if you need to monitor your processed guitar sound in real time. As soon as you switch to playback, turn the latency switch off to conserve power.
- **Oversampling**: This helps reduce unwanted aliasing in the higher frequencies. Aliasing can be easily distinguished as a harsh, high-frequency sound that is very unnatural. By turning the control on (which you should do all the time if you can), you will get the smoothest and most natural sound out of the amp. Just like the No Latency mode, Oversampling mode draws more power from your CPU, but the drain is worth it in sound quality.
- **Treble Booster** (Peak): This treble booster has four frequency bands it can boost: 0.5 kHz, 1 kHz, 2 kHz, and 4 kHz. The toggle switch selects which frequency is the peak frequency.
- **Treble Booster (Type)**: This selects the kind of overall distortion you will get out of the amplifier. You can choose from Original, Crunch, and Clean modes.
- **Volume**: This sets the main output of the amplifier.

There isn't a whole lot more to talk about with the TC Thirty. Having heard a bunch of really good AC-30s, I can say that they did a nice job on this one. It's modeled after a particular amp, and the AC-30s varied from amp to amp, so this is a good re-creation of *one particular* AC-30. If you like the amp they modeled, then you are in luck!

MIDI!

The TC Thirty responds to MIDI automation, so if you plan to play this amp live (through the Powercore Firewire version), then you can attach a MIDI foot controller and tweak aspects of the amp in real time.

We have reached a very nice point now, which is the end of software guitar processors. Now we get to learn what other tools the computer gives the digital guitarist, besides just re-creating a late-'60s Marshall stack.

12 Special Tools: Melodyne

Beyond the plug-ins that enable you to model your guitar tone… beyond the incredible tools you can use to mix your guitar's signal into a polished final form… you can go a step further. A few special tools exist that enable you to do extraordinary things with your guitar in the computer. One such product is Celemony's Melodyne.

What Is Melodyne?

Possibly out of all the definitions in this book, the answer to "What is Melodyne?" may be the hardest to understand. Basically, Melodyne is a studio tool/application/plug-in that allows audio to be treated with the ease of MIDI. Many of you already understand that MIDI is very easy to edit and manipulate. You may also know that audio is typically not as easy to deal with. Melodyne allows audio editing with the same flexibility as MIDI editing.

One of Melodyne's primary uses in the audio community is for vocals. Melodyne is an amazing tool for editing and manipulating the human voice, correcting pitch, and doing various other tasks. For the guitarist, the Melodyne tool palette is nothing short of mind-blowing. Imagine being able to make note-by-note changes to solos, enhance or limit vibrato, or even change your solo from a major key to a minor key with just a click. These are some of the features that make Melodyne so unique. Rather than talk about it in theory, let's take you through the basics of the program and show you how this works.

As an application, Melodyne is a bit of a chameleon. It works as a stand-alone program that you can use to record audio, apply plug-in effects (both audio effects and virtual instrument MIDI plug-ins), and edit your audio. In this way, Melodyne is a DAW just like Cubase or Logic. It also integrates into your existing sequencer of choice as a plug-in of sorts called the Melodyne Bridge, allowing you to either work in Melodyne or integrate Melodyne into your favorite DAW. Most users will use Melodyne as a super plug-in in their host of choice. We are going to look at it from both sides, because Melodyne's versatility in this area is one of its strongest points.

Melodyne is a true cross-platform application, running equally well on Windows or Macintosh.

On the Windows side, the Melodyne Bridge plug-in supports VST for Cubase and Live, RTAS for Pro Tools, and DirectX for Sonar, Vegas, and other Direct X-supported DAWs. It also supports the Rewire protocol, allowing it to integrate into Propellerhead's Reason and other Rewire-enabled applications. For high-end users, it also supports Direct I/O for Pro Tools TDM Hardware Interfaces.

On the Mac side, Melodyne fully supports OSX's CoreAudio and all Macintosh plug-in formats (RTAS, VST, and AudioUnit), so that no matter what application you use on the Macintosh (Logic, Live, Cubase, Nuendo, Pro Tools, etc.), the Melodyne Bridge integrates into your DAW of choice.

As a stand-alone program, hardware support is standard for both Mac and Windows: ASIO, DirectX, CoreAudio, and Direct I/O for Digidesign hardware.

Melodyne ships in three versions: the Studio version, the Cre8 version, and the Uno version. Each version gives you the power of Melodyne, but the lesser versions impose restrictions on the number of tracks you can work with. In the sections below, I will focus on the flagship Studio version.

Melodyne Basics

Let's start with the stand alone application first, as it's easier to show Melodyne's functions independently of any host application. When you launch Melodyne and start a new session, you are faced with Figure 12.1, which is Melodyne's default screen.

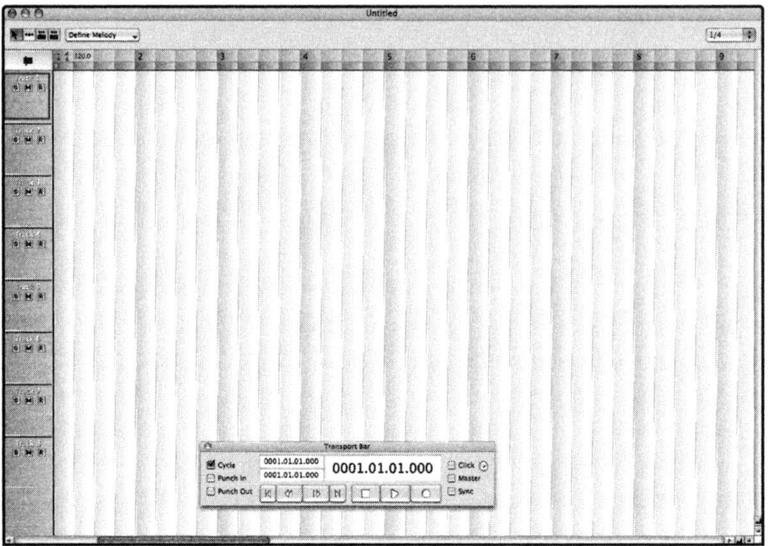

Figure 12.1
Default Melodyne screen.

With the descending track markings on the left side of the screen, you can see why Melodyne is a capable DAW, as it's structured like many other DAWs. With each track, you find buttons for Solo, Mute, and Record (see Figure 12.2).

Figure 12.2
Main track controls.

The presence of a Record button signals that you can record into Melodyne. This is the first thing you will do, which is to record a simple guitar part into Melodyne. In order to do this, you need to make sure that your guitar signal is routed correctly into the program. The first step is to make sure that your audio interface is selected in the preferences of the application, as seen in Figure 12.3. In my case, since I'm using Mac OSX, I chose my CoreAudio device in the Device Driver section.

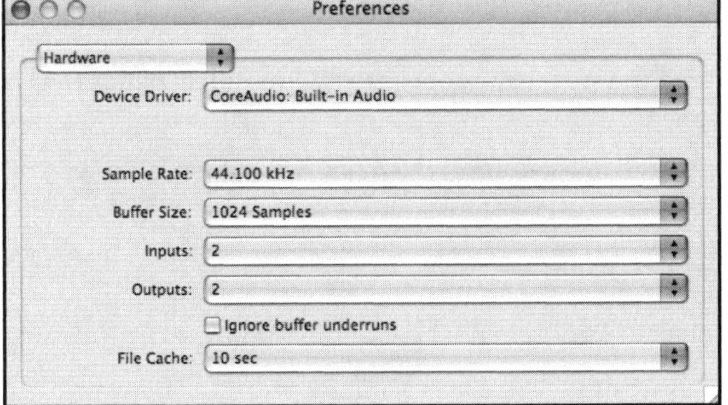

Figure 12.3
Audio interface selection via Melodyne's preferences.

Since we are looking at the Preferences selection for our hardware interfaces, let's look at a few more preference settings. Here you can set the sampling rate and bit depth, as well as the number of inputs/outputs and hardware buffer size. Again, all of these controls are what you'd expect to see in any other audio program. Now that you have that all set up, the last thing to do before you can record is launch the Mixer and route the correct input to your track. You can launch the mixer by selecting Mixer in the Windows menu, or by using the key combination Shift+Command+m on the Mac or Shift+Alt+m on Windows. Doing so will launch the Mixer, as pictured in Figure 12.4.

This Mixer gives you access to all the tracks in Melodyne: their volume levels, pan, effects inserts, solo, mute, pan, and auxiliary effects. Again, exactly what you'd expect to see in a

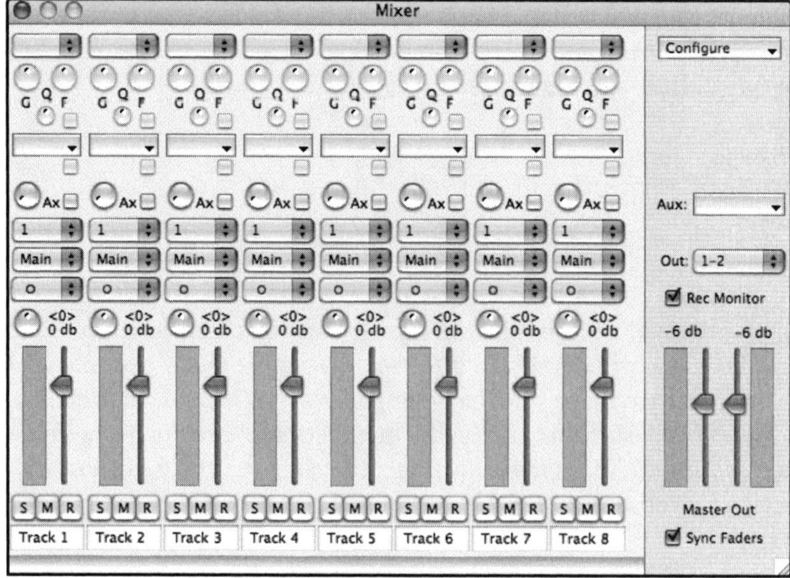

Figure 12.4
Melodyne's Mixer.

DAW's mixer—because, well, it *is* a DAW; it just happens to pull off a few things DAWs only dream of!

The part of the Mixer window you need to focus on is the input and output selection for each track, as highlighted in Figure 12.5.

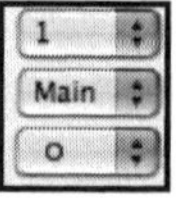

Figure 12.5
Track input and output.

Thankfully, I have my guitar plugged into input one, so I didn't need to change anything. If I had, I could easily have changed the input to wherever my guitar was plugged in.

> **DIRECT?**
> Even though Melodyne is a computer application, it does not require that you bypass your amplifier. You can plug directly into your interface if you get your guitar tone from a plug-in such as Guitar Rig or others. If your signature tone comes from a traditional amplifier, slap a microphone in front of it and feed it into Melodyne. It won't mind either way.

Directly below the input selector is the output selector, which you most likely won't need to change, as most folks use the main outputs of their interface by default. If you utilize different outputs, you can change it here. Below that is the selector for mono or stereo tracks. A single circle is a mono track, while two joined circles denote a stereo track. For most guitar tracks, you'll be recording in mono.

Now that the mixer is set up properly and my guitar is routed into Melodyne correctly, I close the mixer and return back to the main screen to start recording. On track one, I click the R button, which enables recording on the track. On the Transport bar, I simply press Record and then start playing to begin Melodyne. I play a rather lame pentatonic scale into Melodyne. When I'm done, I need to hit Stop! What happens now is the cool part. By this point in the book, you have seen what typical digital audio waveforms look like. For a comparison, Figure 12.6 shows you what this exact short pentatonic clip looks like in every other digital audio program.

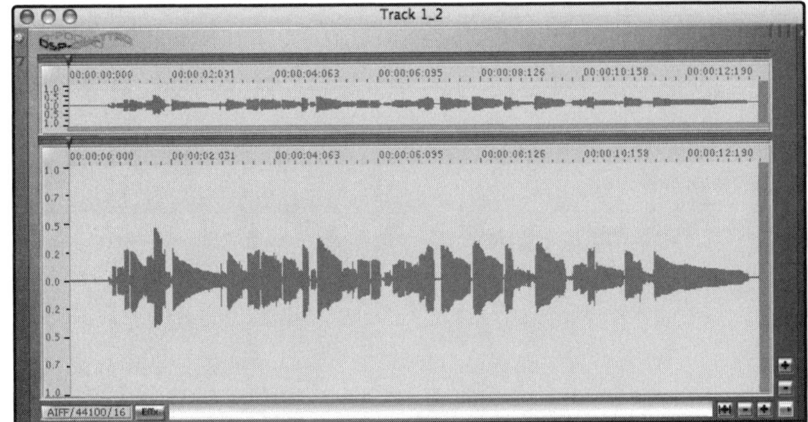

Figure 12.6
A typical digital audio waveform.

This waveform shows you some helpful things, such as loudness on the vertical axis, length of the clip, and silences in the clip if they are there. What if I wanted to single out one note? What if I needed to make edits? Traditionally, I would have to scrub around the file and find the exact point of error, *carefully* trim the note out, artfully punch in and out, and repair my mistake. Figure 12.7 shows how Melodyne looks directly after I play the notes in.

Compare Figures 12.6 and 12.7 against each other. Do they really look that different? Not yet, so we have to do one more thing to engage Melodyne. We need to have Melodyne detect the pitch. This is done via the Detect Melody command. At the top of the main Melodyne screen is a pull-down menu named Define Melody, as shown in Figure 12.8.

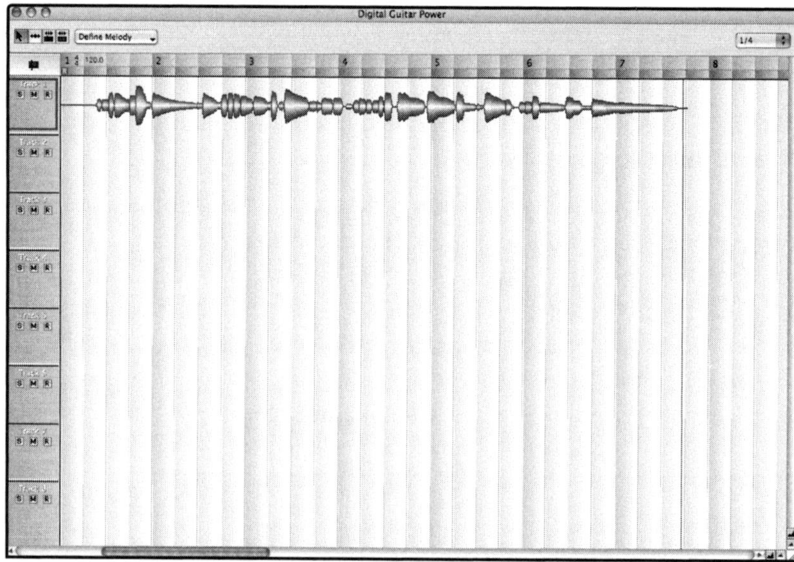

Figure 12.7
Melodyne's original representation of the audio.

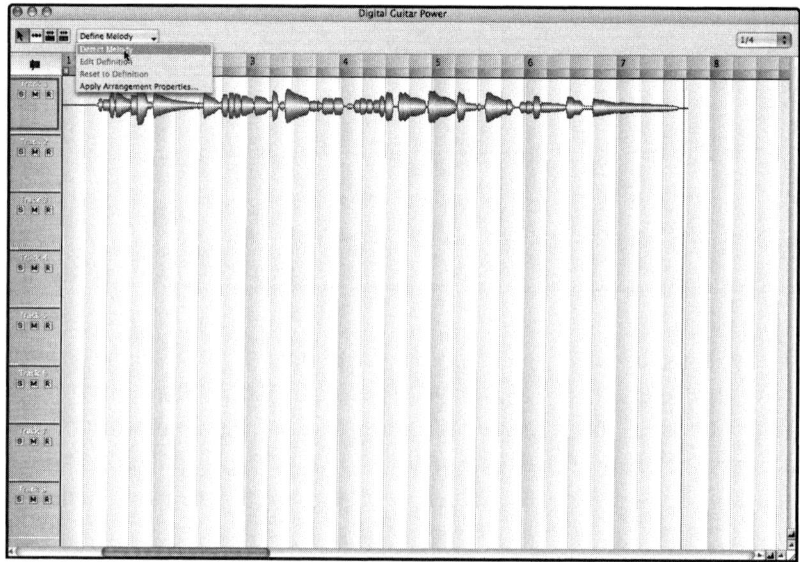

Figure 12.8
The Define Melody parameter box.

By clicking Define Melody, you bring up a pull-down menu with a few functions. The one you want to know about is the Detect Melody command, which is the first choice shown in Figure 12.9.

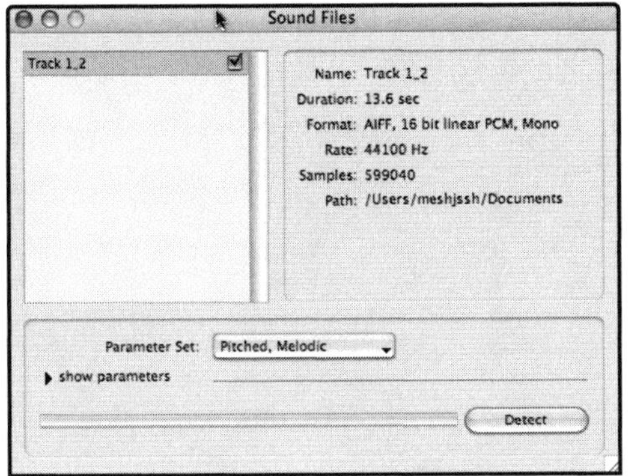

Figure 12.9
The Detect Melody command.

Now, in order for this to work, you have to select the notes that you want Melodyne to look at. In this case, it's our small guitar solo. We can simply select all the notes in the track by using the Select All command or by single-clicking the track box on the left side. Single-clicking the track box will highlight all the notes for the melody, as shown in Figure 12.10.

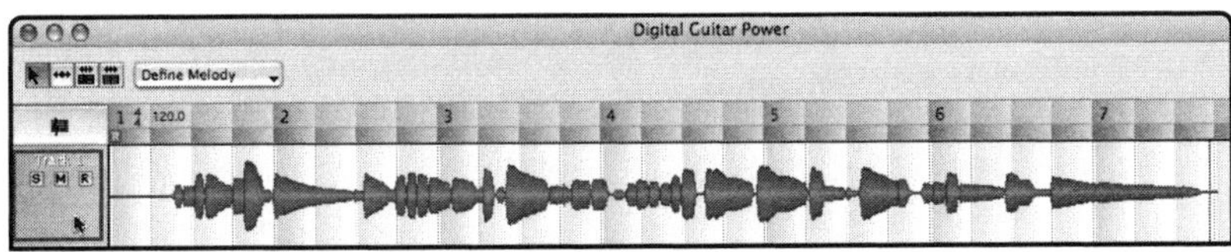

Figure 12.10
Single-click highlighted notes.

Now that we have the notes highlighted, we can use the Detect Melody command to analyze the melody. We can simply click the Define Melody tab and select Detect Melody (see Figure 12.11).

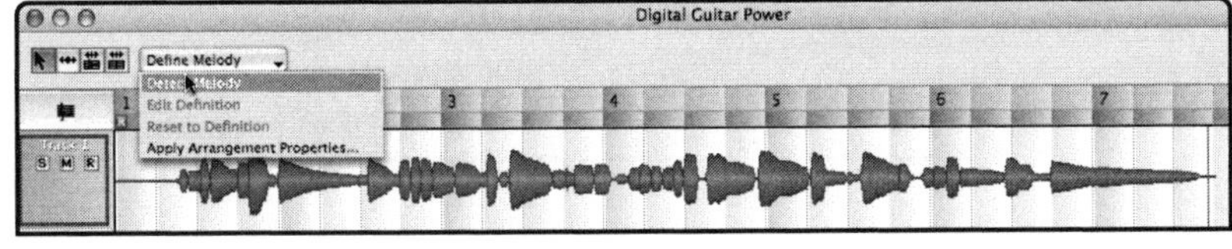

Figure 12.11
Detecting our melody.

Activating this command brings up another window, called the Sound File window, as seen in Figure 12.12.

The Sound File window gives you information about your audio file, such as the file name, its duration, its sample rate, and so on. In the lower-middle pane of that window is the box for Parameter Set, which is where you are going to select which kind of melody this is so that Melodyne can accurately analyze it.

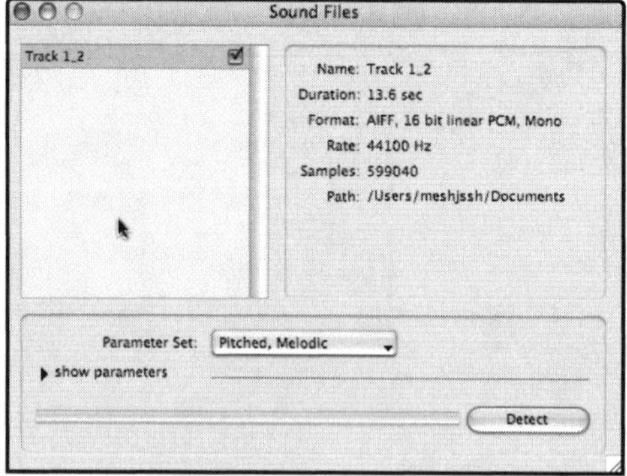

Figure 12.12
The Sound File window.

There are many choices for the type of melody you are detecting. The menus are grouped based on instrument types. Melodyne will do a good job just using standard settings, but you would be wise to select the correct instrument, as this will aid in Melodyne's pitch detection process. Since our melody is guitar, let's navigate to the Plucked/Guitar setting, shown in Figure 12.13.

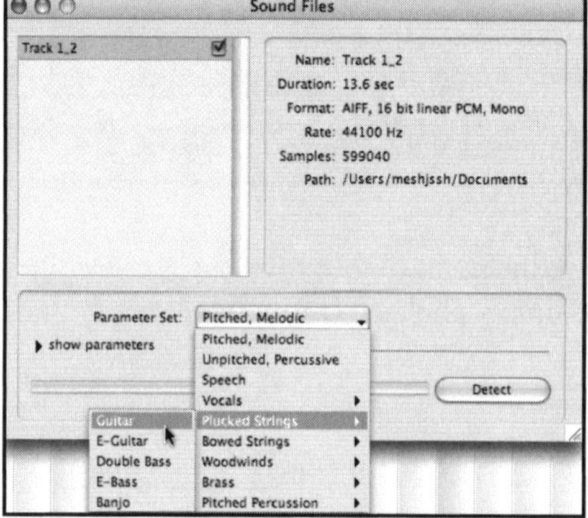

Figure 12.13
Instrument Selection window.

CHORDS?

What kind of musical material will Melodyne work with? Simply, anything that's played one note at a time, or monophonic. Melodyne's detection engine is based around single pitches, so playing chords will confuse Melodyne. If you are working with single-note guitar solos, great, Melodyne will handle this with ease. If your solo contains mixed elements, such as sections with chords and sections on single notes, you can simply cut the original audio file into sections on your DAW and only let Melodyne work with the single notes.

After you have selected the Detect button, the waveform displaying your melody is transformed from a generic waveform (although not *that generic* as Melodyne by default makes it look a bit nicer) into a very different-looking wave. Now you have information up and down, showing the different pitches that make up your melody. Melodyne has detected the individual pitches and is now displaying them as such. Figure 12.14 shows the result of your detection process.

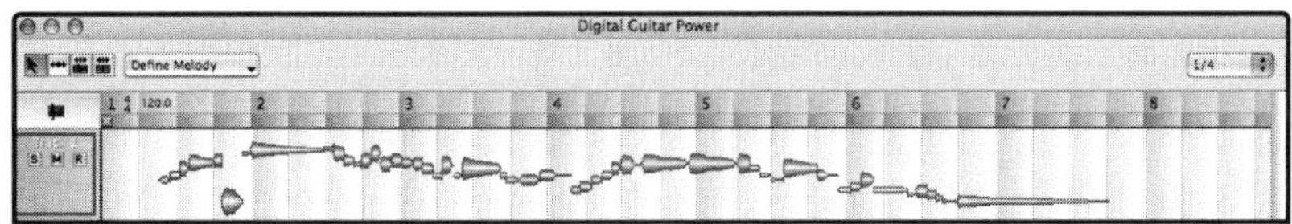

Figure 12.14
Detected pitches.

With the pitches detected, you can now move on to editing your melody. Before we do so, let's look at one more very cool way that Melodyne displays its information. In the upper-left corner of Melodyne's window is a small G clef with a note after it. This button toggles Show Score Notes, shown in Figure 12.15.

Figure 12.15
Show Score Notes.

Toggling this button places a standard musical staff on the screen and shows you the individual pitches and rhythm in standard notation for those of you who prefer to view standard notation. Figure 12.16 shows the result of showing our score notes.

Figure 12.16
Standard notation from an audio file.

Audio Editing

Now that you have your sample riff recorded into Melodyne, you can start to have fun with it and see the real power of this application. Each note is represented individually now because you detected the melody. If you double-click on the tracks clip, you enter the Editor window, as pictured in Figure 12.17.

The Editor window is where you will start having fun. On the left side, you have note names, showing you exactly what you played as it lines up to pitch; exactly like MIDI is represented, but this time it's audio. This style of displaying data is often referred to as piano roll editing. The only catch is that now you are working with audio, instead of MIDI, which has been until now, the only element that is viewed in a piano roll style.

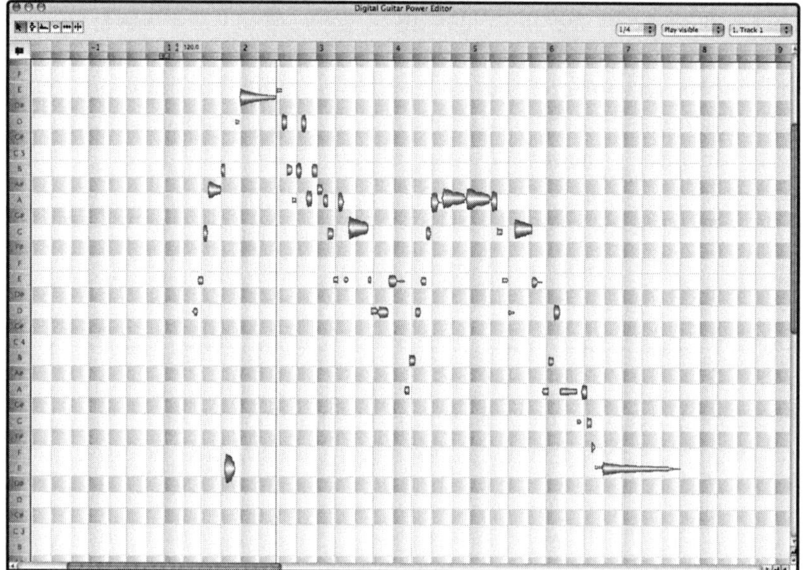

Figure 12.17
The Editor window.

Once you have converted your audio into Melodyne and detected its melody, you can start having a bit of fun. Melodyne shows each pitch separately. This is the place where you can do one of two things, either repair or create.

Repair

We are going to ask Melodyne to help us fix a note we performed less than gracefully. For example, imagine that the solo I played was inspired: the flow of the solo was great, pacing was there, and the tone and microphone placement was killer. All was well, except for one note. I hit one stupid note that is going to ruin my day. Now, this was an improvised solo. I could go back and redo the whole thing, but I may lose the vibe I had originally. Plus, now I'm already thinking about how close I was to a good take. Since it's just one note, I am going to opt to change it with Melodyne.

> **IN THE GOOD OLD DAYS**
>
> Before impressive studio tools like Melodyne were around, it was tougher to edit single notes out of solos. In the days of tape recording, this required cutting and splicing with a razor blade—very precise editing. It is possible to do this kind of work without the help of Melodyne, but it is a challenge, to say the least. One of the most difficult parts of audio editing is figuring out what part of the waveform corresponds to what note. Melodyne takes that guesswork away for you.

Double-clicking the waveform brings us into the Editor window, which is where I'm going to do this work. Across the top of the Editor window, in the upper-left corner, are rows of buttons that allow me to access various functions. The Edit Pitch button, second from the left, is the one I want to click (see Figure 12.18).

Figure 12.18
The Edit Pitch button.

Once we have selected the Edit Pitch button, the notes take on a slightly different appearance; we now see the transitions from note to note. Better yet, we can now start to make some changes. Across the top of the window is a row of flip-down menus for controlling some of the features of the pitch editing. As it is now, I can simply drag any note up and down to correct it, but this does not ensure that I am in tune. Figure 12.19 shows our melody in its unaltered form.

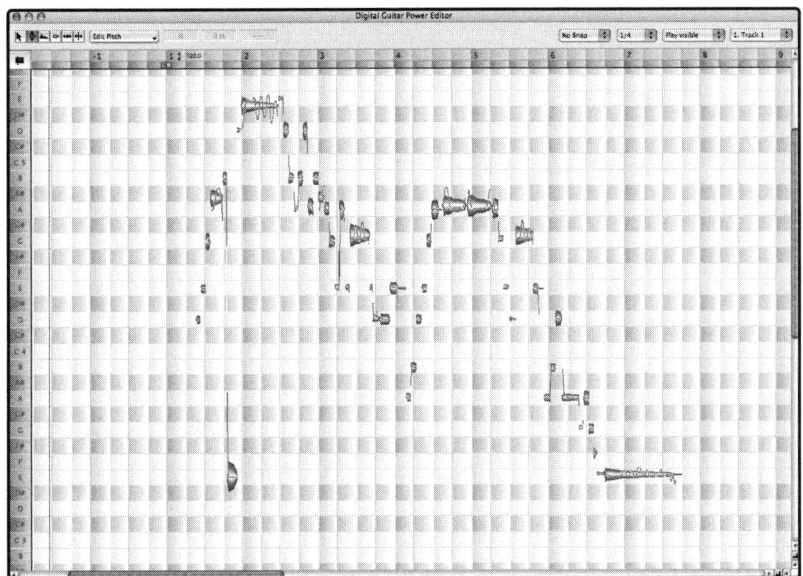

Figure 12.19
Edit Pitch variables.

Currently, the first button is set to No Snap. I would like to have it "snap" the pitch dead center in tune when I move it. I simply press down and toggle the button to Note Snap, as seen in Figure 12.20.

What the Note Snap is doing is showing where each of my notes should be. It does this by showing a blue box around where the pitch should be. In the example, I was fairly in tune. I could, if I wanted, perfect each of the notes and snap them fully into place. But, in my

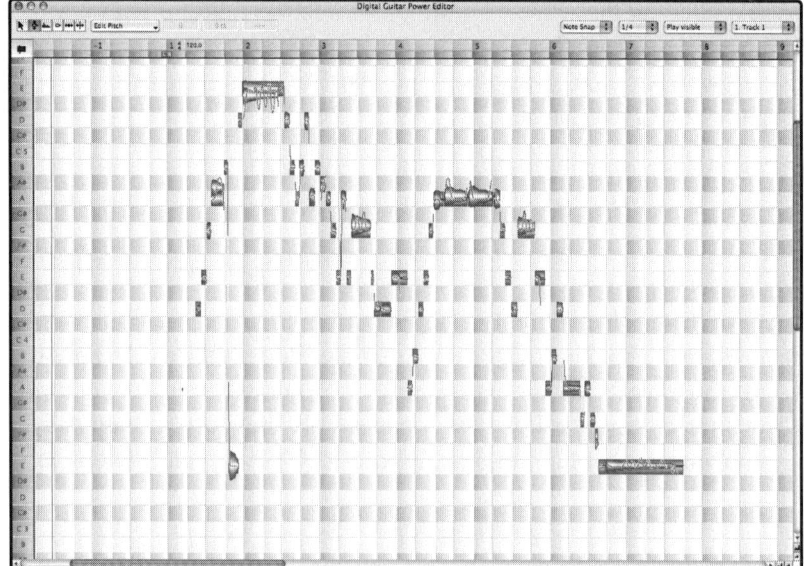

Figure 12.20
Note Snap.

case, the tuning is just fine. The issue was an errant note, and it will just make my bum note perfectly in tune. That won't work in this case. Although it is good to know when you have a note that is simply out of tune, Melodyne will place the pitch back in tune using the Note Snap feature.

Let's outline what the choices for pitch quantization are in Melodyne and their functions:

- **No Snap**: You can move the note up and down without any relative constraints. This may be useful for retaining the phrasing of a section that had some acceptable "out-of-tune-ness."
- **Note Snap**: Snaps the note in tune to its closest pitch..
- **Scale Snap**: Snaps notes to predetermined scales (which you can choose). This is very handy for doing harmony parts, to ensure that your harmony is diatonic.
- **Note Step**: Allows you to move notes anywhere, regardless of scale, and have them snap into tune wherever you drop them.
- **Scale Step**: Allows you to step notes through a scale without having them snap to the closest note in the scale.

Looking at the above list, the Note Snap function seems to work best for us. We do know what key we are in, but in this instance, it's just the one note, and being able to drag it up, semitone by semitone.

In our example, it was the fourth note that I butchered. I made the ugly mistake of playing an A# instead of an A. I can simply click on it (making sure that Note Step is selected) and drag it down to the E: one semitone down. Figures 12.21 and 12.22 show the before and after versions.

Figure 12.21
Mistake identified.

Figure 12.22
Mistake corrected!

Now, in this case, I only had one mistake and no tuning was needed, besides repairing the notes. I could very easily perfect the tuning of any one note. For example, I could fix a bend that didn't quite make it. There are many ways that Melodyne can help to salvage performances. Let's shift our focus to the creative aspects of Melodyne. Pitch correction has been around for a while now. Although other pitch correction methods may not be as unique and intuitive as Melodyne's, the concept is not new. Let's look at the creative uses for Melodyne.

Creative Uses

Melodyne is an amazing creative tool that allows you to start out with a performance and end up with something else entirely. Through the use of Melodyne's tools, you can edit performance aspects, such as vibrato, note length, and overall phrasing. You can also alter the melodic and harmonic content of your music as well. This is where Melodyne's creative potential comes into focus.

Phrasing is a very important part of guitar playing. By phrasing, I am talking about the subtle changes in pitch and vibrato that make each player's signature sound unique. Melodyne lets you take control over vibrato, allowing you to fine-tune aspects of your performance.

Changing Vibrato (Phrasing)

Vibrato is simply defined as a fluctuation in pitch. For guitar players, vibrato is a unique and personal part of our sound. Melodyne allows vibrato to be edited as if it were a simple function of the sound. No other editor allows you to separate vibrato from pitch like this. Let's use a new example, Figure 12.23, which shows a melody I have recorded into Melodyne.

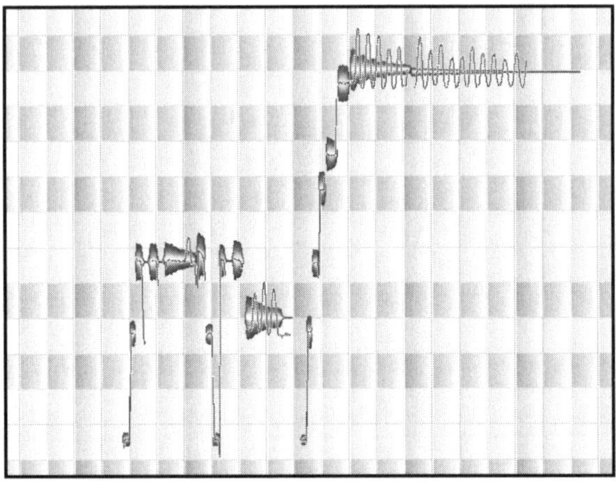

Figure 12.23
Vibrato example.

I purposely was very liberal about vibrato, even at times totally overdoing the amount of vibrato used! In the example above, vibrato is shown with the wavy line in the center of each note. The wideness of the vibrato (intensity) is shown by the number of waves and their relative height.

Notice that the different notes have different amounts of vibrato; this is normal in guitar phrasing. We are going to focus on my last note. I went a touch overboard. Figure 12.24 shows a close-up of the display.

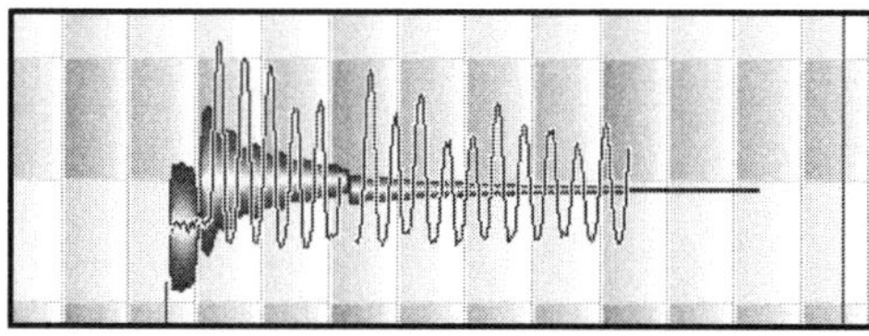

Figure 12.24
Errant vibrato close-up.

Now, in order to tame this vibrato, we are going to stay within our Edit Pitch mode in Melodyne.

> **POWER TIP**
> While you can access any of the editing modes via the top panel on the Edit window, you can get the same view by simply right-clicking to call up the window. For you Mac users with a lonely one-button mouse, Ctrl-Click does the same thing. This is a timesaver for sure, as you can click and change edit modes anywhere you are.

Within our Edit Pitch mode, we need to call the Pitch Align. You can find it by clicking and holding down the Edit Pitch button (either on the toolbar or by using the tip above). Doing so will reveal a submenu of four choices. You want to select the second choice, Pitch Align, as shown in Figure 12.25.

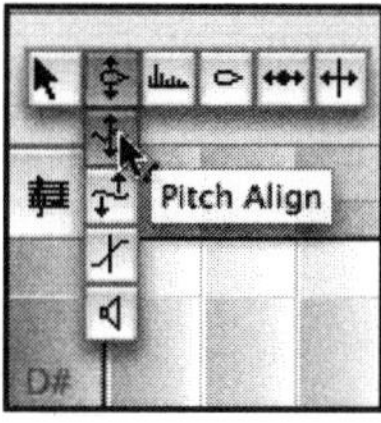

Figure 12.25
Pitch Align.

Thankfully, Melodyne gives you visual feedback as to where you are and what tool you are selecting. Selecting the Pitch Align function changes the mouse's appearance to Figure 12.26.

Figure 12.26
The Pitch Align cursor.

Now that you are in the mode, let's go over to the last note. With the Pitch Align cursor alive, you can go over and edit the vibrato Simply click and drag the vibrato up to increase it (which would be overkill here), or click and drag down to tame the vibrato. Figure 12.27 shows the final product.

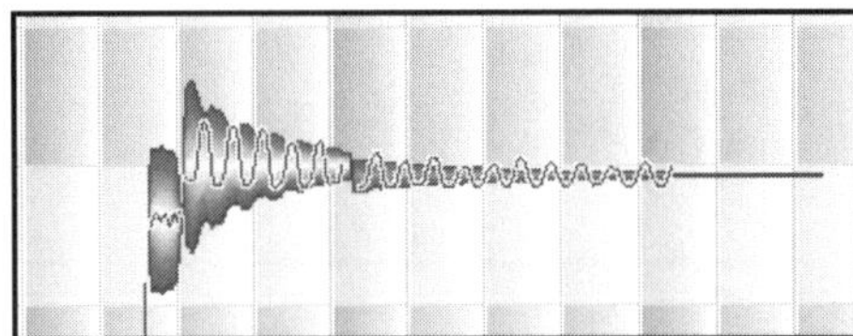

Figure 12.27
Vibrato tamed!

I used visual cues and trial and error to find the right balance between the original phrasing and polishing up the performance. Always play back your work to make sure it sounds the way you want it to. Using the Pitch Align tool, you can totally remove any vibrato. Why would you want to do that? We will rediscover the answer to that when we talk about pitch-to-MIDI conversion, another Melodyne tool. There are definitely instances where vibrato isn't needed. Many players have a hard time shutting it off. With Melodyne, you can choose whether or not you want it there in the first place.

Note-by-Note Volume

The ability to change the volume, or gain, of a digital audio file may not seem that exciting. It's one of the first things computers were able to achieve. However, with Melodyne, gain changes take on a new direction. Since each note is separated, it is very easy to hone in on one note and change the volume of that single note. On a regular DAW, the waveform would be visible, and through trial and error, you could find the note and automate its volume down. It's much easier to do this with Melodyne because the notes are totally separated.

Amplitude, or loudness, is always shown on the vertical axis (up and down), so the higher the peak of a note, the louder it is. In Figure 12.28, you can see that my phrase has one note that is sticking out from the rest (hint: taller is louder). I guess I just played a bit too loudly.

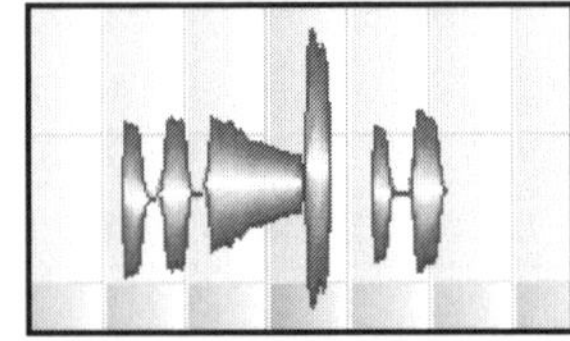

Figure 12.28
The loud note.

To change the amplitude of the note, I have to call up my toolbox or look in the upper-left corner of my editor window. The Edit Amplitude button looks like Figure 12.29.

Figure 12.29
Edit Amplitude.

By selecting it, I can now click on any one note, or a group of notes, and simply pull the volume up and down.

SELECTIVE COMPRESSION

Compression could have been used in this example to tame the peaks from note to note. However, when only a few notes are affected, it's much easier to manually tame the peaks to ensure that the rest of your selection is unaffected.

By taking the amplitude of the errant notes and fixing them by simply sliding them down to better match the other pitches, I am left with the progression shown in Figure 12.30, which looks and sounds much better.

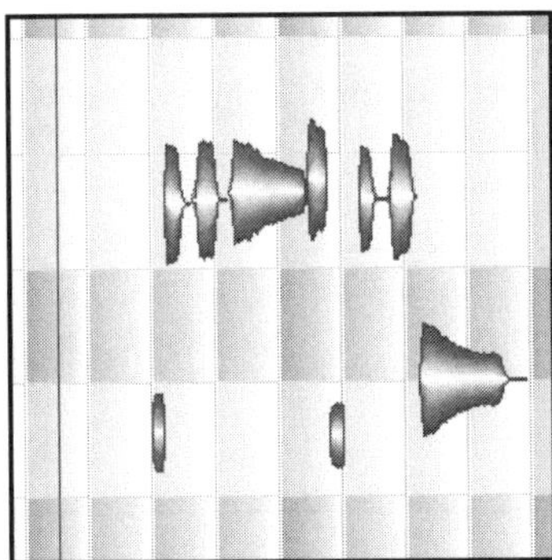

Figure 12.30
Volume adjusted.

Another dynamic tool that Melodyne gives you is access to the transitions from note to note. This is a very souped-up Cross Fade editor in some ways. You can also mute individual notes in a phrase using the Mute tool. This opens up many creative uses for changing not only the dynamic flow of the work, but also the content, by muting notes and altering the transitions from note to note.

Note Lengthening

As you start to edit your work with Melodyne, especially when using the dynamics options, you may find yourself wanting to change other aspects of your performance. The length of a pitch is something that is so easy to change in the MIDI world and so difficult to do in the audio world. Again, Melodyne helps you here with time-stretching options.

Let's imagine a scenario: I've successfully recorded a solo part. But I have decided that I want to change some aspects of it. I alter some of the pitches to taste, and I'm at a point at which I'd like to cut the phrase short; I have about three notes too many. I could simply trim the audio file, but I'd be left with a gap at the end. What I'd like to do is make the last note longer and add some vibrato so it fits in the way that I would usually phrase a note like that.

To do this, I simply bring up the Stretch Notes tool, which is found under the Move Notes toolbox, as shown in Figure 12.31.

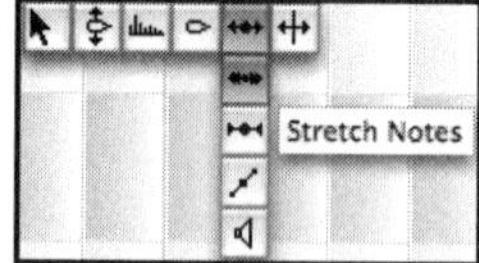

Figure 12.31
The Stretch Notes tool.

Once I have selected the tool, I can grab the end of any particular pitch and pull it out as far as I want. This is called time stretching. This artificial lengthening of a note can sometimes have a negative effect on the quality of the sound. Melodyne does a fine job of allowing me to drag the note out over 300% of its original size with no noticeable difference in sound quality. Figures 12.32 and 12.33 show the before and after versions of my work using note lengthening in Melodyne.

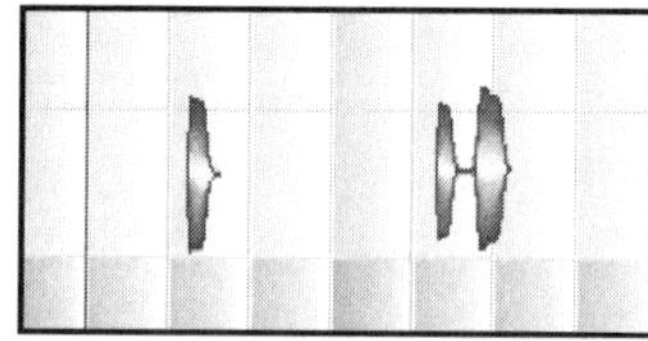

Figure 12.32
Before note lengthening.

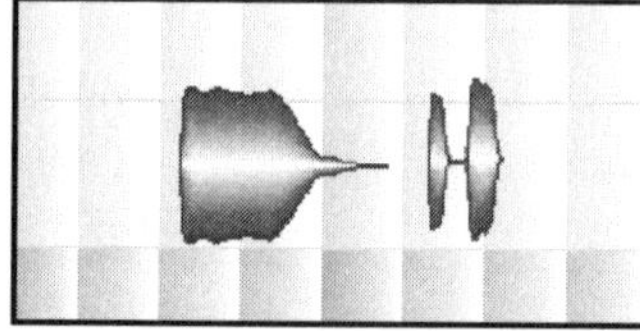

Figure 12.33
After note lengthening.

The result is a phrase that sounds very organic, even though I have edited this on the most microcosmic of levels.

Harmony Tools

Harmony is loosely defined as "the vertical aspect of music." We have dealt with single-line melodies in Melodyne, looking at the horizontal aspects, such as pitch and time. Melodyne also has some powerful tools for dealing with harmony, which we will explore now.

Changing The Tonality

Tonality refers to the key or scale that you are playing in. Melodyne allows you to change recorded solos or licks after the fact. This means that you can play something in a minor key and have Melodyne put it into a major key, or any scale that you define.

To do so, we have to look at the key feature of the Editor window.

By key feature, I mean the selector that defines which key to snap the notes to. Normally, when you edit in Melodyne, you don't necessarily *need* to know the key. You could simply do it by ear. In the case of adjusting the harmony, you could also do that by ear, but assigning the key makes our lives much easier.

In the Edit window, along the left vertical side, are a bunch of note names. These notes allow you to align notes in a piano-roll style. This will allow you to edit notes individually, but you want to change the scale. In order to change all of your notes and have them adhere to a new scale, you have to do a few things. First, you need to enter the Edit Pitch mode using the toolbox shown in Figure 12.34.

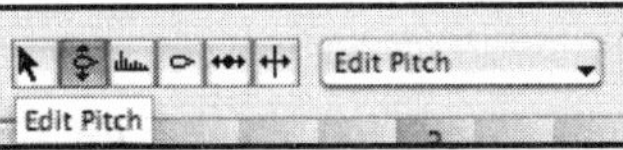

Figure 12.34
Edit Pitch.

We have one more step to do: Snap to scale. Across the toolbar on the Edit window is an extra parameter. By default, it reads No Snap, but for our purposes, we changed it to Scale Snap, as shown in Figure 12.35.

Figure 12.35
No Snap.

We need to toggle that dialog box to Scale Snap. Once we have done that, the Editor window's vertical column of notes takes on a different role. By default, it will highlight the C notes, as seen in Figure 12.36. This indicates that the notes are going to snap to the key of C major.

I can click on any of the keys across the left side to change the key. However, simply selecting a new key will not make any audible result. What it will do is project a ghost image on the notes as to where they should be for that key. I am going to select D major (my original example was played in C major). You will now see which notes no longer fit into the key of D major (D E F# G A B C# D) with a ghost image, as shown in Figure 12.37.

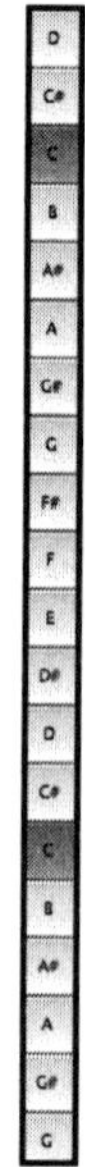

Figure 12.36
Scale Snap in C major.

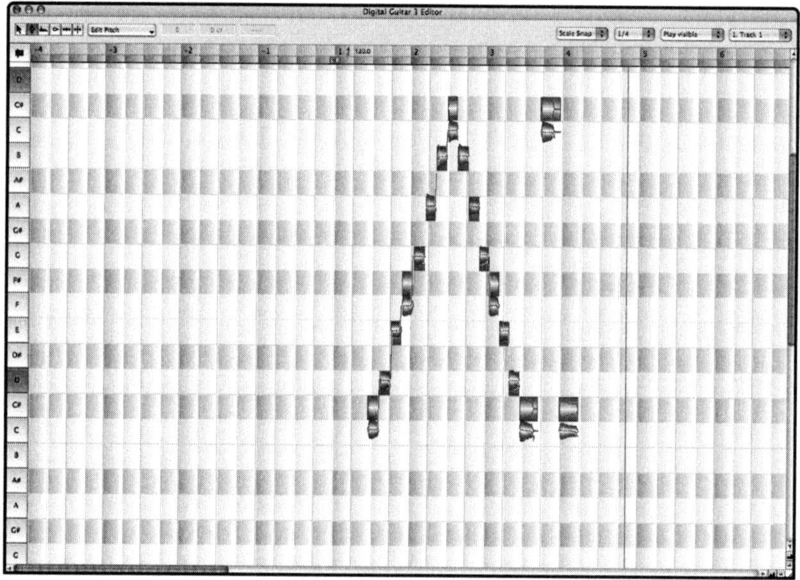

Figure 12.37
Scale Snap ghost images.

For any of the notes that are showing ghost images, I can simply double-click on them to snap them to the new key. This will not necessarily transpose the material into D major, but it will conform the notes to the key. To do a transposition, you have to move all the notes, and this is best done using the Scale Step function and moving them all up two steps, from C to C# and then to D. What this function is good for is taking preexisting material or licks that are very close to working, but just need note-by-note adjustments.

I find that Scale Snap does a great job changing from a major key to a minor key of the same letter. I'll use my original example in C major that we have been working with in this section. To change into a minor key snap, I need to Shift-click the keys across the left vertical side. The result can be seen in Figure 12.38.

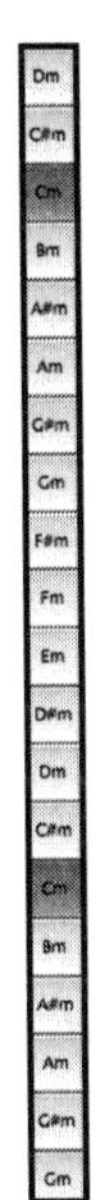

Figure 12.38
Minor key note snap choices.

I will now select Cm (for C minor), and you will see that many of my notes are shown with the ghost image in Figure 12.39.

Now I select all the notes (Edit+Select All), double-click with the Edit Pitch tool selected, and bang—all my notes conform to C minor. I have transposed my music into a minor key. This is very handy for creative edits and music arrangements. The next thing to talk about is how to crate harmony and polyphony (many notes at once) simply in Melodyne.

Instant Harmony

One of the cool things you can do in Melodyne is take existing material and harmonize it. For you non-theory folks, harmonizing a line is when you add a second guitar part that follows the original melody, only a few notes away. This way you can very easily take an existing part and add a second part in harmony!

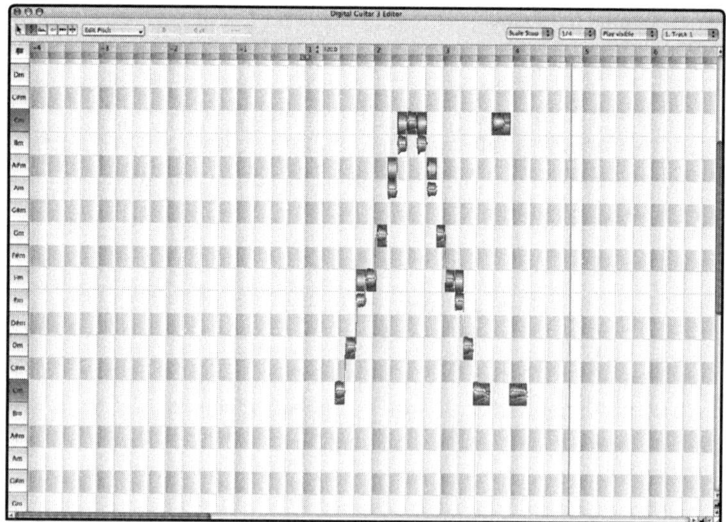

Figure 12.39
C minor note snaps.

First, you need to enter the Edit Pitch mode with Scale Snap on. Make sure the correct key is selected across the left side. Once you have done this, select all the visible notes and copy them with the Edit+Copy command. Now, you need to enter a second track. This can be done on the left-to-right toolbar that runs across the Edit window. By default, it lists the track you are editing, which is Track 1. You need to select Track 2; once you have done this, you can paste the notes into the second track using the Edit+Paste command. The result looks like Figure 12.40.

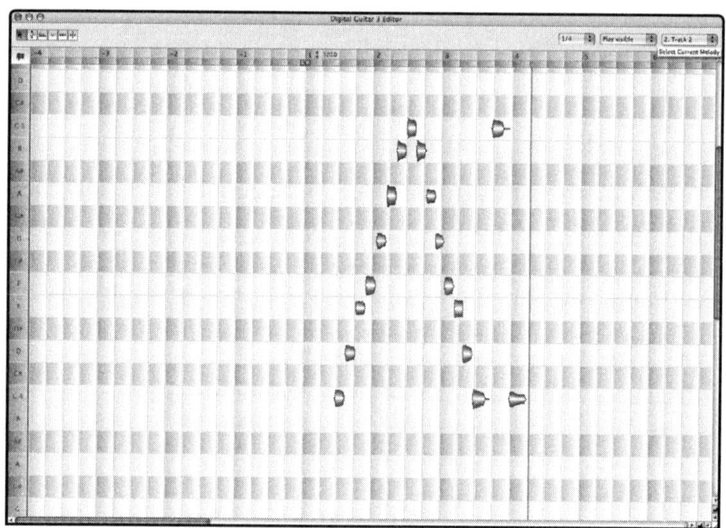

Figure 12.40
Pasting into a new track.

You'll notice that you can still see Track 1, but it's a bit in the background. The other issue is that my notes are not lining up. I choose the Move Notes tool and align them over the original notes. Once that is complete, I go back to the Edit Pitch mode with my Scale Snap on and select all the notes (Edit+Select All). Now that all the notes are selected and the Scale Snap is working, I can pull any of the notes up, and they will all follow to the correct key. I simply drag the notes three steps higher to create harmony at a third—a common way of harmonizing notes. I play it back to make sure that everything sounds nice, and I am greeted with a great-sounding harmony. This was so easy! The result is seen in Figure 12.41.

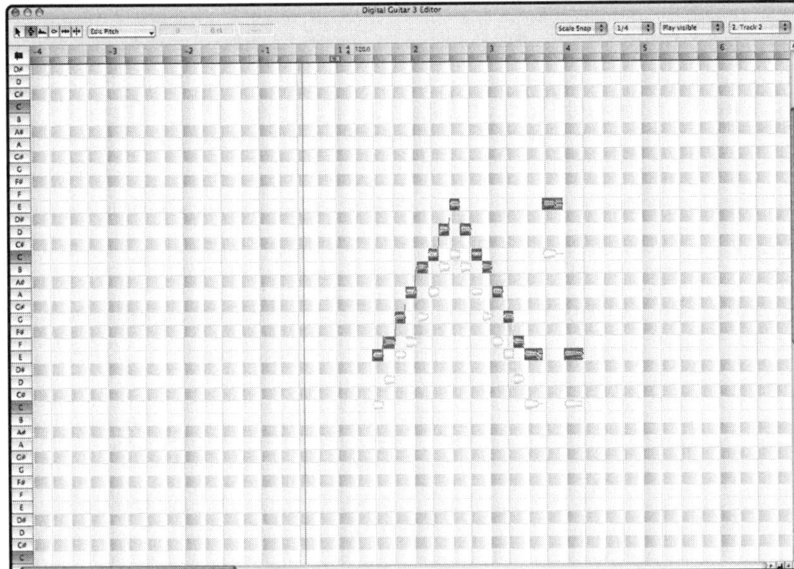

Figure 12.41
Instant harmony.

As long as your Scale Snap is turned on, the new material will remain in the same key as the original, ensuring that your material plays in musical and harmonic sync with the rest of the material.

We have only scratched the surface of what can be done here, but some creative experimentation will yield some impressive results.

> **MINUTE CHORDS**
> Want to make a quick three-part harmony that sounds like instant chords? Simply follow the routine above, this time creating a third track and harmonizing that track another third above. The result will give you three-note triads in the key you are working on. It's a very rich effect!

Using the MelodyneBridge Plug-in

Melodyne by itself is a capable DAW. You can record into the application, add effects, mix, and even use virtual instrument synthesizer plug-ins. Despite this, many of us still prefer to work in the DAW application we are used to. Whether it's Pro Tools, Cubase, or anything else, we like to work where we are comfortable. Melodyne allows you to stay where you are happy, using a technology called the MelodyneBridge. Simply, the MelodyneBridge is a plug-in for your host sequencer of choice that allows you to send audio from your DAW to Melodyne for editing and back to the host at the end. This way, you can track in your favorite program and use Melodyne as needed in your arrangement.

Doing so is very simple. Here is a simple arrangement in Logic Express that I have set up with a few loop tracks and two tracks of guitar. The last track is a solo guitar that could use some help from Melodyne. Here are the steps needed to work with the MelodyneBridge plug-in:

1. Launch your preferred DAW first. Make sure Melodyne is off.
2. Get your tracks the way you want them.
3. Insert the MelodyneBridge plug-in on the audio track.

Now that you have instantiated MelodyneBridge, you can launch Melodyne, the application. Upon startup, you will get a new screen, which you can see in Figure 12.42, that asks you how you want Melodyne to connect with the host application.

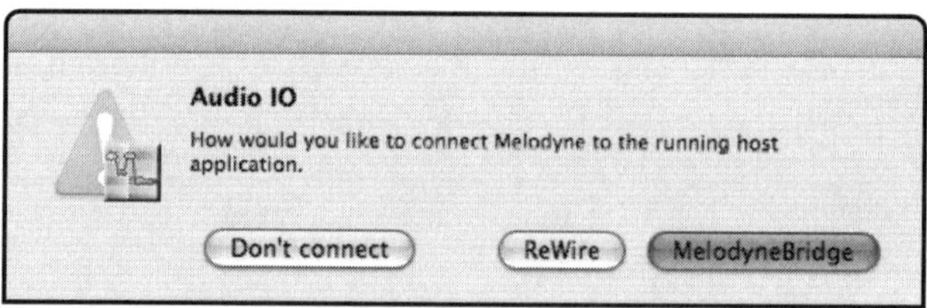

Figure 12.42
MelodyneBridge.

When Melodyne starts, it detects that MelodyneBridge is running and wants to know how to connect to it, if at all. Since you are going to connect, you simply press MelodyneBridge. It now prompts you for a location to save the audio files. Choose the same folder as your original arrangement in your DAW (wherever you saved it). Once this is done, create a new arrangement in Melodyne (File+New) and go back to your host, in this case, Logic Express. Figure 12.43 shows the MelodyneBridge plug-in after Melodyne is started.

There are two important things to hit on here. First is the Mode box. This can be toggled from Record to Playback by clicking on it. Recording allows you to send audio from Logic Express (or your host) to Melodyne for processing. Playback allows the audio from Melodyne to come back into Logic. Second is the list of tracks. In my arrangement, only four tracks are present, and

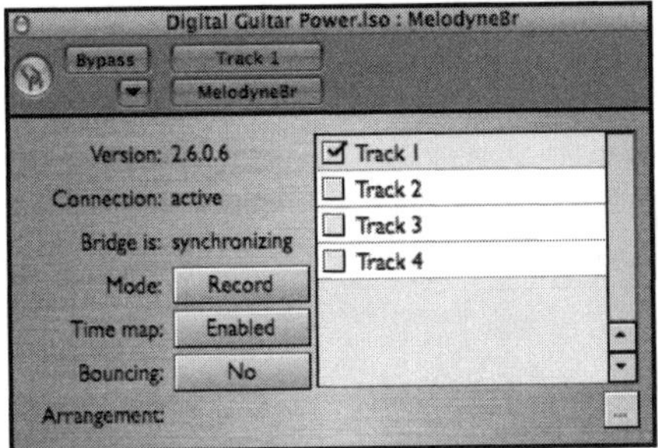

Figure 12.43
MelodyneBridge plug-in.

only one of them is suitable for Melodyne. In this case, I check off Track 1 with the checkbox. Now, as long as the plug-in is set to Record, we are in good shape.

When you are in MelodyneBridge mode, your main DAW acts as the "master commander"—the transport controls both the host *and* Melodyne. As long as I'm in Record mode, simply clicking Play will stream the audio into Melodyne until I click Stop. The result in Melodyne after clicking Stop is shown in Figure 12.44.

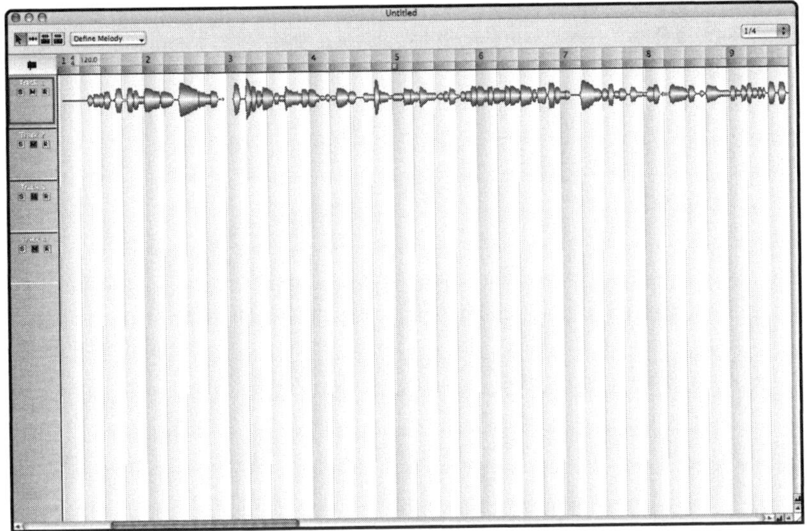

Figure 12.44
Melodyne after a successful bridge.

My audio is now in Melodyne, and I can detect the melody as usual and tweak it to taste. After clicking Stop on Logic's transport, the MelodyneBridge plug-in automatically switches to Playback, which means that any changes made in Melodyne will play through Logic. Just as before, Logic's transport still acts as a main control and keeps both applications in perfect synchronization.

> **JUST A BIT**
> There is no need to stream a whole long track into Melodyne if you only intend to work on a small section of material. When in Record mode, simply start the transport at the beginning of the section you want to edit, and stop it as soon as you are finished. When in Playback mode, your DAW will play back the mixture of original audio and streamed audio from Melodyne automatically.

After you have made all your tweaks, you want to place the music in Melodyne permanently in Logic. To do so, you need to switch the last box in the MelodyneBridge plug-in to Bounce On, which upon playback replaces the original audio with the Melodyne parts. Once this is done, Logic reflects the new changes, and you don't need to have Melodyne running anymore. The bridge is a very transparent and easy way to work. The ability to synchronize both systems and use Melodyne as a super-editor is one of the strengths of the MelodyneBridge function. Most users will probably work this way, as it allows you to work in your own environment. Of course, the MelodyneBridge plug-in is available for all major DAWs on Mac and PC.

> **WIRED IN**
> MelodyneBridge also functions as a Rewire host, allowing it to control a rewire slave application, such as Reason. As a Reason user, this will give you powerful time-stretching and pitch-based tools, even though Reason is a MIDI program, not an audio one. Melodyne can act as both a Rewire master and a Rewire slave.

> **NOT JUST FOR GUITAR**
> With all this talk about Melodyne and guitar, we are forgetting that Melodyne is amazing at processing voice! It also has superior beat detection and time-stretching effects that make it ideal for working with drum tracks and aligning them with your music. Melodyne is a multifaceted program that gives guitar players power, but the program will have uses in other parts of your studio as well.

Converting Pitch to MIDI

For guitarists, controlling MIDI instruments with our guitars is akin to the Holy Grail. We have all looked for it at some point, and few of us have found it. In this book, you will explore how to get MIDI happening on your guitar, but as long as you have Melodyne, you might as well look at yet another trick Melodyne has up its sleeve: pitch-to-MIDI conversion.

Now, before you get too excited, I should clarify. Melodyne's pitch-to-MIDI converter does not work in real time like the Roland systems do. However, any material that you have in Melodyne is analyzed for pitch, amplitude, and vibrato. These elements translate perfectly into MIDI notes, with MIDI velocity and pitch bend information (your standard trifecta of MIDI techniques).

For a practical example of how you might use this, imagine that you have recorded a guitar part into your DAW, or even directly into Melodyne. This part may or may not need any fixing. After you get your mix going, you think to yourself, "Wow, wouldn't this be cool if it was doubled by a synth?"

Now, you *could* go back and retrack the part through a guitar synth system, but what if you don't own one? Moreover, what if you want it to be *exactly* the same as the original part, dynamics and phrasing included? In this case, Melodyne is your best bet.

From the handy Editor window, once you have detected the melody into pitches, you can very easily translate the information to MIDI. You can do this in a few ways. First, in the File menu, you can choose Export, as seen in Figure 12.45.

Figure 12.45
The Export window.

The window itself allows you to export more than MIDI—you can also export individual tracks. For our purposes, we need to make our Export window look like Figure 12.46 to get the correct MIDI file for export.

Figure 12.46
Export Window Settings.

Once this is complete, you will be left with MIDI files at the destination you choose. You can now import these into your DAW and set up a synth plug-in or external MIDI gear, and you will have instant guitar-to-MIDI conversion.

BREEZE
I have intentionally breezed over this function in Melodyne. When we explore MIDI guitar in more detail later in the book, we will revisit Melodyne's pitch-to-MIDI conversion in greater detail throughout the rest of the book.

13 Recording Your Guitar

Up until now, we've been discussing all virtual technology, such as plug-ins and DSP processing devices. But digital guitar does not have to cut out the traditional amplifier. For many of us, recording a real amplifier, or even acoustic guitars, is an important part of the digital guitar puzzle. In this way, "digital" refers to the storage medium only—the guitars will be real, and we'll use either microphones or direct interfaces to capture our sound and get it onto our favorite sequencer. The reality is that no matter how cool and useful any of this technology is, there are times when a real Strat and really loud Marshall are exactly what the doctor ordered. If you're growing up in the digital age, the art of miking an amplifier may be new to you. This chapter is all about putting an edge of reality into your virtual universe.

Why Get Real?

This chapter is about using microphones to capture sound. I guess it's a solid question to ask, "Why do I need to mic my amp when [*insert favorite guitar modeling plug-in*] already does that, and I can just plug into an interface?" Or, "My Brian Moore USB guitar doesn't need an interface; I can just plug it in." Both are legitimate points, but I've got good answers for both of them. First, every plug-in is trying to emulate the real thing—if you already have the sound you want, why try to re-create it? Second, even in the age of plug-ins, direct sounds usually lack something that a real microphone can give you. You can approximate this with some good preamps that serve as direct boxes, and even with a bit of EQ on the way in, but most agree that a microphone gives you something no straight wire can, which is air. If you can get more out of your plug-ins, then why not? Last, what about acoustic guitars? You get my point: Real guitar is just that, real, and digital guitar is about embracing it from all angles and using it to your best advantage. Let's start with microphones.

Microphones

A microphone is a simple device that converts sound to electricity. All microphones essentially do this in the same manner. Sound waves move air molecules, and the microphone inducts current from this movement of air. There are three main types of microphones: dynamic, condenser, and ribbon microphones. Each one translates sound waves into electricity, but they do this in different ways. Let's talk about how each microphone does its job.

Dynamic Microphones

Dynamic microphones are probably the most common microphones in the world. Just about every guitarist knows the Shure SM-57 microphone—that's a dynamic microphone. What makes it dynamic is the way that it produces electricity. A dynamic microphone is essentially an induction circuit, which coincidentally is how a guitar's pickup and most loudspeakers work. A dynamic microphone is, in fact, a backwards speaker—and yes, if you're crazy enough, you can use a speaker as a microphone, too!

In a dynamic microphone, there is a small coil, called the induction coil, which is suspended in front of a magnet. When the coil moves back and forth due to the movement of air hitting it, it induces current, meaning that it makes electricity all on its own. It does not require any external power, but the amount of current it makes is very small which is why microphones require preamplification in order to gain proper level. Figure 13.1 is a picture of another very popular dynamic microphone, the Sennheiser e609.

Figure 13.1
The Sennheiser e609 dynamic microphone.

Dynamic microphones have a few things going for them. First, they are on the whole very cheap. You can get a good dynamic microphone for under $100 and a really sensational one for less than $200. The venerable SM-57 sells for about $75 in most major stores, and that microphone has literally recorded millions of guitar amps. Second, they can handle very loud sounds without distorting or becoming damaged. This is also called sound pressure level or SPL. Dynamic mics can take ear-splitting volumes with ease because of their very durable moving voice coils. This is another reason they are used on guitar amps, because as you may remember, your amp goes to 11.

The last thing they have going for them is a frequency response that is very well suited to guitar. Most dynamic microphones do not have a full range, such as 20 Hz to 20 kHz, as other microphones do. This is fine because a guitar does not cover the full frequency range. The fundamental pitch of the guitar starts around 80 Hz and goes up to about 1.3 kHz at its upper end (not including harmonics). When you include the harmonics and overtones, the typical signal reaches about 5 kHz. Not to mention that most speakers in guitar amps can't reproduce sound over 5 kHz anyway, which is why dynamic mics are perfect for the job. These factors make dynamic microphones great for some miking purposes, but not ideal for others. They are great on amplifiers, but not perfect for acoustic guitars. For everything else, we have two other types of microphones to look at. Next up is the condenser microphone.

Condenser Microphones

The condenser microphone is the quintessential studio microphone. You can see a very famous condenser microphone, the Neumann TLM-103 large diaphragm condenser, in Figure 13.2.

Figure 13.2
The Neumann TLM-103 large diaphragm condenser microphone.

Condenser microphones work very differently than dynamic microphones with respect to their mechanics. A condenser microphone is essentially a capacitor. One element in the microphone is a thin membrane that vibrates with the changing sound pressure. This element is called the diaphragm. The diaphragm is suspended in front of a stationary back plate of metal. This back plate has polarizing voltage applied to it. When the diaphragm moves, its distance from the back plate (which is stationary) induces a very small current. Because the back plate needs voltage applied to it, this is where the term "phantom power" comes from. All condenser microphones require phantom power, either from your mixer, recording interface, or a dedicated power box. Traditional phantom power is always 48 volts. Tube condenser mics, a special subset of condenser mics, have their own power supplies that charge the tube inside the microphone and the microphone's stationary back plate. Without this voltage, the microphone will do nothing!

Condenser microphones have a few things going for them. First, they have a very accurate frequency response. Most good condensers can pick up the complete range of human hearing (20 Hz to 20 kHz), which makes them very accurate for reproducing exactly what you put in front of them. Also, some condenser mics use transformers that color the sound (affect the frequency range), and this coloration is typically a sought-after sound, which is another reason why condenser mics are so popular. This is the reason that condensers are used in studios and most importantly for voice—where accurate reproduction is a must. Condensers can handle very loud sound pressure, but not as loud as dynamics. You have to try very hard to overload a condenser, but it can be done. Contrary to popular belief, you cannot hurt a condenser microphone with too much sound level; if you want to hurt a condenser microphone, drop it on a concrete floor. The main difference between condenser microphones and dynamics is the capability of some condensers to utilize multiple *polar patterns*. A polar pattern refers to *the direction* in which the microphone can capture sound. We are going to get into polar patterns very shortly. On the downside, condenser microphones are usually more expensive than their dynamic counterparts. Sure, you can find a cheap condenser microphone, but the really good ones are going to cost you as much as a new relic Strat.

Because of their wide frequency response, condensers sound very different on guitar amps than dynamic microphones do and are the best choice (usually) on acoustic guitars. Condensers are also good general-instrument microphones for a home studio. You can use them almost anywhere.

Next is the ribbon microphone, an underutilized "secret weapon" for digital recording.

Ribbon Microphones

A ribbon microphone is closest to a dynamic microphone in construction, but instead of using a moving coil, two very thin sheets of metal (usually coated with mylar) are suspended between the poles of a magnet. These thin ribbons induce current as they move back and forth. Like dynamic microphones, they are induction microphones, but they sound very different. Like dynamic microphones, ribbons don't require external power and put out a very weak amount of electricity—noticeably less than a dynamic or condenser microphone, so you'll need a really beefy preamp.

Ribbons are more expensive and more fragile, and there are fewer of them on the market. Traditionally, they have been very expensive, but that is changing now with the introduction of some lower-cost ribbon microphones. Negatives aside, ribbon microphones have one big thing going for them, which is character. They output a warm signal, full of character. Digital recording is very honest about what you present it with; it will reproduce exactly what you feed it. Cold and clinical microphones will sound exactly the same way when played back. Back in the analog days, tape added some character to *everything* that came through it. With digital, you get a much clearer picture of what's really there. Ribbon mics are wonderful for digital recordings, and they sound exceptional on guitar amps. Even though they are expensive, they are definitely worth an audition if you're taking your recorded tone seriously.

Ribbon microphones have one more unique feature: They hear sound in a distinct "figure 8" pattern. This "figure 8" is a type of polar pattern.

Polar Patterns

A polar pattern is the direction in which a microphone hears sound. This factor can influence your decision not only to purchase the best microphone for yourself, but also to choose the right microphone for the job.

Cardiod

The first polar pattern is the most utilized: the cardiod pattern, as seen in Figure 13.3.

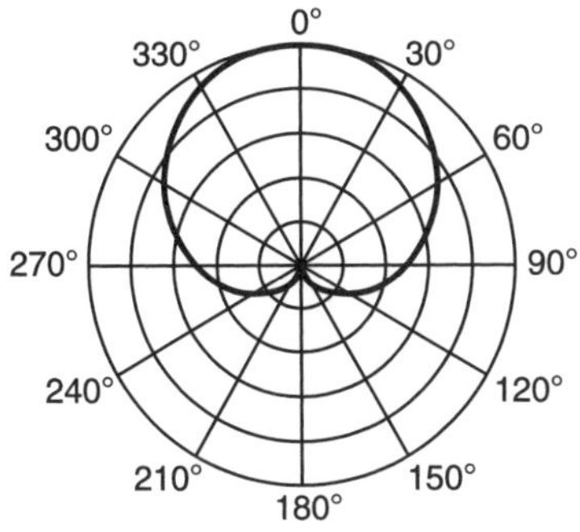

Figure 13.3
The cardiod polar pattern. The microphone is dead center in the middle of the circle, and the sound source is coming from the right, at zero degrees on the circle.

This polar pattern has been referred to as the "heart" pattern. Basically, the microphone hears what's pointed at its capsule, directly in front of it. Because the circle does not extend behind the head of the microphone, it rejects the majority of sounds coming from behind it. This makes this microphone extremely directional. Directionality is great when you want to minimize bleed from other nearby instruments, such as a live band. The cardiod pattern is found on virtually all dynamic microphones and virtually all condensers.

There are two subsets of the cardiod pattern: the supercardiod and the hypercardiod. Both follow the same principle as the cardiod, where the front of the microphone hears the sound and the back rejects sound. As you can see from Figures 13.4 and 13.5, the super- and hypercardiod microphones only differ in the amount of noise they reject from the back.

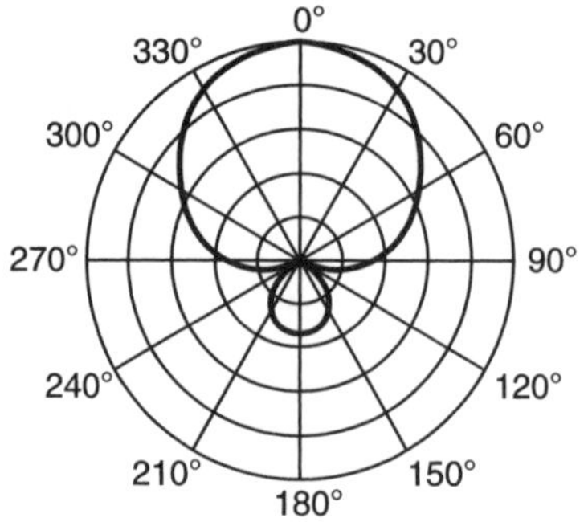

Figure 13.4
The supercardiod polar pattern. The microphone is dead center in the middle of the circle, and the sound source is coming from the right, at zero degrees on the circle.

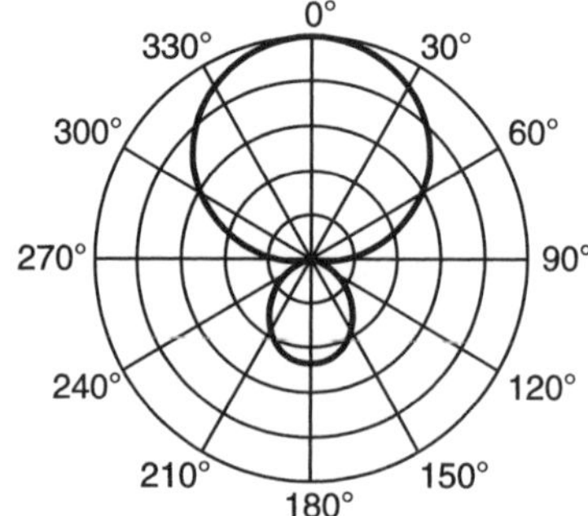

Figure 13.5
The hypercardiod polar pattern. The microphone is dead center in the middle of the circle, and the sound source is coming from the right, at zero degrees on the circle.

Traditional cardiod patterns are the most common, but hyper- and supercardiod variations are useful when you really need to isolate only the sound coming directly into the head of the microphone and reject as much other noise as possible.

Omnidirectional

The next polar pattern is the omnidirectional ("omni" means "all"). This is a microphone polar pattern that can hear equally in all directions. Figure 13.6 shows the omnidirectional polar pattern.

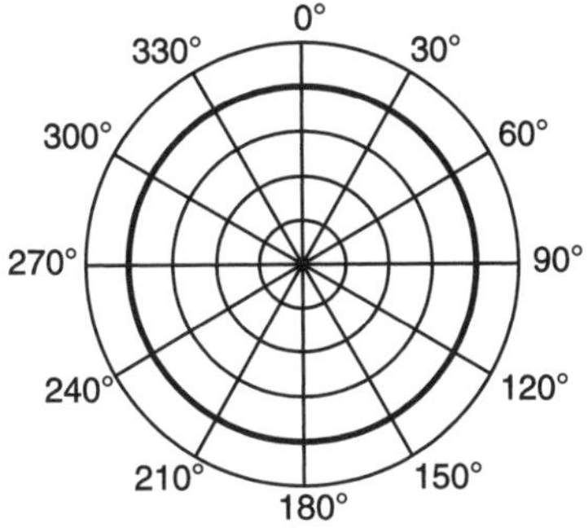

Figure 13.6
The omnidirectional polar pattern. The microphone is dead center in the middle of the circle, and the sound source is coming from the right, at zero degrees on the circle.

Omnidirectional microphones are extremely true to the source they record. Many call them "ears with wires." Since the omnidirectional microphone hears from all sides, you get not only the source, but also the dynamics and natural reverberation of the room you are recording in. My all-time favorite microphones for recording anything are the Earthworks brand of omnidirectional microphones. I use them almost everywhere I can because of their pristine image and exacting reproduction of exactly what I throw at them. Omnis have a bad reputation because they impart so much of the room in the sound, and if your room sounds bad, the omni will not be kind. But also keep in mind that an omnidirectional mic imparts no proximity effect, so you can minimize the room by miking an instrument extremely close-up. That being said, no matter how close to a source you get, you will always get some of the room in the sound when using an omni. My favorite mic, the Earthworks QTC1, is shown in Figure 13.7.

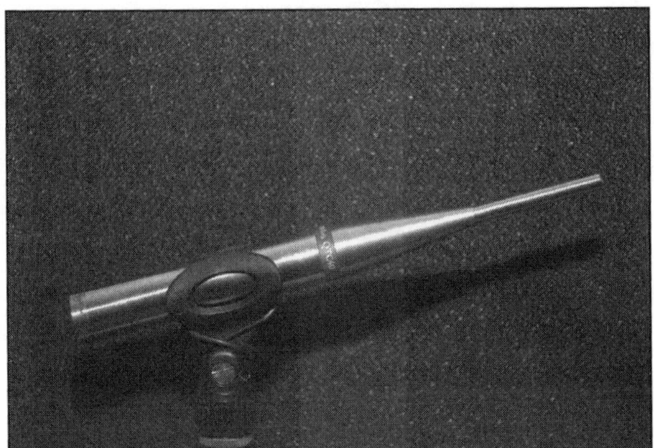

Figure 13.7
The Earthworks QTC1 omnidirectional microphone.

Figure 8

Figure 8 microphones are unique in that they only hear sound equally from the sides. They are often referred to as side address microphones. You see them a lot on talk shows. Figure 13.8 shows the polar pattern for a figure 8 microphone.

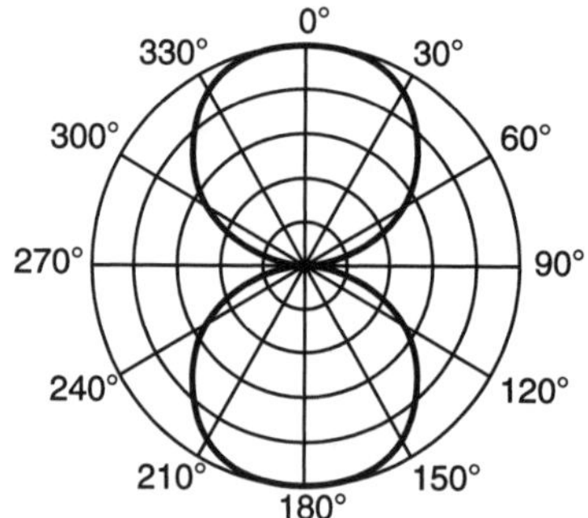

Figure 13.8
The figure 8 polar pattern. The microphone is dead center in the middle of the circle, and the sound source is coming from the right, at zero degrees on the circle.

Microphones that utilize the figure 8 pattern include some condenser microphones that support multi-pattern, and almost every ribbon microphone, by design.

COME A LITTLE CLOSER

All directional microphones (cardiods in all varieties and figure 8 microphones) suffer from something called the proximity effect. This effect is simple: The closer you place a microphone to a sound source, the more exaggerated the bass response becomes. If you place a directional microphone very close to an amp or a voice, you will get an unnatural bass boost, one that is not present in the original source. On vocals, it can make the sound a bit more robust, but on amps it can simply bloat the bass. People place directional microphones very close to the sound sources for a direct sound that rejects much of the background noise, but they will get this proximity effect.

The only microphones that do not suffer from this are omnidirectional microphones. All claims about the omnidirectional being annoying, in regards to hearing a car door close outside the studio, go away when you can stick one less than an inch from the grill of an amplifier with no proximity effect. The closeness to the source eliminates the omni's ability to hear much else, due to signal-to-noise ratio. The higher the sound pressure of the amp, the less the mic is able to hear anything else, and the result is that the sound is exactly as it was, and better yet, it has no proximity effect.

Now that you have a solid grasp on the ways that microphones hear sound, as we progress through the rest of the chapter, you'll have a better understanding of the kinds of microphones you can choose for different situations, and why.

USB

All of the microphones we've discussed require a separate preamp and interface to send sound into your computer. If you plan to primarily use direct recording and occasionally record with a traditional microphone, there is a new type of microphone on the market that may interest you: the USB microphone. This is essentially a microphone with a built-in preamplifier and analog-to-digital (A/D)

> converter. Currently, Blue is making the Snowball USB microphone, and Samson makes the C01U USB condenser microphone. If you are trying to record on the cheap and need a very convenient way to do so, take a look at these new mics. They don't require interfaces or preamps, they don't require drivers either, and they are true plug and play. If you are just getting into recording real sounds, a USB mic may be just what the doctor ordered.
>
> On a side note, Blue sent me a Snowball USB mic to test for this book. I thought it was so cool that I took it hostage and refused to return it to them. I keep it in my laptop bag with me at all times so I can simply record anything, anytime I need to. The sound quality is not the same as a Neumann u47 FET, but I have made some fine, impromptu location recordings with it.

Miking an Amplifier

Miking an amplifier is a basic recording technique. Unfortunately, many players just throw a microphone in front of a speaker, decide that "it's good enough," and never try to experiment with placement and microphone type. Miking an amplifier is an art, and there's a bit about it to discuss here.

The first thing to talk about is your microphone choice. We have talked about dynamic, condenser, and ribbon microphones as the three main types of microphones you encounter in the recording process. Which microphone should you choose? Well, this is a hard one! It *depends*... Dynamic microphones almost always hear in a cardiod pattern, meaning that they hear what you point them at, and they hear little from the back and sides. Dynamic mics may be a solid choice if you are miking other instruments in a live room and need the "rejection" that cardiods give you. We have also discussed that dynamic mics aren't exactly the best when it comes to accurate sound reproduction. Now, that may not be a negative thing. Each microphone's frequency response is different, and while a dynamic mic may not be "true like your ear," it may accentuate the principal parts of the guitar's spectrum, so it may be a good thing in the end.

Condenser microphones will give you a different sound than the dynamic microphones. You will hear a broader frequency range than with a dynamic, which may or may not please you. Both dynamics and condensers (in cardiod patterns) will exhibit the proximity effect, so you will get a bass boost no matter which one you use.

Many condenser microphones have the ability to utilize multiple polar patterns. Some mics, like the AKG 414, can utilize every polar pattern! When using a condenser, definitely try to switch it into omnidirectional mode and listen to the difference. Omnidirectional mics take into account the room you are recording in, so if you have other instruments present, it will hear them and the room you are recording in (which can be both a blessing and a curse). But, since omnis have no proximity effect, you can move them *very* close to the source without fear of proximity effect. And since you are so close to a loud source, signal-to-noise ratio takes over, and you basically block out the other sounds.

Your last choice is the ribbon microphone. Remember that ribbon microphones nearly always utilize a figure 8 pattern, so you will have to point the microphone sideways (either side) to get a proper signal into the microphone. As I've said before, digital recordings greatly benefit from the smooth and warm pickup of a ribbon microphone. I was absolutely stunned when I heard my first nice ribbon microphone (a Royer Ribbon) on a standard guitar cab.

No matter what you choose to do, the placement of the microphone and distance is a major consideration in mic placement. The good ol' SM-57 isn't still around for no reason. You can get a fine sound if you know how to place it.

Placement and Distance

In the next chapter, we are going to discuss mixing techniques specific to guitar, but this section on how to place the microphone is more important than any mixing trick you can learn. Get the idea out of your head forever that you will "fix it in the mix." You won't. The sound you get when the sound hits the microphone and goes to your recording source is about 90% of what you will end up with, so you have to get the sound right *while* recording and not expect to fix it later.

Microphone Placement

Where you place a microphone on an amplifier/speaker has a dramatic effect on what the microphone hears and what your final sound is going to be. We have talked about on-axis versus off-axis in regard to plug-ins and their ability to re-create different miking techniques. Now it's time to learn about what you can do in the studio to get different tones.

First, let's look at a miked speaker, shown in Figure 13.9.

Figure 13.9
A Flite Sound 12-inch speaker cabinet miked dead center, on-axis, with a Blue 8-Ball condenser microphone.

Speakers have a main cone right in the middle. If you point the microphone there, that's referred to as on-axis. This gives you a particular sound. As a general rule, you will get your brightest sound, as in full of high frequencies, the closer to dead center on-axis you are. As you move to the right or left side of the speaker, away from the center, the frequency response changes pretty radically. You will notice that the sound gets warmer and less harsh as you move away from the center of the speaker. This is EQ for dummies. Without even having to touch a dial, you are able to capture different sounds simply by moving the microphone around. Figure 13.10 shows more of an "edge" miking style.

Figure 13.10
A Flite Sound 12-inch speaker miked on its edge, on-axis, with a Blue 8-Ball condenser microphone.

> **MOVE**
> You really need to move the microphone around. I'm not kidding about this. Even if you are recording all alone, you need to experiment as much as you can. I use small pieces of tape on the grilles of amps to mark which positions I have miked, and I do several different takes of the same guitar part with the microphone at various spots. Then I listen to each one and decide which one sounds best. It may take me a good hour or so to get the sound I want. The result is a sound on tape, or disc for that matter, that needs very little in terms of mixing. Get the sound right the first time and use microphone placement as your ultimate EQ. Really, this is the best opportunity to get the sounds correct, rather than trying to "fix them in the mix," which is my least favorite phrase in recording.

There are other things you can experiment with. Let's run down a list of things you should be trying:

- **Microphone distance**: As you move the microphone farther back from the amp, you get a sense of space, air, and distance. The room that you are in will become part of the sound, and you may get a natural ambient effect. Not to mention that the farther back you are from the amp, the less proximity effect you will have to deal with later. Proximity effect can be a good thing, or it can bloat the bass of your recordings. You can nip this one in the bud right here and now.

- **Multiple mics**: Aren't sure which microphone to use? If you have inputs and preamps available, set up a few. Try a few that are all recording the same thing, and play them back separately to see which one you like best. This is usually the best way to find out how one microphone sounds compared to another. Be careful that you choose one mic and not a mixture. If you do choose a mixture, you may have issues due to phase cancellation of mics that are too close together, which can lead to comb filtering and other less-than-desirable effects.
- **Near and far**: Do you really listen to your amp with your ear one-half of an inch from the speaker? No, I didn't think so. So why would you record it that way? All sounds interact with the rooms they are recorded in, and close-miking pretty much destroys all hope of getting any air or room sound in there. Here's a good trick: Put one microphone close up, place a condenser, preferably an omni microphone, a few feet back from the amp, and record both mics. In your DAW, mix both mics together. Because the distant microphone will receive the audible signal a bit later (sound takes time to travel through the air), the second condenser will be slightly delayed (free delay effect), and its signal will be full of room (free reverb). By finding a good mix of your close and distant microphone source, you can get a wide, expansive image. Remember my mantra: Get it right at the mics and mixing will go so much easier.
- **Don't fear the omni**: So many engineers are scared of omni microphones because they "hear too much" and can be a pain. What omnis have going for them is super-flat frequency response and no proximity effect. Throw up a pair of omnis (they work better in spaced pairs) fairly close to your amp, and be prepared to be shocked and amazed that your amp finally sounds *exactly* the same on tape as it does in the room. And because you're using omnis, you'll get some room ambience (free reverb) and you'll have less mixing to do later.
- **Experiment**: Try stuff. Mic the back of the amp. Mic the side of the amp. Place the microphone above it. You'll never know how things sound until you try them. There are few, if any, rules for recording, and you may be amazed at what things sound like.

Reamping

Reamping is a fairly simple idea: It simply means to reamplify a signal and capture it again. Reamping can come in two flavors. The first is to take the output of a computer plug-in, send it out of your interface, and back through a real amp. This is done with a special piece of hardware called a reamping box. The function of this box is to convert the line-level output of your interface back into a high-impedance source that your guitar amplifier can accept. You can run the sound through a clean amp and mic the amp. You will get a sense of realism that way, and the natural color of the amp will come through. Not to mention that you can have fun with microphone choice and placement to affect the overall sound. When you go back into the computer, you can run it through a super-warm preamp to color the sound even more. Many times, doing this will take the edge off digital guitar tones and leave you with a much more realistic signal.

The second way I reamp is by miking my studio monitors while mixing. I don't like to go back through an amplifier again because I feel that it's too much color. I can get the color I want in the computer, but what I can't get in the computer is real space. I use my studio monitors as amplifiers and mic them using a variety of different microphones to add some real ambience to the track. I then mix the original track with the reamped track to get a proper balance of my original source (the plug-in) with the reamped track, which provides me with some great ambience. The fact that I use an extremely flat omni microphone (an Earthworks QTC40) with a Neve preamp doesn't hurt the sound much, either.

Marc's Expert Tip: Don't Be So Direct!

The majority of guitar emulation plug-ins are expecting you to plug your guitar directly into an interface and the plug-in will take care of the rest. While I do this live for convenience, when I record in the studio, I never run direct. I simply take my amp, set it to a clean sound, and place a really good microphone in front of it (my beloved Royer Ribbon). I run the good microphone into a really good preamp (my beloved Neve Portico) and run that through Guitar Rig. The difference is shocking. The direct signal sounds much flatter and more lifeless than the miked version. If you can swing this, I would highly recommend it, because it gives you a much more realistic sound—at least to my ears it does.

Now for the last part about recording guitar, let's talk about the acoustic guitar, something we haven't given much attention to.

Recording Acoustic Guitar

Okay, folks. Recording acoustic guitar is the hardest to get right. Many engineers consider this to be second only to piano in terms of miking difficulty. I would have to concur.

Let's talk about microphones. I can tell you with almost absolute certainty that a dynamic microphone is a bad idea. It simply doesn't have the frequency response needed to capture the full range of an acoustic guitar. You're going to want a condenser or a ribbon microphone for a good acoustic sound. Cardiod patterns will work fine, but if you have a good room, an omnidirectional mic will give you the most realistic image possible.

As for technique, there are a bunch of ways to go here. You're going to want to record an acoustic guitar in stereo with two microphones. The reason for this is that an acoustic guitar radiates sound in a whole bunch of different directions, and one microphone simply won't give you the full sound you want. Here is a list of common techniques for two-microphone recording:

- **Spaced pair**: Take a pair of mics, space them equally in front of your guitar, and record. This works very well with omnidirectional microphones.
- **X/Y**: X/Y technique involves crossing the heads of two microphones 90 degrees from each other, so that the right microphone hears the left channel and vice versa. You'll want to use cardiod (or super, or hyper) mics for this job because directionality is important. You can place these mics in front of the guitar and get a wide stereo image this way.
- **Non-adjacent pairs**: Record with two mics (they don't have to be the same matched pair). Use one mic near the sound hole for the direct sound and place the other microphone closer to the neck/headstock region to get some ambience and a slightly mellower sound.

Without a doubt, mic placement is key here. Even more than miking an amp, acoustic guitars have sweet spots, and there is no excuse for not moving that mic around until you find a good spot.

What about piezo pickups? Many acoustic guitars have amplified outputs using piezo (pressure crystal) pickups embedded in their saddles. Should you use them? Well, if you've heard a piezo, you'll agree that it sounds sort of like an acoustic guitar, but nowhere near as good as a real microphone does. Does this mean that you shouldn't use them? Alone, no. In conjunction with normal stereo miking techniques, yes! Try to record your guitar with three tracks. Use two microphones and the direct piezo feed, and blend them together. The piezo has a sharp and crisp sound that, when dialed in with your signal, can add a very nice dimension.

TRIFECTA!

For the ultimate digital guitar experience, check out a Godin acoustic guitar that is equipped with a piezo pickup and a 13-pin MIDI pickup. You can record all three at the same time: acoustic sound via traditional microphones, direct piezo sound, *and* MIDI into your sequencer for further manipulation or virtual instruments later on. Talk about getting all angles of the digital guitar puzzle! Other companies may offer guitars that do all three, but Godin is a notable company for bringing all aspects into one guitar.

Now that we have talked about all the different ways to mic your guitars, we need to talk about specific tips and tricks for mixing guitars. On to Chapter 14!

14 Mixing Strategies for Guitar

We can't possibly teach you how to mix a full band in one chapter; most books have a difficult time doing that in 20 chapters. This section is geared toward showing you a few specific techniques, such as how to replace the hardware effects in your guitar signal chain with virtual effects, how to deal with EQ issues when you mix guitar tracks within your DAW, and some neat tips and tricks to help your recorded guitar tracks simply sound better.

Replacing Effects

Many guitar players are starting to replicate their hardware-based guitar effect units in the computer with plug-ins. We've seen that the vast majority of guitar plug-ins deal mainly with emulating amplifiers and stompbox-style guitar effects. You may have better-sounding and more flexible choices within your DAW, or as purchases you can make separately.

When adding effects to a traditional guitar amplifier, you can do it in one of two ways: stompbox-style before the amp input, or in an effects loop.

Replicating Inline Effects in a DAW

In the DAW world, stompbox-style effects are typically considered insert effects. Let's take a look at two popular programs, Logic and Cubase, and see how they deal with insert effects. Since most DAWs are meant to emulate mixing boards in traditional analog studios, you'll find channels complete with volume faders in both programs. Figure 14.1 shows Logic's channel strip with an inline or insert Chorus plug-in (this plug-in is included with Logic Pro).

Your signal first passes through the Insert plug-in; then the channel sends the affected signal to the output. Using an inline effect like this does not necessarily mean that you'll get a flood of chorus, however. Within most Insert plug-ins, you will find either a level control or a mix control. These controls will set how much of the effect is applied to your sound. In the case

Figure 14.1
A single channel strip in Logic with a Chorus plug-in as an insert effect.

of the Chorus plug-in, you have a mix control, as seen in Figure 14.2. The mix control allows you to get a good ratio of affected versus unaffected sound and to balance your chorus as you see fit.

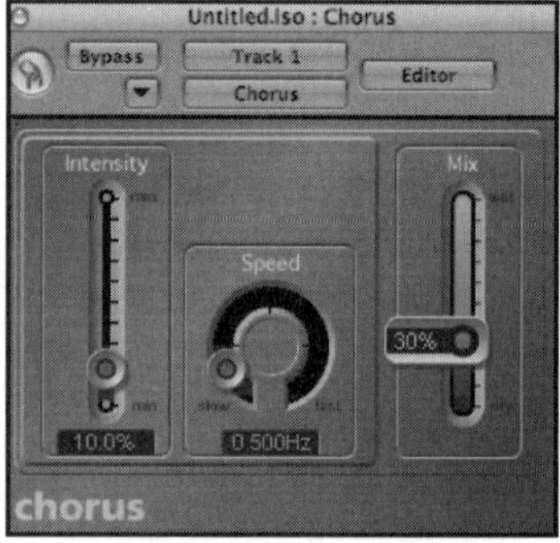

Figure 14.2
A close-up view of Logic's Chorus plug-in.

On a Chorus stompbox, such as the popular Boss CE-5, you'll find the same Mix control simply listed as Level. This holds true for the vast majority of stompbox-style guitar pedals—you'll most likely see Level on the hardware units and Mix on the plug-ins, but of course nothing is absolute. As you can see in Figure 14.2, all the controls you'd expect to see in a Chorus unit, whether virtual or real, are included.

In Logic, the insert effects affect the signal in a top-down order, meaning that your signal flows from the first effect to the second effect, starting at the top of the channel strip. The same rules will apply in the virtual world because quite simply, the virtual software programs are trying to re-create the good old analog-style working environments. For example, when you create chains of stompboxes in traditional guitar rigs, you pay fairly careful attention to which effect came in which order. Certain rules like “Wah-wah first, reverb last, and distortion in the middle” are fairly tried-and-true placements. This is what you want to re-create in the channel strip.

Switching to Cubase, you’ll find a very similar-looking mixer with some different cosmetic treatments. Cubase is a bit different in that its main mixer can be configured to show different views. In Figure 14.3, I have it showing EQ only.

Figure 14.3
Cubase’s mixer showing EQ only.

I can also have Cubase show insert effects, as in Figure 14.4.

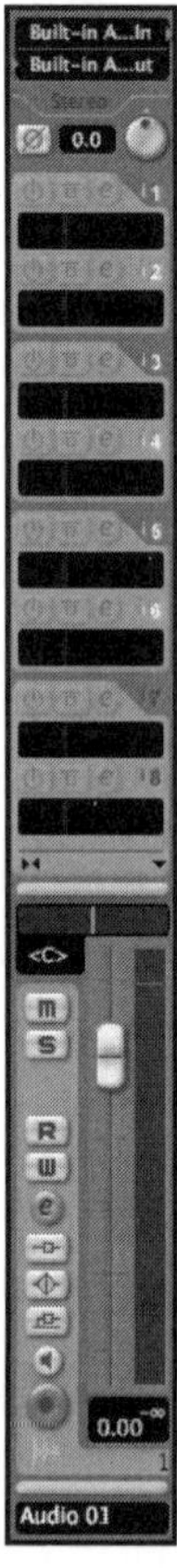

Figure 14.4
Cubase's mixer showing insert effects only.

There is no way to access more than one track component at a time in the Cubase mixer; however, Cubase has a separate window called Channel Settings, which gives you access to a single track's Volume, Pan, Insert, and Send effects (more on Send effects later). Figure 14.5 shows this window configured with a Chorus and Delay effect as insert effects (inline effects).

Within this view, my inserts are on the left side, EQ is in the middle, and Send effects are on the right side. This view makes it very easy to see what's going on with my track. Just like Logic, Cubase processes its insert effects from top to bottom. So the order of effects is crucial! Set this up just as you would in the real world.

This may seem overly simplified, but you can build effects chains like this that sound as good as or many times better than your stompboxes—and these effects never need batteries. Back in Chapter 11, we talked about the Universal Audio UAD card as a DSP card solution that contains

Figure 14.5
Cubase's Channel Settings channel overview window.

an amp emulator called Nigel. I've never loved Nigel as an amp emulator, but the effects that come as part of the UAD card are just fantastic. Of considerable interest to guitarists are the new Roland emulations. The UAD card contains emulations of the old CE-1 Chorus, which is still sought after (see Figure 14.6), and the Dimension-D Chorus (see Figure 14.7). These effects are pretty much spot-on re-creations of hardware that is no longer made and difficult to find. This is a great example of how the digital world has made things a bit better for us guitarists.

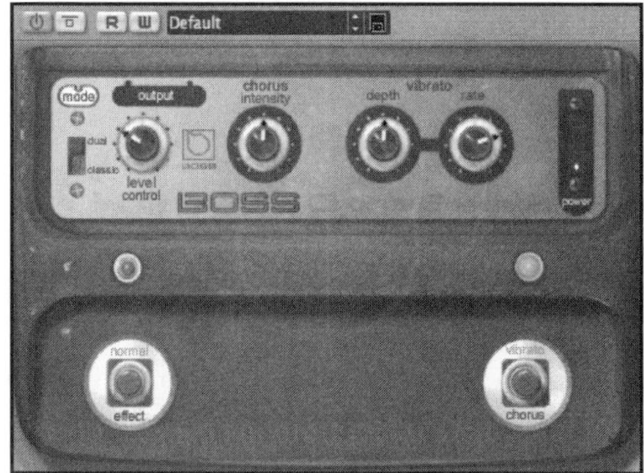

Figure 14.6
Universal Audio's Roland CE-1 Chorus Pedal.

Figure 14.7
Universal Audio's Roland Dimension D Chorus.

CHOICE

Every sequencer or DAW program will come with a selection of included effects. These will cover the basic effects you'll need to get started. You are almost sure to find at least one Reverb, Chorus, Delay, Compression, Distortion, Flange, Phase, and other "bread and butter" effects in any DAW program you buy. The quality of the plug-ins depends on the program, but as a whole, they are more than adequate. If you are looking to extend your system, you're in luck! The effects market has made a dramatic shift towards plug-ins in the past few years, and your choices of aftermarket plug-ins for sound processing are more abundant than ever.

I love the DSP cards, like UAD and Powercore, because their effects are very high-quality and you can run them without penalty on your computer. Waves has had a reputation for quality plug-ins since the early days of digital audio, and they still make some fantastic products. Other companies worth looking at are URS, Audio Ease, Nomad Factory, PSP Audioware, Wave Arts, and others. Honestly, there are so many good plug-ins now that it's hard to say "get this one." Thankfully, many of them have demos, and you owe it to yourself to check out as many of them as you can.

Replicating Effect Loops in a DAW

The other way to add effects to an amplifier is by using an effects loop (if your amp has one, which many modern amplifiers do). An effects loop works completely differently than insert effects. An insert effect, as you learned earlier, lets your signal pass directly through the effect before it hits the amp. An effects loop is a bit different. Typically, on the back of your amp, you have a send and return jack (this signifies an effects loop), and perhaps also an effects loop mix knob. The send jack sends your amplifier's signal to an effects unit. The signal is then processed by the unit, and the processed output is fed back into the amplifier via the return jack.

This design is very different than insert effects, for a number of reasons. First, your original signal is both sent to the effects processor and sent out of the amp unaffected. The Mix knob allows you to mix your dry signal with the affected signal. This is a bit different than taking an insert effect and just turning the Mix knob down. When you run the signal through a pedal into an amplifier, no matter what you do, its circuitry will have some effect on your sound, even when the mix is way down. By using an effects loop, you retain your original tone and the effects loop sound is mixed in at the very end. You can control the amount of pure/affected signal with greater precision.

Effects loops are most often used with rack-mounted effects processors that specialize in time-based effects such as Delay, Chorus, Reverb, and other multi-effects units, such as the TC Electronic G-Major processor we discussed earlier. Generally, effects that require control of wet/dry work best in effects loops.

Now, how do we do this in the virtual world? Actually, not all that differently! We are going to learn about buses, which are the equivalent to parallel effect loops.

A bus is simply a path for audio to take. In the studio, a bus is a multifunction tool. You can use it as a submix, sending several channels to a single volume fader (for a drum submix, for instance). In this case, we are going to use a bus channel as an effects loop. Let's take a look at Logic's channel strip again, and this time, pay attention to the section labeled Sends, as seen in Figure 14.8.

Figure 14.8
Logic's channel strip, this time showing an active Send to Bus 1 and a rotary Send knob.

The Sends section sends a copy of your audio signal to an available bus. In Figure 14.8, I have sent my signal to Bus 1. Next to each bus slot is a rotary dial, which chooses how much of your signal is sent to the bus.

On the actual Bus 1, you would add an insert effect. In this case, I'm using Altiverb, a high-end convolution reverb. I add that as an insert effect, as seen in Figure 14.9.

Now, here's how it works. On our original track, the Send dial that controls how much of our signal to send to the bus is essentially controlling the bus's input. On the bus itself, you always set the plug-ins to 100% Wet signal, because you do wet/dry mix differently. Wet/dry mix is handled by the volume fader on the bus channel. By making the bus louder, you get more reverb in the mix, but by decreasing it, you get the opposite effect. On the original track, your Send can be either pre-fader or post-fader. If your Send is pre-fader, you can add more dry sound by adding more level with its volume fader. If your send is post-fader, turning up your fader adds both dry and affected signal. In this way, you have re-created an effects loop. You can simply run a few buses for various effects, such as reverb, relay, or other effects, when you want to have more precise control over levels and wet/dry mix.

Figure 14.9
Our actual Bus 1, containing the Altiverb convolution reverb effect.

> **JUST ONE**
> Unless you have a good reason to do otherwise, only insert one effect on a single bus. Each bus ideally should be relegated to the duty of the plug-in you assign to it. You can get some interesting effects if you chain inserts together on buses, but the general wisdom is that you should do it one at a time. Also of note, you can use a reverb bus to service multiple tracks in order to save CPU power! You can do this with any bus effect, not just reverb—although reverb is notoriously CPU-intensive.

Busing works essentially the same in almost all other applications. You will almost always find a Send control of some sort on your tracks. Cubase does not call these bus tracks, but instead refers to them as FX tracks. Even though their name is different, their function is identical in every way. The reason that most DAWs work this way is that they are trying to re-create the mixing board, which has Send and Receive knobs and buses its effects this very way.

Marc's Top 5 Reasons to Use Plug-ins

I absolutely love plug-ins. I have basically sold all my hardware and use plug-ins instead. Let me give you a Letterman-style Top 5 list of why you should use plug-ins—in no particular order. (I know he uses 10, but I only have 5.)

1. You can use the same plug-in more than once in the same project. Actually, you can use it as many times as your computer's CPU can handle. Try that with a distortion pedal!
2. You can automate the functions of your plug-ins after the fact, using host-based automation, adding a sense of movement, and changing your sound dynamically as the song progresses.
3. The current breed of digital plug-ins sounds better than the cheap stompbox pedals that you use. Nothing against the Boss Reverb pedal, but convolution reverb is an unfair comparison. Boutique pedals still have their place, and you can still use them if you wish.
4. Plug-ins are often improved with updates. Manufacturers find ways to make them sound better and work more efficiently. Most of the time, these updates are free, and if significant advances are made, you may have to pay a small fee to upgrade to the newer version.
5. There are tons of free plug-ins out there. I mean, completely free. You name the effect, and chances are you can find a freeware version of it. The shocking part is that many of these free plug-ins sound incredible and offer you sound options you simply can't get anywhere else. A quick Internet search for "freeware audio plug-ins" will yield pages and pages of results. Happy hunting.

How to EQ Guitar

The art of equalizing the guitar comes down to your knowledge of a few key factors. First, you need to ask yourself, "Why am I trying to EQ it?" You need to have a specific-purpose sonic goal, or you're just going to affect the sound adversely. Adding or reducing frequencies in a sound is always a destructive process in my opinion, and you want to do the best you can to avoid unnecessary EQ. There are a bunch of really valid reasons to EQ. Let's list a few of them now. You may need to EQ if:

- You have a pronounced proximity effect from your microphone placement.
- Your guitar seems overly muddy and lacks clarity.
- Your guitar is fighting with another instrument in the same mix.
- You need to get rid of noise in your guitar signal.

As you can see, there are many valid reasons to work with EQ. The next trick is understanding more about the guitar's frequency range.

The Guitar's Frequency Range

Before we go any further, let me explain sounding about sound. Every note has a fundamental frequency. This is the main pitch you can measure when you state that "the low E string on the guitar has a frequency of 82 Hz." Now, if I were to pluck the low E string of a guitar and put it through a scope that showed the frequency range, I would certainly see a lot of activity at

82 Hz, but there would be other information there as well. To see exactly what else is going on, I load up a free plug-in called Inspector by Elemental Audio (which is totally free and runs on Mac and PC). Inspector lets me look at the frequency range of my audio. Figure 14.10 shows my single 82 Hz low E.

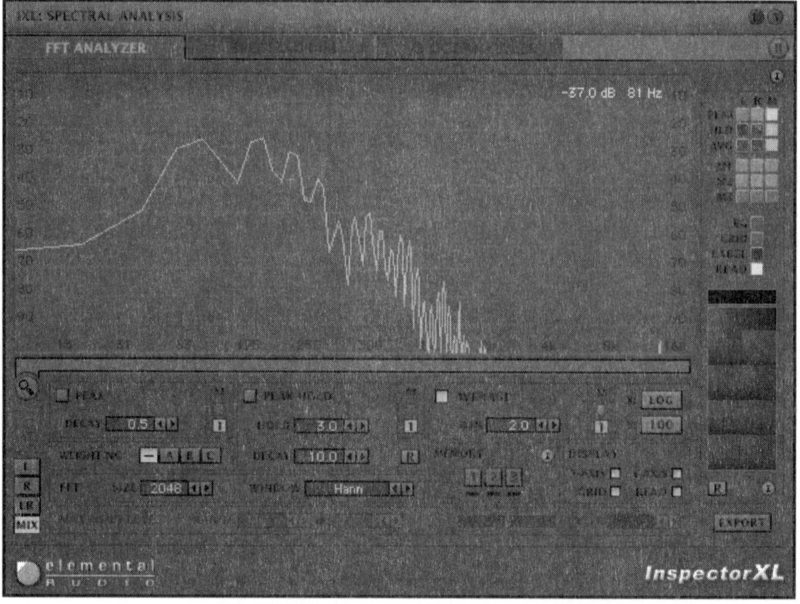

Figure 14.10
Inspector displaying my low E at 82 Hz.

You can clearly see information at 82 Hz, that's where the largest vertical spike is, but you can also see information in the higher-frequency bands. Of course, nothing is as loud as the fundamental frequency, but there is more than just 82 Hz there. Put simply, any single pitch actually contains other frequencies mixed in with the fundamental. These are called *overtones*.

The reason you went to all that trouble is because the range of the guitar is 82 Hz (low E) to 1.3 kHz (24th fret, high E string). This is only the fundamental range of the guitar. The overtones will push the frequencies higher. Even more importantly, distortion and microphone coloration will add to your sound as well. You can work from the following assumptions: The EQ-able range of the guitar is generally from 80 Hz to 5 kHz. As we will get into later, you can EQ much higher than 5 kHz, but it will only have a limited effect. In the last section, we discussed a bunch of reasons you may want to EQ. Let's go through those and look at how you might succeed.

EQ Practices

Let's talk about practical examples for EQ. There will always be engineers who can turn "magic" knobs and get great sounds in seconds, but certain equalization techniques can be taught here in this book, without having a specific sound in front of you.

Proximity Effect

Whether you've actually miked an amp or are using a virtual plug-in with cabinet and microphone emulation, you will probably encounter proximity effect. As you'll remember, proximity effect is an exaggeration of bass frequencies due to very close miking with a cardiod (any cardiod type) or figure 8 pattern microphone. Proximity effect can be really cool, but most times it causes a few problems. First, it can make your lower frequencies sound indistinct, muddy, and inflated. The second thing it can do is start interfering with other instruments (which we will talk about soon). Getting rid of it is fairly easy. You know that unless you're drop-tuning your guitar, the lowest fundamental pitch will be around 80 Hz. You can simply cut the frequencies below that point to carve that effect away. Let me show you how I got rid of proximity effect with a simple EQ plug-in. I used the UAD Cambridge EQ, because it's one of my favorite EQs. However, every DAW comes with EQ, and you'll be able to get these results with almost any EQ. Figure 14.11 shows my settings.

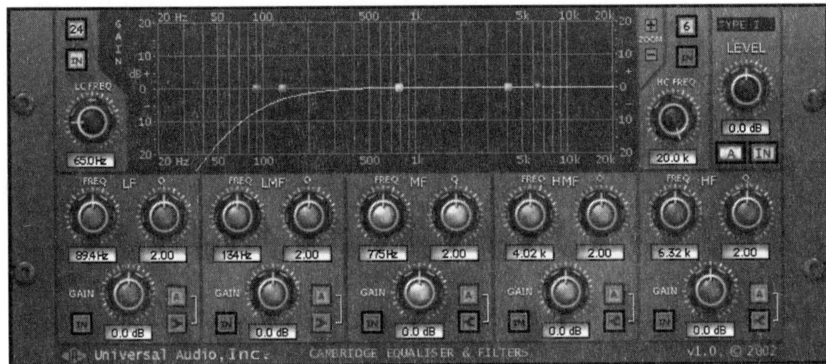

Figure 14.11
Getting rid of proximity effect.

This particular EQ has a lot to look at, but I simply executed a Low Cut filter, also known as a Roll Off filter. In the top left of Figure 14.11, I set the LC Frequency to 65 Hz, which simply means that any sound below 65 Hz will be turned down. I had to experiment a bit with the frequency. Proximity effect is never the same twice, because each mic is different and elements like distance from the source and axis angle will contribute to exactly how much proximity effect you encounter. In general, you want to start rolling off as high as 80 Hz, and sometimes as low as 50 Hz. Your ears will tell you for sure.

Your Guitar Is Overly Muddy and Lacks Clarity

These are two different problems. If it's too muddy, either from proximity effect or because you simply have a "bassy" tone, you can do a roll-off at a higher frequency, say around 120 Hz or so. Keep in mind that when you remove frequencies, you thin out the tone. You may want to boost some frequencies above 120 Hz to increase the clarity of the other frequencies. This part is pretty variable, as I'm not sitting in front of your speakers, hearing *your sound*. What can help is using that Inspector plug-in we discussed earlier in this chapter to view your frequencies. You can learn a lot by looking at what's there and adjusting based on what you see or hear.

As for clarity, you are now in an amorphous world of EQ terms. These terms are thrown around often, such as "punchy," "brilliant," "present," "muddy," and "clear." What do they mean? I really don't know what they mean, and they seem to mean different things to different people. You have to quantify what exactly you aren't hearing and try to get it to come out. I can give you some vague ranges so you can experiment with them on your own. Here is a list of EQ terms and some general ranges.

- **Sub-Bass/Thump**: The area from 40–80 Hz
- **Bass Range**: 80 Hz to around 250 Hz
- **Low-Mid**: 250–500 Hz
- **Mids**: 500–1.5 kHz
- **Hi-Mid**: 1.5–3.5 kHz
- **Presence**: 3.5–6 kHz
- **High**: 6–10 kHz
- **Sheen**: 10–15 kHz
- **Air**: 15–20 kHz

Use these frequencies as a *very* general guideline that may help you sculpt your sounds the way you want them.

Marc's EQ Tip: Go Easy!

When using EQ, especially parametric EQs in a computer, it's very easy to go overboard with the amount of boosting or cutting you are doing. While there may be great reasons to boost or cut something aggressively, let me offer you this tip:

Don't boost or cut anything more than 2 dB in any direction at first. Anything more than 2 dB is a big move. See if you can solve your problems with gentle changes before you start going extreme. I personally find EQ a destructive process and try to do it sparingly, opting instead to get the sound as good as I can at the source, either in the amp modeler or with the mic/speaker combination. If I do have to EQ, I try to go easy. I see many young engineers make severe cuts in EQ, and while there are no rules to engineering, if you can do it with less, you'll get more. Also, remember that when you boost any frequency, you are adding level to the signal, and that can possibly cause digital distortion (the worst kind) and raise the noise floor. These are all things to consider.

Your Guitar Is Fighting with Another Instrument in the Mix

This happens *all* the time and is completely par for the course. You get your sound crafted exactly as you want it, and then you lay the rest of the band in, and all of a sudden the guitar and bass guitar are competing for space. It's not always the bass. Sometimes it's the vocals or the drums. But let's start with the main culprit, which is the bass. The bass guitar has a frequency range that starts at 41 Hz and goes right up through the middle of the guitar's range. Once you get to the second octave of the bass, you are right in the same range as the guitar. Think of EQ like a puzzle. You have the full range of frequencies, from lowest to highest, and each instrument needs to take its own part as best as it can. If you have a lot of overlap, you get mud, bloat, and other nasty sounds! What you lose is the clarity of the instruments.

To help rectify this, you can simply roll off some of the guitar's lower frequencies a bit. The bass usually doesn't play much above the 200 Hz range (unless you're John Pattitucci), so you can make room for it by gently rolling the guitar off around 150 Hz to leave room for the bass guitar. If this only makes it a bit better, you can boost the bass guitar slightly around 100 Hz or so to bring out the parts that may have been lost in your conflict. When I do this kind of EQ carving, I like to use equal and opposite reactions in my mixing style. If I open up a range of frequencies for the bass, I try to boost that range a bit in the bass just a touch to bring it out.

Depending on your mix, your guitar at its highest ranges may interfere with the drums, vocals, or piano. Carving all the instruments together will make everything better. There are tons of books on general mixing techniques you can read, but nothing beats getting your hands dirty and playing with tracks. Using tools like Inspector will help you visualize each instrument and its range, so that you can make more informed decisions about what to cut/boost and when to do it. As you get more experience, you'll find that you go to the visual plug-in less and less, and go right to the EQ knob. Talk about learning!

❊ **Expert Tip: Focus and Then Remove**

Orren Merton, author of *Guitar Rig 2 Power!* (Course Technology, 2006) and other titles, offers the following tips on EQing guitars to fit into a mix:

"The first thing I recommend is to focus on what this particular guitar part is supposed to do. Is it the meat of the song? Is it adding high-end sizzle? Is it carrying the low end? Whatever it may be, you need to identify the role that this particular guitar track has in your song.

"Once you know what your guitar track needs to do, start removing all those frequencies that it doesn't need for that task. For example, if your guitar is the meat of a song, the mid-ranges are the most important frequencies, so you can cut the highs and lows. If a track is designed to add distortion and sizzle, you can get rid of most of the low end (the bass adds the low-end grit).

"This way, you can actually do some pretty drastic cutting of your guitar track to make room for other instruments, while still maintaining the position and effect that you want the guitar to have."

Noise

EQ is great for getting rid of noise. There are two kinds of noise we will deal with here: hiss and buzz. Let's start with buzz. Anyone who's ever owned a Strat knows about buzz. AC electricity alternates back and forth 60 times a second, or at a rate of 60 Hz. When a guitar buzzes, it's going to buzz at 60 Hz and its overtones. To get rid of it, all you have to do is remove 60 Hz and its overtones from the sound. This is actually easy to do. The overtones are always twice the original frequency. If I remove 60 Hz, 120 Hz, 240 Hz, and 480 Hz (all multiples of the original 60 Hz hum), then I can squash the hum. Figure 14.12 shows how I did it with an EQ.

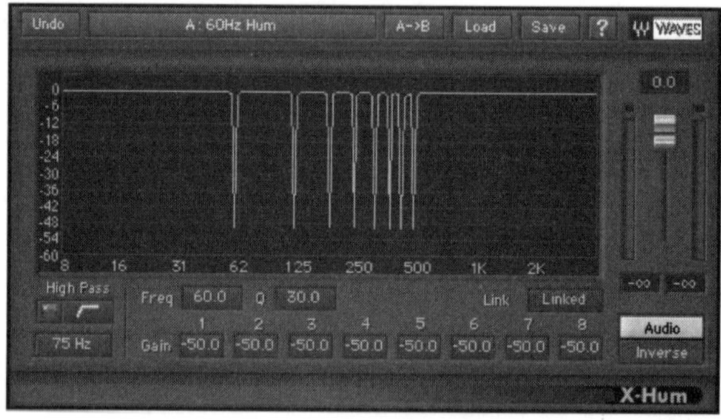

Figure 14.12
Getting rid of 60-cycle hum.

The trick to doing this and not destroying your sound is to make the individual cuts very sharp. By sharp, I mean that you only want to cut 60 Hz and not alter other frequencies around it. You do this by setting the bandwidth or Q as high as possible. This allows you to make the most surgical cuts. By attacking not only 60 Hz, but also its overtones, I was able to get rid of the hum completely.

Expert Tip: Star Grounding

Orren Merton chimes in with another tip, this time on a tried-and-true method to eliminate powerline hum:

"AC line hum can seem like a nearly insurmountable problem, and in some cases, like old or faulty wiring, it is. But one tried-and-true method of reducing or eliminating hum is called *star grounding*. The basic idea is that the hum you are hearing is caused by different devices all going through different grounds. So you want all your equipment to go through the same ground. To do this, plug one power strip into one wall outlet. When you need more outlets, rather than using another wall outlet, plug another power strip into that first power strip. The goal is that no matter how many devices you have, all eventually will be terminating in the one plug from the initial power strip.

"It may seem counterintuitive to have so many devices hanging off a single plug, and it's true that if the building's power is really old, you might blow a fuse that way. But in general, it's no harder on your circuit breaker to have 10 devices on one plug than it is to have 10 devices on four plugs, if they are all on the same circuit anyway. At least if you use the star grounding method, you stand a fighting chance of keeping hum down, or eliminating it altogether."

As for hiss, that's a bit harder to quantify. A 60-cycle hum is endemic to power lines, but hiss can take many forms and can live at higher frequencies. Typically, hiss is fairly high in the spectrum, usually above 10 kHz. Sometimes, it helps to look at your sound on a tool such as Inspector, but in general, getting rid of hiss is something that you need to be careful of. Since hiss is often referred to as broadband noise, it's hard to get rid of without getting rid of musical frequencies. There are a few tools that can take care of this. Waves has an excellent suite of tools for this, including an X-Noise plug-in, as seen in Figure 14.13.

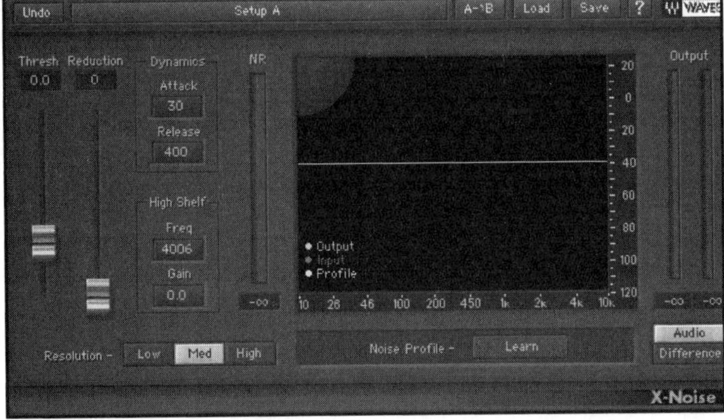

Figure 14.13
Waves X-Noise plug-in detects noise automatically and filters it out.

Realize that noise reducers are specialized EQs, and no matter how intelligent they are, you will still remove frequencies from the sound. When possible, I try to get rid of the hiss during the recording process. I have seen what noise reducers do to my overall sound, and I usually opt for a retake instead of trying to remove the noise. With that said, if you have the most incredible solo and you have to work with that take, it's good to know that you have some options.

Mixing Tips and Tricks

I'm not a big fan of mixing "tricks," for a good reason: every mix is unique. It's really hard to tell you to do X and have it work, because of the particulars that go into every song and every particular sound. However, there are a few tricks that are less about mixing and more along the lines of philosophy. Or else they're vague enough that I can offer them here with the hope that you can mold them to your particular situation.

Tip 1: Real Delay

I learned this trick from a great friend and gifted California-based engineer, Mark Robinson. The basic idea is that these tips can make guitar tracks seem more full. Here's how you do it:

1. Duplicate your track.
2. Take the duplicated track and delay it 20 ms or so (depends on taste). You can delay it by simply moving the track in time 20 milliseconds using your DAW to move the physical audio ahead in time.
3. Pan the duplicated track in the opposite direction of your original.
4. Keep the volume level of your duplicate track very low in relation to the original.

It's a simple enough trick, but oh, does it work! The trick seems to be that the second track is delayed and very low in volume; the resulting effect is a cross between a late reflection and some sort of special specialization effect. Try it, you may like it! If you notice that your guitar sound has become hollow on the second track, you may be experiencing phase issues, which is causing comb filtering. You can fix that in a few ways. First, change the amount of delay and see if that makes it better. If not, flip the phase of the second track so that it no longer interferes with the original track.

Tip 2: Motion

I have found that no matter what you do, static mixes are just that: static. I try to automate a few parameters in my guitar plug-in or EQ to keep things in motion. I typically adjust reverb, EQ levels, and gain settings. To do so, I set up an automation track and slowly draw in a curve with subtle changes over the course of the song. Small changes over the song's length give a sense of motion and help guitar parts sound better, in my opinion. If the patches are heavily affected, I may automate those as well. Now, as to how much movement I'm going to do, it's very small. Just a bit up and down over a long period of time. You'd be amazed at how small changes over the course of a tune can make your tracks sound more alive. This is one that you will have fun with.

Tip 3: Mono

With the exception of miking acoustic instruments with pairs of mics, the vast majority of guitar amps are ***mono***! Many of the new guitar simulators put out a stereo signal. I find this almost impossible to mix with. When I hear a band play live, guitar comes from the part of the stage where the amp is located physically on the stage. Some live sound engineers may play it through a PA and pan it dead center, but that's hardly stereo. I always mix my guitar tracks in mono. If I need some extended "width," I use the delay trick to widen up the mix a bit, but when I've mixed in stereo, the guitar sits too front and center and eats up the center of the mix where the vocals should be! So when mixing with guitar plug-ins, try folding back to mono and seeing how it sounds. You may be caught by the early allure of stereo guitar tracks, but they are very hard to mix well.

> **Expert Tip: Double-Tracking Guitars**
>
> Orren Merton lends his expertise once more with his thoughts on double-tracking:
>
> "Ever wonder why that Led Zeppelin or Green Day song sounds so huge? Usually, it's because they have recorded the same guitar part more than one time. The traditional way to double-track guitars is to play the exact same guitar part twice, but through different guitars or amps (or in the case of software, amp models). Be sure to record each guitar in mono (or if you use more than one mic, each mic should have its own mono track). For a really pronounced effect, the different tracks are then panned hard left and hard right. Each guitar will sound just different enough to be unique, but close enough to the others to blend into one huge guitar tone."

Tip 4: Frankenstein Amps

This last trick only came into being in the last few years, and was only made possible with amp modeling plug-ins. Here is where I got the idea: I love the sounds of different amps, but I can rarely find one amp that does it all. I constantly find myself saying that I love the sound of Marshall top end, I love Mesa Boogie bass, and Fender has wonderful midrange. So I thought to myself, what if I tried all the amps at once? So I opened three plug-ins, set up three duplicate tracks, and mixed them together. The result: a wall of sound, but not that great "wall of sound" that Pink Floyd achieved. It was a muddy mess. Then it dawned on me: If I liked the bass of the Boogie, I shouldn't hear the mid and upper range of it. If I liked the mids of the Fender, cut out the lows and highs. The same with the Marshall: If the highs were so great, I didn't need to hear the mid and bottom.

What I ended up doing was using EQs with very dramatic cuts to notch out the amps. On the Boogie, I killed anything above 1 kHz. On the Fender, I filtered out 20 Hz to 1 kHz and rolled off the frequencies from 20 kHz down to 3 kHz, which only left me that middle band of 1 kHz to 3 kHz of the Fender. On the Marshall, I cut everything below 3 kHz, so I was left with only its top end. I was able to take the parts of the amps that I needed.

I mixed all three tracks together into one track and blended them to taste. The higher frequencies tended to cut a bit more than I expected, so I had to do some leveling between the amps to get the sound I wanted. Once I got it basically right, I bounced them into a single track and did some subtle EQing to make it sound like I had one amp and not a hack job of three. A bit of reverb went a long way toward smoothing out the differences between the amps. It's funny, though, because in the end I got the most unique sound I'd ever had. I had that tight Boogie bottom I loved, the smooth midrange of the Fender, and the highs of the Marshall.

The next step is important: Once I had the amp the way I wanted it, I ran it through a very clean analog preamp, essentially reamping the signal through my best monitors with my best microphones. This way, I was able to add air to the signal and make everything work the way I wanted it to.

This is by far my most unusual trick, and I never thought it would work, but boy, it worked great! Try it, you might just be surprised.

15 MIDI Guitar

If there's ever been a Holy Grail for guitar players, it would have to be a quest for a workable MIDI guitar solution. After countless years and countless designs, guitar players had eventually become frustrated because MIDI guitar never worked like they felt it should—certainly, triggering MIDI via a guitar *never* worked nearly as well as it did for the keyboardists.

There are many contributing factors to "MIDI guitar" becoming dirty words in the guitar player's vocabulary. We need to go through their history to see what went wrong and what turned so many guitar players off to the idea. Thankfully, this is the age of technology, and we are now in a place where MIDI guitar finally works. Now, more than ever, due to the popularity of computer-based sequencers and virtual instruments, guitar players need to catch up and harness the powerful world of MIDI—at over 20 years old, a standard that simply refuses to die. If you've tried MIDI guitar and failed in the past, now is the time to take a serious look at it. Companies like Roland, Brian Moore, Starr Labs, and RMC are forging the way into the next great age of guitar: The guitar as a controller.

The History of MIDI Guitar

Before we can truly get into the history of MIDI guitar, we need to back up a bit and look at the history of synthesizers—more importantly, keyboard controllers.

Electronic or synthetic music has been around since the '50s. In the '60s, synthesizers evolved into monster pieces of modular equipment that filled an entire room. To trigger these sounds, the designers went with the simplest interface they could think of, which was the piano's keyboard. Quite simply, a piano's keyboard could easily be made into a synthesizer controller. Back then, synthesizers responded to voltage, not MIDI commands (MIDI came later). A piano's keyboard could easily send a specific voltage upon keypress and trigger the synth. Each key was assigned a different voltage and made its own unique sound, and you were able to play the keyboard as a controller instrument. From this design, the first controller was born.

You need to think of the simplicity of a keystroke with a keyboard controller. The key goes up and down. All you need is a circuit that is able to sense the key going down to send the information to the synth to play. In reverse, as you release the key, the synth is told to stop making sound. It really is a simple design. Since you can't mistake one key for another (they all have their own unique sensors), the design worked very well and continues to do so. In the old days, velocity, or musical dynamics, were not transmitted. This was a flaw in the original design. It was eventually worked out, though.

The only problem was that the guitar was and is a very popular instrument due to its size, portability, and low cost of ownership, so there are many guitar players in the world, possibly even more than pianists. A guitar is *much* cheaper and *much* more portable. Trust me on this one, let it sit. While the keyboard is a very universal instrument, not everyone can play it. For a long time, the guitar players sat back and watched the keyboard players have all the fun. When MIDI eventually came into being and the amazing world of computer-aided music opened up, we were green with envy, to say the least. Surely, there had to be some way to get a "guitar synth" working.

Non-MIDI Guitar Synths

Before MIDI was created in August 1983, synthesis was analog, meaning that notes were triggered in the analog domain through voltages—just like the original keyboard controllers. Before MIDI, electronic music consisted of oscillators and filters—no samples, no DSP, just plain old analog goodness. This usually involved some sort of pitch-to-voltage scheme, where each frequency on the guitar had a corresponding voltage that ran into a VCO (voltage-controlled oscillator), and the VCO was responsible for the sound, both for keyboard controllers and guitar controllers. The first guitar synth was the APR Avatar, which made its debut in 1977. It consisted of a hardware unit that was the synth, and a pickup that you attached to your guitar (not unlike what the Roland GK pickups do now). It was very expensive at $3,000 and didn't work that well because it had many tracking glitches and was generally slow. The glitches could include notes you never played, "ghost notes," and the tracking caused an audible delay from the time you plucked the string until the sound actually came out. But it was the first of its kind, and there is some pride in being the first to do anything. It used pitch-to-voltage technology, but wasn't particularly efficient at doing so. Only 300 units were ever made, and it nearly bankrupted the company and led to its eventual demise (ouch!).

Next up was Roland. In 1978, just one year after the Avatar came out, Roland debuted its GR-500 analog guitar synthesizer, shown in Figure 15.1.

This was Roland's first foray into the technology, and it worked pretty well, but it still was not good enough to enchant guitar players. The bulky system and limited sonic choices didn't help its popularity—neither did the high price tag. It also came with a guitar that you had to use (pictured in Figure 15.1), and many guitar players still wouldn't part with their Les Pauls, no matter what the product!

Figure 15.1
The Roland GR-500.

After the GR-500 came the simpler and smaller GR-100, which had fewer synthesizer features than the GR-500 but was more compact and affordable. The GR-100 is pictured in Figure 15.2.

With the introduction of the GR-100 came some new guitars that worked with it. Roland introduced three guitar versions: one modeled after a Strat, one modeled after an SG, and one modeled after a Telecaster. All three models had the built-in electronics to interface with the GR-100 series and the embedded pickup. This at least gave guitarists some choice of which guitar to use. An early Roland guitar (made by Ibanez, incidentally) is pictured in Figure 15.3.

Notice the extra switches and electronics on the instrument; these controlled functions on the floor synthesizer units.

The GR-100 was better, but it still did not cut the mustard because of its limited sonic sculpting. There was little you could do with it and few parameters to tweak. The tracking was much better, but the unit wasn't as functional as players wanted it to be. Roland responded with the GR-300, arguably the best analog guitar synth ever made. Not only did it track really fast (I know—I still have mine), but it also allowed you to sculpt your sound in interesting ways using the onboard

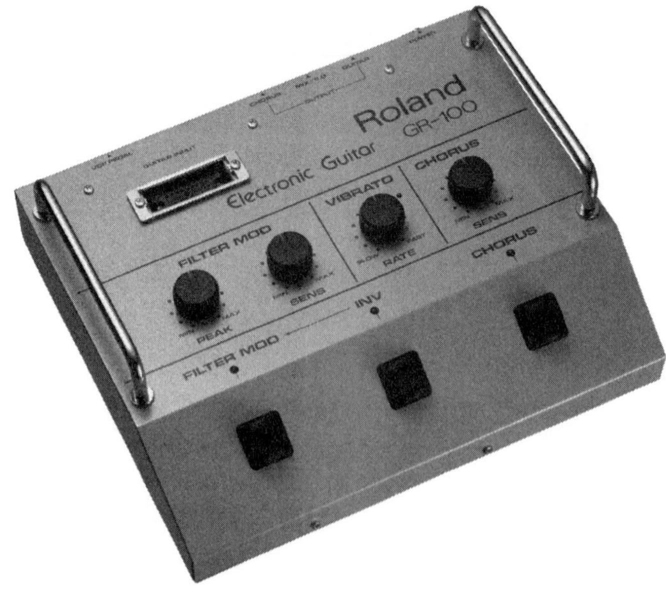

Figure 15.2
The Roland GR-100.

Figure 15.3
The Roland G-303 MIDI guitar.

filtering and modulation settings. The GR-300, pictured in Figure 15.4, could connect to any of the GR series of guitars introduced with the GR-100.

Figure 15.4
The Roland GR-300.

The GR-300 remains to many, the best, most playable guitar synth that does not use MIDI technology. The synth is musical, responds well to dynamics, and most of all is fun as heck to play.

> **GR-300 LISTENING**
>
> Would you like to hear the GR-300? A few notable players continue to use the GR-300 to this day. The most notable is Pat Metheny. He debuted the GR-300 on a track titled "Are You Going with Me?" on his 1982 release *Offramp*. The soaring trumpet-like sound you hear on the final solo is Pat wailing on his GR-300. Pat continues to use this synth today, and it remains one of his trademark sounds.
>
> The only downside is that the GR-300 is an analog-based synth, so it can only reproduce a few different timbres. That being said, Metheny has used it so much that it's become "his thing," and it's hard to play it and not hear "Hey, you got the Metheny sound." Nevertheless, it is a great synth.

The great divide was that the GR-300 did not output MIDI; it was strictly an analog synth. In 1983, Sequential Circuits released the first keyboard with an onboard MIDI interface, and MIDI became the focus. Within the span of a few years, not only did MIDI become a standard, but computer software started popping up to support it. Some of those early programs have modern derivatives that are still around today (Cubase, Logic, SONAR, and more). By the mid-'80s, we started seeing familiar names like Cubase, Emagic, and Cakewalk.

The Shift to MIDI

Facing increasing pressure, Roland abandoned the analog guitar synth and in 1984 moved on to the GR-700, the first guitar synth with a MIDI output, pictured in Figure 15.5.

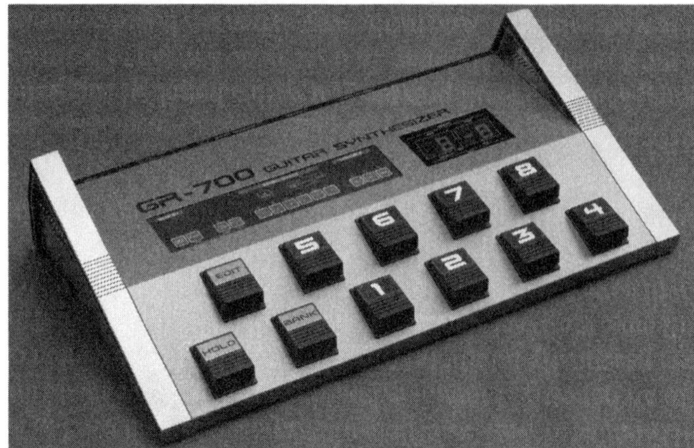

Figure 15.5
The Roland GR-700.

Coupled with the GR-700 was the G-707 guitar, pictured in Figure 15.6.

So you probably want to know how this worked, since the predecessor GR-300 worked so well. Well, in all honesty, it had some major issues. To understand the complexity of the situation, we have to talk about a man named Nyquist.

Nyquist

Harry Nyquist was an engineer who worked at AT&T and Bell Labs. He did some very important work on sound and the sampling of sound that is particularly relevant to MIDI guitarists. Nyquist published a paper, which devised what is now called the Nyquist Theorem. That theorem goes as follows:

When sampling a signal (converting an analog signal to digital), the sampling frequency must be greater than twice the input signal bandwidth in order to be able to reconstruct the original perfectly from the sampled version.

What this means to us is that in order for a guitar synthesizer to know what pitch you are playing, it has to listen to at least two cycles of its waveform. Only when it's done that computation can it tell the embedded synthesizer what note to play. The synthesizer may add additional delays as well. But in the early days, for the engine to know what you were playing, it had to listen to

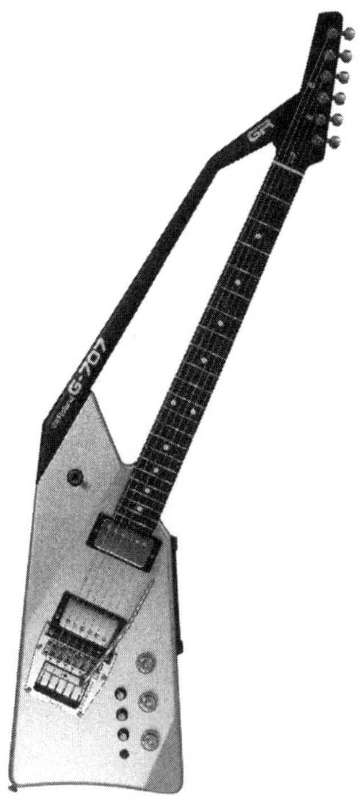

Figure 15.6
The Roland G-707.

two full cycles of each note—slower for low notes and faster for higher notes, due to the difference in their frequencies.

Lower notes have longer cycles and take longer to process. The GR-700 took between 24 and 35 milliseconds to trigger its lowest notes! That is a long time to wait, and this is exactly what turned guitar players off so much.

Now, companies are using predictive technology, where the synthesizer begins to convert to MIDI before the first wave completes. Average latency on modern units is less than one millisecond on the high strings and about 6 to 8 milliseconds on the lower strings.

This latency only affected pitch-to-MIDI conversion systems. Older systems, such as the GR-300, relied on pitch-to-voltage and didn't require computation to determine what note you were playing. This is why the old systems tracked so well, compared to the GR-700 that immediately followed.

Latency

Latency is the ultimate dirty word for the MIDI guitarist. Yeah, back when MIDI guitar first came to be, latency was an issue. This seems to be around the time when most players tried it. It's also the time when most players made up their minds about MIDI and never came back to check out what was really going on with the technology.

Latency is tied to more than just Nyquist. The speed of the data processing has a lot to do with this. How fast was your computer in 1983? Did you even own one then? So, if your computer was a dog compared to the machines available now, can't you expect things to get better as technology improves? You bet you can.

Turns out that there are ways around Nyquist. As technology improved, the MIDI converters became smarter and, more importantly, much faster. Every incarnation of MIDI guitar units was faster than the last. As computers have become faster, so have the pitch-to-MIDI algorithms.

Nowadays, modern units use pitch prediction, and they can figure out what note you're playing before the note even makes one full cycle. Latency on modern units is about 6 ms at the slowest (low E) and is virtually undetectable on the higher strings. Will it get even better? No doubt.

Anyone Else?

So far, we have talked about Roland and Arp as companies who were pivotal players in the synth guitar game. Arp was first, and Roland followed quickly. The GR-700 was the first MIDI guitar synth, but after 1983, the floodgates opened. Not only did the music industry as a whole go nuts over the technology of MIDI, but every guitar manufacturer wanted a slice of the MIDI guitar pie. Here is a list of companies that have at one time or another embarked upon the MIDI guitar thing:

- **Casio**: Guitars that had built-in MIDI converters and onboard sounds. These actually worked pretty well and had standard five-pin outputs.
- **Shadow**: They make a stick-on pickup that attaches to any guitar and converts to MIDI. It's still in production.
- **Gibson**: Gibson simply slapped its name on a Shadow pickup system and called it their own. It is electronically identical to the Shadow in every way.
- **Yamaha**: Yamaha has been in the game for a long time. They still manufacture the G50 converter and their own line of pickups (which are simply rebranded Axon technology). Over the years, they've marketed guitar-shaped controllers, such as the G-10, which are no longer in production.
- **Zeta**: Zeta made a guitar with wired frets that negated the need for pitch detection. Sadly, it was expensive, was hard to repair, and is no longer in production.
- **IVL Pitchrider**: Yet another rack-mounted converter with stick-on pickup. This at one time bore the name "Kramer," and Kramer had guitars with the pickups built in.
- **K-Muse Photon**: Not much info about this one. It used optical sensors to detect the movement of the strings and was used by John McLaughlin.

- **Passac Sentinent**: Another rack/pickup system.
- **Ibanez**: Ibanez had a guitar and converter system. Their guitar looked like a huge shark fin and tracked poorly. Incidentally, they made all of Roland's guitars and many of Casio's MIDI guitars.
- **Stepp**: A very expensive guitar-shaped MIDI controller that went out of business quickly. Ironically, these units tracked perfectly, but were expensive and out of the reach of most players.
- **Synthaxe**: The Synthaxe was another controller shaped like a guitar. It had wired frets, dummy strings that you could play and bend, breath control, etc. It cost as much as a small car and worked perfectly. This company also went out of business. Allan Holdsworth still uses his (and plays more notes per second than most), as does Futureman of Bela Fleck & The Flecktones (although it's been modified into a drum controller).
- **Suzuki**: A guitar-like controller that verged on being a toy. It had plastic strings and very limited onboard sounds, but did have a MIDI out.
- **MIDIAxe**: Made by VirtualDSP, this was a conversion system built into a guitar. Parker and Brian Moore used this system in the '90s. The guitars had a five-pin MIDI output. Tracking was decent, but not up to snuff, and they went south for the winter and never came back.
- **Parker MIDIFly**: Simply a Parker Nitefly model with the MIDIAxe electronics built in. When VirtualDSP went under, so did production of the MIDIFly.
- **Korg**: Another rack/pickup solution that's no longer in production.
- **The Beetle Quantar:** I only know that this existed and was very similar to the Yamaha G-10 in that it was a guitar-shaped MIDI controller. It's also not in production anymore.
- **Axon**: Axon, who is now owned by Terratec, has the AX 100 mk II rack-mounted guitar-to-MIDI converter. It uses the Roland GK-style pickup and works quite well. Among the current offerings, it's one that has stayed around for quite a while.
- **Starr Labs**: Since 1992, Starr Labs has been making guitar-shaped MIDI controllers that have buttons instead of a fingerboard. You can choose to pick either real strings or tap percussive pads. The system has zero latency, is very fast, and allows polyphony on a single string. It has an onboard computer and is highly programmable.
- **Fender**: Fender makes a Strat with a Roland pickup installed into the guitar.
- **RMC**: RMC makes the Polydrive, a piezo saddle-based pickup system that greatly increases the speed and accuracy of any pitch-to-MIDI system available today. No matter how fast your converter is, the RMC will make it faster and less prone to errors.

- **Graph Tech**: Graph Tech makes the Ghost saddle system, which is similar to the RMC 13-pin solution. The main difference is that it allows separate output for each string.
- **Godin**: A high-end guitar company that makes many of its guitars with the embedded RMC pickup system.
- **Ovation**: This guitar had the Shadow pickup built into it, but is no longer made.
- **Brian Moore Guitars**: Brian Moore makes various guitars that have the RMC pickup built in. They have affordable guitars in their iGuitar line and also have a high-end custom shop. They now manufacture the world's first guitar with a USB connection that passes audio and MIDI along the same cable, converting pitch to MIDI inside the guitar.

That's quite a long list. Even though most of the devices are no longer in production, the remaining list breaks down into a few small camps. The first is Roland's 13-pin standard. Roland's GK pickup uses a 13-pin cable to transmit the information to the converter. Roland, Axon, and Yamaha all interface with pickups that use the 13-pin standard that Roland established. Of all the guitar companies making guitars, the majority of them provide a 13-pin output to interface with a Roland-compatible interface. The second group is the non-guitar controllers. The Starr Labs Ztar is the best and longest-lived example of this. The third group is made up of devices that convert to MIDI internally, either the Brian Moore iGuitar.USB or the Shadow pickup/converter unit.

We're now going to break the current MIDI guitar list into sections and talk about what's actually available today.

Roland's Perseverance

I absolutely have to hand it to Roland. They have been at this since 1978 (coincidentally the year of my blessed birth) and have never given up on guitar synthesis in any way. They have continued to innovate and push the boundaries of tracking, even when the going was tough in the '80s and the technology wasn't on their side. They stuck it out when other companies simply bailed. There was a time in the late '80s and early '90s when MIDI was falling out of favor. Audio was becoming easier to manipulate on the computer. Pro Tools became standard, and throughout the '90s, other programs made audio production at home feasible. MIDI was definitely still around, but was starting to feel its age in the wake of this easier audio manipulation. Then came virtual instruments and samplers in the late '90s, which both relied on MIDI to function. Now more than ever, audio and virtual instruments are ruling the home and professional studio market. MIDI's place seems even more solidified than it did in the '80s when the first wave of MIDI rolled in.

Back to Roland. The development of its synths seemed to take a big turn with the GK1 pickup, which was a pickup that you could attach to any guitar. This made many guitar players feel a bit better because they could choose their own sounds. Roland's development went in two directions. The first were all-in-one boxes. These boxes contained sampled sounds and could also output to MIDI, but the focus of these boxes was the onboard sounds, and the outgoing MIDI stream had more of a delay than the internal sounds. This progressed from the GR-50 to the GR-1, the GR-09, the GR-30, the GR-33, and now to the GR-20. These were all floor controllers or rack interfaces that converted to MIDI through a 13-pin cable and had onboard sounds. Each incarnation was faster than the last, and the latency has dropped by leaps and bounds in recent years. The GR-20 boasts latency on the first string of under 1.5 ms. Yeah, you read that right, under 1.5 milliseconds from the time you pick until it comes out. I dare you to complain about that number.

The other direction that Roland took was with converters that contained no sounds, but simply converted the incoming pitch signals into MIDI and passed them right out the rear MIDI jacks. These boxes contained no sounds, and they were the best way to interface with a computer. This started with the GM-70 to the GI-10 and finally the GI-20, which remains the current top-of-the-line MIDI converter out there. I personally use one every day. It's fast and accurate, and it's leaps beyond what used to be available. The GI-20 is the first truly usable guitar synth that plays with you and not against you. It's pictured in Figure 15.7.

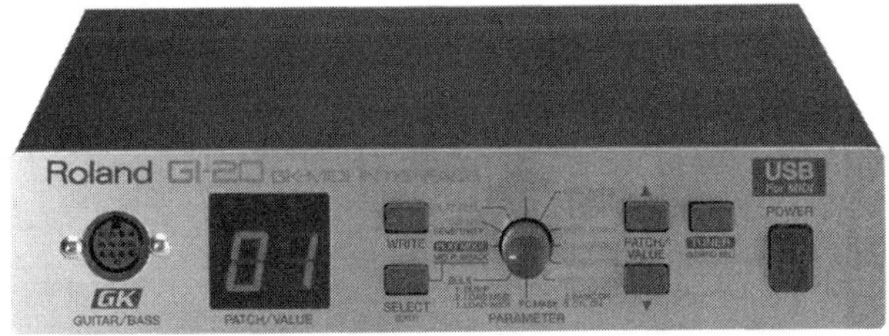

Figure 15.7
The Roland GI-20.

The GI-20, in addition to outputting MIDI through the standard five-pin MIDI jack, also contains a USB connection for a direct connection to a PC or Mac. The USB is even a bit faster than the standard MIDI. Couple this with a box that is easily programmable and can be set for your playing style, and you have a winning box. The GR-20 is simply the GI-20's pitch-detection engine, with onboard sounds for those who want to play the boxes live. For 27 years, Roland has kept the flame alive and standardized many aspects of MIDI guitar, such as the design of the GK pickup and the standard of the 13-pin connection that all companies use now. Go Roland!

Add MIDI to Any Guitar

You can add MIDI to any guitar with a stick-on hex pickup. The pickup itself is composed of a long strip of six elements that sense the sound (just like a normal pickup does), one element for each string (unlike a normal pickup). This thin strip attaches right next to the bridge of your guitar, between the bridge and the rear pickup. Currently, three companies make them: Roland, Yamaha, and Axon. They are basically identical in function, only different in subtle aesthetic design and mounting options. They all attach to the guitar in one of two ways. You can attach a pickup non-permanently with either double-sided tape or Velcro, so you can take it on and off. While this does not mar your guitar in any way, it's not the best for the pickup. The pickup itself needs to be stable and as close to the strings as possible. Tape and Velcro tend to slip and can be hard to adjust and reposition.

The other installation method is to have a professional install the pickup. That involves drilling two holes in your guitar. This sounds painful, but it allows for the most stable attachment, and with the height adjustment you will get (via springs), you can get a much better position on the pickup. The height and position of the pickup is *critical* to the tracking. It needs to be as close to the strings as possible and not move around at all. If at all possible, have it permanently mounted on a guitar you don't care so much about, until you are sure you're going to stick with MIDI.

The other end of the pickup attaches to the control unit, which contains controls for volume, patch selection, and the connector for the 13-pin cable. This attaches by screwing into your rear strap button, so it's not harming the guitar. Figure 15.8 shows the GK-3 pickup, Roland's current offering.

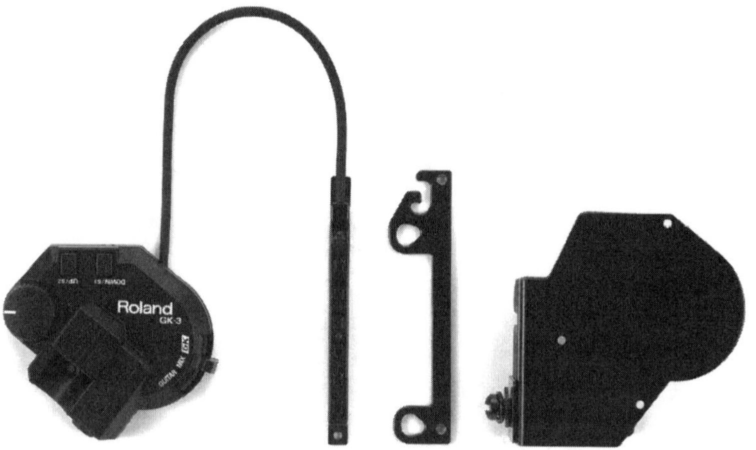

Figure 15.8
The Roland GK-3.

With this method, you can add MIDI to any guitar, assuming that you have a MIDI converter that accepts the 13-pin input. With the add-on pickups, you can add a MIDI guitar system to any instrument you already own. Because of the standardization of the 13-pin system, you can install any pickup and use it with any of the current offerings (Roland, Axon, Yamaha). This is a good way to go for most users; however, for pitch-to-MIDI conversion, there are actually faster and more accurate systems that utilize the 13-pin standard. Let's look at those.

The next step up from the stick-on MIDI pickups is a very permanent solution: the RMC Polydrive pickup. RMC is a company, founded by Richard McClish in California, that makes high-quality piezo pickups that give you an acoustic guitar sound on your electric guitars. (They also make traditional piezo pickups for acoustics as well.) The RMC Polydrive works with a piezo pickup that is mounted in the saddle of the bridge, which is the most efficient means of string contact. The string literally rests on the pickup. This is very different than the GK pickup, which uses a magnetic pickup to grab the pitches. The height of the magnets in relation to the strings can affect tracking. With the RMC system, you use a piezo element embedded in the saddles that passes through its electronics into a 13-pin connector on the side of the instrument.

You gain a major enhancement with this system; it tracks faster and more accurately than the GK series of pickups. Of course, there are a few downsides. It's a permanent modification of your guitar and requires a fairly complex installation procedure. The 13-pin connector is routed into the side of your guitar, and the electronics are concealed within the instrument as well. It also adds a new volume knob and two dipswitches for preset control onto the face of the instrument. There is no add-on pickup floating there. Besides the extra volume knob and dipswitches, this installation is much less obtrusive than a stick-on pickup. The guitar has a far cleaner appearance.

Now, if routing out your '59 Goldtop Les Paul scares you, you may want to investigate a few companies that build guitars with the RMC system built-in. The two best examples of this are Godin and Brian Moore Guitars.

Godin has been making high-end, high-quality guitars for years. You can order the RMC option on just about any guitar, including electric steel-string guitars and nylon-string guitars. The only downside is that Godin guitars are not cheap. But if you are looking for a guitar like that and you'd like the added convenience of the best in MIDI pickups, Godin is a good place to look. Godina also makes nylon-string MIDI guitars and left-handed versions.

Brian Moore is currently the largest supplier of 13-pin-equipped, RMC-enabled guitars in the world. Their guitars are also affordable. You can get a MIDI guitar for about $699 street price with the 13-pin option. They have more expensive models as you go up their ranks, but the entry-level i1000 iGuitars have the same RMC Polydrive as the stunning custom shop models. That's a very good option if you are serious about MIDI guitar and don't want to alter your own instruments. Brian Moore happens to make really nice guitars. I've been playing them exclusively since 2002 and can't say enough good things about them. The RMC is the same everywhere, so the guitar tracks perfectly through my Roland GI-20, but it's also a nice guitar. Since Brian Moore has been making 13-pin guitars for some time, you may even be able to score a used instrument on the cheap! Figure 15.9 shows a Brian Moore i2.13 MIDI guitar with the RMC pickup installed. (Actually, this is one of my guitars.)

Figure 15.9
My Brian Moore.

Of all the RMC-equipped guitars, the Brian Moore iGuitar is the most affordable, but according to RMC's site, over 20 different companies will install the Polydrive 13-pin system in their guitars, so you have many options. If you are using a 13-pin-compatible product, RMC is the way to go.

As for Brian Moore, in 2006 they pulled a rabbit out of their hat with the iGuitar.USB, which eliminates the need for a 13-pin converter box. Intrigued? Read on.

The iGuitar.USB

Earlier in the book, we talked about the original Brian Moore iGuitar.USB, which has a built-in analog-to-digital converter inside and passes this information along a single USB cable, removing the need for an interface or preamp. This simple USB cable allows you to plug and play into your computer with just a guitar. Of course, as soon as that came out, the next logical question was, "When is it going to pass MIDI?" Well, the time has come. The iGuitar.USB is now available with a MIDI option. This totally removes the need for any external hardware. The guitar is still driven by an RMC Polydrive system, but the conversion to MIDI is done inside the guitar through a patented process. This results in MIDI conversion that is every bit as fast as or faster than the 13-pin systems.

A single USB cable now carries three different signals: magnetic audio, piezo audio, and MIDI. You simply plug the guitar into a USB port, and you are all set to go. Of course, this means that you will be using software synthesizers inside a computer. The soft synth is a really exciting aspect of digital guitar. It represents the future, but for those of you who aren't taking laptops on stage, this may remain a studio device. If you need to use hardware synths that require a 5-pin MIDI cable, the Brian Moore guitar still supports the 13-pin output, which you can couple with your existing MIDI hardware/synths and samplers.

The guitar itself looks no different, and you can still get it with the traditional 13-pin output, so you can interface with your preexisting boxes when you're not at a computer. This is the beginning of a new revolution where students, musicians, and composers can simply play without the need for all the extra boxes. No more preamps, no more converters; simply do it all inside the guitar for the ultimate home studio production experience.

Keep in mind that this is also a traditional guitar with pickups, so you can access your favorite amp simulators, or even plug into a real amp (imagine that). It's a guitar with a whole lot more! Since the iGuitar.USB looks no different than any other guitar, there's no need to show a picture of it. Figure 15.9 looks the same; just add a USB jack, and you're all set.

The Starr Labs Ztar

So far, our talk about MIDI guitar has basically centered on the marriage of a traditional guitar and MIDI technology. Now it's time to look at an alternative controller: the Starr Labs Ztar (see Figure 15.10). The Ztar is not a guitar and was never intended to be one.

Figure 15.10
The Starr Labs Ztar.

Looks kind of like a guitar, right? We'll it's a guitar-shaped controller, but in theory it's closer to a keyboard than anything else.

The instrument has a fingerboard that consists of six lines of 24 velocity-sensitive keys. These keys are shaped like frets, and you play them the same way—simply press down. That's the fingerboard that every Ztar shares. Since it has a neck and the keys are straight lines, it looks and plays like a guitar, but there are no strings per se, just buttons. The plus side of buttons is that like a keyboard controller, there is no pitch detection involved, so there is zero latency involved in triggering notes.

The body of the Ztar can be built a few ways. The first way is with a row of six string triggers. These triggers can be plucked with a pick or fingers and are velocity-sensitive. When you activate the strings, they control the fretboard just like you'd expect. Pluck a string, and that string comes alive and any button you press (or don't press, in the case of an open string) will play. The string triggers use photoelectric strobes to sense the movement and velocity of the string and translate that into MIDI note velocity.

The other option is to have a row of six raised rubber ribs, which are velocity-sensitive pads. You simply tap or hold the pads down to activate the strings. This option is very cool, but if you are coming from playing guitar, go with the string triggers because they will feel as close to a guitar as possible. This is the shortest learning curve. The pads can be very cool for other things, like triggering notes that you can hold indefinitely and adding afterpressure, which allows you to change the dynamics of a note already triggered.

The Ztar can operate in a few ways. The first way is with triggers on (whichever you choose, strings or pads). In this case, the fingerboard won't respond unless you trigger it first. This is a typical guitar style, and the Ztar does quite well in this mode. Again, it's not a guitar, and you can't copy Stevie Ray-style blues licks with it. Because the buttons on the neck that act as frets don't bend, they simply press down. Starr Labs makes a whammy bar option, and each instrument has a joystick for bending notes. But it will never give you that organic feel of pushing a metal string up into tune, although it tracks perfectly and is very clean for note entry.

The second mode is triggers-off mode. This mode allows you to play from the fingerboard and activate notes by simply pressing them down with your fretting hand. This mode is unbelievably fast for note entry. Since each of the keys is velocity-sensitive, you can play with two hands, which greatly expands the range of what a typical guitarist can do (that is, as long as you only play one note on each string).

The last mode is poly mode, short for polyphonic mode, which lifts the restriction of "one note per string." The minute you enter poly mode, you lose your open strings (as those are triggered from strings), but you gain the ability to play as many notes on the same string as you feel like. Imagine being able to play actual piano-style, voicing with tightly knit clusters of notes not possible on the guitar at all. It is possible with a bit of work. Don't expect to get the Ztar on a

Monday and be Bill Evans by Friday, because two-handed playing takes work, and none of us are used to being able to play more than one note on the same string.

The Ztar itself is a computer and can be highly programmed. You can break up the fingerboard into rectangular zones, each with a different sound. You can freely retune the instrument with the press of a button. You can add a breath controller for more realistic wind instrument sounds. It's a full-featured MIDI controller in the shape of a guitar. But again, it is not a guitar and takes some getting used to. It's not for everyone, but if you're looking to take your playing beyond the realms of ordinary guitar, the Ztar may be worth a look.

The Ztar is available in a bunch of different configurations, with the Z6, pictured in Figure 15.11, being the most guitarist-friendly version. It retails for around $2,000.

Figure 15.11
The Z6.

For those who do more of the two-hand tapping thing, the Mini-Z is built for you. It's much smaller, and the fingerboard is right out in front of you to make two-handed playing easier. The Mini-Z (the Ztar I own) is pictured in Figure 15.12.

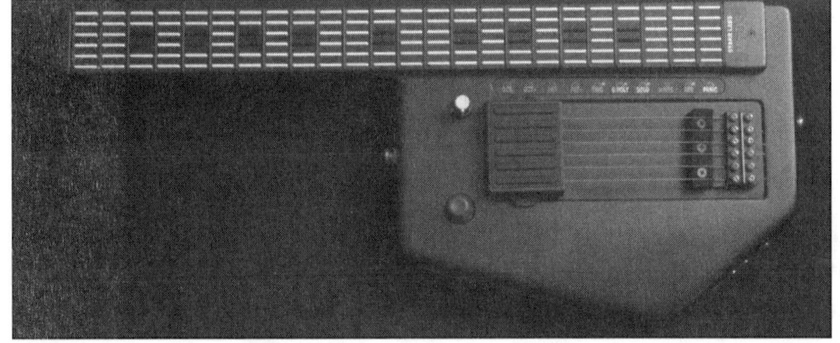

Figure 15.12
The Mini-Z.

New to the lineup is the Z7, a cheaper, slimmed-down Ztar with a USB interface for direct connection to the computer. Ztars traditionally have been expensive (around $2,000 and up), but the Z7 is only around $1,000. It's aimed at guitarists who want to give this technology a shot (see Figure 15.13).

Figure 15.13
The Z7.

The Ztar definitely isn't for everybody, but the fact that it's been around for over 15 years and is the only surviving non-MIDI guitar says something about it. It's a rare beast, and you can only order it directly from the company—trust me, stores like Sam Ash do not carry these on the floor! Some famous Ztar players include Allan Holdsworth, Vernon Reid, Stanley Jordan, and even little old me.

Tips for More Successful MIDI Guitar

Now we come to perhaps the most important part of this chapter: how to make MIDI guitar work as smoothly as possible. There are a bunch of things I can show you that will definitely make life easier for you. The first thing, you won't like it at all.

MIDI guitar works really well now. The conversion is accurate; the latency in MIDI conversion is usually quicker than playing through an amp simulator on your computer. Make no mistake about it—the virtual studio world is far too exciting to allow 6 ms of latency (or better) to stand in your way. The point is that it's now at a stage where it's musical and workable. The technology that is available now works very, very well.

So what's still wrong with MIDI guitar for some folks? Well, the problem, my friend, is you. That's right. It's your fault. Allow me to explain.

As you know by now, MIDI guitar (with the exception of the Ztar) relies in pitch-to-MIDI conversion. In other words, the conversion system "listens" to you play, "hears" the notes, detects the pitch, and spits MIDI notes out. Now, on a keyboard instrument, you don't have that. Each key has its own switch—as long as you've pressed the correct key, you get what you asked for.

MIDI guitar won't be accurate unless you are. Let's say you're playing a line of notes and you brush against a string, or by accident your pick grabs another string. The MIDI converter is going to convert everything you play, including your slop. Every open string you fail to mute, every bend you execute that ends up sounding another string, will convert into a MIDI note. Thankfully, now it will convert your mistakes faster than ever before.

Do you see my point? Players have been asking for more accurate and faster conversion for years. And now, we finally have it. It's fast and accurate, and it's exposing our weakness. Simply put, if MIDI guitar is giving you a high degree of errors, you need to look at your general technique on the instrument. How clean are your notes? Remember, you asked for accurate conversion. Some folks think that this accuracy should in some way be deductive—that the converter should know that you didn't mean to hit that other note. It won't ever be that. The most successful MIDI guitarists I know are clean players. Many, including myself, find that MIDI guitar has actually improved their playing. To track accurately when playing MIDI guitar, I paid more attention to pick detail and general muting early on, and now when I play regular guitar, I'm more accurate than ever.

The guitar is, without a doubt, an instrument full of *great* nuances and inflections. In order to get MIDI guitar to work as efficiently as possible, you need to look at how you play the instrument. In all honestly, I think keyboard controllers have made things wholly unfair for us. A switch is practically infallible. Any pitch-to-MIDI devices that come out in the future (trumpet, sax) will have the exact same issue: they will only convert what they hear. Maybe one day, MIDI guitar will have a "no bad note" function, and it will analyze your playing in real time and deduce that you didn't mean to play that note. For now, slow down and look at how you physically play the instrument. MIDI guitar is a gift, and you should not look this gift horse in the mouth! Be happy you have it and learn how to make the best of it—it just may help you to be a better player in the end.

That being said, I can still provide you with a bunch of suggestions in the interim to help you get the most out of MIDI guitar. In no way do I mean to belittle your playing; you just have to make a few adjustments. And by the way, when keyboard controllers first came out, piano players complained that it "didn't feel like a Steinway," so you're not alone. Everyone compromises for the computer, and it's fully worth it. No matter what you do, there is a small adjustment period —not just to your technique, but to the MIDI guitar thing itself. However, I can tell you that now more than ever, the transition to successful MIDI guitar is easier than ever.

Strings

The kind of strings you put on your guitar will greatly affect the quality of conversion! That's right, something as simple as a guitar string can have a *huge* impact on how well the converter does.

First, try this: Run your finger up and down your low E string. Hear that shrieking? Yes, that's called string noise. You get that because your fingers rub against the coils of the strings, producing harmonics. Now, any good MIDI guitar converter will hear those harmonics and try to convert them to notes. You'll end up with glitches and notes you didn't intend! I have found a way around this: get rid of coiled strings.

String manufacturers make two kinds of strings to help you with this. The first is called a ground wound string, which has about half the height of the string coils ground down, so you get much less string noise. In my tests with ground wound strings, I noticed fewer glitches immediately. For use as standard guitar strings, they sound a bit "darker" than normal strings, but not terribly so. The other kind of string is a flat wound, which has *no* coils on the lower strings. Instead, the strings are wrapped with flat ribbons, and they are completely smooth to the touch. This smoothness means that your strings don't suffer at *all* from string noise when you move up and down them. For me, this was the ticket to virtually perfect tracking. Coincidentally, I'm a jazz player and happen to like the much darker and warmer sound that flat wound strings give me.

The only downside to flat wound strings is that they won't sound right for rock guitar performance when you turn your MIDI guitar off. If you can designate one of your guitars as a MIDI-only guitar, then throw on a set of flat wound strings and be amazed at how much cleaner your conversion goes. I use .011 gauge La Bella flat wound strings on my MIDI guitars, and the difference is wonderful. If at all possible, try either ground wound or flat wound strings for a week and see how you feel.

SQUEAK

Here's a personal anecdote about just how bad string squeak is and what you can learn from it. When I was getting my undergraduate degree in classical guitar, I was playing a piece for a friend (a pianist), and she remarked, "Sounds great, but what about the squeaks?" My answer was, "Well, the guitar kind of does that." To her it was very annoying, but to me, it was simply part of the sound of the guitar, it squeaks and there is very little you can do about it—or so I thought.

I did a bit of research and found out that string manufacturers make recording strings that are polished and have their windings ground down to eliminate noise. Unfortunately, the sound quality that emerged from the new strings wasn't as full on the bass strings, so I went back to normal strings as a result. That process was what led me to consider such a string for MIDI guitar, which I was having similar problems with at that time.

Muting

Muting is a part of guitar playing. Oddly, many players never learn to mute correctly. But proper muting is essential to getting clean MIDI guitar output. Thankfully, muting isn't difficult at all.

The physics behind muting are essential. When you play notes on your guitar, other open strings may "sympathetically" vibrate because they are in a related overtone series. For a good example of this, play your high E string open. Notice that your A string is making noise, as is your lowest E string. Both are playing "by themselves," without you actually plucking them. Without getting into a physics discussion, both the A and E are strongly sympathetic to the high E and are going to ring. Unless you want that open string to translate to MIDI and show up in your sequencer or sound module, you need to mute that puppy!

Simply use the palm of your hand to lightly mute the lower strings of your guitar. When playing the lower strings, I let my pinky rest on the top strings to keep them quiet, but usually, this is not an issue.

A studio trick for extreme muting is to tie a handkerchief or sock around the nut/first fret region. This only works if you're *not* using open strings in your performance. The handkerchief will mute all of the open strings. I've never needed to use it, but for critical work, you may want to try it.

BEND ME

When you bend a string, you always push other strings along with the string you are bending. When you release the bend, the other affected strings may suddenly start to ring. You need to mute carefully when you bend so that the other strings don't get detected! You can mute with the palm of your picking hand, or, if you're really sneaky like me, while your third finger is bending, lay your first finger down across the other strings to keep them quiet. It works very well, but requires a bit of practice.

Ghost Notes and Double Triggers

The two most endemic problems when dealing with MIDI guitar are ghost notes and double triggers. Let's start with ghost notes.

Ghost notes are those little "x" notes you see in guitar tablature. They're a bit hard to define. Sometimes, they occur when you drag your pick across the strings for effect. Sometimes, they're an accident. Sometimes, they're on purpose. Either way, they are going to show up in your MIDI output stream, and you don't want them there. You either have to adapt your technique when using MIDI, or, in the case of MIDI sequencing, take those notes out manually, which you will learn about in the next section. Ghost notes are generally annoying, but can be dealt with by paying closer attention to your performance. This is another aspect where you may gain some very useful playing skills in the name of clean MIDI guitar.

A double trigger is when you intend to play one note and you get two very quick notes, one on top of the other. Double triggers are clearly identifiable as right/left hand coordination issues. Most guitar players lead with their fretting hands, not their picking hands. As such, you fret notes a microsecond before you pick them. Now, when you press a string down with your fretting hand, you may cause the string to start ringing. That tapping might start the MIDI conversion. Of course, you're going to strike the string a millisecond later, and bingo, you've got a double trigger. Double triggers fall into a larger group of issues called synchronization. Ideally, when you play the guitar, both hands should be right in sync. If this is true, you won't get any double triggers (or hardly any).

Even though this is not a guitar method book, I will throw in one piece of music for you to practice (see Figure 15.14). This is a great synchronization drill. Play it up and down a few minutes each day. The things to keep in mind are that you should only go as fast as you can play cleanly, and just realize that your pinky is always the issue, because it's usually hitting a touch too late. If you can designate this to sound clean, and better yet, if you can put it into a sequencer and have it come out clean, you are well on your way to making MIDI guitar work for you.

Figure 15.14
Chromatic synchronization drill.

For the record, I do this exercise every day, regardless of how much MIDI guitar work I do. It's become my warmup, and I learned it from John Petrucci of Dream Theater. It's been the one thing that has helped me more than anything else.

Since we are talking about cleaning up sequences and getting MIDI to look right, let's go over to a sequencer and look at what MIDI guitar may look like on your screen.

Cleaning Up Sequences

Playing MIDI guitar live is one thing, but when you do it with a computer sequencer, you usually notice things like ghost notes and double triggers, since they are clearly visible onscreen. I am going to load up Cubase and simply play for about 10 seconds. I'm also going to be as sloppy as possible! I want mistakes we can look at and clearly identify. Here is the result of my 10-second trip back to being 16 years old (see Figure 15.15).

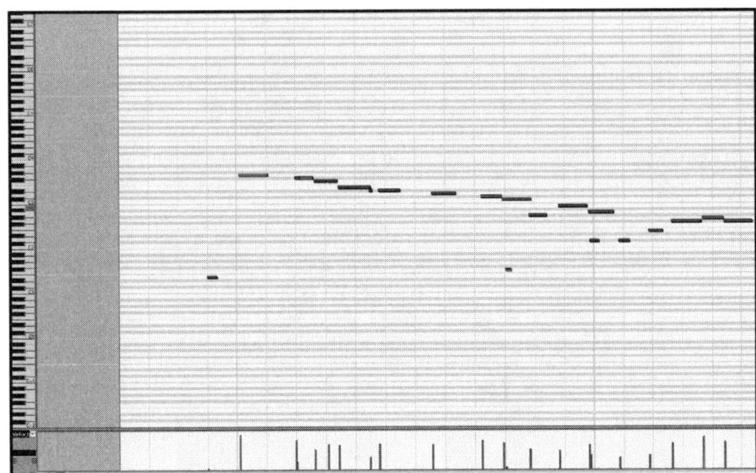

Figure 15.15
MIDI guitar in sequence.

So let's take a closer look at a few spots. First, depending on the material, you can deduce some mistakes right off the bat. I was playing a solo on the upper strings, which means that any low notes probably exist because I wasn't muting. You can see them clearly in Figure 15.16.

All of the higher notes are the ones I meant to play. Those few lower notes (coincidentally Es and As) are simply open notes. I can easily delete them. Already this is looking cleaner. Let's now look for double triggers. These are harder to spot because they happen on the same note. In the Sequence editor, you have to look for a region split, a spot where one note stops and a new one takes over. In this case, it's a small black line between two notes, as shown in Figure 15.17.

Now, we have to think about this one. There are two notes within a split second of each other. Which one is correct? To get a better idea, you need to bring the concept of MIDI velocity into this. MIDI velocity is what tells you how loud your pitches will play back. MIDI velocity goes from 0–127 at its fullest.

I can make Cubase show me the velocity of the notes as well. Let's look at that. Figure 15.18 shows the velocity directly below the notes (higher lines are higher-velocity).

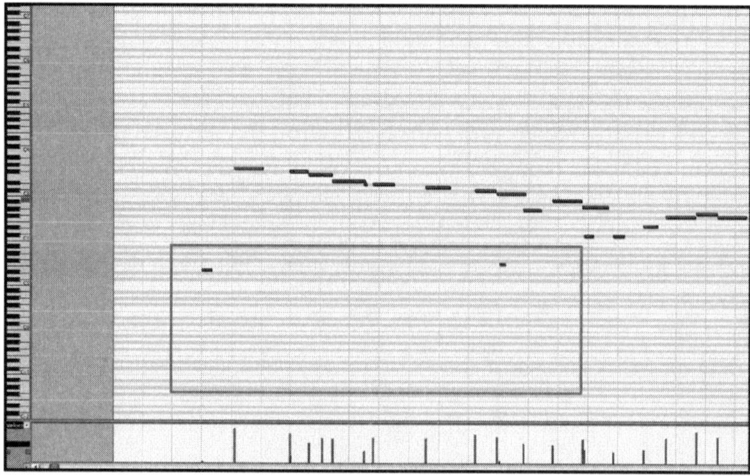

Figure 15.16
Notes that do not belong!

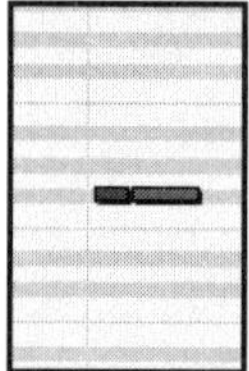

Figure 15.17
Pesky double triggers exposed!

I have two notes, one with a velocity of 20 and one with a velocity of 97. Which one do you think is the correct one? The louder one, of course, because that was my pick strike. So if we get rid of the first note (the weak one), we should come to the proper sound. I play back the sequence and all is well.

Another great features that companies are implementing are automatic MIDI guitar features. Sibelius, Finale, and Cakewalk have MIDI guitar deglitch options that allow you to ignore low-velocity notes, eliminate double triggers, and automatically clean up your sequences while you input. Other programs, like Cubase and Logic, allow you to set up conditions in their advanced MIDI editors to disallow velocities under a certain range you specify. This can act as a deglitch double-note killer, but you have to program it yourself. Sibelius, Finale, and Cakewalk have done the process for you already.

LOW VELOCITY

Low-velocity notes are usually indicative of errant notes, or glitches in the MIDI spectrum. As a general rule, I usually take out anything with a MIDI velocity below 25. A velocity of 25/127 is most likely a glitch. I believe that my softest strike is about 35. But you can test that for yourself: see how low you

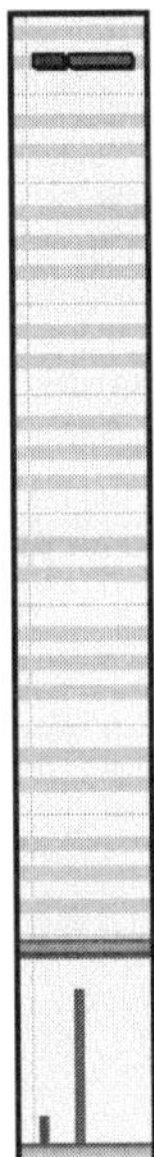

Figure 15.18
Showing velocity.

can play and then use that as a cutoff number. If your lowest velocity is around 50, then look at notes under 45 or so as errant notes, and try muting those notes or removing them altogether.

You can fix wrong notes this way and quantize note timing (applying a rhythmic grid for your notes to adhere to) to clean up some of your timing. MIDI allows you *great* flexibility and control over the final product. I have one last tip for you in the following sidebar.

SLOW DOWN

One of the gems about MIDI is that it's not audio. You can record at any tempo you desire. I find that for accuracy, especially with very difficult parts, recording at a lower tempo makes just about everything better. When you are done, simply speed up to the faster tempo and you'll be all set. Slower tempos usually result in cleaner sequences anyway, so it's a good practice to get into. There is nothing wrong with slowing down for accuracy's sake.

We've gone through a lot of great tips to help you get the most out of your MIDI guitar. The last thing we should look at is finger style playing, which has some challenges of its own.

Finger Style MIDI Guitar Secrets

I have made it no secret that I also play classical guitar. Because of this, I end up playing MIDI guitar finger style without a pick. There are a few significant challenges involved with this kind of playing. Most have been outlined in the chapter, and I will simply list them again as food for thought, but there are a few new issues I'll mention here.

Here is a list of endemic issues for finger style players, especially nylon string players:

- **Finger squeaks**: Most players using MIDI guitar like this are using nylon strings, which have very loud bass strings, and they can be noisy. When in doubt, try to purchase a set of polished or recording strings to ease the noise.
- **Open strings**: When you play finger style, open strings are part of your sound, and the resonance you get from the sympathetic strings is a vital part of your sound. When you sequence this information, depending on the synth that you play it back with, you may or may not like the results. You may have to edit the sequence data to remove or shorten the ringing open strings. Muting is harder, too.
- **Fingernails**: Many players use their fingernails or slip on fingerpicks to pluck the notes. If your fingernails aren't nicely sanded and polished with a clean edge, the ripples in your nails can create double, even triple triggers. Grab any book on classical guitar playing and learn to shape your nails to alleviate this problem.
- **Plucking/preparing**: When playing finger style, many players let their right-hand fingers rest on the strings prior to plucking a note. When you plant your finger, you may end up with an audible click or noise that may convert to MIDI. I have found that if you plant with the flesh of your fingertip and not the hard nail surface, this problem goes away.

I hope you've enjoyed this MIDI guitar primer. Now we can explore a few chapters showing you all the cool doors you've just opened with this newfound knowledge. Next up: Notation!

16 Music Notation

One of the most impressive perks of using a MIDI guitar system is how well it integrates with music notation programs. Guitar players typically have typically had a hard time with music notation. This is not due to lack of will or general inelegance. The guitar happens to be a complicated instrument to learn to read music on. There are multiple positions that play the exact same pitch, and unlike the piano's black and white repeating structure, the guitar has few visual clues to aid players as to what notes they are playing. Position markers only visually mark locations on the fingerboard, not concrete pitch names. The fact is that the majority of guitar players don't know the majority of their notes. In contrast, a non-piano player with a three-minute pep talk can name every key on a keyboard, due to its repeating visual structure. Not only does MIDI guitar make notation much easier, but it can even assist in how you learn the instrument. We are going to look at the two dominant music notation software programs: Sibelius and Finale.

Why MIDI Guitar?

What does MIDI guitar have to do with notation? Both Sibelius and Finale support traditional notation and tablature without the use of a MIDI guitar. Both allow you to enter notes with your computer's keyboard or with a mouse click. Both allow you to open tab files from the Internet and create your own tab files without a MIDI guitar. So, if these programs are so capable without the help of a MIDI guitar, then why bother?

I can show you exactly why with a very simple demonstration. Let's say that I want to create a single note. Just one note, an E—top of the treble staff. Okay, so I go into Sibelius, set up a staff with a treble and a tab staff, and enter an E whole note with my mouse (no guitar involved). I then copy the note to the tab staff. The result is Figure 16.1.

The treble staff is showing the correct pitch. I wanted an E, and I got an E. But the tab staff is showing something odd. It's showing an open first string. That's not where I envisioned it. I wanted a second string, fifth fret E. Okay. No big deal, I can go to the tab staff, edit the note, and force it onto the first string to look like Figure 16.2.

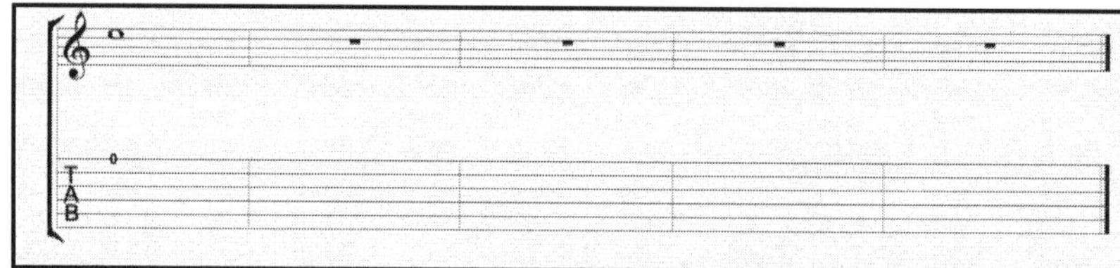

Figure 16.1
Basic notation.

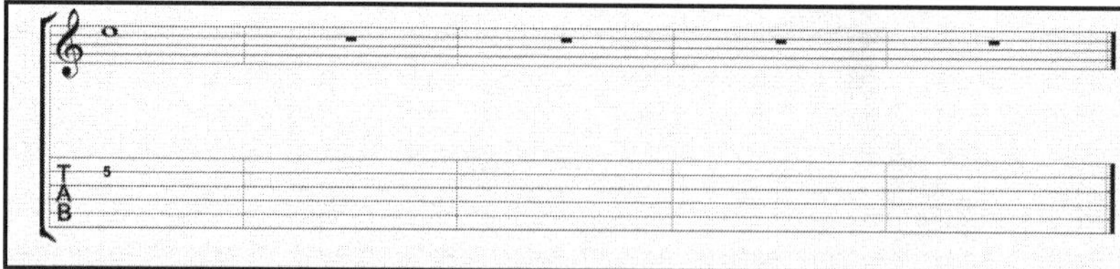

Figure 16.2
The correct E.

Now, that took several steps. First, I had to use the mouse to place the note, convert to tab, and then fix it. Why didn't it get it right the first time? Well, the guitar is a complex instrument in that you can play the same written pitch in many different places on the neck. For example, a high E can be played five or six different ways (depending on how many strings you have). That's right, the same note can be played in other locations on the neck and still sound exactly the same.

How is the software supposed to know which one you wanted? One way around it is to start with the tablature staff and add the note you want in the location you want. That will get you the right location, and you can copy that to the notation staff, but what about rhythm? I can make your life simpler.

A MIDI guitar sends out its MIDI information on specific channels. The MIDI specification allows for 16 different channels through one MIDI cable. Because of this, a MIDI guitar can force each string to transmit on its own channel. String one plays through channel one, and so on. That means that if the program is smart enough to understand that an E on channel two should go to the second string, you're golden. And these programs are smart enough. They take the incoming MIDI information and store it along with the notation. When you go to convert to tab, it has this extra data stored behind the scenes and places the note on the same string that you played it on. To demonstrate, I will play the top space E on every string using my MIDI guitar and convert to tab. Figure 16.3 is the result.

Now, the treble staff isn't too exciting to look at. All I see is the same note repeated over and over again. But the tablature staff is very cool. That's exactly where I played those notes.

This is exactly why MIDI guitar and notation go hand in hand—because no other method offers you this level of accuracy. Imagine preparing a scale sheet for a student, or writing down some licks, simply by playing your guitar and letting the software print it out exactly as you played

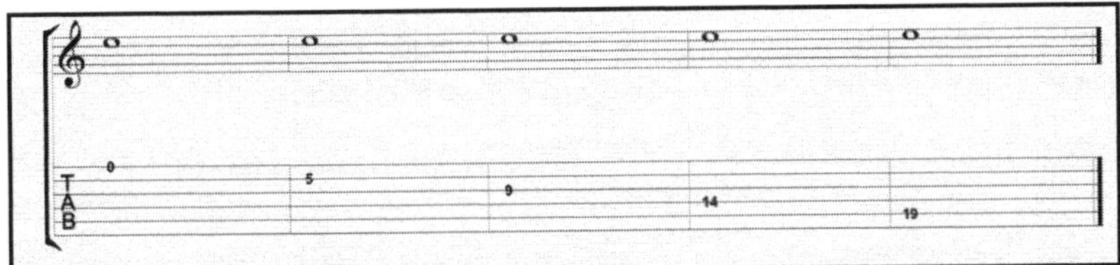

Figure 16.3
Multiple Es.

it. That's why MIDI guitar is so important, because not only will you have better access to notation, but you can also use it as a learning tool, which we will find out more about as we progress through this chapter.

Let's go through Sibelius now and see how to set it up for MIDI guitar and what it can do for us.

> **UBER TIP!**
> When working with a notation program, accuracy of input is key. I have found that setting up your guitar-to-MIDI converter differently for notation programs is important. In a sequencer, you'd want dynamics and nuances to shine through as clear as day. In notation programs, nuances can lead to mistakes in notation. On my GI-20, I turn each string's input sensitivity down to 1—the lowest setting. I find that with this setting, my notes go in much cleaner with fewer ghost notes and mistakes. Of course, you need to turn the input sensitivity back to normal when you play synth sounds. But for notation, try this trick; it really helped me get the most out of my MIDI guitar notation tools.

Setting Up Sibelius

Since this section is not intended to be a complete setup guide for Sibelius, let's just assume that you can operate the program enough to get a blank score up. The next thing we need to look at is how to explore the specific guitar features of the program.

First, you need to make sure that your input device is hooked in. I'm using the Roland GI-20 Interface, hooked up to my computer by a USB cable. In Sibelius, you need to access your Playback and Input Devices list to make sure that the GI-20 (or whatever interface you use) is set up and turned on. The setup window is shown in Figure 16.4.

In the upper-right section, you see a list of my input devices available. I highlighted the GI-20 to activate it. Directly below that is an input monitor light. This allows me to double-check that information is passing into Sibelius. Once that's all set, look at the lower half of the same screen, as seen in Figure 16.5.

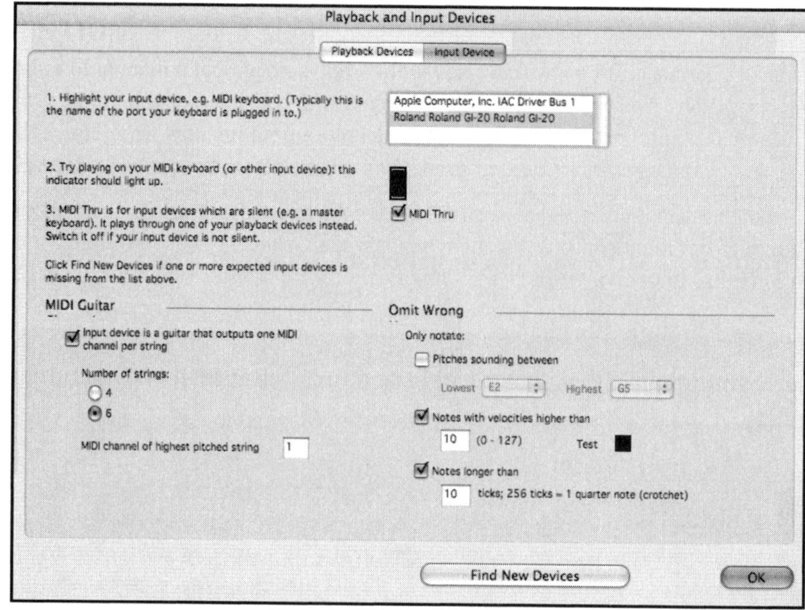

Figure 16.4
MIDI device setup in Sibelius.

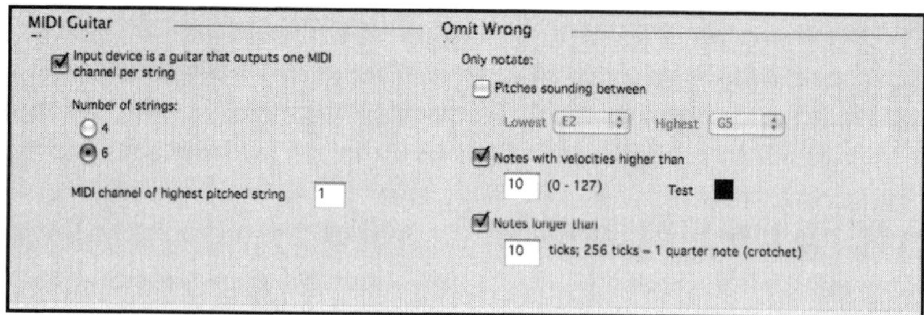

Figure 16.5
MIDI guitar features.

This screen is what sets Sibelius apart from other traditional notation programs. We have specific features to help ensure the most accurate MIDI guitar input. This first section to look at is the left side under the MIDI guitar heading. There is a checkbox that signifies that your MIDI guitar is sending each string on a separate channel. This is needed because of how Sibelius will make sure that your notes are tabbed correctly on the right string. If you're not sure if your interface supports sending out a separate channel for each string, check with them. Roland's and Terratec's converters definitely do, although you may have to set this up on the device first—more on that in a bit.

Below this checkbox, you will see a choice for the number of strings, either four (bass guitar) or six (guitar). Currently, Sibelius only supports four- or six-string MIDI guitar devices. Chapman sticks and other custom MIDI controllers are not supported past the sixth string. The last thing to set up is the MIDI channel of your highest-pitched string, i.e., your high E string. By default this is 1, and unless you have some special setup inside of your pitch-to-MIDI converter, there is no need to change this. Now that this is done, you can direct your attention to the Omit Wrong heading on the right side of the window.

Omit Wrong just sounds good, like Sibelius wants to help us! As we have detailed in Chapter 15, "MIDI Guitar," the two most common goofs that MIDI guitar can spit out are ghost notes and double triggers. We also identified that ghost notes tend to have very low velocity. MIDI velocity is expressed in numbers ranging from 1–127, with 127 being the maximum loudness. In Sibelius, you can choose to ignore and not notate notes with velocities lower than a certain number. You can, of course, change this number. It chooses 10 as a default value, and that may work for you, but if not, you can always change it. What this means is that as MIDI streams in, anything with a MIDI velocity under 10 will not notate, eliminating your ghost notes.

Double triggers are also a common problem. Sibelius has an answer for that as well! Double triggers tend to be very short notes, so Sibelius allows you to ignore very short notes. It does so by using MIDI tick, which is equal to 1/256th of any given quarter note (which is *very* short). For example, at 60 beats per minute, a tick would last only .003 of a second—really short! The default value is 10 ticks, which is three-tenths of a second, and should take care of many of your double triggers. Again, you can go back and change the settings as you need to. It's nice to see a notation program embrace MIDI guitar like this and give you some help.

Now that you have your MIDI guitar all set up, you need to look at exactly how you can enter notes. Our blank score has both a traditional treble cleft and a tablature staff beneath it. You can enter notes in either the treble staff or the tab staff. No matter which way you start entering, you can easily copy between the two parts.

Sibelius has a few ways to enter information. The first is called step time. In step time, you choose your note value from the computer's numeric keypad, as shown in Figure 16.6.

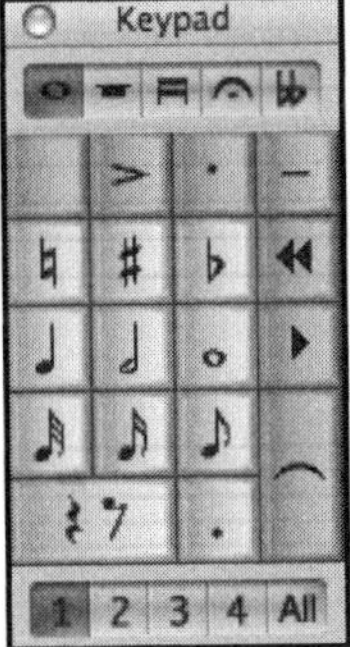

Figure 16.6
Keypad entry.

Each of the keys on your computer's numeric keypad corresponds to a common musical note. You can simply choose the type of note you are going to play and then play the MIDI guitar, and you will get automatic results.

The other way is to play to a click track and record in real time, just the way you might with a DAW/Sequencer. Sibelius calls this Flexi Time input.

Sibelius offers a similar transport controller, allowing you to control tempo and record on and off Figure 16.7 shows Sibelius' transport.

Figure 16.7
Transport.

From the transport, you can set up your tempo to play at a speed that suits you. Now, unlike a sequencer, the output of your real-time playing may look *very* messy. Playing to a notation program is a bit of an art, thankfully. Sibelius gives you some ways to quantize and clean up your inputted notes.

First, when you are inputting pitches to a click track, Sibelius uses math to align your notes to a predetermined grid and notate it as best as it can. Now, as human beings, we are probably going to make some mistakes and play notes that aren't perfectly in time, and Sibelius may misrepresent them. To overcome this, there are two ways to fix notation. The first happens before you even play a note.

The grid that Sibelius sets up can be programmed to only work with simple note divisions (eighth, quarter, sixteenth notes) instead of trying to notate everything it sees. To do this, you need to access the Flexi-time options, as seen in Figure 16.8.

These options may seem a bit confusing, but if you know that you're only inputting simple notes and not using triplets, you can set your minimum value to whatever value you know will be the fastest you play (usually an eighth or sixteenth note), and you can disallow triplets if your input will not feature them. By enacting these measures, you can greatly improve the quality of your input.

Once you've gotten the information into Sibelius, copying from staff to staff is as easy as copying, cutting, and pasting.

I started notating on the treble staff. If I select all and copy the information using copy and paste, I get the identical music in the tab staff, but this time with the correct fingerings I played it with. I can even have my tab staff display rhythms for more accurate reading. Figure 16.9 is the result of my hard work in a short eight-measure excerpt—nothing fancy, but I did the whole thing in about one minute, including copying from staff to staff.

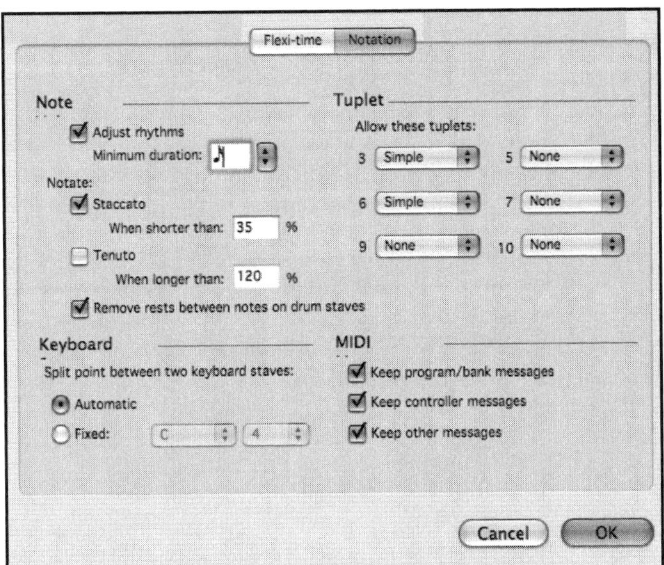

Figure 16.8
Flexi-time options.

From there I can go deeper into Sibelius, add chord symbols, dynamics, you name it! As we will learn later in this chapter, you will also be able to take your work and export it as MIDI to take into your favorite DAW for further music creation. There is a lot more to these programs than meets the eye!

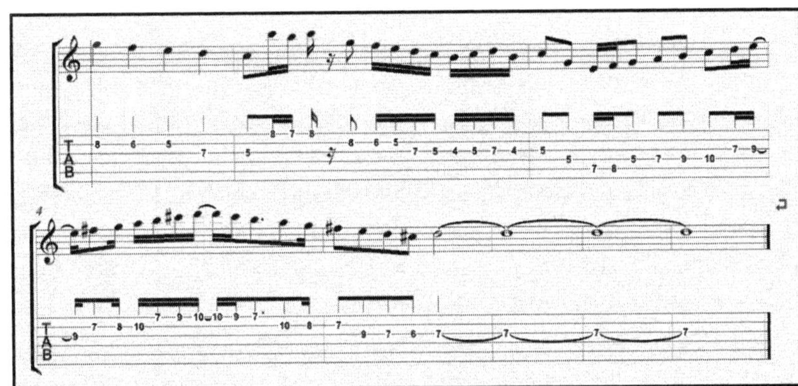

Figure 16.9
Creating a tab and staff score.

Expert Tip: Marc's Step Entry Trick

When I notate guitar, I never play to the click track. Even on keyboard, I've only seen a few people get it in cleanly the first time, one of them a Sibelius employee, Robin Hodson, who can get music into Sibelius perfectly, every time. In a DAW, minute differences in tempo may sound "human," but in a notation program, you want clean output that any musician can read. What I do is use step time input, but I do it with a twist.

Instead of using one hand on my numeric keypad, I use a program called MIDIPipe, which converts incoming MIDI information into keystrokes. I use my Behringer foot pedal and assign the note values to the buttons on the unit. Using a custom-made script, I have MIDIKeys convert the foot presses into the numeric keypad on-screen. This way my guitar is in my hands the whole time, and I simply select the note value with my feet and keep playing. It's super-fast! MIDIKeys is a Mac application, but for you Windows folks, you can use Bome's MIDI Translator for the same result.

Setting Up Finale

Finale is very similar to Sibelius. They are both top-shelf notation programs, and both allow you the same basic functionality. In Finale, you can also set up the program to listen to your MIDI guitar strings for accurate tablature.

To set this up, after you have launched Finale and set up your score (with a single treble staff and a tab staff), you need to access Tablature MIDI Channels to set up Finale to hear your input on the correct channels. You can access this through the MIDI pull-down menu. The Tablature MIDI Channels window is shown in Figure 16.10.

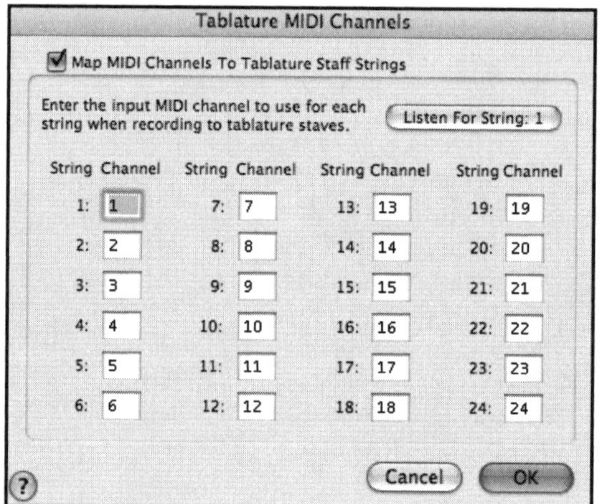

Figure 16.10
MIDI device setup in Finale.

In this window, you can see that by default, strings 1–6 are mapped to MIDI channels 1–6. If this is not how your instrument is set up, you can use the Listen for String feature and assign the strings as you need to. When you have set this up properly, Finale will notate the tab staff, according to exactly how you played.

Sibelius adds options for cleaning up your note entry, namely it can ignore small note values (double triggers) and low-velocity notes (ghost notes). Unfortunately, at the time of this writing, Finale does not support either of those features. But as history has shown between Sibelius and Finale, competition is good. When one company comes out with a feature, the other usually matches it. Maybe soon Finale will adopt these changes.

Entering notes can be done either on the staff or on the tablature, and easily copied back and forth. Just like Sibelius, you can enter notes in Simple Entry mode or the faster Speedy Entry mode, using your guitar for pitches and the keypad for note values, or you can use the Hyperscribe Tool and play into the staff in real time. Since Finale lacks some of the features to aid MIDI guitarists, Hyperscribe mode may result in a higher degree of mistakes—this depends on the accuracy of your technique, though. It's not impossible to clean up the notation afterwards, but it's simpler to get it right the first time.

I will use Hyperscribe to notate a few notes and chords in the tab staff and then copy my work to the notation staff to see what my music looks like in standard notation (see Figure 16.11).

Figure 16.11
Finale's staff and tablature.

To move the parts from tablature to the staff, I need to use Finale's Mass Edit tool and select and move from the tab staff to the notation. You can work in either direction you feel is best, tab first or notation.

After that, you can go ahead and use Finale to add dynamics and other musical markings to your score. Both Finale and Sibelius support guitarist notations for bends, slides, and other useful symbols, if you plan to do serious notation and transcription.

NO MIDI?

In Finale, there is an option for MicNotator, which is a feature that allows Finale to notate based on incoming audio signals, much like a pitch-to-MIDI converter. It works decently on woodwind and brass instruments, but I found that when using it for guitar, it was nearly impossible to get accurate results. Not to mention that you lose all the cool MIDI implementation with tablature when inputting notes this way. Nevertheless, if you own Finale and don't own a MIDI guitar system, you might want to investigate this option to see if it works for you.

Learning with Notation

One of my favorite parts about notation programs paired with MIDI guitars is the ability to learn with them. We all know that guitarists aren't known the world over for their sight-reading skills. Many of my students use MIDI guitar and notation programs to help improve their reading skills. The real boon here is the capability for the programs themselves to translate notation into tab and vice versa.

Let's use an example from an online resource. There are thousands, if not millions, of free MIDI files on the Internet that you can download. You can download classical-style pieces, popular melodies, or pretty much anything else. A quick Google search for "free MIDI files" will give you a solid starting point. Both Finale and Sibelius can open these files and display them as notation. In this example, I'm going to grab a simple melody of "Jingle Bells" online and open it in Sibelius. The basic, bare melody is shown in Figure 16.12.

Figure 16.12
The "Jingle Bells" melody.

The first thing you can do is simply cut and paste it onto the tab staff, as shown in Figure 16.13.

Figure 16.13
The "Jingle Bells" staff and tablature.

Now that you have it on the tab staff, a non-music reader can at least play it, but we can do much better than that. If you want to learn the names of the notes, Sibelius ships with plug-ins that allow you to do specific actions. One of these actions will name the notes in the treble staff for you automatically. A quick run of the Add Note Names plug-in yields Figure 16.14.

Figure 16.14
Adding note names.

Imagine being able to do this with any melody, simply playing something into the tablature staff first, converting it to notation, and adding the note names. This way, you can learn to see the pitches with names, and with a bit of work, you'll be on your way as a music reader.

> **RHYTHM!**
> When I was a struggling music reader, notation programs helped me learn to read rhythms that I had a hard time counting out myself. I would simply enter them as notation, and the program would play them back perfectly each time. I could alter the tempo to make my learning easier. Over time, I would test myself by creating random rhythmic groupings in notation (all on a single pitch) and trying to figure them out. When in doubt, Sibelius could just play it back for me. After a while, I learned to associate visual rhythms with sounds. It was like having a teacher there to play any rhythm I asked. I learned immensely from this technique.

Now we can do some cooler stuff. What about naming chords that you play in? Chord theory is very complex and can take many years to figure out. As long as you can play the chords with your MIDI guitar, Sibelius can name them!

Here is an example in tablatures of some jazz chords I played. Some of these chords are simple, and some are very hard to name. I played them into Figure 16.15 so you could see the raw tablature.

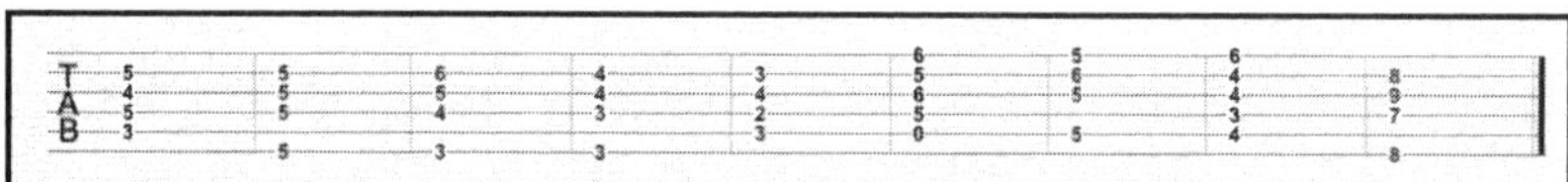

Figure 16.15
Chord naming, step one.

Now, again using one of Sibelius's plug-ins, I can have it automatically name the chords for me. The plug-in that I am using is called Add Chord Symbols. When I bring up the plug-in, I have a window of choices, as seen in Figure 16.16.

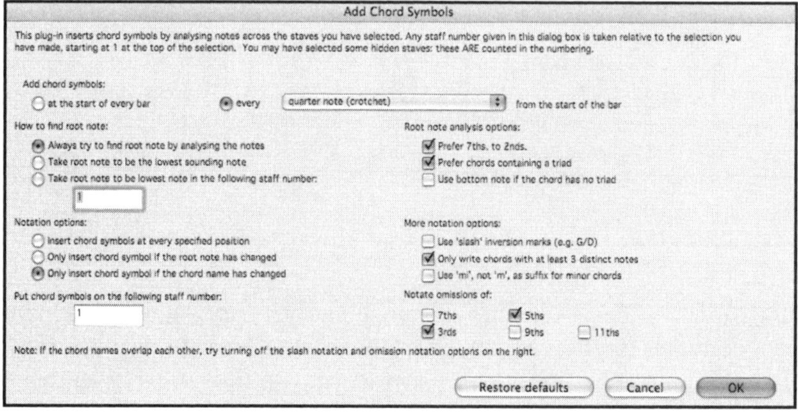

Figure 16.16
Name the chords!

In the dialog box that comes up, you are given a bunch of choices. The only one I will change is the checkmark to Take Root Note as Lowest Sounding Pitch, since most guitar chords are played this way—but you can change this behavior if the chords come out looking very odd.

A simple run of the plug-in gives me Figure 16.17, perfectly naming the exact chords I played with my MIDI guitar.

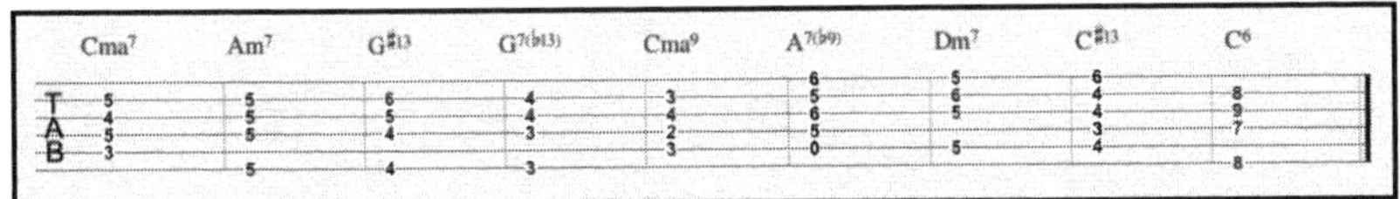

Figure 16.17
Chord naming success.

As you can see, notation programs are incredible tools when mixed with MIDI guitars. They can help you professionally as well as personally.

Versions

Sibelius and Finale exist in a few different versions. Let's look at Sibelius and their product offerings:

- **Sibelius 4**: This is the flagship program that has all the features you'd expect in a professional scorewriter. Tablature, lyrics, chord boxes, you name it. You can compose anything from a lead sheet to a full symphony!
- **Sibelius G7**: This is a guitar-friendly version of Sibelius. It is basically Sibelius with a few twists. The most visible difference is that you can enter notes on a virtual fretboard view, without the need for a MIDI guitar. You can't do a full symphony on it because the program is limited to common instruments like guitar, piano, drums, and vocals, but it's wonderful for guitar parts, lyric sheets, lead sheets, and chord diagrams. It also costs about one-quarter as much as the full version of Sibelius. The Fretboard view is a strong feature, especially if you don't have MIDI guitar and need to enter notes on a score using your neck as a guide.
- **Sibelius Student**: This is the entry-level version of Sibelius. It is based on the full version of Sibelius, but restricts the number of parts you can write at once and limits a few of the features. This version includes guitar tablature tools and chord diagrams as well.

Just a quick note regarding Sibelius G7. The Fretboard view is very unique among notation programs, so I wanted to show it to you. Figure 16.18 shows the Fretboard view in G7.

With this virtual fretboard, you can enter notes and chords one at a time. Alternately, you can look at any piece of notation and watch where it plays back on the fingerboard. The fretboard can even display a 4-, 5-, or 6-string bass neck for you MIDI bass players out there.

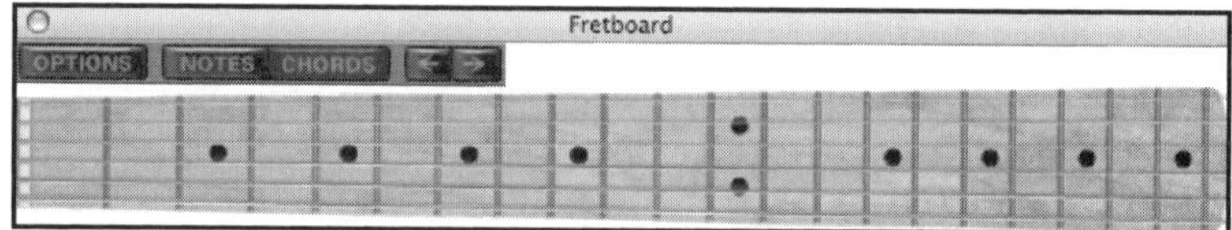

Figure 16.18
Sibelius G7 Fretboard view.

Expert Tip: Lefty Fretboards in SONAR!

Orren Merton, author of *Guitar Rig 2 Power!* (Course Technology, 2006) and *Logic Pro 7 Power!* (Course Technology, 2004), among other audio technology books, offers the following tip for left-handed MIDI guitarists who are interested in Notation:

"If you're a lefty who plays left-handed guitars like I do, you know that our fretboard is reversed from a right-handed fretboard. This means that if both a right-handed and a left-handed guitar were to be positioned so that the headstock faced to the right, the top string on a right-handed guitar would be the low E string, but the top string on a left-handed guitar would be the high E string. This means that if you want to use Sibelius G7 to input notes onto the fretboard, you're going to have a bit of translating to do.

"Cakewalk, however, makes this easier for us lefties. SONAR also has a Fretboard view in its Notation editor; however, it allows you to choose which string will appear at the top and which one is at the bottom. This way, you can enter your notes onto a left-handed fretboard. Unfortunately for Mac-based lefties, SONAR is currently Windows only."

Finale has a distinct product line with multiple offerings. Let's detail what Finale has to offer:

- **Finale Year**: Each year, Finale releases its flagship program with a new year in the title. Now it's 2006 and next year they will release a 2007 version, and so on. Finale is a robust, powerful program that is popular. It has all the features you'd expect from a top-of-the-line notation program.
- **Finale Allegro**: Finale Allegro is the reduced-price/reduced-feature set version of Finale. You can only work on 32 staffs at once, but it includes all of the guitar features of Finale 2006.
- **Finale has Guitar**: Finale has released a guitar-friendly version of Finale, but sadly, it has seen few updates. On the Mac side, it hasn't even been ported to OSX, although it will run on XP. You get all the same functionality in Allegro, so if you want a lower-cost version of Finale, go with Allegro.
- **Finale PrintMusic**: This is an even more cut-down version of Finale for those who need basic notation without all of the power tools, although it does include tab and chord grids for guitar music.

- **Finale Songwriter**: This is aimed at the entry-level notation user. It is a simple, basic program to use, but still contains all the guitar-specific notations, such as tab and chord shapes.
- **Finale Notepad**: Notepad is a free version of Finale that anyone can download from the Internet for free. It allows you to work with a maximum of eight staffs, and you can do rudimentary guitar tab notation.

As you can see, there's quite a bit to choose from. As to which you'll like, thankfully both Sibelius and Finale have free demos. I chose Sibelius for its ease of use and guitar-specific features that I needed in my life. You will come to your own conclusions. Either way, it's pretty clear that these impressive programs are made even better with the addition of MIDI guitar.

17 Virtual Instruments

A virtual instrument is simply an instrument whose sound output isn't generated by a hardware box, such as a keyboard synthesizer. It's an instrument that is playable via MIDI and that resides as software in your computer. Virtual instruments come in many forms, but they share one thing in common: every sound they make is generated in your computer. They are the future, and you, the MIDI guitarist, are going to get a taste of what keyboard players have been enjoying for years—the future of sound. For the MIDI guitarist, this opens up countless doors for sonic experimentation and composition.

What Virtual Instruments Do

Virtual instruments simply re-create sound synthetically, but instead of doing it with specialized DSP chips inside of hardware units, they do it entirely using your computer's CPU. There are a few exceptions, the most notable being Powercore, which is able to run virtual instruments off its own DSP chips.

A virtual instrument doesn't differ that greatly from any other plug-in we use, except it does not affect incoming audio; it actually responds to incoming MIDI signals and produces sound based on them. For the MIDI guitarist, this can unlock some absolutely amazing and truly stunning sounds! Forget the built-in sounds on your Roland guitar synth; the majority, if not all, virtual instruments will blow away what you already have now. As a MIDI guitarist, these instruments can be used in the studio or onstage to broaden the reach and depth of your playing. Virtual instruments, on the whole, are starting to replace the hardware-based keyboard/sampler/synth workstations.

My plan here is to offer you a survey of what's out there without writing a novella about each plug-in. I am picking and choosing a very small cross-section of what's already out there. The field of virtual instruments has grown to a pretty spectacular size, and there are simply too many to include here. I could honestly do a whole book on this topic. Let's simply start with the goal of showing you what's out there for you.

Samplers

A sampler is a fairly simple instrument. Instead of trying to re-create sound using electronic synthesis, why not record the sounds as audio files that can be played back with MIDI input? Based on the accuracy of the audio recording, samplers can be very realistic-sounding.

Before we talk about a few of the dominant samplers, let's talk about the two most important things that you look for in a good sampler or sample instrument: multi-sampling and velocity layers. Multi-sampling means that a significant number of MIDI keys have their own separate recorded audio files associated with them. Early samplers simply had a few audio files that were pitch-stretched across the range of notes. The newer and more accurate samplers have a separate audio file for each. This results in a more accurate representation of an acoustic instrument. A velocity layer is a particular sample that's triggered based on a velocity range. For example, a trumpet sounds different when played quietly than when it's played loudly. A sampler that allows many velocity layers lets you record an instrument at different volume levels and match them to MIDI velocity (0–127) for a more realistic sound. The higher the number of velocity layers present in a sample, the more realistic that sample will sound.

What makes a sampler special is its ability to manipulate prerecorded samples or those you make on your own, if you are inclined to record your own samples in another program. Samplers currently only allow you to assemble instruments, not record them. There are virtual instruments that simply play back samples and give you no way to edit them. These playback-only samplers are great for sounds that may not need a lot of tweaking, like orchestral sounds, for example.

On the PC-only side, Tascams GigaStudio has been a favorite for many years. There are two dominant cross-platform samplers on the market: Kontakt by Native Instruments and Halion by Steinberg.

Let's start with Kontakt (see Figure 17.1).

Kontakt boasts a pretty impressive list of features, such as the ability to import samples from almost any library (meaning that if you're coming from one of the proprietary hardware formats like AKAI of Kurzweil, it can decode and read them), so you don't lose your investment in third-party sample discs. It also offers built-in effects, including convolution reverb, a generous synthesizer section for shaping and manipulation of your samples, and support for up to 16 channels of surround sound samples! Kontakt makes it easy for you to make your own sampled instruments with its easy drag-and-drop Mapping Editor, seen in Figure 17.2.

From the Mapping Editor, you can place individual samples to trigger specific MIDI notes, and set up velocity layers for the most realistic sampling experience. You can even perform pitch shifting, beat matching, and other advanced sampling techniques. Kontakt 2 has brought an impressive scripting language to the world of samplers, allowing you to program aspects of your sample's performance, such as scripts like auto harmonize, pitch randomization, pitch inversion, and many other unique tools. Speaking of samples, Kontakt ships with over 16 gigabytes of

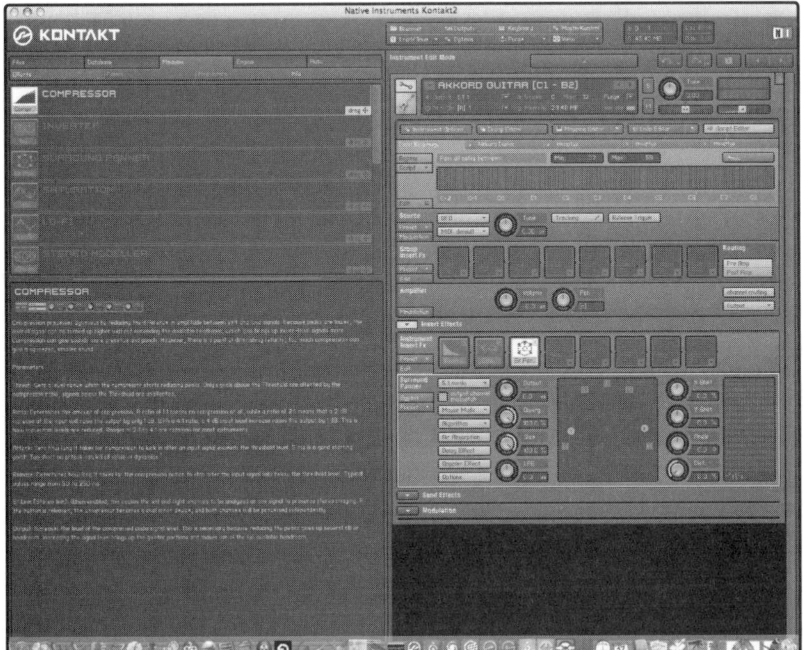

Figure 17.1
Kontakt 2's main sampler window.

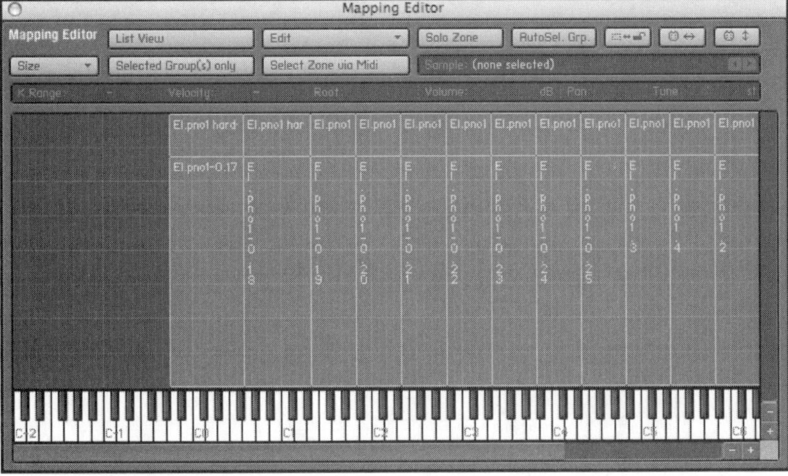

Figure 17.2
Kontak's simple-to-use sample Mapping Editor.

included samples, including a special 16-bit version of the Vienna Philharmonic Orchestra (not every instrument, but enough to get you going). You'll find a varied selection of acoustic, electronic, and off-the-wall sounds in Kontakt.

Next up is Steinberg's Halion. Halion is also a cross-platform sampler, supporting both Mac and PC. It will run in RTAS format, so if you use only Pro Tools, you'll need a VST-RTAS wrapper (like FXPansion's), or else look elsewhere for your sampler. Halion ships in a few different versions, but its flagship is simply Halion, as pictured in Figure 17.3.

Figure 17.3
Steinberg's Halion main view.

Halion also ships in a player-only version, which forgoes the ability to edit samples (useful for a composer who simply wants to have sounds), and a string edition, which includes a very high-quality library of string samples (perfect for string composers and film scorers). Just like you'd expect from a top-of-the-line sampler, Halion allows you to shape the sound with effects and synthesizer-like controls, as well as map the samples as you see fit. Figure 17.4 is a shot of Halion's sound page.

Figure 17.4
Halion's sound page. Here is where you can edit and control the sound, shape, and timbre of your sampled instruments.

Halion also imports a great number of third-party sample formats. Check with Steinberg to see the current list of imported samples.

The last sampler we will cover is Logic's EXS24mkII, but not in this section. Logic is a bit unique in that it includes a plethora of virtual instruments with the program. Because of that, Logic is getting its own section at the end of this chapter.

Additive Synthesizers

The three popular methods for producing sounds electronically are additive synthesis, subtractive synthesis, and FM synthesis. Additive synthesis adds multiple sinusoidal waveforms together, with varying degrees of harmonics, to create musical timbres. Fourier, the father of mathematical analysis, theorized that all sounds are combinations and additions of simple sine waves that, when added together, make more complex sounds. Additive synthesis has a very unique sound. One of the coolest additive synthesizers out there is the Cameleon 5000, by Camel Audio, which at its heart is an additive synthesizer. Figure 17.5 shows the Cameleon in action.

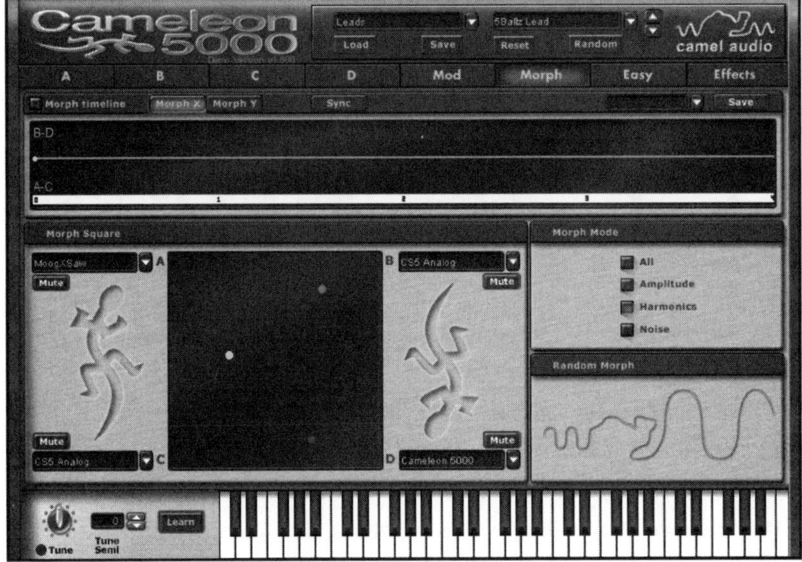

Figure 17.5
Camel Audio's Cameleon 5000 additive synthesizer.

The Cameleon is highly programmable, allowing you to morph between presets and even add audio files as the basis for your synthesis. You have a great deal of control over the harmonics of each individual wave (four of them), and you can create some amazing sounds that range from ethereal to leads to pads and basses. It's actually pretty amazing what you can make by adding four simple sounds together—the palette seems unending. Figure 17.6 is a shot of the control you have over any of the four sounds that add to the final sound.

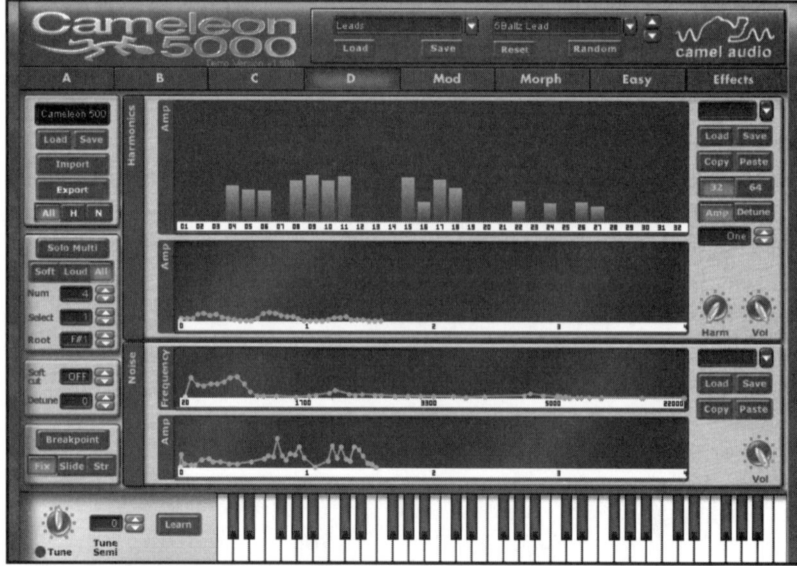

Figure 17.6
Tweaking the harmonics and noise shaping for a single sinusoidal waveshape in Cameleon.

A complete modulation section allows you to link MIDI velocity from your guitar to affect parameters in the synth in real time—such as changing the harmonic content with your picking attack. Of course, with a MIDI foot controller, you can automate through MIDI Learn and change the sound dynamically as you go along. It's a really neat synth, one that constantly inspires me to play non-guitarist phrases every time I plug into it.

Other popular additive synthesizer plug-ins are Expert Sleeper's Additive Synth, VirSyn's Cube, and Casual Agency's Additive Synth.

Subtractive Synthesizers

Subtractive synthesis is one of the oldest and most popular forms of synthesis. If you've ever used or heard a Moog synthesizer, you know about a subtractive synth in some form. Not to mention that the sound of subtractive synthesis is all over records you hear every day—from Nine Inch Nails to Rush to Pink Floyd. The early guitar synths, such as the GR-100 and the GR-300, used subtractive synthesis for their sound generation. Subtractive synthesis works very simply. You start off with a sound oscillator, which can generate a sine wave, square wave, saw tooth wave, or some other variation. The oscillator makes a frequency-rich sound. In order to shape the sound and transform it into other timbres, you simply take away some of the harmonic content through filtering. Subtractive synthesizers may use multiple oscillators, so you can mix and match different source sounds and filter them to taste. Finding a synth in the virtual world that specializes in subtractive synthesis only can be a tall order, since so many synths do multi-synthesis. For this one, we'll look at the legendary Minimoog, which has been re-created in plug-in form by Arturia. Figure 15.7 shows the Minimoog V in action.

Figure 17.7
One of the most famous subtractive synth modules in the world, the Minimoog V, in plug-in form by Arturia.

The visuals are true to the original. There are three oscillators, each of which can have a different waveshape. Next to them is a mixer that allows you to control the independent levels of each oscillator. Next to that is the subtractive part of this synth, where you can filter out the frequencies you don't want until you end up with a final sound you're happy with.

Arturia has a very neat hidden back panel that exposes an arpeggiator, a chorus, a synchable LFO (for old-school vibrato), a delay module, and a modulation section where you can route incoming MIDI values to affect the synth as you play it. Figure 17.8 shows these hidden sections.

In truth, this plug-in belongs in the "Individual Instrument Re-creations" section later in this chapter, but it's such a great example of subtractive synthesis that I decided, what the heck. Logic has some subtractive-only synths as well, which are covered in Logic's section later in this chapter.

Figure 17.8
The hidden back panel exposes a whole bunch of goodies.

FM Synthesizers

Ever heard of a Yamaha DX7? Good, then you've heard of FM, or Frequency Modulation, synthesis. FM synthesis was invented at Stanford University and later licensed to Yamaha for their legendary DX-7 keyboard. FM synthesis is quite a bit different than the other synthesis methods we discussed before. At its heart, FM synthesis uses a simple waveform called the carrier, and the modulator modulates this carrier frequency, resulting in a new waveform. Honestly, the mechanics of FM synthesis aren't that simple, but the sound speaks for itself. The '80s were dominated by the sounds of the Yamaha DX7. Its bell-like tones and strings were recorded more times than we care to admit. Thankfully, in the virtual world, we have a great example of an FM synth: FM7 by Native Instruments. Figure 17.9 shows the interface of FM7.

What makes FM7 so amazing is that it looks and acts in most ways like the original DX7. If you can use a DX series keyboard, you can use the FM7—it even imports the DX7's presets! For us guitar players, FM7 is a way to tap into that particular sound and add it to our production, or even use it live to add in keyboard-type parts. While other synths may adopt FM as one of their means of generating sounds, FM7 is one of the true emulations of the venerable DX7 and is well worth looking at.

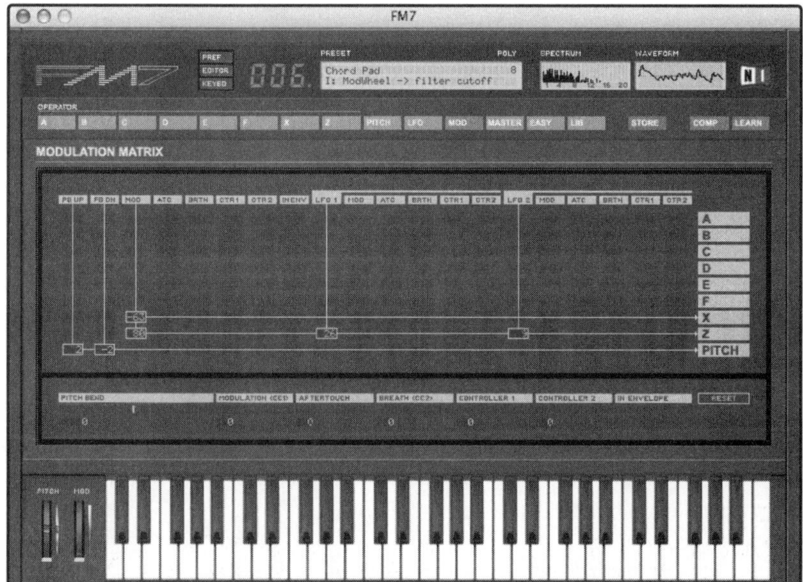

Figure 17.9
Native Instruments' FM7 Synthesizer's Modulation Matrix.

Figure 17.10
Native Instruments FM7—single operator controls.

Multi-Synths

Up until now, we have discussed synthesizers based exclusively on either subtractive, additive, or FM synthesis. Here are some synth plug-ins that incorporate elements of all of the major synthesis methods, and several synths that push the boundaries of what a synth is. We're going to look at three great examples of multi-synths: Motu's MX4, U-He's Zebra 2, and Native Instruments' Absynth. While there are many plug-ins on the market that fall under the multi-synth umbrella, these synths will give us a clear example of what goes into a full-featured multi-synth.

Let's start with Motu's MX4, which is a multi-oscillator synthesizer drawing on additive, FM, and subtractive synthesis, with advanced filtering and arpeggiators/pattern generators.

Figure 17.11
MX4 main/patch view.

What makes MX4 special and unique is its use of multiple methods of synthesis at once. MX4 uses a combination of wavetable, FM, AM, and traditional subtractive synthesis. One really cool feature is that you can route an audio signal into MX4 and process it with MX4's synthesis engine! That means you can play your regular guitar tone and shape it with synth filters. Even better is combining MIDI guitar and audio guitar input for some extremely expressive sounds. As you'd expect from a top-shelf multi-synth, there are tons of ways to make this synth act dynamically. Filters and modulators can be mapped to input levels and other controllers. There is even a built-in step sequencer and arpeggiators! It's a really neat synth.

Now let's look at Native Instruments' modular synth monster, Absynth. At its heart, this is a three-oscillator synthesizer with a few tricks up its sleeve. What makes Absynth modular is that

Figure 17.12
MX4's modulation possibilities.

any of the three oscillator sections can contain subtractive, FM, ring modulated, fractalized, samples, granular synthesis, and audio input. Just like MX4, Absynth allows you to use traditional audio inputs and manipulate them with other synthetic sounds. Figure 17.13 shows the patch window where you can design your own custom synth using any combination of the oscillators, each with its own filter and modulator.

Another notable feature of Absynth is that it allows you to draw your own oscillator waveshapes. Most synths have the standard stock of saw, triangle, sine, and other typical waveshapes. Absynth enables you to draw your own waveshape and use it as an oscillator waveform! Figure 17.14 shows a custom waveshape.

Of course, Absynth does a lot more than this. Its envelope features are basically unparalleled in the industry, and its surround sound implementation is also amazing. It's not surprising that Absynth has become a staple for composers and film-scoring professionals. One more aspect to mention is that you can specify which MIDI notes are taken by which oscillator in the special Note Scaling window, allowing you to set part of your guitar to one oscillator and another range to a different oscillator. Absynth is definitely worth investigation!

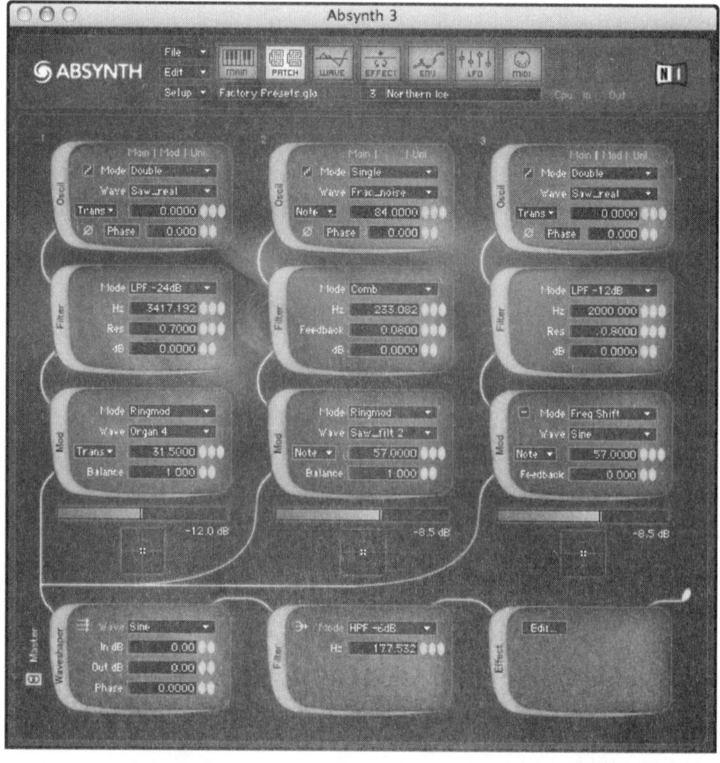

Figure 17.13
Absynth's Patch window, where you construct your synthetic sounds based on oscillator choices, filters, and modulators.

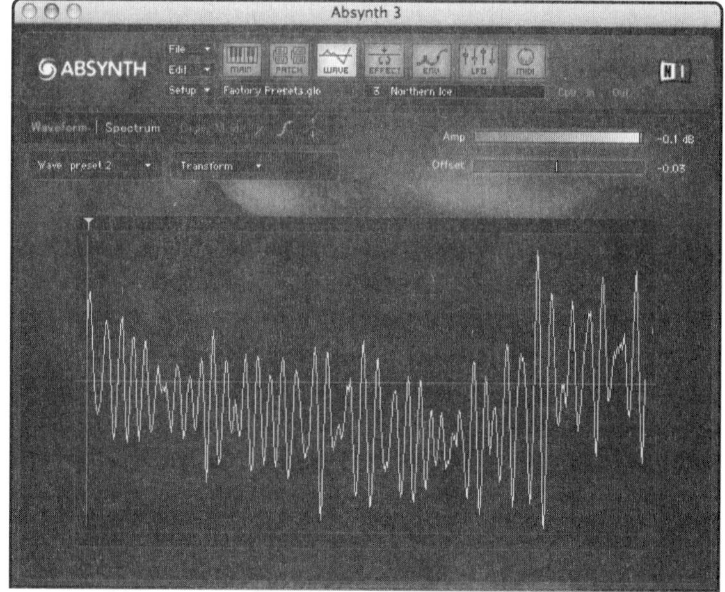

Figure 17.14
Custom waveshape in Absynth.

> **TRY B4 U BUY**
>
> Many of the synths talked about here are ones that I own. However, many others I have experienced using the free demos. Almost every plug-in I discuss in this chapter has some sort of demo you can download. You should definitely take advantage of that and try this stuff out before you go dropping money. Some of the virtual instruments I've used are now on my list of " must-haves," due to my ability to preview them in demo form. So, use Google, find some virtual instruments, and try them out—don't just take my word for it.

Many of the plug-ins we're talking about here have come from large music companies with large staffs of programmers working day and night to bring you the future. What a breath of fresh air it is to find a single developer pushing the limits of musical programming. One such developer is Urs Heckman, head of u-he software. Heckman is a frequent forum contributor to a Web site that I moderate, and I've seen his work mature at an incredible rate. His newest synth plug-in, Zebra 2, is another multi-synth that demands your attention.

Zebra 2, which is a cross-platform hybrid synth, is just phenomenal, and it's even more impressive when you realize that one man did this on his own! Figure 17.15 shows Zebra's main synthesis window.

Figure 17.15
Urs Heckman's Zebra main synthesis window.

The list of what Zebra can do is quite long. It's a traditional subtractive synth; it's got FM and AM oscillators, noise generation, comb filtering, ring modulation, and more. It's also got integrated effects in its own grid-like configuration.

What sets Zebra apart is the extent to which Heckman takes the concept of modularity. Within the main synthesis window, you can drag and drop the modules in any order so that the signal flow goes in the direction you want. Figure 17.16 shows the grid and the top-down processing order. You can freely move the objects around to change their processing order. This is a pretty revolutionary way to approach a modular synth, and it yields an amazing amount of control and sound manipulation.

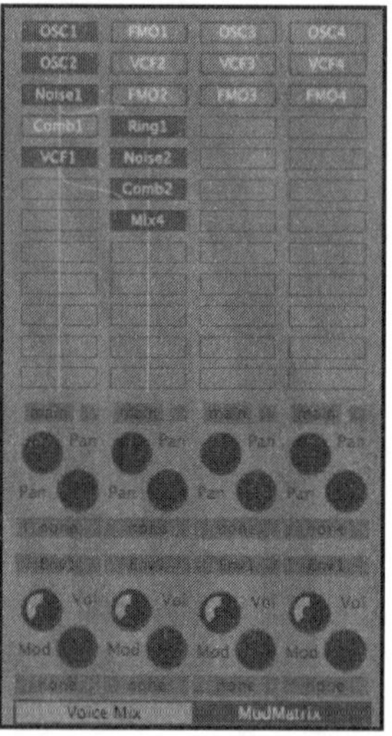

Figure 17.16
Zebra's synthesis grid. Drag and drop to your heart's content!

Of course, what synth would be complete without a full complement of effects and a highly configurable modulation matrix? Yeah, Zebra's got those too. Zebra is an amazing example of the future of synthesis— borrowing from the past while using the future to break down barriers that are present in the hardware. Zebra 2 will make it into my live rig just as soon as possible.

Individual Instrument Re-creations

One of the things that virtual instruments are great for is re-creating instruments. These instruments can be classical hardware synths, long out of production, that you can *only* find in virtual form, or meticulously sampled acoustic instruments, allowing you to play a nine-foot grand piano from the comfort of your desk. With virtual instruments, all of this and more is possible.

Acoustic Instruments

The role of these virtual instruments is to re-create the sound of a real instrument. There are lots of different examples, but piano seems to be one of the "Holy Grails" of virtual instruments, and it's also one of the hardest to get right. We are going to look at one grand piano example and one electric piano example, a re-creation of the mighty Fender Rhodes electric piano.

Both instruments here are sample-based, meaning they are based on acoustic samples. These don't fit in the sampler section because the samples are hidden from you. As a guitarist, piano is one of the things I use all the time during gigs because when mixed with traditional guitar sounds, it sounds like you have a piano player (minus all that great Bill Evans' voicing).

Our acoustic piano is The Grand 2 by Steinberg. The Grand is based on two different sampled grand pianos. The work that goes into these instruments is staggering. Each key is sampled individually, typically at 5–8 different velocity layers, and edited together to make a cohesive, real-sounding instrument. Elements like sustain pedal resonance, response curves, and mechanical noises (hammers, keys) make The Grand one of the better pianos you can use. As with all sample-based instruments, the library of audio files needed to power this instrument can be quite large. In the case of The Grand, you'll need three gigabytes of free hard disk space. While playing the piano, you get an overview of the main screen, which isn't much to look at, as seen in Figure 17.17.

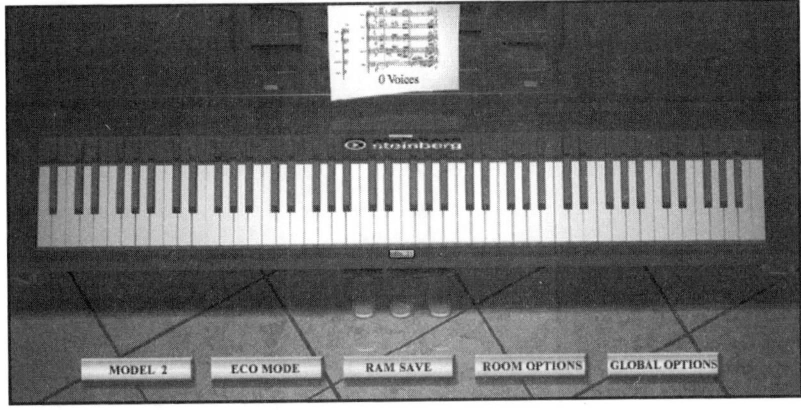

Figure 17.17
The Grand 2's main window view.

You can also easily edit finer parameters of the piano by accessing global options that allow you to tweak the instrument to your tastes, as seen in Figure 17.18. You can edit elements like velocity curves, tuning, and other features.

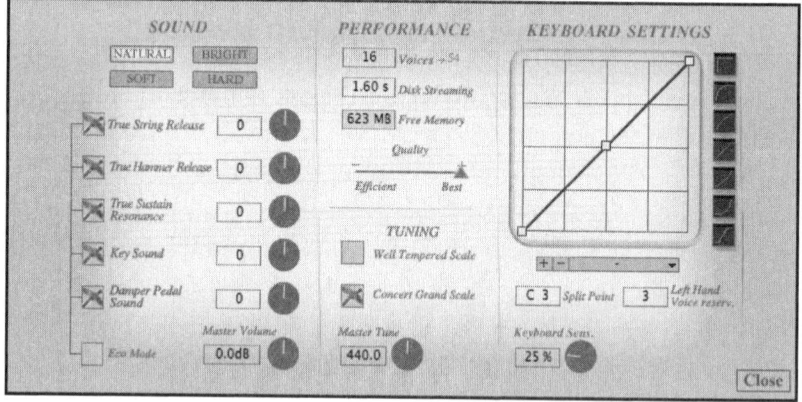

Figure 17.18
Get inside The Grand and tweak parameters such as velocity curves, resonance, and other settings to make the piano suit you.

You can also alter the content of the acoustic space in which you are playing, to simulate different-sized halls and match them to your particular song or live venue. This can be done by accessing the room options, as seen in Figure 17.19.

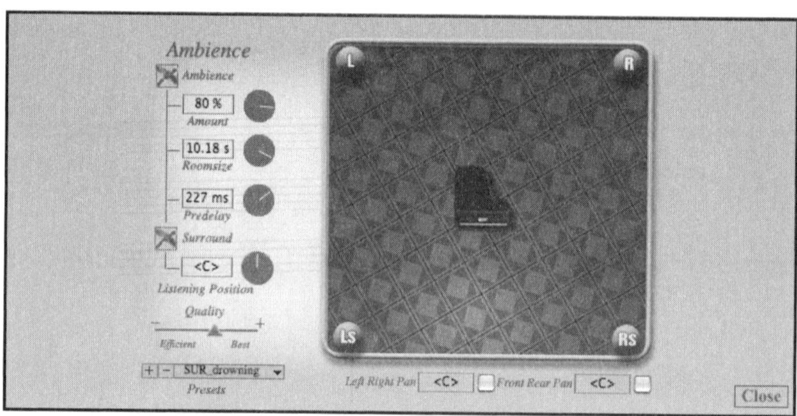

Figure 17.19
Room/reverb settings in The Grand 2.

Other popular acoustic piano virtual instruments are Native Instruments' Akoustik Piano, Art Vista's Virtual Grand Piano, Synthogy's Ivory, and EastWest's Bosendorfer 290.

When it comes to electric pianos, Native Instruments' Elektrik Piano is a pretty amazing piece. This sample-based instrument models four classic electric pianos: the Rhodes MKI + MKII, a Honer Clavinet, and the Wurlitzer A200. This instrument is a player's dream, and the interface is as spartan as the real instruments are—there are few parameters to tweak on the real instruments, so why add more? Figure 17.20 shows the simple interface.

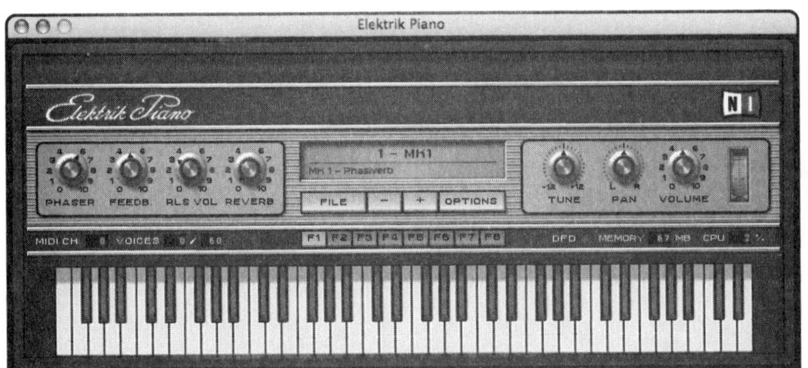

Figure 17.20
Native Instruments' easy-to-use Elektrik Piano.

You can load up any eight variations on the four sampled pianos into any of the eight slots across the top of the instrument. This instrument is also sample-based, so within each category, the different electric pianos are sampled with different reverbs, effects, and adjusted parameters. As is common with a sampled instrument of this type, at least three gigabytes of free space is needed to load the library. The sound speaks for itself. MIDI guitarists may have a hard time matching the exacting response needed to play acoustic piano in a highly realistic fashion, but the particular envelope of the electric piano seems to lend itself to guitar style very well.

Other popular electric piano instruments are Applied Acoustics' Lounge Lizard and the Scarbee '73 Rhodes samples.

Of course, there's more to life than just pianos. Spectrasonics makes Trilogy, an amazing electric and acoustic bass instrument. FXPansion has its BFD virtual drum sets. EastWest even has instruments that cover ethnic and world instruments (RA) and choirs (symphonic choirs). The choir is so advanced that you can type text into it, and it sings back! Traditional orchestras will be covered in the next section. Acoustic instruments may be the most challenging instruments to sample correctly, but the current crop are making believers out of many. Not to mention the convenience of being able to produce highly realistic instrument sounds from the comfort of your own home!

Analog Synthesizer Emulations

Many of us may never get the chance to play with analog synthesizers, due to their high cost and limited availability. Thankfully for us, plug-ins are allowing a new generation of players to experience the magic of the original analog synthesizers that shaped music. These plug-ins do such a good job of it, even the most discriminating players are looking at the new plug-ins with a sense of awe. "How did they do that?"

We are going to look at two re-creations of classical analog synths: Native Instruments' Pro 53 and Arturia's ARP2600V.

Native Instruments' Pro 53 is a re-creation of the legendary Prophet 5 synthesizer, made by Sequential Circuits. There isn't much to say about this one, Native Instruments absolutely nailed the sound of the original. As you can see in Figure 17.21, they nailed the visuals as well! It is a re-creation in every sense of the word. It's a fat-sounding synth and is a total blast to use. Considering that the plug-in sells for about $200, it's a steal when you price out a vintage Prophet 5!

Figure 17.21
Native Instruments' Pro 53's authentic on-screen emulation.

Arturia's ARP2600V is a re-creation of one of the most successful semi-modular synthesizers in history, the ARP2600. The 2600 consisted of a keyboard trigger, a fairly advanced analog sequencer, and the heart of the unit: the patchable, modular synthesizer section. Arturia did a spectacular job of re-creating not only the sound of the unit, but the aesthetic functionality as well. Figure 17.22 shows the main keyboard register and sequencer.

Figure 17.22
Arturia's ARP2600V keyboard and analog sequencer.

Figure 17.23 shows the modular synthesis section, complete with virtual patch chords that you can add and remove at will. The 2600 is a three-oscillator synth with voltage-controlled filters, effects, and everything you expect to see in a modular synthesizer of the era.

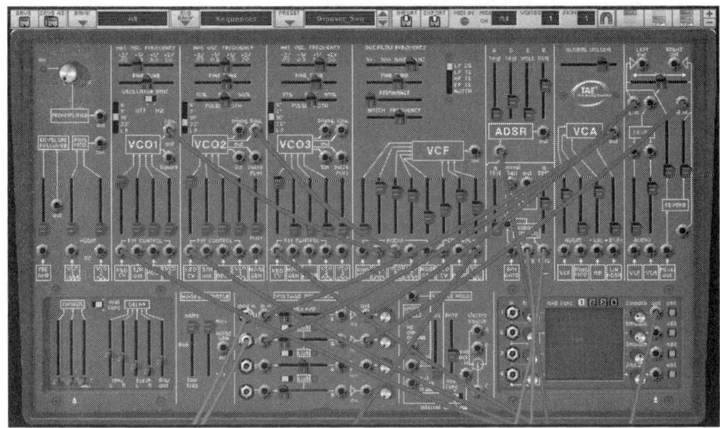

Figure 17.23
The 2600V's synthesizer section, complete with virtual patch cables. Ah, the good old days of patching a modular synth!

Keep in mind that the 2600 was never MIDI-equipped, so the plug-in version actually adds to the functionality of the unit. Try that with the original unit!

Reaktor

Native Instruments has been mentioned a lot in this section, and with good reason, because they are one of the most innovative and experienced virtual instrument companies. Their first product, Generator, was a major leap forward in virtual synthesizer technology. What makes Generator unique is its approach to synthesis. Instead of providing you with an instrument, it gives you the building blocks of virtual synthesis as modules, and you can simply build the instrument you want. It's a bit like Lego for synthesizer designers. Generator was eventually merged with another product called Transformer and was renamed Reaktor. It gets its own category here for one simple reason: it defies categorization. Because of its open architecture and robust building materials, folks have made just about every possible electronic musical instrument using Reaktor. All forms of synthesis, physical modeling, sampling, audio effects—someone even made a car racing game in Reaktor!

You can use Reaktor as a host for instruments of all types without even needing to get involved in the building side of things. If you are so inclined, you can open the hood and peer deep into the abyss that is Reaktor programming. Luckily, Native Instruments has a library where user-created instruments can be shared for free with other registered users. To date, there are more than 2,000 free instruments for Reaktor.

What's an instrument? Within Reaktor, one instrument can be a physical model of a flute played with a steam engine (crazy as it sounds), as seen in Figure 17.24.

Figure 17.24
Steampipe 2, Reaktor's amazing, physically modeled steam/flute instrument.

Another instrument could be a self-playing synth, like Skrewell, screaming all sorts of unusual effects, as shown in Figure 17.25.

Another instrument could be a simple subtractive synthesizer on steroids, Carbon 2, as seen in Figure 17.26.

What's amazing about Reaktor is its ability not to be pigeonholed into any one thing. Buying one plug-in gets you over 2,000 different instruments that truly defy categorization. For those of you brave souls who want to see "under the hood" of Reaktor, I humbly show you the structure view. Figure 17.27 shows you the first basic level.

Simply clicking into any module will take you a level deeper, as shown in Figure 17.28.

Each part can be accessed in another sublayer if you click again, as shown in Figure 17.29.

As you can see, Reaktor is a synthesizer programming environment. Some folks spend months making these instruments. Personally, I am not a builder at all—actually, the structure view freaks me out! I've been able to make some rudimentary instruments, but some of the supreme Reaktor builders find ways to twist the program into doing things even the original developers never thought were possible.

Another instrument that is a lot like Reaktor is Tassman 4 by Applied Acoustics Systems.

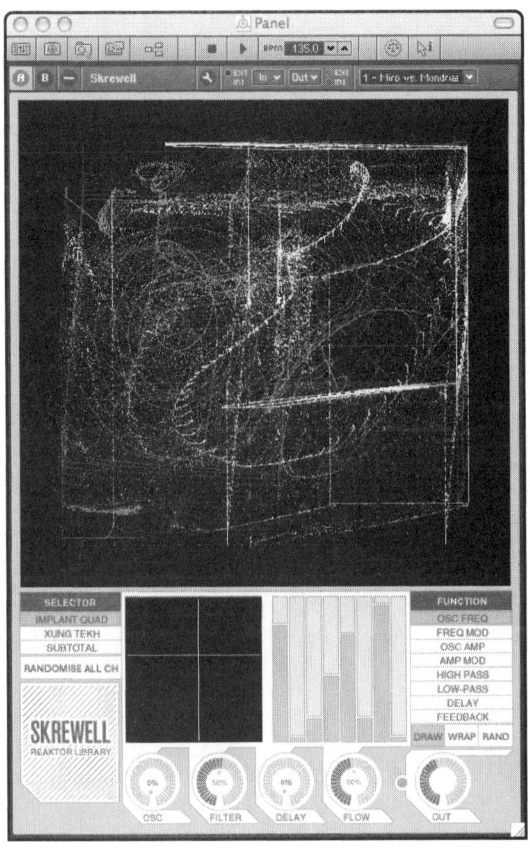

Figure 17.25
The self-playing mad machine that is Skrewell!

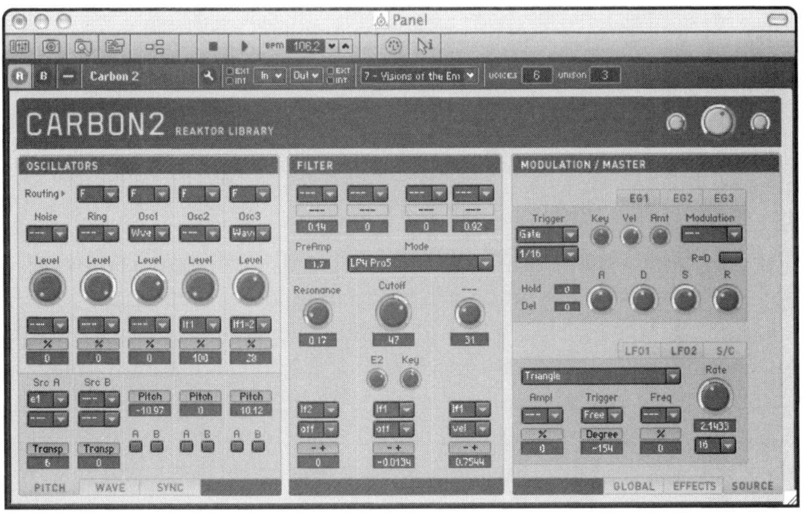

Figure 17.26
Carbon 2, a mighty, mighty synth!

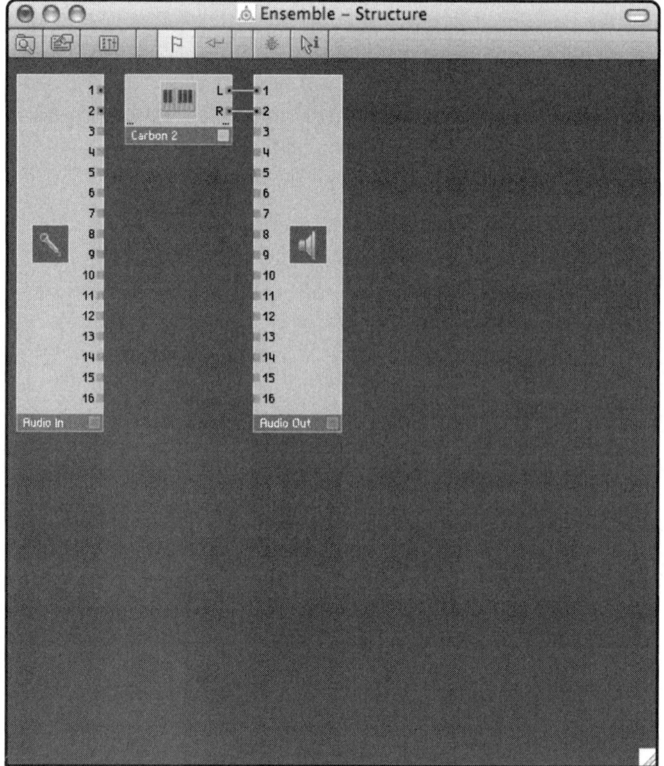

Figure 17.27
Reaktor's structure view, level one.

On a side note, one of my favorite lead sounds for jazz improvisation is taken from Reaktor (the Steampipe 2 Ensemble), and I use it as much as I can. It reacts perfectly to MIDI guitar, and like any good virtual instrument should, it makes me feel like I'm not playing guitar and changes how I play. This is the real power of these virtual instruments. They are more than just software—they are instruments in every sense of the word. Earlier we mentioned the term "physical modeling." Let's explore a bit about physical modeling and see what makes it so unique.

Physical Modeling

Physical modeling is a fairly new idea in synthesis. Instead of using traditional models of waveform or frequency modulated syntheses to make timbres, a physical model is a complex mathematical model of an instrument. What makes physical models so cool is that they are very expressive. Think of the way a string sounds different as you pluck it harder. In a traditional synthesis or sampling environment, you'd either need to resample at different velocity layers or figure out some way to modulate the sound. In a physical model, this is built into the model. Physical models are much harder to design since each model is very specific to its instrument.

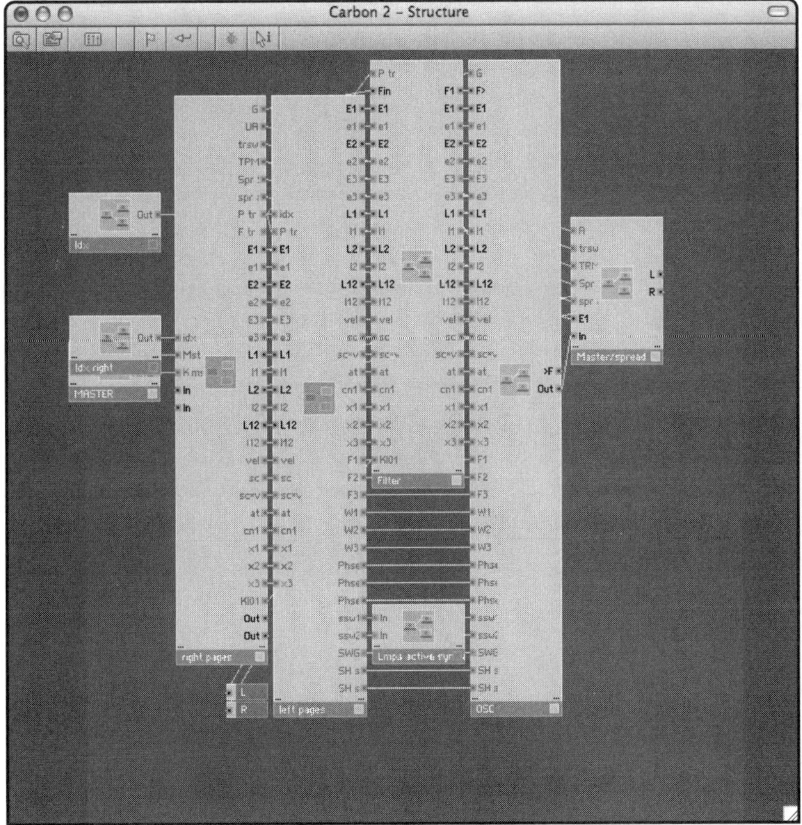

Figure 17.28
Delving deeper into Reaktor's structure view.

Yamaha once had an incredible piece of hardware, the VLZ synth, that was a physical modeler, but we are here to talk about plug-ins.

Applied Acoustics has one of the better physical modeling studios: Tassman. Tassman is often thought of as a Reaktor-type application, and although they are both very modular, Reaktor is a different thing. Tassman allows the creation of models in a much simpler way than Reaktor. Tassman is also specifically a physical modeler—that's its one job, whereas Reaktor does all sorts of stuff.

Tassman is great for synth guitar because it's so amazingly expressive and reacts to this type of playing. As you know by now, MIDI guitar is very expressive and sends out a great deal of controller information. Tassman is wonderful about bringing the nuances out. Figure 17.30 shows the main screen of Tassman in action.

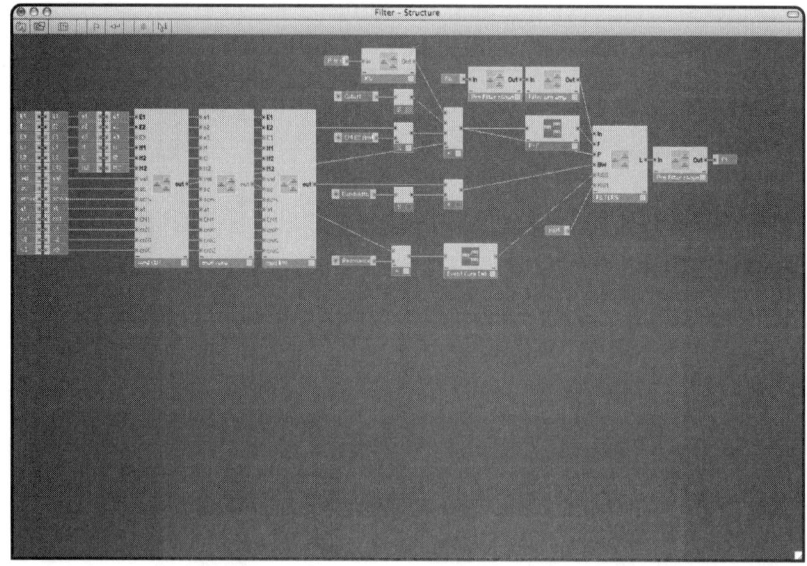

Figure 17.29
Micro-level modules in Reaktor's structure view.

Figure 17.30
Tassman's main modeling window with controls.

As stated before, Tassman is modular, so if you want to get beyond the presets, you can build amazing models of your own. Figure 17.31 is the modular Builder window in Tassman. It's similar to Reaktor in its structure, but a bit less scary.

I find myself gravitating towards physical modeling more and more because the technology is just so exciting. Even though samples may sound more "real," there is something about the expressiveness of physical modeling that makes up for other flaws. Samples are notoriously dry

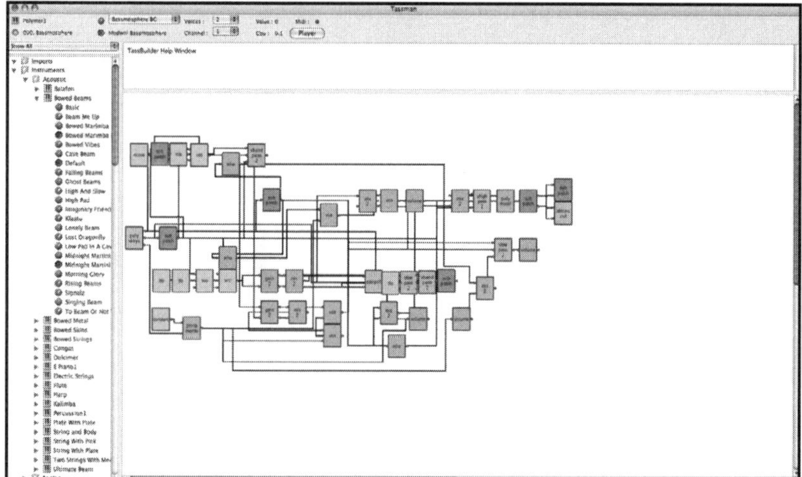

Figure 17.31
Building on the component level in Tassman.

and require a great deal of programming to get right. Physical models feel like instruments; you simply play them.

Applied Acoustics has a new physical modeler, String Studio, that boasts some of the most realistic string models I've ever heard. You dig in and the instrument digs back; it's pretty wild.

Other physical modelers include Ugo's String Theory and Synapse Audio's Plucked String.

Logic Pro

It's a fact that Logic Pro is a DAW. It's also a bit more than just a DAW. It is one of the most complete virtual instrument collections to be found anywhere. They pretty much threw everything they could at Logic Pro, and there is an included plug-in for just about everything. The reason I am giving Logic Pro its own section is that it's a Mac-only application and the virtual instruments are hard-coded into the program—you can't use them in other parts of the system or in other programs. Simply put, Logic Pro is self-contained. The list of virtual instruments is pretty exhaustive, so rather than go into a long discussion about them, let's just tell you briefly what it has. A quick note that two virtual instruments will be left out: Ultrabeat (a drum machine and step sequencer) and the EVOC 20 Vocoder. Each of these instruments is incredible in its own right, and you will find tons of uses for them both in your studio, but they don't necessarily lend themselves to being controlled by a MIDI guitar. If you own Logic, you know how cool these instruments are already—I don't have to sell you on them!

I have used many DAWs in my life, and I find that each has its strengths and weaknesses. I come back to Logic time and time again because of the virtual instruments. They are simply fantastic.

Let's Start with the Simpler, Subtractive Synthesizers

We start with the ES M, which is a single-oscillator, monophonic subtractive synthesizer that excels in bass sounds (although I've gotten mine to do much more). It's a basic and very easy-to-use synth, and it is also a great way to get started learning about synthesis. ES M is pictured in Figure 17.32.

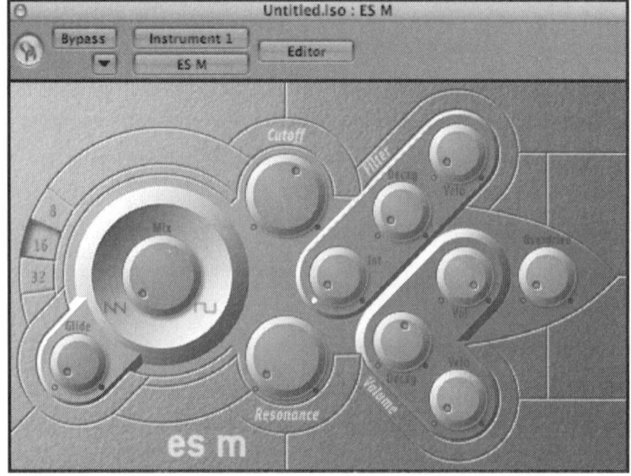

Figure 17.32
The ES M Mono Synth.

Next is the ES P, which is an eight-voice polyphonic synth, and is a bit more complex than the ES E. Six different oscillators are available, each with its own level controls, allowing you to mix any combination of the six timbres together. An eight-voice synth is great for guitar, as you can easily use one voice for each string. The ES P is shown in Figure 17.33.

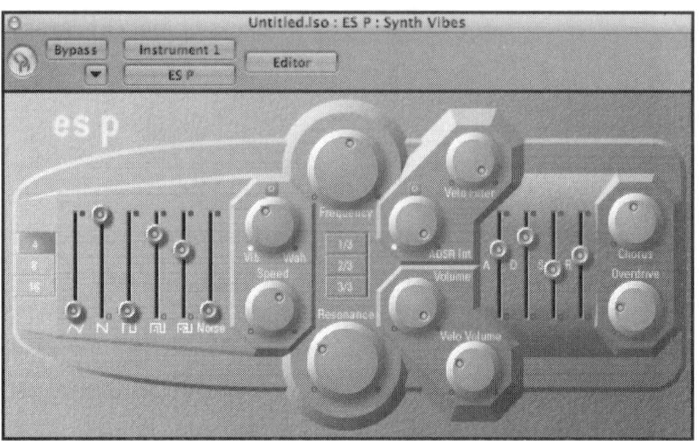

Figure 17.33
ES P, an eight-voice polyphonic synth.

Next is the ES E, which is another eight-voice polyphonic synth. The ES-E uses only one oscillator at a time, which switches between pulse and saw wave shapes. It was intended for pad type/atmospheric sounds. Simple filtering controls allow you to shape your tone. The ES E is pictured in Figure 17.34.

Figure 17.34
The ES E, another eight-voice polyphonic synth in Logic.

Advanced Subtractive Synthesizers, ES 1 and ES 2

The ES 1, shown in Figure 17.35, is as appealing sonically as it is visually. A combination of wave

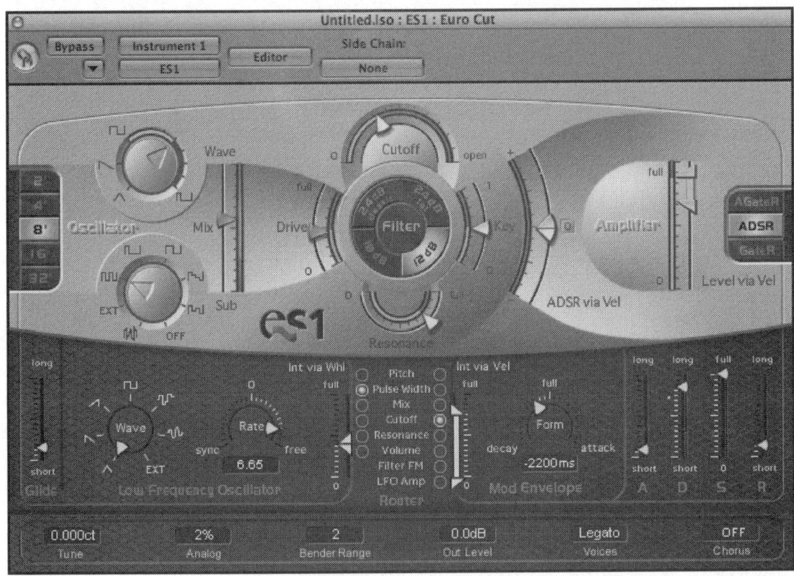

Figure 17.35
Logic's robust ES 1 synth.

shapes, LFOs, and traditional sound envelope controls make this synth very chameleon-like. This was the first synth I used live with a MIDI guitar, and it still remains one of my favorites. The filtering section is extremely rich-sounding, and the synth itself can be set up to modulate parameters via velocity, giving you a dynamically changing sound as you play. ES 1 covers about any sound you can imagine, from leads to pads, basses to percussive sounds.

The ES 2, shown in Figure 17.36, is the successor to the popular ES 2, and as you can see, the bar was raised on this one. The ES 2 is a three-oscillator (like the venerable Minimoog) with an extensive modulation environment. The range of sounds you can pull out of this beast is really amazing. Integrated effects such as Distortion, Delay, Chorus, Flange, and Phaser add more tools to your sonic arsenal. The filtering section is also dynamic, fat, and very fun to work with. This puppy has lots of parameters you can modulate based on velocity and pitch to make your sounds dynamic, a must for the MIDI guitarist.

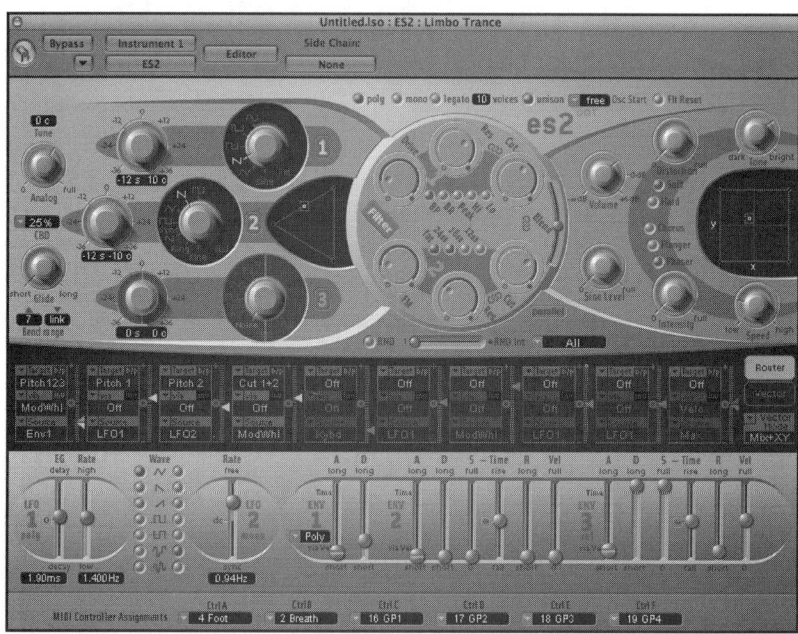

Figure 17.36
Logic's impressive ES 2 synth.

Traditional FM-Style EFM 1 and Totally Unique Sculpture

What studio would be complete without an FM-style synth? Logic Pro version 7 saw the introduction of the EFM 1 synth, shown in Figure 17.37. This simple FM-style synth should not fool you with its spartan interface—it yields some very cool sounds. It has everything you'd expect from an FM synth: your pads, bells, atmospheres, and keyboard sounds.

Also new in Logic 7 is Sculpture, which may be one of the most advanced synths ever created. It's based on component modeling, which is basically physical modeling. In Sculpture, the models are based either on a vibrating string or a vibrating bar, but boy did they do a lot with just those two models! A look at the interface of Sculpture in Figure 17.38 shows you the extent

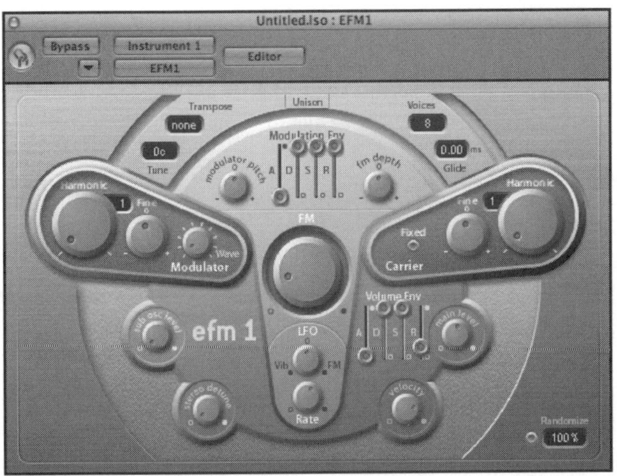

Figure 17.37
Logic's take on FM synthesis: the EFM 1.

of this synth and its beautifully designed layout. Sculpture's uniqueness lies in how the models are utilized. String and bar models are quickly transformed into sounds beyond imagination. The usual complement of synth filtering and modulation is included, but with more unique twists and turns than I can discuss. I could go on for 10 pages about Sculpture, but I will spare you. It's one of the most unique synths I've ever used, and its ability to morph sounds from one to the other has yet to be rivaled anywhere. Period.

Figure 17.38
Logic's innovative Sculpture synthesizer.

Logic Virtual Keyboard Collection

Our keyboard collection starts with a good Rhodes, the EVP88, shown in Figure 17.39. This

Figure 17.39
Logic's electric piano, the EVP88.

EVP88 is actually based on 15 different models of classic electronic keyboards. Tremolo, Chorus, Phaser, Overdrive, and EQ help shape your tones, and each model has specific controls for its timbre and tuning. The EVP88 is not a sampled piano; instead, it is all modeling and synthesis, which makes its convincing sound even that much more impressive. Jazz legend Herbie Hancock retired his Rhodes from use and went virtual, employing the EVP88 for his live gigs. That's a pretty serious endorsement!

Now let's look at the EVB3, Logic's Hammond B3 model, as seen in Figure 17.40. This one is pretty simple to show and explain. Everything you'd expect to find in a B3 organ is present: Drawbars, Leslie Effects, EQ, Tone-wheel Leakage, Brakes, Vibrato, and Percussion. What sells this organ is its highly realistic sound, which is also not sampled, but all synthetically modeled. The EVB3 simply does its job and does it well.

Last is the EVD6, a re-creation of the legendary Honer Clavinet D6. You know the sound of the cavinet from Stevie Wonder's classic, "Higher Ground"? Figure 17.41 shows the plug-in that re-creates this sound in action. This particular model is one of the most realistic in the collection; the accuracy of the modeling is amazing. This is truly a fun instrument to play live with. Get your funk here!

Figure 17.40
You want a Hammond? Look no further than the EVB3.

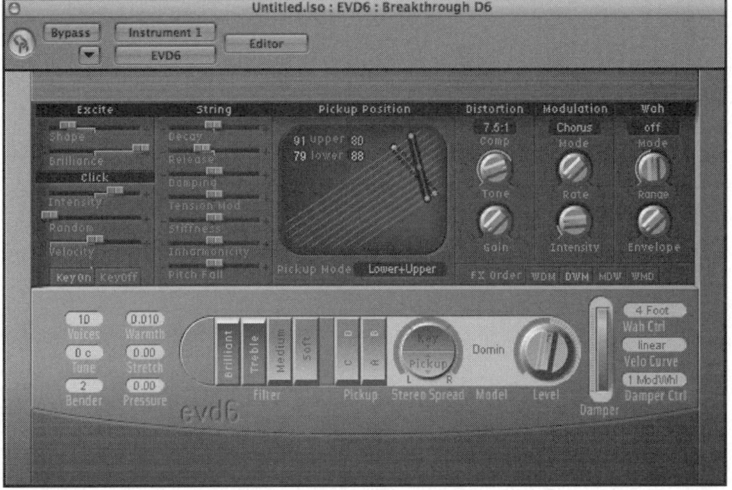

Figure 17.41
Heaps of funk: The EVD6 clavinet!

Sampler: EXS24 mkII

The EXS24 is Logic's built-in sampler, shown in Figure 17.42. ESX24 has all that you'd expect from a modern sampler: an impressive included sound library, the ability to import third-party sample formats (Akai, Giga, SampleCell, SoundFont, and DLS), extensive modulation, envelope and filter controls, and an advanced sampler editor/keymap editor, shown in Figure 17.43.

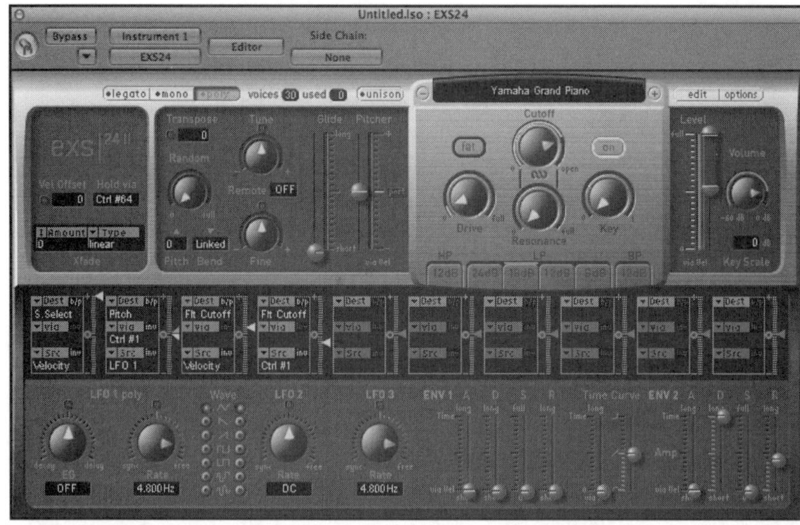

Figure 17.42
Logic's sampler: The ESX24 mkII.

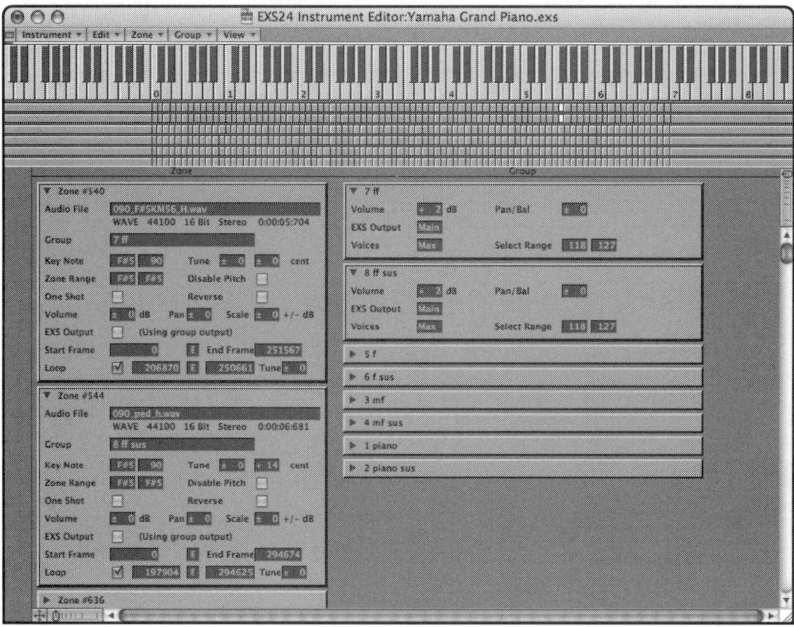

Figure 17.43
The EXS24's sample mapping editor.

The EXS24 has always had one huge plus going for it—it's efficient. You can run a bunch of them at once with extensive modulation and other parameters active, and your computer will still have plenty of computing power left over for other duties.

As you can see, Logic included pretty much anything you'd need to create music with. Unfortunately, you will also be limited to using its amazing facilities inside of Logic because you can't take the plug-ins into Cubase, for example.

AMAZING

You know what's amazing? We just showed you the power of plug-in virtual instruments. If this were hardware, I would need a whole house to fit it all in, and it would bankrupt me. Not to mention upkeep of all the delicate electronics. The fact that I can run them all from a laptop will continue to amaze me, and it should wow you as well. Welcome to the future, it's pretty cool here. Grab that MIDI guitar and break some new ground—music could certainly use the help.

The last thing we are going to explore is the last part of the digital guitar puzzle, which is how to pull this off live. Read on, read on!

18 Digital Guitar Live!

The focus of this book has been on studio applications of digital guitar technology. If you want to ride the cutting edge of digital guitar, you need to take your rig on the road with you. This chapter will detail exactly how you can harness the power of digital guitar away from the confines of your home studio.

Getting Started

To fully explore digital guitar live, you need to take your computer with you. In just about every case, this will involve a laptop computer. Some musicians have taken the new iMac G5s on stage with them, but for 99.9% of musicians who use computers onstage, laptops are it.

Guitar players are certainly not leading the charge here. The first musicians to employ laptops onstage were electronic musicians and DJs. It's actually more common to see Apple Powerbooks at electronic music shows than old MIDI hardware like Roland 303s and 808s (although we are seeing mixtures of software and hardware). For the past several years, electronic musicians have been the test bed for the stability and usability of laptop setups. Knowing quite a few of these musicians and even participating in their shows, I can pass on some wisdom of how they are able to pull off such a feat!

The first thing that laptop-based musicians look for is a stable platform. Crashing onstage is certainly not an attractive option for anyone. Apple Powerbooks are more common onstage. This is no slight against the Windows platform, but I've seen far more glowing Apple logos onstage than Windows laptops. That's not to say that I've never seen Windows laptops working really well. A good friend of mine, Richard Devine, employs his Windows laptop in all his live shows without a hitch.

I believe that part of the Apple vs. Windows debate has more to do with software than just hardware. I'm not sure you can quantify which is more stable. I can only comment on what I see onstage. For some artists, there were more attractive software options on the Mac side at first, but as we're on the final chapter of this book, you are surely aware that both platforms have wonderful music software.

Also, in the early days, Apple hardware was capable of lower latencies than their Windows counterparts. This has also changed with the new crop of ASIO-based Firewire and USB hardware, but history has set some precedents and many artists still go to the Mac because it's so prevalent, even though XP can attain lower latencies that OSX. Never fear, as you know from this book already, it really doesn't matter which you choose. Pick the one that you like the best.

Our Questions

We guitarists have a different set of requirements. Electronic musicians may trigger samples or soft-synths live. That is one thing, but audio processing is another thing.

In order to take your laptop onstage, you will need to work a few things out. The first is the audio interface you will use. You will need something that is very stable and can operate at low latencies. The interface also needs to have preamplified inputs so your guitar can reach the appropriate level into the computer. Honestly, there are so many good interfaces out there; you should post to a few online forums to poll some users who may be in the same boat as you. Laptop guitar is new and cutting-edge, but there are certainly people doing it who can lend some valuable advice. I personally love small, bus-powered interfaces that run class-compliant without needing drivers at all, such as the Presonus Firebox. Web sites such as www.kvr.com and www.osxaudio.com may link you up with similar artists using interfaces in a live setting. Interface advice doesn't necessarily have to come from a guitarist, you know.

Once you have the interface figured out, you need to decide on software. Which of the many capable virtual amplifiers do you want to use? Are you going to run this through a sequencer, or will you use it stand-alone, like Native Instruments Guitar Rig 2? The other choice is to use a real amp for guitar sounds and a laptop for MIDI guitar. This was my first foray into the virtual world. The Guitar Rig-type software was integrated into my setup a year or so later. In that time, my amp did double duty, providing real tones and amplifying my synths. If this sounds like where you may be headed, it's a very realistic possibility and can be easily done.

The next question is control. How are you going to control your presets and tone in real time? Just because the computer is doing the processing doesn't mean you need to or should sacrifice the ability to turn effects on and off, operate Wah-wahs, and so on. Are you looking for an all-in-one solution like Native Instruments' Guitar Rig and their interface/pedal, or do you have a preferred MIDI-based foot controller?

Next up is the MIDI guitar. Are you going to use one? If so, which system are you going to use and how are you going to interface it with your computer? If you are going to trigger software instruments in addition to your sound, which ones are you going to use? Which host will you run them in and is your laptop powerful enough for all of this? If you aren't comfortable taking your laptop on the road, MIDI guitar can work without a computer, either triggering the internal sounds of your converter unit or slaving to a hardware module or sampler.

What about amplification? Are you taking the outputs of your interface into your Fender Twin? Maybe, maybe not. Digital guitar has a new set of rules, and amplifiers and cabinets have some different requirements than normal guitar amps do. This is especially true if you are using virtual instruments that have a much fuller range than a typical guitar's signal, because you will need a speaker with a fuller range than most speakers available for guitarists.

The last issue that you need to deal with is security. Laptops are easily stolen. How are you going to secure yours on set breaks and on those much-needed trips to the bar?

These are all aspects of being a digital guitarist that you may have to deal with. Thankfully, I am one of the brave few who has been doing this for years and have endured many "war stories" over the years. I am here to tell you that not only is it possible, but it also allows you some luxuries that the average guitarist simply won't have.

Let's go over each of these aspects in greater detail, and at the end, I will show you my setup as one example of how you can do this.

Live Audio Interfaces

As for which interface to use, this really depends on your needs. There are a slew of Firewire and USB interfaces that are well suited to guitarists. The main selling points you need to look for are low latency, at least one preamplified input, and of course, the type of outputs, either RCA or quarter-inch, so that you can interface with your amplifier. I personally recommend that you go with an interface that is bus-powered—that is, self-powered from your laptop. The Presonus Firebox, M-Audio FastTrack, and Metric Halo ULN-2 are examples of bus-powered interfaces.

The other factor is drivers. Each audio interface will need some sort of driver to access your computer's digital audio applications. Each manufacturer is responsible for designing and implementing its own drivers. Certain companies are famous for releasing stable drivers, while other manufacturers simply aren't as successful. This is another area in which the online bulletin boards are very helpful. Ask around if you have an interface in mind. You may get some very valuable opinions based on real-world testing. Personally, I find interfaces that don't rely on drivers can save your life, as they simply plug-and-play and take the guesswork out of drivers and compatibility. Look for the term "class-compliant."

Sound quality is another issue. An audio interface is responsible for two critical aspects: A/D conversion and D/A conversion. Simply, the interface has to convert your analog sound into digital information that the computer can process, and then convert it back to analog again for amplification. The quality of this digital conversion (in either direction) is critical to getting a good sound. Cheap converters will ultimately sound cheap, especially when internal preamps are used. It doesn't matter how good your guitar software is if it's not giving you a faithful reproduction of your original sound.

You definitely get what you pay for here, but I don't mean to be elitist. A $200 guitar amp won't sound as good as a '68 Superlead, but you can get a good sound out of a budget interface. I don't mean to suggest that without spending big bucks you're doomed to sound like a rank amateur! But I do mean that when you compare an entry-level interface with a high-end one, you will notice the differences. A lot of this depends on the type of music you play. I play jazz, so clarity is essential. For louder rock bands, it may not be as much of a consideration. For the record, I played a professional gig with a budget interface once because I was having driver issues, and no one complained, so there you have it.

The two notable exceptions when it comes to interfaces are the Rig Kontrol pedal, shown in Figure 18.1, which takes care of your interface, preamps, and outputs and is bus-powered (you also get foot control). More on that later.

Figure 18.1
Rig Kontrol II.

The other exception is the Brian Moore iGuitar.USB, which allows you to plug in directly to your computer onstage. The only problem with the USB solution is that USB cables aren't very long, and your computer will still need a separate audio interface for its output because the iGuitar.USB is an input-only device. Since you have to carry a second interface, you might as well just use the guitar's normal quarter-inch output jack into a preamp/interface and leave the USB option for home use. That being said, if you are using a laptop, how far away from it do you expect to stand?

More and more, we are seeing interfaces designed for the guitarist. Companies like Edirol, Yamaha, Presonus, RME, Metric Halo, M-Audio, Digidesign, MOTU, and others make interfaces that will work well for you due to the inclusion of guitar-optimized inputs and preamps. Once you get your interface settled, you need to decide on some software.

Software

The software that you ultimately choose is a personal decision. Thankfully, almost all audio programs have demo versions, so you can "try before you buy." What's very important is how you are going to access these plug-ins live. In a studio environment, you are working with a sequencer and typically other things are going on, such as other recorded tracks and so on. In our case, we are using the plug-ins for live processing, essentially using the computer as an effects box, similar to a pedal or a rack-mounted piece of gear. We will be using the computer as a hub for all of our audio or MIDI synths, and this needs to happen within a host environment. You probably won't be playing against other tracks, so you'll want to give your computer as much free power as possible to run your software of choice.

The complication is that you need to run your plug-ins from within a sequencer, which means you have to bring a full-fledged sequencer with you. As you know, some sequencers are protected with dongle copy protection, and that may be a deterrent for you—it was for me. Dongles scare me because they are very easily stolen or lost. I can secure my laptop with a security cable, but dongles still make me uncomfortable. Also, how stable is the sequencer for longer periods of use? You can't have the program crash in the middle of a two-hour gig, so you need to take the proper preparations to ensure that your chosen platform is running as smoothly as possible.

Host programs, like any DAW we have mentioned, usually incur extra latency in your signal, and this has to be factored into your sound. Native Instruments' Guitar Rig is the only software choice right now that allows you to run the full-fledged program without an extra host program. This application runs without a host, which is called running stand-alone. Boy, there are a lot of elements that go into the process of selecting the perfect combination of software, host sequencer, hardware, etc. If you take it step by step and test each part out well before you try your first live gig with it, you'll be happy you took all the extra time.

BURN IN

When selecting any program to use in a live setting, you really want to make sure that there won't be any surprises. You may want to try a burn in session. This term "burning in" comes from electronics testing, where they left equipment on for a few days to test for failure. My idea of a burn in is to leave the program and sequencer running for a few days straight with some loops running over and over again, constantly pressing on foot pedals and such. Basically, I want to make sure that it runs for a long period of time and if there is a bug anywhere in the software, I need to know if it's a deal-breaker, or if I can simply avoid that action. I ran Logic Express for four days straight before I decided that it was stable enough for live use! It hasn't crashed on me in three years of using the system and hundreds of hours onstage!

Control

As for control, guitar players are used to foot control of amp and pedal functions. If you're going to take the proverbial "show on the road," you're not going to be able to get by without it. As for control, you have a few options. The first is an externally based MIDI foot controller. Most, if not all of the major guitar plug-ins, are able to link to an external MIDI foot controller to change presets and manipulate the on-screen functions. There are a few popular foot controllers on the market: The Behringer FCB 1010 (see Figure 18.2), the Digital Music Ground Control Plus, the Yamaha MFC10, the DigiTech Control 8, and the Roland FC-200.

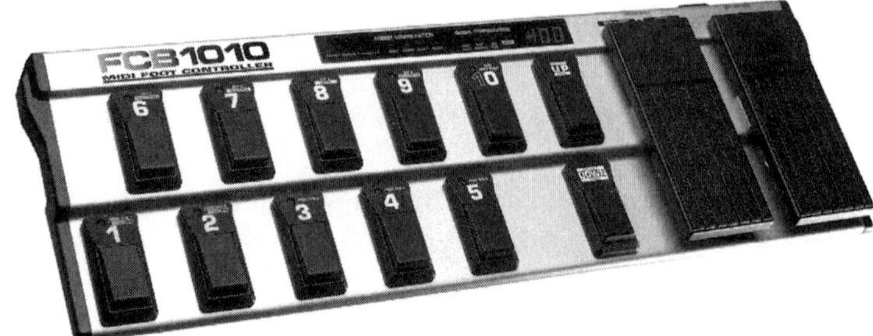

Figure 18.2
The Behringer FCB1010.

The controller has a very simple job to do—send MIDI messages based on your feet completing a simple circuit. The foot controllers have two types of pedals: on/off pedals and expression controllers. The on/off pedals are just that; they send one MIDI message, either on or off, or program change-to-change presets. They can change a preset or active/deactivate a preset effect or stompbox. The expression controllers are variable foot controllers that send a varying signal. A good analogy is a volume pedal or a Wah-wah. Based on where the pedal is rocked in its full range, a different value is sent. These expression pedals are great for performing actions such as distortion saturation, volume pedal, Wah-wah pedals, reverb depth, chorus rate, etc. In short, any parameter in your setup that can change over time can be set up to respond to your expression controls.

The pedals themselves have some onboard functionality that allows you to program what each button and controller actually does. This is handy for hardware-based units (such as rack-mounted MIDI tone generators that respond to fixed parameters), but in this day of MIDI Learn within plug-ins, where you can simply tell the program to listen for your pedal and automatically route a pedal to a software component, programming hardware isn't as necessary as it used to be. I don't see much sense in it. I go into Guitar Rig and set up for the five or six presets that I use, which buttons control, which parameters, and what the expression controller does. This way, I can have a unique setup that does not rely on settings in my foot controller, which could become corrupt or lost somehow (all due to Murphy's Law).

The pedals simply need power and a MIDI interface to interface with your computer/laptop. You can get a simple 1×1 MIDI interface that runs on USB for this purpose. Just plug the cables in, power up the unit, and you are good to go.

My foot controller (the Behringer) has 10 dedicated buttons, preset up/down, and two expression controllers. I set mine up statically. This means that button 1 is always distortion on/off, and so on. Regardless of whether or not my preset has distortion in it, I keep it the same so that no matter what preset I'm on, I know what I can change. I even have the pedals labeled with glow-in-the-dark label strips that tell me what things are, but at this point, I know what they do by heart. In Guitar Rig, it is really easy to set up a configuration like this. As for the expression controllers, the left one is always Wah-wah, and the right is always master volume—two very important functions for me.

With Guitar Rig 2, you get a new pedal, which acts as an input/output device and also as a floor controller. All other systems require third-party MIDI foot controllers. In any event, no matter what you choose, you have some very simple options for controlling your new, cutting-edge rig in the old-school way of pressing buttons!

MIDI Guitar

Live digital guitar is so much cooler with MIDI guitar in the equation. The question you need to ask yourself is: How are you going to integrate this into your rig? Are you thinking of using a stand-alone guitar-to-MIDI converter, like the Roland GR-20 or the Axon AX100 mk II, and simply taking the outputs of the units and running them alongside your amp?

The other option is to trigger soft-synthesizers from your laptop. In the last chapter, I detailed exactly how cool the current offerings are in the software world. If you plan to do this, you need to nail down a few things before going ahead.

If you are triggering samples from the computer directly, boxes that do not contain built-in sounds, such as the GI-20, send MIDI out faster than units that contain built-in sounds. So if tracking and speed are key issues for you—and they should be—then you want to look at a stand-alone MIDI guitar converter.

If you're going to take the plunge on a Ztar or the new Brian Moore USB guitars that send MIDI, great, they work very well! They simply remove one step in your onstage rig by eliminating the need for a guitar-to-MIDI converter. In the case of the Ztar, you'll need a real guitar onstage as well. I keep my Ztar on a stand and use it when I need it, going back and forth from guitar to Ztar and back again. Ultimately, this is why the iGuitar gets more work in my setup—I can do MIDI and guitar in the same instrument. I still use the Ztar live, but for Ztar-only pieces.

Software synthesizers can be very demanding on your system. Exactly how demanding running a software synthesizer will be depends on the system you are running, which plug-ins, and which guitar simulator you have. Readily available technological improvements, such as abundant

RAM and fast hard disks (if you are using samples), will make things better. There is no substitute for giving your computer stress tests and running some clean guitar sounds with string backgrounds and other tasks that will heavily tax your computer.

Changing presets in your synths can be as simple as using one of the foot controllers mentioned in the previous section. However, if you plan to use several different synths loaded up at once and switch between them live, that may take a bit more work. A lot of this depends on your host DAW. In the old days when I used Logic, you couldn't run more than one virtual instrument at the same time. They could all be loaded up, but you simply could not layer the sounds. There were always work arounds at the time, and with Logic this has been taken care of with updates, but each system is different in how it handles this sort of thing. Remember that if you want to have a few sounds loaded, they will tax your CPU simply by being instantiated, whether or not they are playing anything. Some DAWs, such as Digital Performer and Logic, bypass plug-ins that are not receiving information, but others, like Cubase and Nuendo, do not, so you have to determine what's going to work for you based on the speed of your system.

Which sounds will you play? There are a lot of sounds out there now. To say that the market has undergone a virtual instrument explosion is an understatement! The question really is, how many sounds do you need to have going at one time? For me, just like my guitar sounds aren't that complex (I rely on two clean sounds and two distorted/affected sounds), my synth sounds aren't that exotic. I use strings behind clean chords, and I have a screaming lead sound and usually a Rhodes-type piano. I can find all of these in one plug-in, and I simply switch presets of muted and unmuted channels with my foot controller to start and end sounds. I even have a separate expression controller for MIDI volume, even though my guitar has a MIDI volume knob and preset up/down. I still like to control my volume hands-free.

Even though there are thousands of sounds available to you, you need to boil it down to the essentials and not overdo it. Make sure that your choices sound good and come across as realistically as possible. Acoustic pianos rarely sound great on guitar, but electric keyboards do work very well. Percussion can be cool, but usually you have a drummer. Strings are always great, especially when you blend them with regular sounds, particularly on slow tunes.

The last aspect is amplification! Thankfully, amplification will get its own section here. Let's get to it.

Amplification and Speakers

When it comes to amplifying your new rig, you need to keep a few things in mind. First, regular guitar amps are simply not suited for what you are doing now. Remember back in the '80s, when guitar players were in love with racks and used power amps that fed guitar cabinets? They did so for the same reason that we are: a guitar amp is intended for high-impedance, low-level signal. Computers put out line-level signals, and regular amps aren't suited for this. You can reamp with an impedance matcher to better suit the signals together, but you will still run into one major issue: frequency range (which we will discuss in just one minute).

If you still want to run just a single amp, you'd be better off using a keyboard amp, as those are much more suited to your purposes. Even then, a separate power amp is the best way to go. You can feed that into a regular cabinet if all you are doing is digital processing. This isn't to say that running your laptop into a Fender Twin won't work, because it will, but you will lose a lot of the sonic detail gained in DSP processing on a laptop.

A power amp is great because typically power amps are very "clean" and do not impart any additional color on your sound. This is especially important if you've gone to great lengths to craft a sound in your favorite guitar plug-in and emulate cabinets and response. You simply want an amplifier that makes your sound louder and does not color it.

DIRECT APPROACHES

If you are using a soundman or have a PA available, you can take the outputs of your interface and run them into the mixer through the house system. A good engineer will be able to give you a monitor mix of your sound, and their amplifiers and speakers take care of the rest. A PA system, by design, is a full-range system. This is a good option if the venue where you're playing has good equipment and a knowledgeable soundman. I've left my amps and speakers behind the stage on many occasions because this option is simply easier and often can sound much better.

Now, if you're running MIDI guitar and software synthesizers, you need to realize one thing: the guitar signal is not very wide in terms of frequency. The typical guitar speaker is simply a woofer, in that it takes only the lower frequencies and amplifies them. Typically, frequencies higher than about 5 kHz are rolled off and are not present in the final sound. Anyone who's plugged an amplified acoustic guitar into a typical guitar amp knows just how bad it can sound.

That being said, acoustic amps add a second speaker, a tweeter, which takes care of the high frequencies. If you are running synths, they are going to have a very wide frequency range, one that no guitar cabinet will be able to reproduce well. You need a cabinet with a tweeter and a horn. These cabinets are referred to as full-range cabinets. PA and keyboard players typically use full-range cabinets because of the full range of frequencies that they need to amplify. This is why I recommend a keyboard amp if you have to use a combo amp, like a Korg or Roland keyboard amp.

If you are going to use a separate speaker, it's not hard to find full-range cabinets at stores; they just won't have Marshall written on the front of them.

MOTHER OF INVENTION

Necessity being the mother of invention led me on a quest a few years ago when I first started toying with the idea of taking my laptop on the road. The full-range cabinets available on the market were heavy and usually didn't sound great with guitar; the synths sounded great, but everything else was a bit off. I needed something that had a good guitar woofer and a horn/tweeter for my synths.

I found that the trick was having a crossover that was adjustable for frequencies and attenuation/boost. I contacted Flite Sound, a small company in Connecticut that had made a few cabinets for me over the years, and they designed the cabinet I use now. It does all it should—good guitar tones with solid high range for accurate synth reproduction. It's also very light and easy to carry around.

Next up is security. No one likes to have his or her stuff stolen. With a laptop onstage, how are you going to secure it?

Security

If you run a full Marshall stack, the chances of it "walking out" during a set break are very slim. Now, a small laptop computer—*that* may grow legs and walk away on you. Security is a big concern, and there are some easy ways to ensure it.

First, every laptop computer made today has a slot for a security cable. This is a notch in the side of the computer where you can attach a locking mechanism. Several companies make these locks, and they typically have keys of codes to unlock them. I use a Kensington security lock, but you can find locks made by Targus, Belkin, and many other companies. Attached to the locking mechanism is a long, braided-steel cable that you can loop around an immovable object. It's very hard to circumvent this without a lot of effort, and that will usually be noticed.

My speaker cabinet was designed with a steel U-hook protruding from the side of it just for that purpose. Flite Sound had the forethought to provide this especially for the security lock to lock into. Even though it's impossible for someone to take my whole rig, a laptop can be slipped under your arm. My whole rig cannot walk off without being noticed. That being said, I've never had mine stolen, but I know many people who haven't used security cables and have had their laptops stolen.

These cables go for about $20, and you'd be silly not to own one. Some manufacturers even guarantee that if your equipment is stolen, they will reimburse you a portion or a full refund of the cost of your laptop. Either way, secure your laptop, because without it, it will be very hard to play the gig!

Tips That Will Save Your Life When Performing Live

Here are some very important tips to save your life when setting up your live rig and performing live:

- Test! Make sure that before you hit the stage, you've tried your exact setup for at least 20 hours without a single mishap.
- When it comes to computers, redundancy is everything. Bring copies of all your software and updates you have already installed. A quick reinstall on a set break can fix glitchy behavior.
- Bring a spare for each cable you use, including power and speaker cables, and fuses, too. Be prepared, odd things happen at gigs!
- Find a working system and don't touch it. When you find a solution that works, a winning combination of software versions, hardware drivers, and operating system versions, don't touch them. Apple may introduce a new update today. You may see an update for your DAW. Don't even think of installing it until you can give it the old 20-hour test. If it ain't broke, please don't fix it.
- Partition your hard drive and duplicate your running system. This way, if one system freaks out, you can reboot into the other one in a pinch.
- Carry a small spare amp, just in case. I stopped doing this because of my rig, which you'll read about soon, but when things go bad, which they may, you need to have a sound. A cheap amp left in the trunk of your car will bail you out.
- Show up early. When a computer is involved, leave more time up front to get things running, go through your patches, and make sure that everything sounds okay.
- Don't experiment on stage. Don't decide on the set break that you're going to call up Absynth for your new lead sound without testing it first.

This list is not intended to scare you. It's simply the reality of every electronic musician. Be prepared and be smart about how you run your setup, and it will reward you with great sound and enjoyment, gig after gig after gig.

Now, if you were curious, let's go over my current live guitar rig.

My Rig

My rig does change pretty often, but certain parts of it are always the same:

Guitar: Brian Moore Guitars. I endorse them proudly! I currently use a custom hollow-body jazz guitar they made for me. It has regular guitar outputs and 13-pin outputs for my MIDI guitar. I also have another custom shop that has the USB option for recording and a few iGuitars with USB as well.

Audio interface: Metric Halo Firewire ULN-2 interface. These are really good interfaces, not only for live use, but for general recording. They are extremely high-quality in all aspects and sound fabulous.

Amp: I use a Walter Woods amplifier. You can't buy it in stores; it's handmade and only available from Walter himself. It's about the size of a breadbasket, weighs 6 pounds, and runs 600 watts of clean power (which is absurdly loud). The amp is stereo and feeds two cabinets.

Cabinets: Two custom-made speaker cabinets from Flite Sound. Both have 8-inch woofers that fire down into the floor and have tweeters for high-range and synth sounds. I position them about six feet apart for a wide stereo image.

Software: I host everything in Logic Pro. I use Guitar Rig for my guitar's tone and various Native Instrument soft synths for my lead and other sounds. I also use the excellent synthesizers built into Logic Pro for other synth sounds.

MIDI: I use a Roland GI-20 to convert my guitar's signal to MIDI, using a USB connection to my laptop.

Computer: I use an Apple 12-inch Powerbook, 1.33GHz with 1.5 GB of RAM. This will change as soon as a faster computer comes out, but it's working well for now. I use the security cable from the laptop to one of my speaker cabinets to ensure that it won't walk away!

Foot control: I use a Behringer FCB1010 to access and change my sounds via foot control. The MIDI cables run into a small USB MIDI interface attached to the Powerbook.

Misc: I use a Roland/Boss reverb pedal and an A/B footswitch as my redundancy setup. If my computer ever freaks out (which it hasn't), I can hit a switch, my sound goes directly into the amp through the reverb pedal, and I can get a nice clean jazz tone. If I were using distortion, I would bring along a pedal for dirty sounds, but since the majority of my work is jazz, clean tones usually dominate my setup. But I have used the rig on many recordings and sessions where modern tones were called for.

I also use Ableton's Live software for triggering samples/loops and layered recording on certain avant-garde gigs. I can trigger samples from my MIDI guitar and start and stop recording from my foot control. I've created some very "hip" sounds this way and had a great deal of fun doing so. Live has even hosted my MIDI synth lead tones, so I can run all of my work through Live, as well as Logic. I still rely on Logic for its stability, but Live is getting used more and more.

Figure 18.3 is a flowchart showing how everything is set up.

The audio interface, the GI-20, and my amp are all in a four-space rack unit that is prewired; my guitar simply plugs in the front, and I run the speaker leads to the cabinets. With computer boot-up time, I can be ready in about four minutes. I've used the system since 2001 and have never had a crash or a glitch. That's including a very big gig at Lincoln Center in NYC, where I simply could not afford to mess up. I've probably logged over a few hundred hours onstage with this setup—I can't (and won't) think of going back!

I like to hit the A/B pedal just to see what my old tone sounded like, and it's pretty startling to hear the difference. My sound is cleaner though the computer, and the sense of balance is so

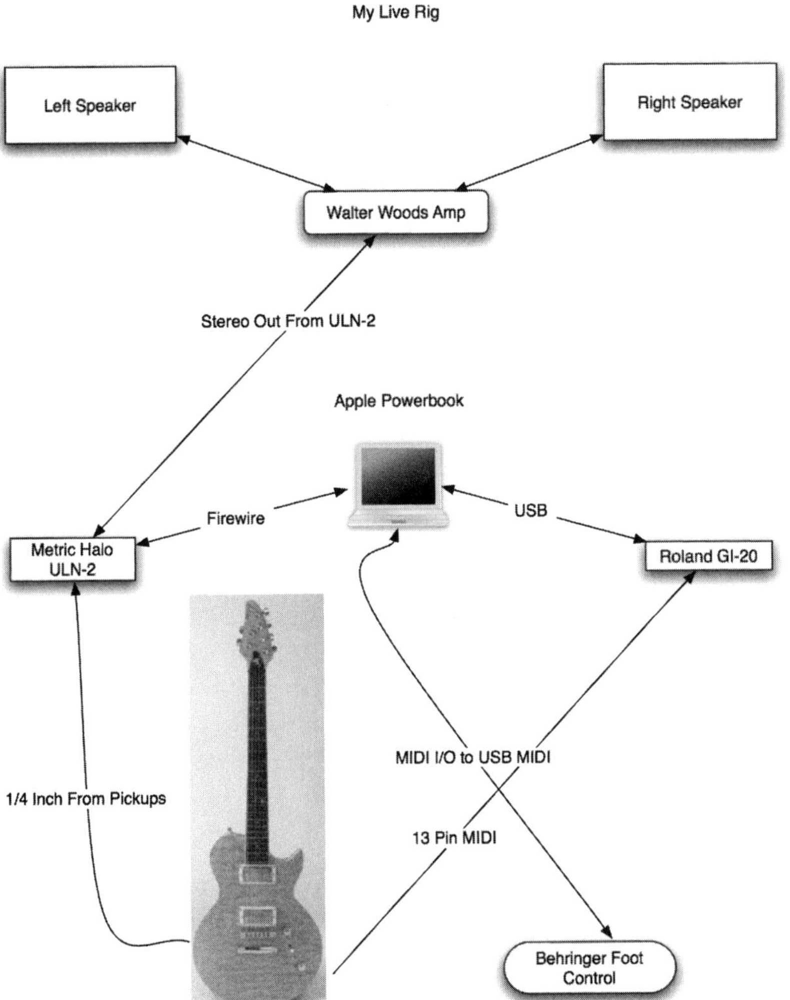

Figure 18.3
My onstage setup.

much better. Not only is it fun to throw in synth sounds during gigs, but it also has added a dimension to my music that I never thought was possible. In short, I won't ever go back; this is just too much fun!

That's it! We did it! I hope you've enjoyed this book. It was a pleasure to bring all this information together for you. Welcome to the future, and I look forward to seeing all your glowing laptops onstage!

Important Terms for the MIDI Guitarist

ASDHR envelope—Short for *A*ttack, *S*ustain, *D*elay, *H*old, and *R*elease. These settings allow you to shape the envelope of the note: how quickly it appears (attack), how long it holds (sustain), how long it takes to sound (delay), how long it should stick around (hold), and how quickly the note should hang around (release). These are your standard envelope-shaping controls found on most synths.

control change—A command that controls elements of the synthesizer such as volume, portamento, and modulation. These are also commonly called Continuous Controllers. There are 128 possible Continuous Controllers. Some are standard, such as CC7 = Volume, while the other CCs can be set from the program.

double trigger—An accidental double hit on a note, one by your finger and the next immediately after, when your pick strikes. This is a common problem with MIDI guitar.

ghost note—An errant note in the MIDI guitar stream, usually a result of playing noise.

LFO—A Low Frequency Oscillator is a synthesizer feature that modulates or changes a parameter in the synth periodically over time. A famous example is an LFO assigned to vary a pitch and give a vibrato effect.

MIDI channel—A MIDI channel is a data path. There are 16 channels in a single MIDI stream. A typical MIDI guitar will use six channels (one for each string), or you can force the guitar to only take up one channel. Typically, you want to use all six channels so that you can edit your information and make the most out of your synths and notation programs.

MIDI note names—Each pitch is represented by its letter (A-G) and a number indicating where on the piano the pitch resides. For example, E2 is your lowest string on the guitar. E5 would be a note three octaves higher.

note on—The command that initiates a MIDI note.

note off—The command that ends a MIDI note.

oscillators—In a traditional synth, the oscillator is responsible for the sound you hear. Oscillators are holdovers from the days of analog synthesis, where differently shaped waves represented different sounds. The common oscillator shapes are sine, square, and sawtooth.

pitch bend—Commands to finely change the tuning of a note — this will allow you to bend notes.

pitch bend range—The maximum range that you can bend a pitch. This number is expressed in semitones (12 per octave). The range on your guitar-to-MIDI controller must match the pitch bend range on the synth sound you are playing. Typically, 12 is the default, as it gives you a full octave. No matter what you choose, it must be the same.

pitch-to-MIDI—The process of transferring audible pitch to MIDI information.

polyphony—Polyphony means multiple notes sounding at once. Most synths have a polyphony setting that dictates how many voices can sound at any one time before cutting off.

program change—A command that changes the patch or sound you are using.

sampler—A sampler is a device that takes incoming MIDI commands and plays back prerecorded audio samples instead of synthetically generated waveforms.

sensitivity—A setting in your guitar-to-MIDI interface that sets how sensitive each string is. Lower-sensitivity settings don't show as much true velocity, but can cut down on mistakes. This makes this setting dynamic. You want it set higher for performance and lower for sequencing when accuracy is key.

tracking—A term used to express the accuracy of a guitar-to-MIDI translator. Tracking can also refer to the speed of the translation.

velocity—A MIDI command that sets the loudness of your pitch, expressed in a value of 0–172.

virtual instrument—A sound-producing device that runs in a virtual environment within your computer.

Index